Lives of Saints

LIVES OF SAINTS

WITH EXCERPTS FROM THEIR WRITINGS

*Selected
and
Illustrated*

INTRODUCTION BY FATHER THOMAS PLASSMANN, O.F.M.

EDITORIAL SUPERVISION BY FATHER JOSEPH VANN, O.F.M.

JOHN J. CRAWLEY & CO., INC.

NEW YORK

NIHIL OBSTAT   John M. A. Fearns, S.T.D., *Censor Librorum*

IMPRIMATUR ✠ Francis Cardinal Spellman *Archbishop of New York*

August 7, 1954

Contents

Illustrations

Acknowledgments

For the right to include the copyrighted items in this volume, the publisher is indebted to the following:

Columbia University Press (Records of Civilization) for selections from Emerton's *Letters of St. Boniface.*

E. P. Dutton & Co., Inc. (Everyman's Library) for St. Louis' Last Testament from De Joinville's *Memoirs of the Crusades;* for a selection from More's *Dialogue of Comfort Against Tribulation;* and for selections from *Letters of St. Catherine of Siena,* translated by Vida D. Scudder.

Harvard University Press (Loeb Classical Library) for selections from *St. Jerome's Select Letters,* translated by F. A. Wright; and for selections from St. Bernard's *The Steps of Humility,* translated by G. B. Burch.

Editor's Note

The text is based on authorized sources, a chief one being Alban Butler's *Lives of the Saints.* Scriptural quotations are generally from the Douay version of the Old Testament and the Confraternity edition of the New Testament.

The two dates that follow the saint's name at the beginning of each Life are the year of his death and the feast day as celebrated in the Roman Catholic Church.

Introduction

There will never be too many "Lives of the Saints." The reason is because the saints are friends of God; they tell us of God; they bring us nearer to God—and the world does need God. In a sense the saints are common property—an interreligious élite, as it were. They have lived their lives; they have said their say and, even though their words or deeds may have jarred their environment, past or present, the common verdict is in their favor. Even those outside the Catholic Church cannot but sense an irresistible attraction towards them. And while this attraction may stem from curiosity, it is apt gradually to engender admiration, if not imitation.

For this reason the saints are the best promoters and champions of the Church. Doctrine and cult, morals and discipline may offer difficulties to the understanding and full appreciation, but when tenets and precepts are seen embodied in flesh and blood, and when mortals behold in one of their own kin and kind "as in a mirror the glory of the Lord," as St. Paul would have it (II Cor. iii, 18), then what might have appeared unbelievable, if not unreasonable, will in time force upon us a clear-cut *fait accompli* and bring all fantasy from its rarefied atmosphere down to the daily drudgery of human existence.

Usually biographies of saints are limited to dates and outstanding events in their lives. This is in keeping with the age-old proverb, *Verbum sonat, exemplum tonat*. For examples are more forceful

ix

than words, and sainthood is proven by the deeds that follow and substantiate the words spoken or pledges made. Nonetheless, the more observant student is anxious to delve into the inner consciousness of the person who has achieved great things and to analyze and coordinate the thoughts and feelings of the soul that found its way from this Valley of Tears to the Mountain of God. To such students the present volume will serve as a welcome aid. The selected excerpts from the writings of certain saints will reveal not only the inner workings of his soul, but will also present a picture of the world in which he lived and moved as well as of his struggles and disappointments, of his triumphs and failures and, lastly, of the wise counsels he left for others.

The present volume has studiously followed approved authors and reliable sources. In her official records of saints, the Church has consistently sought to establish historical truth and accuracy of data, in as far as such was possible in the ever varying trends and vicissitudes of the centuries. The bent for historical, not to say critical evaluation of facts and proofs, was part of the official pattern of the early Church and became crystallized in the days when the canonical writings and apostolic traditions had to be rescued and kept apart from the deluge of apocryphal literature and legendry. Alongside of what was considered the sacrosanct deposit of revealed truth, there came to the fore the lives and sufferings of the "first witnesses to the faith," i.e., the holy martyrs. One of the first pontiffs, St. Clement, set the pace when he divided the City of Rome into seven districts and assigned to each a scribe who would carefully note down the acts of the martyrs. All succeeding pontiffs followed his lead. In fact any unbiased historian will grant that as far as the official attitude of the Church is concerned, there has been throughout the centuries a policy of painstaking care regarding the lives and acts of the Church's predilect children, namely, the martyrs and saints of God. It is safe to say that, in spite of handicaps and obstacles from within and without, this ecclesiastical attitude in regard to careful documentation and evaluation not only preceded but paved the way for modern critical research and investigation.

Proof of this, though the purpose was entirely different, is the history of the official processes of the beatification and canonization of saints. Anyone interested in this rather fascinating subject will read with profit a recent study by Rev. Damian J. Blaher, O.F.M., *The Ordinary Processes in Causes of Beatification and Canonization of Saints* (The Catholic University Press, Washington, D.C., 1949). The author divides his work into two parts: Historical Synopsis and Canonical Commentary. As this author points out, though the spontaneous devotion of the faithful had a large share in the cult of holy men and women, ecclesiastical authority and supervision asserted themselves from the very beginning because no such devotion could survive unless it entered the sphere of liturgical rules and practices over which the bishop and, to some extent, the local clergy exercised charge and final authority.

In early days such titles as "Venerable," "Servant of God," "Blessed," and "Saint" were used promiscuously. Gradually, however, these terms became well defined and were used to denote definite progressive stages in the process. Today every Catholic knows that veneration may be accorded to one who has been officially pronounced Blessed, but such veneration is restricted in various ways. There is no restriction, however, as to the veneration to be accorded to a saint. For a saint is held up by papal decree to the public veneration, intercession and imitation to the Church universal. In so doing, the Holy Father exercises his supreme and infallible authority, for he speaks as the Vicar of Christ, the pastor of all Christendom.

It was a long and arduous road before this stage was reached. The first saint so honored and recognized was St. Ulrich, Bishop of Augsburg, in the year 993. Throughout the previous centuries numerous directive and legislative actions had been taken by ecclesiastical authorities for the purpose of guiding the clergy and the faithful in the proper conduct of paying homage to departed friends of God and of forestalling abuses and excesses, as well as

checking relevant documents and, above all, such miraculous deeds
and events as had been witnessed before or after their death. The
above date, however, gave a new impulse to the formulation of
canonical procedures in this important matter of ecclesiastical
jurisdiction. Since then this formulation has grown apace, so that
at the present time there is hardly a tribunal in the world which
handles its cases with such painstaking care, critical exactitude,
and relentless objectivity as the Sacred Congregation of Rites employs in its usually protracted scrutiny of every cause with all its
phases and items in the process of the beatification and canonization.

The entire life of every candidate for the honors of the altar is
severely tested to determine the existence of heroic virtue; all
pertinent documents and especially the writings of the prospective
saint are carefully examined by the standard of sound and orthodox thinking and teaching; witnesses, wherever available, are called
in to be cross-examined and to testify under oath; alleged miracles
are subjected to relentless medical and other available testimony.
If any flaw is detected a re-examination is ordered; or the case may
be dropped without hope of further appeal. A prosecutor for the
opposition, popularly known as the "devil's advocate," is accorded
full freedom to register his objection. The verdict is rendered,
not by individuals, but by a competent jury in plenary session.
Thus the case proceeds from stage to stage, in accordance with the
titles indicated above, each demanding long intermissions. Only
after the entire cause is approved by the appointed commissions
and the highest dignitaries of the Church, the Holy Father is
approached to render final decision.

It goes without saying that there are many holy people in heaven,
now enjoying the Beatific Vision, whose earthly life was never submitted to such severe scrutiny. And why not? The Catholic takes
his simple answer from the Holy Bible: "Oh, the depth of the riches
of the wisdom and of the knowledge of God. How incomprehensible
are his judgments and how unsearchable are his ways" (Rom. xi,
33). Sainthood is acquired by grace, and grace is the gift of God.

The saints themselves attribute little to their own cooperation, necessary though it be. And if they should seek publicity either before death or after, they would default in an indispensable requisite for sanctity, which is humility. Their whole outlook is gathered up in the words of St. Paul: "For you have died and your life is hidden with Christ in God" (Col. iii, 3). Hence their destiny, both in life and death, is in the hands of God.

The Church, however, considers it her duty to search out and proclaim "the wonderful works of God" (Acts ii, 13) and to hoist on high the examples of her saints for the edification and imitation of her subjects. Mindful of the words of St. Paul, that "star differs from star in glory" (I Cor. xv, 41), she looks about in her vast domain in search for evidence of genuine sanctity. The result is the Catholic calendar of saints. And this calendar is written according to the standard set up by St. Peter, "that God is no respecter of persons" (Acts x, 34).

Every clime and country, every race and nation, every color and tongue, is represented on this glorious list. Sex, age, social rank and any form of distinction or achievement fade into oblivion where the halo, which is the distinctive emblem of recognized sanctity, adorns the brow. True, our statuary or other representations often display some faint symbolic allusion, but this usually indicates the hard way the saints had to walk or the tortures they had to suffer "for my name's sake" (Matt. x, 22). If it be urged that in the early centuries most of the saints were popes or bishops it must be remembered that the historical monuments of those days are scant and sparse. Nevertheless, besides the martyred pontiffs of the first three centuries, a galaxy of holy youths, of lowly men and women has reached us through the Church's Martyrology.

Since the present volume was designed to carry excerpts from the writings of saints, along with an account of their lives and deeds, it will be noted that many of the holy persons included here represent the literary type. The larger catalogue of saints, however, such as the official calendar of saints, shows alongside of popes and bishops, kings and princes, monks and nuns, doctors and **savants**, the humble figures of St. Isidore the farmer, St. Alexius the beggar, St. Zita the domestic servant, St. Tarsicius the holy altar boy, and thus without regard for earthly prestige, whether by design or chance or Providence, the Church manifests herself in her calendar of saints truly as the Church Universal.

Sensitive of the claims, interests and devotions of individuals and groups alike, the Church heartily approves in her saints the power of patronage. This is based on the Doctrine of the Communion of Saints which implies their intercessory powers in behalf of those near and dear to them on earth, or because of some local tie or community of interests. Thus not only every member of the Church receives a patron saint at baptism, but every church, monastery and usually institutions and even cities venerate their patron saint. The geographical survey of both Americas may serve as a colorful commentary to the catalogue of saints. Harking back to medieval days, each guild, craft or trade goes by the name of a saint. In this way an age of faith sought to blend the natural with the supernatural, the material with the spiritual.

The Ecclesiastical Year of the Church intertwines the great feasts of our Lord with the feasts of His saints. With an outlook on eternity, the Church commemorates a saint on the day of his birth, that is, the day of his death, which is his birth to a new life. In proportion to the eminence of sanctity achieved, or to some local significance, a saint's feast is ranked as a simple, semi-double, double, double major or, in case of great distinction, second or first class. The key-feasts of the year bear the name Solemnity. This rank regulates the ceremonial and prayers according to strict liturgical laws. The veneration of saints goes by the technical name of "dulia" (Greek: servitude); the Blessed Virgin Mary receives "hyper-dulia" (the highest form of veneration), while "latria" (Adoration) is accorded only to God. In the Missal and Divine Office the saints are classed and venerated according to well-defined categories, such as Apostles and Evangelists, Martyrs, Confessors of episcopal or non-episcopal rank, Doctors, Virgins and non-Virgins. These categories are indications of hierarchical orders in the celestial Kingdom, where each order has its own "aureola" or crown. The most powerful prayer which the Church has devised to honor her saints, and which goes back to early antiquity is the Litany of All Saints. It is chanted on solemn occasions and on days of prayer and penance. It brings forcibly to mind and heart the unity, solidity and eternity of the army of Christ, the Church triumphant, the Church militant and the Church suffering. Here the voices of millions of souls seem to blend in a rousing chorus of jubilation, intercession, and humble petition—all looking forward to the place where "light will be no more . . . for the Lord God will shed light upon them; and they shall reign forever and ever" (Apoc. xx, 5).

THOMAS PLASSMANN, O.F.M.

SAINT MICHAEL AND THE DRAGON   Guido Reni

The artist, a pupil of the three Caracci cousins, lived in Italy from 1575-1642. His teachers were the founders of the early Baroque school of painting in Italy. The open spacing and three-dimensional effect of this painting are in marked contrast to the crowded flat effect of earlier paintings.

Saint Michael, as one of the Archangels, is always represented with wings and in armor. Often he is shown with a pair of scales, representative of his function in weighing souls.

THE ANNUNCIATION
Fra Angelico

The art of Fra Angelico (1387-1455) has a deep religious content. He joined
the Dominican order in 1407, and his life was spent in the
cloister serving the Church with his art. It is known that each
day before he began to paint, he prayed that he might be
guided by divine inspiration.

Saint Gabriel, the "angel of the Annunciation," wears the
wings of an Archangel. He generally carries a lily or a scroll
with the words "Ave Maria, gratia plena."

Lives of Saints

Saint Ignatius of Antioch
Bishop, Martyr
c. 1 1 7
(February 1)

Ignatius of Antioch, surnamed Theophorus, which in Greek means "God-Bearer," was probably a convert and disciple of St. John the Evangelist. We know nothing of his early life. The fourth-century Church historian, Eusebius, says that the Apostles Peter and Paul, who planted the faith in Antioch, left directions that Ignatius should succeed Evodius as bishop of that city; he states further that Ignatius retained the office for forty years, proving himself in every way an exemplary pastor. During the persecution of the emperor Domitian, whose reign covered the period of 81 to 96, Ignatius kept up the courage of his flock by daily preaching, by prayer and fasting. After Domitian's death there was a cessation of the persecutions during the fifteen months of Nerva's reign, then in Trajan's reign we have records of a number of martyrs, though no general persecution. In an interesting letter to the younger Pliny, then governor of the Black Sea province of Bithynia, Trajan laid down the principle that Christians should be put to death if formally reported, but not otherwise sought out for punishment. The Emperor was a humane man, yet the gratitude which he felt he owed to his own pagan gods for his victories over the Dacians and the Scythians later led him to authorize the death penalty for those Christians who refused to acknowledge these divinities publicly.

There is a legend that the emperor Trajan himself, who wintered in Antioch in the year 115, examined the aged Bishop Ignatius in the year 115, with questions such as these:

3

"Who are you, spirit of evil, who dare disobey my orders and goad others on to their destruction?"

"No one calls Theophorus a spirit of evil," the bishop replied.

"Who is Theophorus?"

"He who bears Christ within him."

"And do we not bear within ourselves the gods who help us against our enemies?"

"You are mistaken when you call gods those who are no better than devils. There is but one God, who created heaven and earth and all that in them is; and one Jesus, made Christ, into whose kingdom I earnestly desire to be admitted."

"Do you mean Him who was crucified under Pontius Pilate?"

"Yes, the same, who by His death has crucified both sin and its author, and who has proclaimed that every malice of the devil shall be trodden underfoot by those who bear Him in their hearts."

"Do you then," asked the Emperor, "bear Christ within you?"

"Yes," said Ignatius, "for it is written, 'I will dwell in them and will walk with them.'"

According to the legend, Trajan ruled that Ignatius should die. He was bound and conveyed to Rome, to be devoured by wild beasts in the Colosseum. From this point on, we are on firm ground, historically speaking, with Ignatius' own letters, seven of which are still extant, to tell us the story. At the seaport of Seleucia they boarded a ship that made many stops along the shores of Asia Minor, instead of proceeding directly to Rome. Some of Ignatius' friends took the direct route west and, reaching Rome before him, awaited his arrival. For a great part of the journey he had as companions a deacon, Philo, and a friend, Agathopus, supposedly the authors of an account of his martyrdom. On shipboard Ignatius was guarded by ten soldiers so brutal that he speaks of them as "ten leopards," and adds that they only grew worse when kindly treated.

Wherever the ship put in, the local Christians sent bishops and priests to meet the venerable bishop, and crowds gathered to receive the benediction of one who was already revered as a martyr.

At Smyrna he met his former fellow disciple, Bishop Polycarp,[1] and delegations came from Ephesus, Magnesia, and Tralles, three ancient cities of Asia Minor which had Christian colonies. Ignatius wrote letters to be carried back to these various churches, exhorting the members to keep in harmony with their bishops and other clergy, to assemble often in prayer, to be meek and humble, and to suffer injuries without protest. He praises them for their zeal against heresy and particularly warns them against the Docetic teaching.[2]

One of his seven extant letters was addressed to the Christians of Rome, whom he passionately entreats to do nothing to prevent his martyrdom. At this time Christianity had a number of influential converts, and some of these highly-placed persons might well have tried to have his sentence mitigated. The contemporary pagan satirist Lucian, who almost certainly was familiar with the life and letters of Ignatius, bears witness in his dialogue, "The Death of Peregrinus," to the devotion of Christians one for another. This work of his is an interesting illustration of the attitude of a learned and skeptical Greek towards the new religion.

The guards were anxious to reach Rome with their prisoner before the great public games were over, for victims of venerable appearance were always an attraction. At Troas, where the boat stopped, Ignatius wrote letters to the Philadelphians,[3] to the Smyrneans, and to Polycarp. From Troas the ship sailed on to the Macedonian port of Neapolis, thence, we are told, to Philippi. The

[1] St. Polycarp, a convert of St. John the Evangelist, was then bishop of Smyrna. One of the last survivors of the generation that heard the teaching of the Apostles, he was martyred in his extreme old age, around the year 155.
[2] The Docetists of the second century, like the Gnostics of whom we shall hear later, were unable to accept the doctrine of the twofold nature of Christ, as the Church had learned it from St. Paul and the other Apostles. If Jesus was truly divine, they felt that he could never have been truly man; they believed the historic Jesus had been a spirit or phantom, with the outward appearance of a man but never in reality knowing hunger, pain, or death.
[3] Philadelphia was in eastern Palestine, beyond the Jordan; it is now known as Amman.

little party crossed Macedonia and Epirus on foot, and took ship
for the trip around Italy. These details, along with the account of
the arrival at Rome, are found in the *Acts of the Martyrs*,[4] but
are not altogether reliable. We are told that as the saint approached
Rome, the faithful came out to meet him, rejoicing in his presence,
but grieving that they were to lose him so soon. He prevented them
from taking steps to obtain his release. According to tradition, he
reached Rome on December 20, the last day of the games, and
was brought at once before the prefect, to whom the Emperor's
letter was delivered. At the prefect's command, the prisoner was
hurried off to the Colosseum, where, we are told, two fierce lions
were let out and Ignatius was at once killed. Thus his prayer for
a martyr's death was answered.

There is evidence that some fragments of the martyr's remains
were taken to Antioch and venerated. St. Jerome, visiting Antioch
nearly three hundred years later, tells us that these remains had
been placed "in a cemetery outside the Daphne gate." It is believed that they were brought back to Rome in 637 to rest in the
church of San Clemente. From the ancient Syrian martyrology we
learn that the martyr's feast was kept in the East on October 17.
St. John Chrysostom,[5] bishop of Constantinople in the fourth century, preached a famous panegyric on Ignatius, but even then
legend was beginning to play its part; he supposes that Ignatius
was appointed to the see of Antioch by the Apostle Peter himself.
Later a whole correspondence was fabricated, including letters purporting to have passed between Ignatius and the Blessed Virgin
Mary, while she still dwelt on earth, after the Ascension of Jesus.

In contrast to these legendary and fictitious elements, the seven

[4] The Acts of the Martyrs (*Acta Martyrum*) include two types of documents, namely, official records of the trials and executions of martyrs, and
accounts of their lives and deaths written, or purporting to be written, by
contemporaries and eyewitnesses. The material to be found in the latter
category varies greatly in value and authenticity.

[5] St. John Chrysostom, born in Antioch about 347, was one of the great
preachers and teachers of the early Church; the Byzantine liturgy bears his
name.

letters described above as written by Ignatius on his way to Rome, which have come down to us in their entirety, are accepted as absolutely authentic by modern scholars. Their great importance is the light they throw on the organization, beliefs, and practices of the Christian Church, about eighty-five years after Christ's death. Ignatius is the first, outside the New Testament writers, to lay stress on the Virgin Birth. To the Ephesians he writes: "And from the prince of this world were hidden Mary's virginity and her child-bearing, in like manner also the death of the Lord." The doctrine of the Trinity, too, he plainly takes for granted, and we detect an approach to later definitions of Christ's nature when we read in the same letter: "There is one Physician of flesh and spirit, begotten and unbegotten, God in man, true life in death, son of Mary and son of God, first suffering and then beyond suffering, Jesus Christ our Lord." No less remarkable are the phrases he uses to describe the Eucharist. It is "the flesh of Christ," "the gift of God," "the medicine of immortality." Repeatedly he emphasizes the loyalty and obedience due the bishop as the transmitter of true apostolic tradition, and the necessity of unity and peace. Finally, it is in his letter to the church of Smyrna that for the first time in Christian literature "the Catholic Church" [6] is spoken of. "Wheresoever," he writes, "the bishop appears, there let the people be, even as wheresoever Christ is, there is the Catholic Church." Ignatius' martyrdom and his important contribution to the development of Church doctrine make it fitting that his name should occur in the Canon of the Mass.

Excerpts from Letters of Ignatius

TO THE EPHESIANS

3.   *I do not command you as if I were someone great, for even though I be bound in the Name, I am not yet perfect in* Jesus Christ. For now I do but begin to be a disciple and I speak

[6] The word Catholic derives from the Greek adjective meaning universal.

to you as to my fellow learners. And it were fitting for me to be anointed by you for the contest,[7] with faith, admonition, patience, long-suffering. But since love does not suffer me to be silent concerning you, I have therefore hastened to exhort you to set yourselves in harmony with the mind of God. For Jesus Christ, our inseparable Life, is the mind of the Father, even as the bishops who are settled in the farthest parts of the earth are the mind of Christ.

4.   Hence it is fitting for you to set yourselves in harmony with the mind of the bishop, as indeed you do. For your noble presbytery, worthy of God, is attuned to the bishop, even as the strings to a lyre. And thus by means of your accord and harmonious love Jesus Christ is sung. Form yourselves one and all into a choir,[8] that blending in concord and taking the keynote of God, you may sing in unison with one voice through Jesus Christ to the Father, that he may hear you and recognize you through your good deeds to be members of His Son. Therefore it is profitable for you to live in blameless unity, that you may always enjoy communion with God. . . .

10.   And for the rest of mankind pray unceasingly—for there is in them hope of repentance, that they may attain unto God. Let them also be instructed by the example of your works. In face of their outbursts of wrath be patient; in face of their arrogant words be humble; meet their revilings with prayers; where they are in error be steadfast in the faith; in face of their violence be gentle. Be not anxious to retaliate on them. Let our forbearance prove us their brethren. Endeavor to imitate the Lord, striving who can suffer the greater wrong, who can be more defrauded, who can be set at naught, that no rank weed of the devil be found in you. In all purity and sobriety abide in Christ Jesus in flesh and in spirit.

TO THE ROMANS

1.   My prayer to God has been heard, and I have been permitted to see your holy faces, so that I have been granted even

[7] This figure of speech is an allusion to the anointing of an athlete before the games.
[8] The allusion here is to the chorus which sang ritual hymns around the altar during a pagan sacrifice.

more than I was asking. For in bonds in Jesus Christ I hope to salute you, if it be God's will that I should be accounted worthy to reach the end. For the beginning is well ordained if I may attain the end and so receive my inheritance without hindrance. For I fear lest your very love should do me wrong. It is easy for you to accomplish whatever you will, but for me it is difficult to attain unto God unless you let me take my own way.

2. . . . Grant me just this privilege of being poured out as an offering to God, while the altar is now prepared; and do you as a choir of love sing praises to the Father in Christ Jesus that he has counted the bishop of Syria worthy to be brought from the land of the sunrise to the sunset. It is good to be setting to the world for God, that I may rise to him. . . .

4. I write to all the churches and charge them all to know that I die willingly for God, if only you do not hinder. I beseech you, do not unreasonably befriend me. Suffer me to become the food of wild beasts, through whom I may attain to God. I am God's grain, and I am ground by the teeth of wild beasts, that I may be found the pure bread of Christ. Rather entice the wild beasts to become my tomb, and to leave no trace of my body, that when I have fallen asleep I may not be a burden to anyone. Then I shall truly be a disciple of Christ, when the world shall not see even my body. Entreat the Lord for me, that by these instruments [9] I may be found a sacrifice to God. I do not order you, as did Peter and Paul. They were Apostles and I am even until now a slave. But if I suffer, I am Jesus Christ's freedman, and in Him I shall arise free. Now in my bonds I am learning to give up all desires. . . .

6. The goals of the earth and the kingdoms of this world shall profit me nothing. It is better for me to die for the sake of Jesus Christ than to reign over the ends of the earth. I seek Him who died for us. I desire Him who rose. My birth-pains are upon me. Forgive me, brethren, hinder me not from entering into life; desire not my death. Consign not to the world one who yearns to be God's; nor tempt me with the things of this life. Suffer me to receive pure light. When I come thither then shall I be a man indeed. Suffer me to be an imitator of the passion of my God. If

9 That is, the wild beasts.

any man has Him dwelling in him, he will understand my desire and feel with me, knowing what constrains me. . . .

TO THE SMYRNEANS

1. I give glory to Jesus Christ, the God who has given you wisdom. For I have perceived that you are firmly settled in unwavering faith, being nailed, as it were, to the cross of the Lord Jesus Christ, fully convinced as touching our Lord that he is truly of the race of David according to the flesh, and Son of God by the Divine will and power, truly born of a virgin, baptized by John that all righteousness might be fulfilled in Him, under Pontius Pilate and Herod the Tetrarch truly nailed up for us in the flesh (of whose fruit are we, even of His most blessed Passion); that He might raise up an ensign to the ages through His resurrection, for his saints and believers, whether Jews or Gentiles, in one body of His church.

4. . . . For if these deeds were wrought by our Lord in mere semblance, then too are my bonds mere semblance. And why moreover have I surrendered myself to death, to face fire, sword, and wild beasts? For to be near the sword is to be near to God, in the midst of wild beasts is in the midst of God, if only it be in the name Jesus Christ, that we may suffer with Him. All things I endure, since He, the perfect man, makes me strong.

(Srawley, *The Epistles of St. Ignatius,* 1919.)

Saints Perpetua, Felicitas, and Companions

Martyrs

2 0 3

(*March 6*)

The record of the *Passion of St. Perpetua, St. Felicitas, and their Companions* is one of the great treasures of martyr literature, an authentic document preserved for us in the actual words of the martyrs and their friends. It was in the great African city of Carthage, in the year 203, during the persecutions ordered by the Emperor Severus,[1] that five catechumens [2] were arrested for their faith. The group consisted of a slave Revocatus, his fellow slave Felicitas, who was expecting the birth of a child, two free men, Saturninus and Secundulus, and a matron of twenty-two, Vivia Perpetua, wife of a man in good position and mother of a small infant. Perpetua's father was a pagan, her mother and two brothers Christians, one of the brothers being a catechumen. These five prisoners were soon joined by one Saturus, who seems to have been their instructor in the faith and who now chose to share their punishment. At first they were all kept under strong guard in a private house. Perpetua wrote a vivid account of what happened.

[1] Severus was a Roman general whose bold military exploits led him to be proclaimed emperor by the army after the death of the licentious Commodus, son of Marcus Aurelius.

[2] A catechumen is the term for a person under instruction preparatory to being received into the Church but as yet not baptized.

"While I was still with my companions, and my father in his affection for me was trying to turn me from my purpose by arguments and so weaken my faith, 'Father,' said I, 'do you see this vessel—water pot or whatever it may be? . . . Can it be called by any other name than what it is?' 'No,' he replied. 'So also I cannot call myself by any other name than what I am—a Christian.' Then my father, provoked by the word 'Christian,' threw himself on me as if he would pluck out my eyes, but he only shook me, and in fact was vanquished. . . . Then I thanked God for the relief of being, for a few days, parted from my father . . . and during those few days we were baptized. The Holy Spirit bade me after the holy rite to pray for nothing but bodily endurance.

"A few days later we were lodged in the prison, and I was much frightened, because I had never known such darkness. What a day of horror! Terrible heat, owing to the crowds! Rough treatment by the soldiers! To crown all I was tormented with anxiety for my baby. But Tertius and Pomponius, those blessed deacons who ministered to us, paid for us to be moved for a few hours to a better part of the prison and we obtained some relief. All went out of the prison and we were left to ourselves. My baby was brought and I nursed him, for already he was faint for want of food. I spoke anxiously to my mother on his behalf and encouraged my brother and commended my son to their care. For I was concerned when I saw their concern for me. For many days I suffered such anxieties, but I obtained leave for my child to remain in the prison with me, and when relieved of my trouble and distress for him, I quickly recovered my health. My prison suddenly became a palace to me and I would rather have been there than anywhere else.

"My brother then said to me: 'Lady sister, you are now greatly honored, so greatly that you may well pray for a vision to show you whether suffering or release is in store for you.' And I, knowing myself to have speech of the Lord for whose sake I was suffering, promised him confidently, 'Tomorrow I will bring you word.' And I prayed and this was shown me. I saw a golden ladder of wonderful length reaching up to heaven, but so narrow that only

one at a time could ascend; and to the sides of the ladder were
fastened all kinds of iron weapons. There were swords, lances,
hooks, daggers, so that if anyone climbed up carelessly or without
looking upwards, he was mangled and his flesh caught on the
weapons. And at the foot of the ladder was a huge dragon which
lay in wait for those going up and sought to frighten them from
the ascent. The first to go up was Saturus, who of his own accord
had given himself up for our sakes, because our faith was of his
building and he was not with us when we were arrested. He reached
the top of the ladder and, turning, said to me: 'Perpetua, I wait
for you, but take care that the dragon does not bite you.' And I
said: 'In the name of Jesus Christ, he will not hurt me.' And the
dragon put out his head gently, as if afraid of me, just at the foot
of the ladder; and as though I were treading on the first step, I trod
on his head. And I went up and saw a vast garden, and sitting in
the midst a tall man with white hair in the dress of a shepherd,
milking sheep; and round about were many thousands clad in
white. He raised his head and looked at me and said: 'Thou art
well come, my child.' And he called me and gave me some curds
of the milk he was milking, and I received them in my joined hands
and ate, and all that were round about said 'Amen.' At the sound
of the word I awoke, still tasting something sweet. I at once told
my brother and we understood that we must suffer, and henceforth
began to have no hope in this world.

"After a few days there was a report that we were to be examined. My father arrived from the city, worn with anxiety, and
came up the hill hoping still to weaken my resolution. 'Daughter,'
he said, 'pity my white hairs! Pity your father, if I deserve you
should call me father, if I have brought you up to this your prime
of life, if I have loved you more than your brothers! Make me
not a reproach to mankind! Look on your mother and your
mother's sister, look on your son who cannot live after you are
gone. Forget your pride; do not make us all wretched! None of us
will ever speak freely again if calamity strikes you.' So spoke my
father in his love for me, kissing my hands and casting himself at

my feet, and with tears calling me by the title not of 'daughter' but of 'lady.' And I grieved for my father's sake, because he alone of all my kindred would not have joy at my martyrdom. And I tried to comfort him, saying, 'What takes place on that platform will be as God shall choose, for assuredly we are not in our own power but in the power of God.' But he departed full of grief.

"The following day, while we were at our dinner, we were suddenly summoned to be examined and went to the forum. The news of the trial spread fast and brought a huge crowd together in the forum. We were placed on a sort of platform before the judge, who was Hilarion, procurator of the province, since the proconsul had lately died. The others were questioned before me and confessed their faith. But when it came to my turn, my father appeared with my child, and drawing me down the steps besought me, 'Have pity on the child.' The judge Hilarion joined with my father and said: 'Spare your father's white hairs. Spare the tender years of your child. Offer sacrifice for the prosperity of the emperors.' I replied, 'No.' 'Are you a Christian?' asked Hilarion, and I answered, 'Yes, I am.' My father then attempted to drag me down from the platform, at which Hilarion commanded that he should be beaten off, and he was struck with a rod. I felt this as much as if I myself had been struck, so deeply did I grieve to see my father treated thus in his old age. The judge then passed sentence on us all and condemned us to the wild beasts, and in great joy we returned to our prison. Then, as my baby was accustomed to the breast, I sent Pomponius the deacon to ask him of my father, who, however, refused to send him. And God so ordered it that the child no longer needed to nurse, nor did my milk incommode me."

Secundulus seems to have died in prison before the examination. Before pronouncing sentence, Hilarion had Saturus, Saturninus, and Revocatus scourged and Perpetua and Felicitas beaten on the face. They were then kept for the gladiatorial shows which were to be given for the soldiers on the festival of Geta, the young prince whom his father Severus had made Caesar four years previously.

While in prison both Perpetua and Saturus had visions which they described in writing in great detail.

The remainder of the story was added by another hand, apparently that of an eyewitness. Felicitas had feared that she might not be allowed to suffer with the rest because pregnant women were not sent into the arena. However, she gave birth in the prison to a daughter whom one of their fellow Christians at once adopted. Pudens, their jailer, was by this time a convert, and did all he could for them. The day before the games they were given the usual last meal, which was called "the free banquet." The martyrs strove to make it an *Agape* or Love Feast,[3] and to those who crowded around them they spoke of the judgments of God and of their own joy in their sufferings. Such calm courage and confidence astonished the pagans and brought about many conversions.

On the day of their martyrdom they set forth from the prison. Behind the men walked the young noblewoman Perpetua, "abashing the gaze of all with the high spirit in her eyes," and beside her the slave Felicitas. At the gates of the amphitheater the attendants tried to force the men to put on the robes of the priests of Saturn and the women the dress symbolic of the goddess Ceres, but they all resisted and the officer allowed them to enter the arena clad as they were. Perpetua was singing, while Revocatus, Saturninus, and Saturus were calling out warnings to the bystanders and even to Hilarion himself, as they walked beneath his balcony, of the coming vengeance of God. The mob cried out that they should be scourged for their boldness. Accordingly, as the martyrs passed in front of the *venatores,* or hunters, each received a lash.

To each one God granted the form of martyrdom he desired. Saturus had hoped to be exposed to several sorts of beasts, that his sufferings might be intensified. He and Revocatus were first attacked half-heartedly by a leopard. Saturus was next exposed to a

---

[3] Agape is the Greek word for brotherly love. It was used to denote one type of early Christian assembly, which included the eating of food together, as well as prayer, singing of psalms, and often the celebration of the Eucharist.

wild boar which turned on his keeper instead. He was then tied up on the bridge in front of a bear, but the animal refused to stir out of his den, and Saturus was reserved for one more encounter. The delay gave him an opportunity to turn and speak to the converted jailer Pudens: "You see that what I desired and foretold has come to pass. Not a beast has touched me! So believe steadfastly in Christ. And see now, I go forth yonder and with one bite from a leopard all will be over." As he had foretold, a leopard was now let out, sprang upon him, and in a moment he was fatally wounded. Seeing the flow of blood, the cruel mob cried out, "He is well baptized now!" Dying, Saturus said to Pudens, "Farewell; remember my faith and me, and let these things not daunt but strengthen you." He then asked for a ring from Pudens' finger, and dipping it in his own blood, returned it to the jailer as a keepsake. Then he expired.

Perpetua and Felicitas were exposed to a mad heifer. Perpetua was tossed first and fell on her back, but raised herself and gathered her torn tunic modestly about her; then, after fastening up her hair, lest she look as if she were in mourning, she rose and went to help Felicitas, who had been badly hurt by the animal. Side by side they stood, expecting another assault, but the sated audience cried out that it was enough. They were therefore led to the gate Sanevivaria, where victims who had not been killed in the arena were despatched by gladiators. Here Perpetua seemed to arouse herself from an ecstasy and could not believe that she had already been exposed to a mad heifer until she saw the marks of her injuries. She then called out to her brother and to the catechumen: "Stand fast in the faith, and love one another. Do not let our sufferings be a stumbling block to you." By this time the fickle populace was clamoring for the women to come back into the open. This they did willingly, and after giving each other the kiss of peace, they were killed by the gladiators. Perpetua had to guide the sword of the nervous executioner to her throat. The story of these martyrs has been given in detail for it is typical of so many others. No saints were more universally honored in all the early Church calendars

INSTRUCTION OF THE VIRGIN   M. Raab
This picture was painted by an itinerant artist for one of the houses of the
Congregation of the Most Holy Redeemer. He has followed the great traditions of art in depicting Saint Anne instructing the young Mary, although
the style is fresh and modern.

This painting uses none of the traditional symbolism. Saint Anne is recognized
by the figure of the young Virgin Mary. Her usual symbol is a nest of birds.

THE MEETING OF JOACHIM AND ANNA
Giotto

The climax of this great painter's work (1266-1337) was the series of frescoes on the lives of the Virgin and Christ which he painted in the Arena Chapel in Padua. This scene shows the meeting of the parents of the Blessed Virgin just after each has been informed separately of the joy to come in the birth of Mary.

Saint Joachim is always shown with the Golden Gate of Jerusalem, before which the meeting with his childless wife took place. Sometimes a basket containing doves is also represented.

and martyrologies. Their names appear not only in the Philocalian Calendar [4] of Rome, but also in the Syriac Calendar. The names of Felicitas and Perpetua occur in the prayer "Nobis quoque peccatoribus" in the Canon of the Mass. In the fourth century their *Acts* were publicly read in the churches of Africa and were so highly esteemed that Augustine, bishop of Hippo, found it necessary to protest against their being placed on a level with the Scriptures.

[4] The Philocalian Calendar, compiled by one Philocalus in the year 354, was the earliest known list of the feasts of martyrs observed by the Roman Church; the Syriac Calendar was drawn up at Antioch towards the end of the fourth century.

Saint Irenaeus
Doctor of the Church
c. 2 0 3
(June 28)

The writings of Irenaeus give him an honored place among the Fathers of the Church for they laid the foundations of Christian theology and, by refuting the errors of the Gnostics,[1] kept the youthful Catholic faith from the danger of corruption by the subtle, pessimistic doctrines of these philosophers. Irenaeus was born, probably about the year 125, in one of the maritime provinces of Asia Minor, where the memory of the Apostles was still cherished and where Christians were already numerous. His education was exceptionally liberal, for, besides a thorough knowledge of the Scriptures, he had an acquaintance with Greek philosophy and literature. Irenaeus had also the privilege of sitting at the feet of men who had known the Apostles. Of these the one who made the deepest impression on him was St. Polycarp, the venerable bishop of Smyrna. All through his life, he told a friend, he could recall

[1] Gnostic is the name applied to a fluctuating set of Eastern dualist beliefs, older than Christianity, though they took over features from Christianity in the course of their spread westward. The Docetists of Ignatius' day may be regarded as a branch of the Gnostics. In general the latter took the view that the creator of the gross world of matter, the God of the Old Testament, was a dark and brutal deity, forever at war with the pure and spiritual God of light, depicted in the New Testament, from whom Jesus had been an emanation. Jesus, therefore, only appeared to be born and die and could never have suffered contamination by mortal flesh. The Gnostic movement, with its denial of Christ's humanity, vexed the Church in one form or another for several centuries. In the Middle Ages it was known as Manichaeism.

every detail of Polycarp's appearance, his voice, and the very words he used when telling what he had heard from John the Evangelist and others who had seen Jesus.

From early times commerce had been brisk between the ports of Asia Minor and the city of Marseilles, at the mouth of the Rhone River. In the second century of the Christian era Levantine traders were conveying their wares up the river as far as Lyons, the most populous city of Gaul and an important mart for all Western Europe. In the train of these Asiatic merchants, many of whom settled in Lyons, came Christian missionaries, who brought the Gospel to the pagan Gauls and founded a vigorous church. Here Irenaeus was sent to serve as priest under the bishop, Pothinus.

The high regard which Irenaeus earned for himself at Lyons was shown in the year 177, when he was chosen to go on a serious mission to Rome. He was the bearer of a letter to Pope Eleutherius, urging him to deal firmly with the Montanist [2] faction in faraway Phrygia, for heresy was now rampant in the East. This mission explains how it was that Irenaeus did not share in the martyrdom of his fellow Christians. A persecution broke out, and some of the leaders of the Lyons church were imprisoned; a few suffered martyrdom. This was in the reign of the philosophical pagan emperor, Marcus Aurelius. Since Lyons was a vital outpost of imperial power, adorned with temples and fine public buildings, the Roman officials perhaps thought it necessary to keep the new religion in check here. When Irenaeus returned from Rome it was to fill the now vacant bishopric. The brief period of persecution was over, and the twenty or more years of his episcopate were fairly peaceful. In addition to his pastoral duties at Lyons, Irenaeus is

[2] The Montanists, followers of a Phrygian priest, Montanus, were a set of Christians who believed in a speedy return of Christ to earth. They practiced a rigid asceticism and accepted as their only authority the revelations of God to each individual soul. They therefore presented serious obstacles to the setting up of an orderly church organization. They are not heard of after the second century.

said to have extended the sphere of Christian influence by sending missionaries to other towns of Gaul—SS. Felix, Fortunatus, and Achilleus to Valence, and SS. Ferrutius and Ferreolus to Besançon. The bishop identified himself with his flock so completely as to speak habitually the native tongue instead of Latin or Greek, and to encourage all priests to do likewise.

The spread of Gnosticism in Gaul led Irenaeus to make a careful study of its tenets, not an easy matter since each Gnostic teacher was inclined to introduce subleties of his own. He was, Tertullian tells us, "a curious explorer of all kinds of learning," and the task interested him. His treatise *Against the Heresies,* in five books, sets forth fully the doctrines of the main dissident sects of the day and then contrasts them with the words of Scripture and the teachings of the Apostles, as preserved not only in sacred writings but by oral tradition in the churches which the Apostles founded. Above all, he cites the authoritative tradition of the Church of Rome, handed down from Peter and Paul through an unbroken succession of bishops. In his theological works Irenaeus especially shows the influence of St. Paul and St. John. An humble, patient man, he writes of controversial matters with a moderation and courtesy unusual in this age of perfervid conviction.

An example of his method is his discussion of one type of Gnostic doctrine, that the visible world was created and is sustained and governed by angelic beings, but not by God, who remains unconnected with it, aloof and unmoved in his own inaccessible sphere. Irenaeus states the theory, develops it to a logical conclusion, and then by an effective *reductio ad absurdum* demonstrates its fallacy. The Christian doctrine of a close continuing relationship between the Triune God and the world He created Irenaeus describes thus: "The Father is above all, and He is the Head of Christ; the Word (*Logos*) is through all things and is Himself the Head of the Church, while the Spirit is in us all, and His is the living water which the Lord gave to those who believe in Him and love Him, and who know that there is one Father above all things and through all things." Irenaeus was convinced that the veil of mystery which enveloped Gnosticism was part of its attraction, and he was determined to "strip the fox," as he expressed it. His book, written in Greek and quickly translated into Latin, was widely circulated, and from this time on Gnosticism presented no serious threat.

Thirteen or fourteen years after his mission to Rome, Irenaeus attempted mediation between another Pope and a body of Christians in Asia Minor called the Quartodecimans,[3] who refused to fix the day of Easter by the method commonly used by Christians. Pope Victor had excommunicated them, and Irenaeus pleaded with him in a beautiful letter to raise the ban, pointing out that these Asiatics were only following their Apostolic tradition, and that the difference of opinion on this minor point had not prevented St. Polycarp and many others from staying in communion. At the end of the fourth century Jerome wrote that many Eastern bishops still adhered to the ancient Jewish calendar.

The date of the death of Irenaeus is usually given as about the year 203. According to a late and dubious tradition he suffered martyrdom under Septimius Severus. His book *Against the Heresies* has come down to us entire in its Latin version; and an Armenian translation of his *Exposition of Apostolic Preaching* has lately been discovered. Though the rest of his writings have perished, in these two works may be found the elements of a complete system of Catholic theology.

Excerpts from Against the Heresies

iii. 1. *We have learned the plan of our salvation entirely* from the men through whom the Gospel came to us. At first they proclaimed it abroad; then later, by the will of God,

[3] The Quartodecimans observed Easter on the second day after the Passover of the Jews, that is, on the fourteenth day of the Jewish month Nisan, regardless of the day of the week on which it fell. The majority of Christians celebrated it on the first Sunday after the first full moon following the Spring equinox.

they wrote it down for us in the Scriptures to be the foundation and pillar of our faith. . . .

2. But when we refute these people [the heretics] out of the Scriptures, they turn and accuse the very Scriptures, on the ground that they are mistaken or not authoritative or not consistent in their narrative, and they say that the truth cannot be learned from them by persons who do not know the tradition, and that that was not transmitted in writing but by word of mouth. . . .

3. Now it is within the power of anyone who cares to find out the truth, to know the tradition of the Apostles, professed throughout the world in every church. We can name those too who were appointed bishops by the Apostles in the churches and their successors down to our own time. . . . But inasmuch as it would be very tedious in a book like this to rehearse the lines of succession in every church, we will put to confusion all those who, either from waywardness or conceit or blindness or obstinacy combine together against the truth, by pointing to the tradition, derived from the Apostles, of that great and illustrious Church founded and organized at Rome by the two glorious Apostles, Peter and Paul, and to the faith declared to mankind and handed down to our own time through its bishops in their succession. For with this Church, because of its more powerful leadership, every church, that is to say, the faithful from everywhere, must needs agree, and in it the tradition that springs from the Apostles has been continuously preserved by men from everywhere. . . .

4. Seeing, therefore, that we have such testimony, we do not need to seek elsewhere the truth which it is easy to find in the Church. For the Apostles, like a rich man at a bank, deposited lavishly with her all aspects of the truth, so that everyone, whoever will, may draw from her the water of life. For she is the door to life, and all others are thieves and robbers. For this reason we must shun them and love the things of the Church with the utmost diligence and keep hold of the tradition of the truth. . . .

This is the course followed by the barbarian peoples [4] who believe in Christ and have salvation written in their hearts by the Spirit without paper or ink, but who guard carefully the ancient tradition. For they believe in one God, the Creator of heaven and

[4] That is, the Gallic provincials among whom Irenaeus was living.

earth and of all things therein through Christ Jesus, the Son of God, who for his surpassing love towards his creation underwent birth from a virgin, uniting man through himself to God, and who suffered under Pontius Pilate and rose again and was received up in splendor, and who shall come in glory, the Saviour of those who are saved and the Judge of those who are judged, to send into eternal fire those who pervert the truth and despise his Father and his coming.

(*The Ante-Nicene Fathers,* Vol. I, 1885.)

Saint Cecilia

Virgin, Martyr

SECOND OR THIRD CENTURY

(*November 22*)

For over a thousand years St. Cecilia has been one of the most venerated martyrs of the early Church; she is among the seven martyrs named in the Canon of the Mass. According to a tradition current at the end of the fifth century, Cecilia was a Roman girl of patrician family, who had been brought up as a Christian. She fasted often, and wore a coarse garment beneath her rich clothing. Although she wished to remain a virgin, her father betrothed her to a young pagan named Valerian. When the wedding day came, Cecilia sat apart from the guests, repeating psalms and praying. After the ceremony, when the guests had departed and she was alone with her husband, Cecilia made known her great desire to remain as she was, saying that she already had a lover, an angel of God, who was very jealous. Valerian, shaken by suspicion, fear, and anger, said to her: "Show me this angel. If he is of God, I shall refrain, as you wish, but if he is a human lover, you both must die." Cecilia answered: "If you believe in the one true and living God and receive the water of baptism, then you shall see the angel." Valerian assented, and following his wife's directions sought out a bishop named Urban, who was in hiding among the tombs of the martyrs, for this was a time of persecutions. Valerian made his profession of faith and the bishop baptized him. When the young husband returned, he found an angel with flaming wings standing beside Cecilia. The angel placed chaplets of roses and lilies on their heads. The brother of Valerian, Tiburtius, was

24

also converted, and after being baptized he too experienced many marvels.

Valerian and Tiburtius devoted themselves to good works in behalf of the Christian community, and they made it their special duty to give proper burial to those Christians who were put to death by order of the prefect Almachius. The two brothers were themselves soon sentenced for refusing to sacrifice to Jupiter. Maximus, a Roman officer charged with their execution, was converted by a vision that came to him in the hour of their death. After professing Christianity, he too suffered martyrdom. The three were buried by the grieving Cecilia, and a little later she herself was sentenced. The prefect came and tried to reason with her, but when he found her firm in the faith and scornful of his threats, he gave an order that she was to be suffocated in her own bathroom. Surviving this attempt on her life, a soldier was sent to behead her. He struck at her neck three times, then left her lying, still alive, for it was against the law to strike a fourth time. She lingered on for three days, during which the Christians who remained in Rome flocked to her house. In dying she bequeathed all her goods to the poor, and her house to the bishop for a Christian place of worship. She was buried in the crypt of the Caecilii at the catacomb of St. Callistus.

The above legend of St. Cecilia dates back, as we have said, to the end of the fifth century. There is no mention of this saint in the *Depositio Martyrum,* but there is a record of an early Roman Christian church founded by a lady of this name. In the ninth century Pope Paschal I moved the remains of many martyrs from the catacombs to new churches within the city; the presumed relics of St. Cecilia, her husband, his brother, and the Roman officer Maximus, were all placed in the church of St. Cecilia. The origin of her veneration as a patron of music is unknown to us. She was not associated with music in the early period or in the account given in the medieval *Golden Legend* by Jacobus Voragine, but artists of later times have delighted in depicting her at the organ, singing God's praise or listening to a choir of angels.

Saint Christopher

Martyr

THIRD CENTURY

(*July 25*)

From the great mass of legendary material, often confused and contradictory, which is associated with the name of St. Christopher, there emerges one clear conception. It is that of a man who is strong, simple, kind, and completely dedicated to one thing: serving the Lord by serving his fellow men. Christopher, according to the ancient and very popular tradition, lived in the province of Lydia, Asia Minor, during the reign of the Emperor Decius. He was a man of enormous size and strength, who had been converted to Christianity by a holy hermit. Having no gift for preaching, fasting, or prayer, the customary practices of the good Christian, he searched for some other way of showing his love of God. An inspiration came to him. He went to a certain stream whose current was so dangerous that travelers were often swept away while trying to ford it. Here Christopher built a hut for shelter, then stationed himself on the bank, and carried across all who came, a sort of human ferry. After he had been laboring in this way for some time, a little child appeared one day, and asked to be carried. Christopher lifted the child in his great arms, placed him on his shoulder, and started across, staff in hand. At every step the load grew more burdensome, and Christopher came near losing his balance in the rushing water. On reaching the other bank, he put the boy down, saying, "Child, thou hast put me in dire peril, and hast weighed so heavily on me that if I had borne the whole weight of the world upon my shoulders it could not have burdened me more heavily."

The boy answered, "Wonder not, Christopher, for not only hast thou borne the whole world on thy shoulders, but Him who created the world"—for the Christ Child, bearing in His own arms the great world, had been Christopher's burden. To prove that this was true, He told Christopher to recross the river and plant his staff in the ground beside his hut and soon it would burst into bloom. Obeying, Christopher was amazed to see this occur, and then he knew how wonderfully he had been favored.

This miracle brought about the conversion of many in those parts, but it aroused the wrath of the pagan king, who had Christopher imprisoned, tortured, and beheaded. In the *Golden Legend* are to be found other stories of the saint which were current in medieval times. Christopher is loved and honored in the churches both of the East and the West. In addition to being the patron and protector of all travelers, he is also invoked against storms and sudden death. In art Christopher is usually shown with his emblems, the Christ Child, a tree in bloom, a torrent; the great artists Dürer and Pollaiuolo are among those who have portrayed him in the act for which he is best known.

Saint Lucy
Virgin, Martyr
3 0 4
(*December 13*)

The traditional story of St. Lucy tells us that she was of noble Greek parentage, born in Syracuse, Sicily, and brought up as a Christian by her mother, Eutychia. Although Lucy, like Cecilia, wished to dedicate herself to God, Eutychia arranged for her a marriage with a young pagan. The mother, who suffered from haemorrhage, was persuaded to make a pilgrimage to Catania, to offer prayers at the tomb of St. Agatha. Lucy accompanied her mother, and their prayers for a cure were answered. Then Lucy made known to Eutychia her desire to give her own share of their fortune to the poor and devote herself to God's service. Eutychia, in gratitude for her cure, gave permission. This so angered the young man to whom Lucy had been unwillingly betrothed that he denounced her as a Christian to the governor, Paschius. The persecutions instituted by the Emperor Diocletian were then at their height, and when Lucy steadfastly clung to her faith, she was sentenced to prostitution in a brothel. God rendered her immovable and the officers were not able to carry her off to the place of evil. An attempt was then made to burn her, but boiling oil and pitch had no power to hurt her or break her strong spirit. At last she was put to death by the sword. At Rome in the sixth century Lucy was honored among the other virgin martyrs, and her name was inserted in the Canon of the Mass. A reference to her sanctity occurs in a letter written by Pope Gregory the Great. In the Middle Ages, she was invoked by persons suffering from eye trouble, perhaps because Lucy (in Italian, Lucia) derives from *lux*, the Latin word for light. The first church writer to give an account of St. Lucy from her *Acts* was the English bishop St. Aldhelm of Sherborne at the end of the seventh century. This saint's relics are venerated at Venice and at Bourges, in France. She is patroness of Syracuse; her emblems are a cord and eyes.

Saint Catherine of Alexandria
Virgin, Martyr

c. 3 1 0

(*November 25*)

From the tenth century onwards veneration for St. Catherine of Alexandria [1] has been widespread in the Church of the East, and from the time of the Crusades this saint has been popular in the West, where many churches have been dedicated to her and her feast day kept with great solemnity, sometimes as a holy-day of obligation. She is listed as one of the Fourteen Holy Helpers of mankind among the saints in Heaven; she is the patroness of young women, philosophers, preachers, theologians, wheelwrights, millers, and other workingmen. She was said to have appeared with Our Lady to St. Dominic and to Blessed Reginald of Orleans; the Dominicans adopted her as their special protectress. Hers was one of the heavenly voices heard by St. Joan of Arc. Artists have painted her with her chief emblem, the wheel, on which by tradition she was tortured; other emblems are a lamb and a sword. Her name continues to be cherished today by the young unmarried women of Paris.

Yet in spite of this veneration, we have few facts that can be relied on concerning Catherine's life. Eusebius,[2] "father of Church

---

[1] Alexandria, the great Egyptian city at the mouth of the Nile, was at this time a center of both pagan and Christian learning. Its Christian activities centered around the great church founded, according to tradition, by the Apostle Mark, with its catechetical school, the first of its kind in Christendom.

[2] Eusebius, bishop of Caesarea, who lived through all the vicissitudes of the years before and succeeding the Edict of Toleration and died about 340, wrote the first history of the Church.

history," writing around the year 320, had heard of a noble young Christian woman of Alexandria whom the Emperor ordered to come to his palace, presumably to become his mistress, and who, on refusing, was punished by banishment and the confiscation of her estates. The story of St. Catherine may have sprung from some brief record such as this, which Christians writing at a later date expanded. The last persecutions of Christians, though short, were severe, and those living in the peace which followed seem to have had a tendency to embellish the traditions of their martyrs that they might not be forgotten.

According to the popular tradition, Catherine was born of a patrician family of Alexandria and from childhood had devoted herself to study. Through her reading she had learned much of Christianity and had been converted by a vision of Our Lady and the Holy Child. When Maxentius [3] began his persecution, Catherine, then a beautiful young girl, went to him and rebuked him boldly for his cruelty. He could not answer her arguments against his pagan gods, and summoned fifty philosophers to confute her. They all confessed themselves won over by her reasoning, and were thereupon burned to death by the enraged Emperor. He then tried to seduce Catherine with an offer of a consort's crown, and when she indignantly refused him, he had her beaten and imprisoned. The Emperor went off to inspect his military forces, and when he got back he discovered that his wife Faustina and a high official, one Porphyrius, had been visiting Catherine and had been converted, along with the soldiers of the guard. They too were put to death, and Catherine was sentenced to be killed on a spiked wheel. When she was fastened to the wheel, her bonds were miraculously loosed and the wheel itself broke, its spikes flying off and killing some of the onlookers. She was then beheaded. The

---

[3] Maxentius was one of several rival emperors who struggled for mastery during the first dozen years of the fourth century. Like the others, he tried to crush what he considered the dangerous institution of the Catholic Church. Some historians are of the opinion that Catherine suffered under his father, Maximian.

modern catherine-wheel, from which sparks fly off in all directions, took its name from the saint's wheel of martyrdom. The text of the *Acts* of this illustrious saint states that her body was carried by angels to Mount Sinai, where a church and monastery were afterwards built in her honor. This legend was, however, unknown to the earliest pilgrims to the mountain. In 527 the Emperor Justinian built a fortified monastery for hermits in that region, and two or three centuries later the story of St. Catherine and the angels began to be circulated.

Saint Agnes

Virgin, Martyr

c. 3 1 4

(*January 21*)

Few legends of saints have been more cherished than that of the virgin martyr Agnes. She was held in high regard by the primitive Christian Church, and her name has remained a symbol of maidenly purity through the ages. According to tradition, Agnes was a Christian girl of Rome, perhaps twelve or thirteen years old, when Diocletian began his persecutions. Like St. Lucy, she was sentenced by a judge to a house of ill fame, but a young man who looked upon her lustfully was stricken blind. Thereafter she was taken out to be burned, but whether she met her death by fire or sword we cannot know with any certainty. Although we have no contemporary sources for the facts of her life and martyrdom, there is little reason to doubt the main outline of the story. References to this young saint appear in many Church writings of later date. St. Ambrose, St. Damasus, and Prudentius all praise her purity and heroism. Her name occurs in the Canon of the Mass. Agnes' crypt was in the Via Nomentana, and the stone covering her remains was carven with the words, *Agna sanctissima* (most holy lamb). A church in her honor is presumed to have been built at Rome in the time of Constantine the Great. In the apse of this basilica, which was rebuilt in the seventh century by Pope Honorius, there is still to be seen the large and beautiful mosaic depicting the saint. St. Agnes is the patroness of young girls and her symbol is, naturally, a lamb. On the anniversary of her martyrdom, the Pope, after high pontifical Mass in her church at Rome, blesses two lambs, and their wool is later woven into the *pallia* worn by archbishops.

33

Saint Blaise

Martyr

c. 3 1 6

(*February 3*)

I t is not known precisely when or where St. Blaise lived, but according to tradition he was a bishop of Sebaste, Armenia, in the early part of the fourth century, and suffered martyrdom under the Roman emperor Licinius, who had commanded the governor of the province, one Agricolaus, to prevent the spread of Christianity in his territory. After this edict had been promulgated, Blaise fled to the mountains and lived in a cave frequented by wild beasts. He used his skill to heal the animals that he found wounded or sick, and when the emperor's hunters, bent on collecting wild animals for the royal games, discovered him in this cave, they carried him off to Agricolaus as a special prize.

On the way, the story goes, they met a poor woman whose pig had been seized by a wolf. At the command of Blaise, the wolf restored the pig to its owner, alive and unhurt. During the course of this journey he also miraculously cured a child who was choking to death on a fishbone. For this reason St. Blaise is often invoked by persons suffering from throat trouble. When he had reached the capital and was in prison awaiting execution, the old woman whose pig he had saved came to see him, bringing two fine wax candles to dispel the gloom of his dark cell. When he was finally killed, he is supposed to have been tortured with an iron comb or rake, and afterwards beheaded. In the West there was no cult honoring St. Blaise prior to the eighth century. One of the Fourteen Holy Helpers, his emblems are an iron comb and a wax taper.

Saint Helena

Widow

3 3 0

(August 18)

Helena, mother of Constantine I, called the Great, was born of humble parents in the Roman province of Moesia, a land on the western shore of the Black Sea. Constantine's father, Constantius Chlorus, who had risen to the throne by way of military success, was also a native of that region. According to St. Ambrose, Helena was an inn-keeper when Constantius lifted her from her lowly position and made her his consort. There exists a legend that she was the daughter of a British king, but there is no historical foundation for this. It is, however, true that Constantius spent some time in Britain putting down a rebellion among the Picts and Scots, and died at York, but it is thought that he had cast off Helena and taken a new wife long before this time. On the death of his father, the young Constantine brought his mother to live at court at Byzantium, the capital of the Eastern Empire. He honored her by giving her the Roman title of Augusta and also had coins struck bearing her image.

Everyone knows the story of Constantine's dramatic conversion. The Church historian, Eusebius, whose *Life of Constantine* is a chief source of information for the period, relates that on the eve of a great battle in the year 312 Constantine had a dream (by some accounts the dream was preceded by a day-time vision) of a flaming cross in the sky, and beneath it were the words, in Greek, "In this sign conquer." He thereupon embraced Christianity and proceeded south to the Tiber, where his victory over the Emperor

35

Maxentius gave him control of the Western Empire. Constantine now effected his mother's conversion, and had his children reared as Christians. Helena became zealous for the faith, using her influence and wealth to extend Christianity. She built many churches and restored shrines; her name is particularly associated with churches at Rome and at Trier, in Gaul. But it is in the Holy Land itself that we have the most authentic record of her activities, which included the construction of great basilicas at Bethlehem and Jerusalem. To clear the Holy Places of the accumulated débris of three centuries was Helena's dearest aim. According to some of the chroniclers, when she was an old woman of nearly eighty, with the help of St. Judas Cyriacus, she cleared the mound that covered the Holy Sepulchre, and in doing so uncovered the True Cross, on which Jesus was crucified. The treasure was then removed to Byzantium, and in the life of *St. Louis* of France we shall read something of its later history. There is, however, no record of this discovery in Eusebius.

Saint Nicholas of Myra

Bishop, Confessor

c. 3 4 2

(*December 6*)

The veneration with which this saint has been honored in both East and West, the number of altars and churches erected in his memory, and the countless stories associated with his name all bear witness to something extraordinary about him. Yet the one fact concerning the life of Nicholas of which we can be absolutely certain is that he was bishop of Myra in the fourth century. According to tradition, he was born at Patara, Lycia, a province of southern Asia Minor where St. Paul had planted the faith. Myra, the capital, was the seat of a bishopric founded by St. Nicander. The accounts of Nicholas given us by the Greek Church all say that he was imprisoned in the reign of Diocletian, whose persecutions, while they lasted, were waged with great severity. Some twenty years after this he appeared at the Council of Nicaea,[1] to join in the condemnation of Arianism. We are also informed that he died at Myra and was buried in his cathedral. Such a wealth of literature has accumulated around Nicholas that we are justified in giving a brief account of some of the popular traditions, which in the main date from medieval times. St. Methodius, patriarch of Constantinople towards the middle of the ninth century, wrote a

[1] Nicaea was a city in Bithynia, now northwestern Turkey, a short distance south of Constantinople. The Council of Nicaea, in 325, was the first oecumenical church council, and was called by the Emperor Constantine to bring about agreement on matters of creed. For more on Arianism, see below, *St. Athanasius*, n. 6.

life of the saint in which he declares that "up to the present the life of the distinguished shepherd has been unknown to the majority of the faithful." Nearly five hundred years had passed since the death of the good St. Nicholas, and Methodius' account, therefore, had to be based more on legend than actual fact.

He was very well brought up, we are told, by pious and virtuous parents, who set him to studying the sacred books at the age of five. His parents died while he was still young, leaving him with a comfortable fortune, which he resolved to use for works of charity. Soon an opportunity came. A citizen of Patara had lost all his money and his three daughters could not find husbands because of their poverty. In despair their wretched father was about to commit them to a life of shame. When Nicholas heard of this, he took a bag of gold and at night tossed it through an open window of the man's house. Here was a dowry for the eldest girl, and she was quickly married. Nicholas did the same for the second and then for the third daughter. On the last occasion the father was watching by the window, and overwhelmed his young benefactor with gratitude.

It happened that Nicholas was in the city of Myra when the clergy and people were meeting together to elect a new bishop, and God directed them to choose him. This was at the time of Diocletian's persecutions at the beginning of the fourth century. The Greek writers go on to say that now, as leader, "the divine Nicholas was seized by the magistrates, tortured, then chained and thrown into prison with other Christians. But when the great and religious Constantine, chosen by God, assumed the imperial diadem of the Romans, the prisoners were released from their bonds and with them the illustrious Nicholas." St. Methodius adds that "thanks to the teaching of St. Nicholas, the metropolis of Myra alone was untouched by the filth of the Arian heresy, which it firmly rejected as a death-dealing poison." He does not speak of Nicholas' presence at the Council of Nicaea, but according to other traditions he was not only there but went so far in his indignation as to slap the arch-heretic Arius in the face! At this, they say, he was deprived of his episcopal insignia and imprisoned, but Our Lord and His Mother appeared and restored to him both his liberty and his office. Nicholas also took strong measures against paganism. He tore down many temples, among them one to the Greek goddess Artemis, which was the chief pagan shrine of the district.

Nicholas was also the guardian of his people in temporal affairs. The governor had been bribed to condemn three innocent men to death. On the day fixed for their execution Nicholas stayed the hand of the executioner and released them. Then he turned to the governor and reproved him so sternly that he repented. There happened to be present that day three imperial officers, Nepotian, Ursus, and Herpylion, on their way to duty in Phrygia. Later, after their return, they were imprisoned on false charges of treason by the prefect and an order was procured from the Emperor Constantine for their death. In their extremity they remembered the bishop of Myra's passion for justice and prayed to God for his intercession. That night Nicholas appeared to Constantine in a dream, ordering him to release the three innocent officers. The prefect had the same dream, and in the morning the two men compared their dreams, then questioned the accused officers. On learning that they had prayed for the intervention of Nicholas, Constantine freed them and sent them to the bishop with a letter asking him to pray for the peace of the world. In the West the story took on more and more fantastic forms; in one version the three officers eventually became three boys murdered by an innkeeper and put into a brine tub from which Nicholas rescued them and restored them to life.

The traditions all agree that Nicholas was buried in his episcopal city of Myra. By the time of Justinian, some two centuries later, his feast was celebrated and there was a church built over his tomb. The ruins of this domed basilica, which stood in the plain where the city was built, were excavated in the nineteenth century. The tremendous popularity of the saint is indicated by an anonymous writer of the tenth century who declares: "The West as well as the East acclaims and glorifies him. Wherever there are people, in the country and the town, in the villages, in the isles, in the farthest parts of the earth, his name is revered and churches are erected in his honor." In 1034 Myra was taken by the Saracens. Several Italian cities made plans to get possession of the relics of the famous Nicholas. The citizens of Bari finally in 1087 carried them off from the lawful Greek custodians and their Moslem masters. A new church was quickly built at Bari and Pope Urban II was present at the enshrining of the relics. Devotion to St. Nicholas now increased and many miracles were attributed to his intercession.

The image of St. Nicholas appeared often on Byzantine seals. Artists painted him usually with the three boys in a tub or else tossing a bag of gold through a window. In the West he has often been invoked by prisoners, and in the East by sailors. One legend has it that during his life-time he appeared off the coast of Lycia to some storm-tossed mariners who invoked his aid, and he brought them safely to port. Sailors in the Aegean and Ionian seas had their "star of St. Nicholas" and wished one another safe voyages with the words, "May St. Nicholas hold the tiller."

From the legend of the three boys may have come the tradition of his love for children, celebrated in both secular and religious observances. In many places there was once a year a ceremonious installation of a "boy bishop." In Germany, Switzerland, and the Netherlands gifts were bestowed on children at Christmas time in St. Nicholas' name. The Dutch Protestant settlers of New Amsterdam made the custom popular on this side of the Atlantic. The Eastern saint was converted into a Nordic magician (Saint Nicholas—Sint Klaes—Santa Claus). His popularity was greatest of all in Russia, where he and St. Andrew were joint national patrons. There was not a church that did not have some sort of shrine in honor of St. Nicholas and the Russian Orthodox Church observes even the feast of the translation of his relics. So many Russian pilgrims came to Bari in Czarist times that the Russian government maintained a church, a hospital, and a hospice there. St.

Nicholas is also patron of Greece, Apulia, Sicily, and Lorraine, of many cities and dioceses. At Rome the basilica of St. Nicholas was founded as early as the end of the sixth or the beginning of the seventh century. In the later Middle Ages four hundred churches were dedicated to him in England alone. St. Nicholas' emblems are children, a mitre, a vessel,

Saint Antony of Egypt
Abbot, Patriarch of Monks

c. 3 5 6

(January 7)

Concerning Antony of Egypt we have more knowledge than of any other saint of this early period, thanks to the biography written by his friend, St. Athanasius. Antony was born in 251 at Coma, a village near Great Heracleopolis in Middle Egypt. His Christian parents wished to protect him from bad examples and kept him closely at home, so that he grew up in ignorance of pagan literature and read no language but his own. At their death, before he had reached the age of twenty, he found himself in possession of a large estate and responsible for the care of a younger sister. Soon afterward, while in church, he heard the text from Matthew xix, 21, in which Christ says to the rich young man, "Go, sell what thou hast, and give to the poor." Antony took this command as meant for himself. He went home and made over to his neighbors about one hundred and twenty acres of good land. He then sold the rest of the estate and gave the money to the needy, saving only what he thought necessary to maintain his sister and himself. Another drastic step was to follow. He heard in church those other words which Christ spoke (Matthew vi, 34), "Do not be anxious about tomorrow." Antony now distributed in alms all his movable property and placed his sister in a "house of virgins," the first reference we have to a Christian nunnery. In her later years this sister was entrusted with the direction of the women in that holy way of life. Antony, now twenty-one and free of worldly care, became a hermit. He retired to a solitary place and occupied him-

42

self with manual labor, prayer, and religious reading. His only food was bread and a little salt, and he drank nothing but water. His bed was a rush mat. He soon became a model of humility, piety, and self-discipline.

However, the devil assailed him by various temptations. He pointed out the joys of family life, the good works Antony might have done in the world with his money, and the futility of the hermit's existence. When repulsed by the young novice, the devil changed his mode of attack, and harassed him night and day with gross and obscene thoughts. Antony resisted by a strict watchfulness over his senses and imagination, controlling them by austere fasts, acts of humility, and prayer. At last Satan himself appeared in visible form, first as a seductive woman, then as a black and terrifying man. Antony remained unmoved, and the fiend confessed himself vanquished.

In quest now of greater solitude, he hid himself in an old tomb in the desert, where a friend brought him a little bread from time to time. Here Satan again attacked him and deafened him with loud noises. Once, Athanasius says, he was so grievously beaten that when his friend arrived he lay almost dead. As Antony came to himself, he called out to the devils, "See, here I am! Do your worst! Nothing shall separate me from Christ my Lord." At this, the demons reappeared and again filled the tomb with a terrible clamor and specters of ravening beasts in hideous shapes until a ray of heavenly light, breaking through, chased them away. "Where wast Thou," Antony cried, "my Lord and my Master? Why wast Thou not here from the beginning of my conflict to give me succor?" "Antony," replied a voice, "I was here the whole time; I stood by thee, and watched thy conflict. And because thou hast manfully withstood thy enemies, I will forever protect thee, and will make thy name famous throughout the earth." At this the saint rose up to pray and give thanks.

It was a common practice at this time for fervent Christians to lead retired lives in penance and contemplation on the outskirts of towns, and in the desert, while others practiced their austerities without withdrawing from their fellow men. In even earlier times we hear of these ascetics.[1] Origen, about 249, wrote that they abstained from flesh, as the disciples of Pythagoras did.[2] Antony lived in his tomb near Coma until about 285. Then, at the age of thirty-five, he set out into the empty desert, crossed the eastern branch of the Nile, and took up his abode in the ruins of an old castle on the top of a mountain. There he lived for almost twenty years, rarely seeing any man except the one who brought him food every six months.

In his fifty-fifth year he came down from his mountain retreat and founded his first monastery, not far from Aphroditopolis. It consisted of scattered cells, each inhabited by a solitary monk; some of the later settlements may have been arranged on more of a community plan. Antony did not stay with any of his foundations long, but visited them all from time to time. These interruptions to his solitude, involving as they did some management of the affairs of others, tended to disturb him. We are told of a temptation to despair, which he overcame by prayer and hard manual labor. Notwithstanding his stringent self-discipline, he always maintained that perfection consisted not in mortification of the flesh but in love of God. He taught his monks to have eternity always present to their minds and to perform every act with all the fervor of their souls, as if it were to be their last.

Antony's later years were spent on Mount Colzim, near the Red Sea. Here he lived on a bit of bread daily, with some dates; in extreme old age, a little oil was added to this meager diet. When he came to his meal, usually taken late in the day, he said he felt a sense of shame, remembering the state of the blessed spirits in Heaven, who praise God without ceasing. He always seemed vigorous and cheerful. Strangers were able to pick him out from among his disciples by the joy which shone in his face. They traveled

---

[1] Ascetic is from the Greek word *askesis,* meaning bodily discipline of all kinds.
[2] The disciples of Pythagoras, a Greek philosopher and mathematician of the sixth century B.C., led abstemious lives in groups apart from ordinary men.

great distances to talk with the celebrated holy man, and it was the duty of Macarius, Antony's companion and disciple, to interview them. If they proved to be spiritual men, Antony would come out and sit in converse. If they were worldly persons, Macarius would entertain them, and Antony would appear only to give a short talk.

In spite of his fame, this saint looked on himself as the least of mankind; he listened carefully to the counsel of others, and declared that he received benefit from speaking with the humblest person. He cultivated a small garden that he might have a few refreshing vegetables to offer his visitors, who were apt to be weary after traveling by camel caravan over long stretches of desert and climbing the mountain. Athanasius also writes of his weaving mats as a daily occupation. He could pray while working, although his practice was to alternate periods of prayer and contemplation with his weaving.

In the year 311, during the persecutions under Maximian, Antony hoped he might be one of those chosen for martyrdom. He went down to Alexandria and made himself conspicuous by encouraging the Christians already imprisoned, and also those who were standing before the judges and at the places of execution. He wore his white hermit's habit openly, within sight of the governor, yet he did nothing provocative and did not come forward and accuse himself, as some impetuous ones did. The next year, when the persecutions abated, he returned to his mountain. In his extreme old age he made another trip to Alexandria, expressly to refute the Arians,[3] and went about preaching that Christ the Son was not a creature, but of the same eternal substance as the Father; and that the impious Arians, who called Him a creature, did not differ from the heathen, "who worshiped and served the creature rather than the Creator." The people flocked to hear him, and even pagans, struck by the dignity of his bearing, gathered around him, saying, "We want to see the man of God." He made many converts and worked several miracles. The governor of

[3] For a fuller account of Arian doctrine, see below, *St. Athanasius*, n. 6.

Egypt invited him to stay longer in the city, but he declined, saying, "Fish die if they are taken from the water; so does a monk wither away if he forsakes his solitude." St. Jerome says that at Alexandria he met the famous blind Christian scholar Didymus, and told him not to regret overmuch the loss of his eyes, physical organs which men shared with the insects, but to rejoice in the treasure of the inner light which the Apostles knew, and by which we may have a vision of God, and kindle the fire of His love in our souls.

Heathen philosophers who disputed with Antony were amazed both at his modesty and at his wisdom. When asked how he could spend his life in solitude without the companionship of books, he replied that nature was his great book. When they criticized his ignorance, he simply asked which was the better, good sense or book learning, and which produced the other. They answered, "Good sense." "Then," said Antony, "it is sufficient of itself." His pagan visitors usually wanted to know the reasons for his faith in Christ. He told them that they degraded their gods by ascribing to them the worst of human passions, whereas the ignominy of the cross, followed by Christ's triumphant Resurrection, was a supreme demonstration of His infinite goodness, to say nothing of His miracles of healing and raising the dead. The Christian's faith in his Almighty God and His works was a more satisfactory basis for religion than the empty sophistries of the Greeks. Antony carried on his discussions with the Greeks through an interpreter. His biographer Athanasius tells us that in spite of his solitary life, "he did not seem to others morose or unapproachable, but met them with a most engaging and friendly air." He writes that no one in trouble ever visited Antony without going away comforted.

When Belacius, the military commander in Egypt, was savagely persecuting the Christians, Antony wrote warning him to leave the servants of Christ in peace. Belacius tore up the letter, spat and trampled on it, and threatened to make Antony his next victim. But five days later, as he was riding with Nestorius, governor of Egypt, the commander's horse began to curvet and prance and crashed against the other. Belacius was thrown and his horse then turned and bit his thigh. In three days he was dead.

The Emperor Constantine and his two sons, Constantius and Constans, once sent Antony a joint letter, recommending themselves to his prayers. Noting the astonishment of some of the monks present, Antony said, "Do not wonder that the Emperor writes to us, even to a man such as I am; rather be astounded that God has communicated with us, and has spoken to us by His Son." Replying to the letter, he exhorted the Emperor and his sons to contempt of the world and to constant remembrance of the final judgment.

St. Jerome mentions seven other letters from Antony to various monasteries, written in the style of the Apostles, and filled with their teachings. As the devil fell by pride, so he assails us most often by temptations to that sin; knowledge of ourselves, Antony said, is the indispensable step by which we go on to the knowledge and love of God. In discourses to his monks he would repeatedly emphasize the importance of rigorous self-examination every evening. Once, when he heard his disciples express amazement at the multitudes who were then embracing the religious life and undertaking austere practices of virtue, he told them tearfully that a time would come when monks would be fond of living in cities and in stately buildings and eating at dainty tables, and would be distinguished from the people of the world solely by the habits they wore. Only a few would then rise to the heights of perfection, though the crowns these few received would be so much the more resplendent since they had attained virtue amid the contagion of bad examples.

A short time before his death Antony made a round of visitations of his scattered communities of monks. This first great "Desert Father" died about the year 356, probably on January 17, the day on which most ancient martyrologies commemorate him, and which the Greek Church kept as a feast. He had lived to the remarkable age of 105, without sickness, his sight unimpaired, his teeth still sound. Two disciples interred Antony's remains according to his instructions, beside his cell. About 561, in the reign of

Justinian, they are said to have been carried to Alexandria, and later, when the Saracens overran Egypt, to Constantinople. During the Crusades they were brought to Vienne, France, by Joscelin, a native of that region, to whom the Emperor at Constantinople had given them. The Bollandists [4] report numerous miracles wrought by Antony's intercession, in particular, the cures of persons suffering from St. Antony's Fire, an epidemic which raged violently in France and other parts of Europe in the eleventh century.

Several orders of Eastern monks may still preserve the general features of Antony's system of ascetic training. Certainly his instructions and his example have lived on as ideals of the monastic life through subsequent centuries.

---

[4] The Bollandists were a group of Jesuit scholars who about 1630 began publishing a definitive edition of the *Acta Sanctorum,* or Lives of the Saints, from the beginning down to their own time. The leader of the original group was one John van Bolland. Their work has been continued to the present day.

THE ESPOUSAL OF THE BLESSED VIRGIN

Raphael

Raphael (1483-1520) painted this picture while he was at Umbria, studying with Perugino. In fact, both master and pupil painted this same subject in very much the same way, but Raphael developed his theme to a much finer conclusion.

Saint Joseph, here depicted placing the wedding ring on the finger of the Virgin Mary, carries in his left hand a rod tipped with almond blossoms. He is sometimes depicted with a saw, axe, hatchet or plane, the emblems of his trade as a carpenter.

THE VISITATION   Ghirlandaio

Domenico Ghirlandaio (1449-1494) painted the everyday life of Florence into his great religious pictures. This scene of Saint Elizabeth saluting the Virgin was one of a series of fourteen illustrating the life of the Virgin and Saint John the Baptist which Ghirlandaio painted under the patronage of a wealthy Florentine family.

Saint Elizabeth is usually depicted saluting the Virgin, who has come to visit her after hearing that she is to bear a child in her old age. Elizabeth, inspired with the knowledge of the greater destiny of Mary's Son, kneels to her young kinswoman.

Saint Athanasius

Bishop, Doctor of the Church

3 7 3

(May 2)

St. Athanasius, known as the "champion of orthodoxy," was born about the year 297, in Alexandria. There is a tradition, related by Rufinus,[1] that he first attracted the notice of Patriarch Alexander as he was playing at baptism on the seashore with other small boys. After watching young Athanasius perform the rite, the prelate called the boys to him and by questioning satisfied himself that the baptisms were valid. He then undertook to have these boys trained for the priesthood. Athanasius received an excellent education, not only in Christian doctrine, but also in Greek literature and philosophy, rhetoric, and jurisprudence. He knew the Scriptures thoroughly, and learned theology from teachers who had been confessors [2] during the terrible persecutions under Maximian.[3] In youth he appears to have formed friendships with several hermits of the desert, especially with the great Antony, whose biography he was to write. He was reader to the patriarch, and in 318 became his secretary. During this period he wrote a dis-

[1] Rufinus was a famous theological and controversial writer of the late fourth century. Born in Aquileia, he became interested in the monastic movement in Egypt, and later went to Palestine. On him, see below, *St. Jerome*, p. 88.

[2] As used here and throughout, confessor means one who suffers ill-treatment for the faith, or who confesses or professes Christ in a public or notable manner.

[3] Emperor Maximian was the father of Maxentius, who is mentioned above, *St. Catherine of Alexandria,* n. 3.

course, *Against the Gentiles*,[4] in which he attempted an explanation of the Incarnation and the doctrine of the Trinity.

In Egypt two strong and often divergent forces had early appeared in the Christian Church: the conservative hierarchy in Alexandria, represented by the patriarch or bishop, and the theologians of the schools, who cared little for tradition and stood for free reasoning on theological subjects. The leaders of the latter party had sometimes been obliged, like the famous Origen,[5] to go into exile. There were also schisms over the distribution of authority in the Church and over doctrinal questions. It was probably about the year 323 that one Arius,[6] a priest of the church of Baucalis, began to teach that Jesus, though more than man, was not eternal God, that he was created in time by the Eternal Father, and could therefore be described only figuratively as the Son of God. The patriarch demanded a written statement of these doctrines. With only two dissenting voices the bishops condemned them as heresy, and deposed Arius, together with eleven priests and deacons of Alexandria. Arius retired to Caesarea, where he continued to propagate his ideas, enlisting the support of Bishop Eusebius of Nicomedia and other Syrian prelates. In Egypt he

[4] At this time, in Christian usage, the word "Gentiles" meant pagans—persons who were neither Christians nor Jews.

[5] Origen (185-254) had been the head of the catechetical school of Alexandria and later, when forced to leave Alexandria, of the school of Caesarea. He tried to formulate a complete Christian philosophy of his own, based on the Scriptures, but developed along Platonic lines. His views always involved him in bitter controversy and afterwards the Church held several of his conclusions to be heretical. See below, *St. Jerome,* p. 88.

[6] Arius and his followers, as opposed to the Docetists and the Gnostics, analyzed the problem of the nature of Christ not by denying His humanity but by diminishing His divinity. They concluded that to call Him eternal, uncreated God, of the same ineffable ever-living substance as God the Creator, was to set up two Gods. Christ was divine, He had come as God's immortal Word to men, but He had been first created in time and was not the equal of His Creator. The New Testament, they said, showed His continual dependence upon the superior power of His Father. The orthodox doctrine of the Trinity was, therefore, untenable.

had already won over many of the metaphysicians, as well as Meletius, bishop of Lycopolis, and leader of a dissident group. Theology being the topic which most deeply engaged men's minds, the Arian controversy interested all classes of the population. The heretical propositions were publicized in the form of songs set to popular tunes, and these were chanted in the forums and carried by sailors from port to port.

Athanasius, as the patriarch's secretary, took a prominent part in this great Church struggle. It is probable that he even composed the encyclical letter announcing the condemnation of Arius. We know that he was present, as an attendant on Alexander, at the famous Council of Nicaea,[7] summoned by the Emperor Constantine to determine matters of dogma. There the sentence against Arius was confirmed, and the confession of faith known as the Nicene Creed promulgated and subscribed. This gathering of churchmen influenced Athanasius deeply, and, as a modern writer has said, the rest of his life was a testimony to the divinity of the Saviour.

Shortly after this Alexander died, and Athanasius succeeded him, although he was not yet thirty. One of his first acts was a tour of his enormous diocese, which included the great monastic settlements, especially the Thebaid.[8] He ordained a bishop for Abyssinia, where the Christian faith had recently been established. Yet in spite of his best efforts, there was strong opposition. The Meletians made common cause with the Arians, and the movement, temporarily discredited by the Council of Nicaea, was soon again rampant in Asia Minor and Egypt.

In 330 the Arian bishop of Nicomedia, Eusebius, returned from his exile and before long had persuaded the aging Constantine to write to Athanasius, bidding him readmit Arius into communion, in the interests of unity. Eusebius sent an ingratiating letter in defense

[7] On the Council of Nicaea, see above, *St. Nicholas of Myra,* n. 1.
[8] The Thebaid was the term given to the region settled by Christian anchorites in the Egyptian desert, especially in the vicinity of Thebes. It lay on the east bank of the Nile, near the site of the modern village of Karnak.

of Arius, but Athanasius held to his conviction that the Church could have no communion with heretics who attacked the divinity of Christ. Then Eusebius wrote the Egyptian Meletians urging them to impeach Athanasius for personal misconduct. They brought charges that he had levied a general tribute of linen for use in his own church, and made other petty accusations. At his trial before the emperor, Athanasius cleared himself and returned in triumph to Alexandria, bearing with him a letter of approval from Constantinople.

His enemies now accused him of having murdered a Meletian bishop named Arsenius, and summoned him to attend a council at Caesarea. Knowing that his supposed victim was in hiding, Athanasius ignored the summons. In 335 an order came from Constantinople to appear before another assembly at Tyre, packed by his opponents and presided over by an Arian who had seized the see of Antioch. Realizing that his condemnation had been decided on, Athanasius abruptly left the council and took ship for Constantinople. There he accosted the emperor as a suppliant in the street and obtained an interview. So completely did he vindicate himself that Constantine summoned the bishops to Constantinople for a retrial of the case. Then, for some unexplained reason, he suddenly changed his mind. Before the first letter arrived, a second was sent, confirming the sentence and banishing Athanasius to Treves. During this first exile, Athanasius kept in touch with his flock by letter.

In 337 Constantine died, shortly after his baptism by Eusebius of Nicomedia, and his empire was divided among his three sons, Constantine II, Constantius, and Constans. Many of the exiled prelates were now recalled. One of the first acts of Constantine II, who had sovereignty over Britain, Spain, and Gaul, was to allow Athanasius to return to his see. Two years later Constantine II was to be killed in battle in Aquileia. The patriarch reentered Alexandria in seeming triumph, but his enemies were as relentless as ever, and Eusebius of Nicomedia had completely won over the Emperor Constantius, within whose portion of the empire Alexandria was situated. New scandals were invented and Athanasius was now accused of raising sedition, promoting bloodshed, and keeping for himself corn intended for the poor. A Church council which met at Antioch again deposed him, and ratified an Arian bishop for Alexandria.

In the midst of all this confusion a Cappadocian priest named Gregory was forcibly installed as patriarch of Alexandria by the city prefect, pagans and Arians having now joined forces against the Catholics. Confronted unceasingly by acts of violence and sacrilege, Athanasius betook himself to Rome to await the hearing of his case by the Pope. A synod was summoned, but the Eusebians who had proposed it failed to appear. The result was a complete vindication of Athanasius, a verdict afterwards endorsed by the Council of Sardica.[9] Nevertheless he found it impossible to return to Alexandria until after the death of Gregory, and then only because Emperor Constantius, on the eve of a war with Persia, thought it politic to propitiate his brother Constans by restoring Athanasius to his see.

After an absence then of eight years, Athanasius was welcomed back to Alexandria in 346, and for three or four years there was comparative peace. But the murder of Constans in 350 removed the most powerful support of orthodoxy, and Constantius, once he found himself ruler of both West and East, set himself to crush the man he now regarded as a personal enemy. At Arles in 353 he obtained the condemnation of Athanasius from a council of Gallic bishops, who seem to have been kept in ignorance of the importance of the issues. Two years later at Milan he met with more opposition from the Italian bishops, but when with his hand on his sword he gave them their choice between condemnation of Athanasius and exile, by far the greater number yielded. The few stubborn bishops were exiled, including the new Pope Liberius. He was sent into isolation in Thrace until, broken in body and spirit, he too gave his consent to the Arian decrees. Athanasius held on for an-

[9] This council, held at modern Sofia in 343, was chiefly notable for its provisions creating a right of appeal to the see of Rome by any deposed bishop.

other year with the support of his own clergy and people. Then one night, as he was celebrating a vigil in the church of St. Thomas, soldiers broke in. Athanasius was instantly surrounded by his people, who swept him out into the safety of darkness; but for six years thereafter he had to live in hiding. His abounding energy now expressed itself in literary composition, and to this period are ascribed his chief writings, including a *History of the Arians,* three letters to Serapion, a defense of his position to Constantius, and a treatise on the synods of Rimini and Seleucia.

The death of Constantius in 361 was followed by another shift in the situation. The new emperor, Julian,[10] a pagan, revoked the sentences of banishment enacted by his predecessors, and Athanasius returned once again to his own city. But it was only for a few months. Julian's plans for a reconquest of the Christian world could make little headway as long as the champion of the Catholic faith ruled in Egypt; he also considered it necessary to banish Athanasius from Alexandria as "a disturber of the peace and an enemy of the gods." During this fourth exile, he seems to have explored the entire Thebaid. He was in Antinopolis when two hermits informed him of the death of Julian, who, it was later ascertained, at that moment was expiring in distant Persia, slain by an enemy's arrow.

The new emperor, Jovian, a soldier of Catholic sympathies, revoked the sentence of banishment and invited Athanasius to Antioch, to expound the doctrine of the Trinity. Jovian's reign lasted only a year, and his successor in the East, Valens, succumbed to Arian pressure in Constantinople and in May, 365, issued an order banishing again all orthodox bishops who had been exiled by Constantius and restored by his successors. Once more the worn and aged prelate was forced to flee. The ecclesiastical

---

[10] Julian, known as the Apostate because he renounced Christianity for a form of philosophic paganism, was a nephew of Constantine the Great, and on Constantius' death was declared emperor. His effort to turn the world back to paganism was seen to be a failure even before his death, and there is a tradition that his dying words were, "Thou hast conquered, O Galilean."

historian, Socrates, tells us that Athanasius hid himself this time
in his father's tomb, but a better-informed writer says that he spent
the months in a villa in a suburb of Alexandria. Four months later
Valens revoked his edict, fearing possibly a rising of the Egyptians,
who were determined to accept no other man as bishop. Joyfully
they escorted him back. Athanasius had spent seventeen years in
exile, but his last years were peaceful. He died in Alexandria on
May 2, 373. His body was twice removed, first to Constantinople,
and then to Venice.

While the theological controversies which marked this period may
seem both complex and remote, they were an important milestone
in the history of the Church, Athanasius rendering an outstanding
service. The statement of Christian doctrine known as the Athana-
sian Creed was probably composed during his life, but not actually
by him. In his works there is deep spiritual feeling and understanding, and as Cardinal Newman said, he stands as "a principal
instrument after the Apostles by which the sacred truths of Christianity have been conveyed and secured to the world."

Excerpts from Life of St. Antony

14. *And so for nearly twenty years he continued training*
himself in solitude, never going forth and but seldom
seen by any. After this, when many were eager to imitate his
discipline and his acquaintances came and began to cast down and
wrench off the door by force, Antony as from a shrine, came forth
as one initiated in the mysteries and filled with the Spirit of
God. . . . Through him the Lord healed the bodily ailments of
many present, and cleansed others from evil spirits. And He gave
grace to Antony in speaking, so that he consoled many that were
sorrowful, and harmonized those who were at variance, exhorting
all to prefer the love of Christ before all that is in the world. . . .
And thus it happened in the end that cells arose even in the
mountains, and the desert was colonized by monks, who came forth

from their own people, and enrolled themselves for citizenship in the heavens.

16. One day when he had gone forth because all the monks had assembled around him and asked to hear words from him, he spoke to them in the Egyptian tongue as follows: "The Scriptures are enough for instruction, but it is a good thing to encourage one another in the faith, and to stir up with words. Wherefore you as children carry that which you know to your father and I as the elder share my knowledge and what experience has taught me with you. Let this especially be the common aim of all, neither to give way having once begun, not to faint in trouble, nor to say, 'We have lived in the discipline a long time;' but rather as though making a beginning daily, let this increase our earnestness. For the whole life of man is very short, measured by the ages to come, wherefore all our time is nothing compared with eternal life. . . .

35. "When therefore the demons come by night to you and wish to tell the future, or say, 'We are the angels,' give no heed, for they lie. Even if they praise your discipline and call you blessed, hear them not, and have no dealings with them, but rather sign yourselves and your houses, and pray, and you shall see them vanish. For they are cowards, and greatly fear the sign of the Lord's Cross, since truly in it the Saviour stripped them and made an example of them. But if they shamelessly stand their ground, capering and changing their forms of appearance, fear them not, nor shrink, nor heed them as though they were good spirits. For the presence either of good or evil can easily be distinguished by the help of God. The vision of the holy ones is not fraught with distraction. . . . But it comes so quietly and gently that immediately joy, gladness, and courage arise in the soul. For the Lord who is our joy is with them, and the power of God the Father. . . .

36. "But the display and attack of evil spirits is fraught with confusion, with din, with sounds and cryings such as the disturbance of boorish youths and robbers would occasion. From which arise in the heart fear, tumult and confusion of thought, dejection, hatred towards them that live a life of discipline, indifference, grief, remembrance of kinsfolk and fear of death, and finally desire of evil things, disregard of virtue and unsettled habits. Whenever, therefore, ye have seen something and are afraid, if your fear is

immediately taken away and in place of it comes joy unspeakable, cheerfulness, courage, renewed strength, calmness of thought, and all those I named before, boldness and love toward God—take courage and pray. For joy and a settled state of soul show the holiness of Him who is present. . . ."

44.   While Antony was thus speaking all rejoiced; in some the love of virtue increased, in others carelessness was thrown aside, the self-conceit of others was ended; and all were persuaded to despise the assaults of the Evil One, and marveled at the grace given to Antony from the Lord for the discerning of spirits. So then the cells in the mountains were like tabernacles, filled with holy bands of men who sang psalms, loved reading, fasted, prayed, rejoiced in the hope of things to come, labored in almsgiving, and preserved love and harmony one with another. And truly it was possible, as it were, to behold a land set by itself filled with piety and justice. For then there were no evil-doers nor injured, nor the reproaches of the tax-gatherers; but instead a multitude of ascetics; and the one purpose of them all was to strive for virtue. . . .

72.   And Antony was also exceedingly prudent, and the wonder was that although he was not learned, he was a ready-witted and sagacious man.

74.   (Greek philosophers come and ask to hear the reasons for his faith.) Antony stopped for a little and first pitying their ignorance, said through an interpreter: (By making your gods out of nature, the sun, the moon, the sky, the sea) you are worshiping the thing created instead of the Creator. For if because creation is beautiful you composed such legends, still it was fitting you should stop short at admiration and not make gods of the things created, lest you give the honor that is the Maker's to the things he made. . . .

78.   "We Christians have religious truth based not on Greek philosophical arguments but on the power of faith given us by God through Jesus Christ. And to show that this statement is true, behold now, without being learned, we believe in God, knowing through His works His providence over all things. To show how effective is our faith, see how the portents of the idols among you are being done away with, while our faith is extending everywhere. . . .

79. "Tell us, where are your oracles now? Where are the charms of the Egyptians, where the delusions of the magicians? When did all these things cease and grow weak except when the cross of Christ arose? Is it then a fit subject for mockery, and not rather the things brought to nought by it and convicted of weakness? For this is a marvelous thing, that your religion was never persecuted, but was even honored by men in every city, while the followers of Christ are persecuted, and still our side flourishes and multiplies over yours; yours though praised and honored, perishes while the faith and the teaching of Christ, though mocked by you and often persecuted by kings has filled the world. . . ."

(*Select Library of Nicene and Post-Nicene Fathers.* Series II. v. 4. 1892.)

Saint Monica

Widow

3 8 7

(*May 4*)

Our knowledge of Monica comes almost entirely from the writings of her much-loved son, the great Doctor of the Church, St. Augustine of Hippo. His relationship with his mother was a close one, especially during Monica's last years. In Book IX of St. Augustine's *Confessions* he gives us many details of her life, and expresses his gratitude for her devotion in moving terms. Monica was born about the year 332 in Tagaste, North Africa, of a Christian family of some substance. We are given one episode of her childhood which suggests a possible origin for her firmness of will. She was sometimes sent down to the cellar to draw wine for the family, and fell into the habit of taking secret sips. She developed such a passion for wine that before long she was drinking great draughts of it whenever opportunity offered. One day a family slave who had been spying on the little girl denounced her as a wine-bibber, and Monica, covered with shame, gave up the habit. Soon afterwards she was baptized, and thenceforth seems to have led a life of irreproachable virtue.

As soon as Monica had reached marriageable age, her parents found a husband for her, the pagan Patricius. He was a man of violent temper and their home could scarcely have been a happy one. Monica endured his outbursts with the utmost patience, although he was critical of Christians and their practices. The daily example of her gentleness and kindness finally had its rewards, and a year before his death, which occurred when Augustine was seventeen, Patricius accepted his wife's faith. Monica and Patricius had three children, Navigius, who seems to have been an exemplary son, Augustine, and Perpetua, a daughter, who became a religious. Augustine, the more brilliant of the sons, was sent to Carthage, so that he might develop his talents and become a man of culture. He took to learning naturally but he also spent time in youthful carousing. This caused his mother great anguish, and when he returned to Tagaste, she disapproved so strongly both of his loose living and of his espousal of the popular heresy of Manichaeism that she refused at first to allow him to live at home. She relented only after having seen a vision. One day as she was weeping over his behavior, a figure appeared and asked her the cause of her grief. She answered, and a voice issued from the mysterious figure, telling her to dry her tears; then she heard the words, "Your son is with you." Monica related this story to Augustine, and he replied that they might easily be together if she gave up her faith, for that was the main obstacle keeping them apart. Quickly she retorted, "He did not say I was with you: he said that you were with me." Augustine was impressed by the quick answer and never forgot it. Although his conversion was not to take place for nine long years, Monica did not lose faith. She continually fasted, prayed, and wept on his behalf. She implored the local bishop for help in winning him over, and he counseled her to be patient, saying, "God's time will come." Monica persisted in importuning him, and the bishop uttered the words which have often been quoted: "Go now, I beg you; it is not possible that the son of so many tears should perish."

Augustine was twenty-nine and a successful teacher when he decided to go to Rome. Monica opposed the move, fearing that his conversion would be indefinitely postponed. Her son went on with his plan, and set off with his young mistress and little son Adeodatus for the seaport. His mother followed him there, and when he saw that she intended to accompany him, he outwitted her by a deception as to the time of sailing. He embarked while she was spending the night praying in a church. Although this grieved her deeply, Monica was still not discouraged about her wayward son, for she continued on to Rome. The ship on which she took passage was tossed about by a storm, and she cheered those on board by her serene confidence in God's mercy. On reaching Rome, Monica learned that her son had gone to Milan. There he had come under the influence of the great Bishop Ambrose. When his mother finally found him in the northern city, he had given up Manichaeism, although he was not yet a Christian. Monica's friendship with Ambrose is worth touching upon. She apparently made a friend of this eminent churchman and he entertained the highest opinion of her. Here in Milan, as at home in North Africa, Monica was foremost among the women in all charitable works, and also in her devotions. The bishop, however, persuaded her to give up some of the customs practiced by the Christians of her homeland, for they were derived from ancient pagan rites; carrying food and wine to the tombs of the martyrs was one of the customs which Monica now relinquished.

The joyous day of Augustine's conversion, which will be fully described in the life of that saint, came at last. For some time his mother had been trying to end her son s illicit relationship of so many years' standing. She hoped to find a suitable bride for him, but after his mistress went back to Africa Augustine informed her that he would now adopt a celibate life and devote himself to God's service. The *Confessions* give us glimpses of the period of preparation preceding his baptism. The time was passed in the house of a friend, where a close-knit group, consisting of his mother, brother, Adeodatus, and a few companions occupied themselves with discussions of religion and philosophy. At Easter, when Bishop Ambrose baptized Augustine, his mother's cup was full to overflowing.

Augustine and the members of his family now set out for their return to Tagaste. At the port of Ostia, Monica fell ill. She knew that her work had been accomplished and that life would soon be over. Her exaltation of spirit was such that her sons were unaware of the approach of death. As Monica's strength failed, she said to

Augustine: "I do not know what there is left for me to do or why I am still here, all my hopes in this world being now fulfilled. All I wished for was that I might see you a Catholic and a child of Heaven. God granted me even more than this in making you despise earthly felicity and consecrate yourself to His service." Shortly afterwards they asked her if she did not fear to die so far from home, for she had earlier expressed a desire to be buried beside her husband in Tagaste. Now, with beautiful simplicity, she replied, "Nothing is far from God," and indicated that she was content to be buried where she died. Monica's death plunged her children into the deepest grief, and Augustine, "the son of so many tears," in the *Confessions* implores his readers' prayers for his parents. It is the prayers of Monica herself that have been invoked by generations of the faithful who honor her as a special patroness of married women and as an example for Christian motherhood. Her relics are alleged to have been transferred from Ostia to Rome, to rest in the church of San Agostino. Her emblems are a girdle and tears.

Saint Ambrose
Bishop, Confessor, Doctor of the Church

3 9 7

(December 7)

S t. Ambrose was a small man with pale yellow hair like a
nimbus. In the violence and confusion of his time, he stood
out courageously resisting evil, strengthening the Church, and
administering it with extraordinary ability. His learning gained for
him the title of Doctor of the Church. He was born into the
Roman governing class, his father being prefect of southern Gaul,
the vast territory which included Britain, the Mediterranean
islands, and the lands stretching from the Alps to Spain and
Portugal. His birthplace was the palace at Treves,[1] and the date
was about the year 340. After the death of his father, his mother,
a woman of piety and intellect, returned with her children to
Rome, where she gave careful thought to their rearing. A daughter,
Marcellina, became a consecrated virgin. Young Ambrose studied
Greek, and showed promise as an orator and poet. He went on to
a mastery of law, and as a young pleader attracted the notice of
Anicius Probus, prefect of Italy, and of the pagan Symmachus,
prefect of Rome. Probus appointed him assessor, an office he filled
with dignity. Then in 372, when Ambrose was barely thirty, the
Western Emperor, Valentinian I, chose him as consular prefect
of Liguria and Aemilia. The office gave him full consular rank,
with his residence at Milan.[2] When he left Rome for his new post,

[1] Treves, or Trier, an ancient German city on the Moselle River, was at this
time the military headquarters on the northern border of the Empire.

[2] Milan was now the administrative capital of the West, the imperial court
having been moved there in 303, under Maximian.

Probus dismissed him with these prophetic words, "Go and govern more like a bishop than a judge."

When Ambrose had governed at Milan for two years, the bishop, an Arian, died, and the city was torn by strife over the election of a successor, some demanding an Arian, others a Catholic. Ambrose, as the responsible civil official, went to the church where the voting was to take place, and urged the people to make their choice like good Christians, without disorder. A voice suddenly called out, "Ambrose, bishop!" The whole gathering took up the cry, and both Catholics and Arians then and there proclaimed him bishop of Milan. The outburst astounded Ambrose, for though he was a professing Christian, he was still unbaptized and therefore not eligible for the office. In view of the popular vote, the other bishops of the province agreed to ratify the election, at which Ambrose sadly remarked, "Emotion has now overruled canon law." The bishop-elect tried unsuccessfully to escape from the city.

A report went to Valentinian, whose consent was necessary if an imperial officer was to be made a bishop. Ambrose also wrote, asking to be excused, but Valentinian replied that it gave him the greatest pleasure to have chosen a prefect fit for the episcopal office, and sent orders to the vicar of the province to hold a formal election. Meanwhile, Ambrose was hiding in the house of a senator, who, on hearing the imperial decision, gave Ambrose up. He was baptized, and a week later, on December 7, 374, was consecrated. The new bishop now gave his possessions to the poor and his lands to the Church, reserving only a small income for the use of his sister Marcellina. All care of temporal matters was delegated to a brother, and he began to serve his diocese with energy and devotion. In a letter to the emperor he complained of the behavior of certain imperial magistrates, to which Valentinian in all humility replied: "I have long been acquainted with your freedom of speech, which did not hinder me from consenting to your election. Continue to apply to our sins the remedies prescribed by divine law."

Very conscious of his ignorance of theology, Ambrose began to

ZACHARIAS WRITING THE NAME OF SAINT JOHN

Studio of Fra Angelico

It was customary for master painters such as Fra Angelico (1387-1455) to gather about them a group of students and assistants who painted much of the preliminary material which the master finished. Such a painting is this. It is not known which parts, if any, are the work of Fra Angelico himself.

Saint Zacharias is identified by the thurible, the symbol of his priestly function. According to the Gospel of Saint Luke, Zacharias was burning incense on the altar when the Angel of the Lord announced to him that his wife would bear a son who should be called John.

THE BAPTISM OF JESUS
After Doré

Gustave Doré (1833-1883) whose culminating work was the several hundred
illustrations he did for the Bible was not successful in his
native Paris. The materialistic Parisians jeered at his choice of
a subject, and it was not until his works were displayed in
London and the United States that he received acclaim.

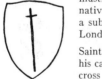

Saint John the Baptist can almost always be recognized from
his camel's-hair garment. The long slender staff tipped with a
cross is also characteristic.

study the Scriptures and the works of religious writers, particularly Origen and Basil,[3] putting himself under the tutelage of Simplician, a learned priest. The great issue of the day was the Arian heresy, and Ambrose labored to rid his diocese of it. From the beginning he was at the service of the people, giving them regular and careful instruction. He led a life of extreme simplicity, entertaining little, and excusing himself from banquets. Every day he offered the Eucharist. Certain things he rigorously avoided: he would persuade no one to be a soldier, he would take no hand in match-making, and would recommend no one to a place at court.

When Augustine of Hippo came to live at Milan, he called on the bishop, and in time the two became great friends. Augustine went often to hear Ambrose preach, and was at last baptized by him. One of Ambrose's topics was the blessing and virtue of virginity, when chosen for God's sake. At the request of Marcellina, he made a popular manual of his sermons on this subject. Mothers are said to have tried to keep their daughters from hearing him, and some accused him of trying to depopulate the empire! Ambrose would retort, "What man ever wanted to marry and could not find a wife?" He declared that the population was greatest where maidenhood was most esteemed. It was his contention that wars, and not virgins, were responsible for the destruction of the race.

Valentinian I died in 375, leaving two heirs, Gratian, a boy of sixteen, by his first wife, and a four-year-old, known as Valentinian II, by Justina, his second wife. Gratian took as his share the provinces beyond the Alps, turning over to his brother, or, rather, to Justina, as regent, Illyricum, North Africa, and Italy. In the East, where his uncle Valens was emperor, there was now an invasion of Goths, and Gratian determined to go to his uncle's aid. But in order to guard against contamination by Arians, of whom Valens was an active protector, he asked Ambrose to instruct him

---

[3] St. Basil, bishop of Caesarea, was the defender of his province against the Arian heresy, defying the emperor in the process. Basil is famous for his doctrinal writings, his monastic rule, and the liturgy which still bears his name in the Eastern rite. On Origen, see above, *St. Athanasius*, n. 5.

concerning the heresy. Ambrose accordingly wrote for him in 377 the treatise entitled, *To Gratian, on the Faith.* The following year Valens was defeated and killed in the battle of Adrianople and an orthodox Spanish general, Theodosius, vanquished the Goths. In 379 Gratian recognized him as Emperor of the East. Meanwhile other Goths had advanced westward to Illyricum and had taken thousands of captives. To ransom them, Ambrose first laid out all the money he could raise and then melted down gold vessels belonging to the Church.[4] When the Arians attacked him for what they called his sacrilege, he answered, "If the Church has gold, it is in order to use it to save men's souls, not to hoard it."

After the murder of Gratian, in 383, the Empress Justina begged Ambrose to go and negotiate with the brutal usurper Maximus and prevail on him not to attack Italy or to jeopardize her young son Valentinian's rights. Ambrose went up to Treves and induced Maximus to confine his conquests to Gaul, Spain, and Britain. Historians have called it the first occasion on which a Christian minister was asked to intervene in a matter of high politics; in this case, to vindicate right and order against armed aggression.

Ambrose now gained a victory in another affair. A group of pagan senators at Rome, headed by Quintus Aurelius Symmachus, son and successor of the city prefect who had been Ambrose's patron, petitioned Valentinian to restore the altar of the Goddess of Victory, removed by Gratian, to its old place in the senate-house, claiming that Rome had fallen on evil days since the ancient cult had been abandoned. Symmachus, in his discourse, attributed Rome's former triumphs and grandeur to the power of the goddess, and ended with the persuasive appeal, which is still heard today, "What does it matter how one seeks for the truth? There must be more than one road to the great mystery." Ambrose replied eloquently; he ridiculed the notion that what the Roman soldiers had achieved in the past by valor had been dependent on the reports of the augurs as to the state of the entrails of sacrificed animals. Rising to great heights of rhetoric, he spoke as by the

[4] This is a precedent often cited in Church history.

mouth of Rome herself, bewailing past errors, but not ashamed to change with a changing world. Symmachus and his friends should learn the mysteries of nature from the God who created it. Instead of imploring their emperors to give their gods peace, they should ask God to give the emperors peace. When both addresses, that of Symmachus and that of Ambrose, were read before Valentinian, he said simply: "My father did not take away the altar, nor was he asked to put it back. I therefore follow him in changing nothing that was done before my time."

At a council in Aquileia, in 382, Ambrose had effected the deposition of two Arian bishops, in spite of Justina's opposition. Justina, not easily vanquished, persuaded Valentinian, who was now fourteen years old, to demand the Portian basilica, situated just outside the city, for the use of the Arians, who had chosen Auxentius as their bishop. Ambrose replied that he would not surrender a temple of God to heretics. Now Valentinian demanded the larger new basilica of the Apostles, in the city. Still Ambrose would not yield. Although he had most of the citizenry and soldiers on his side, he was careful not to precipitate violence, and would not officiate in either of the churches. He was preaching in a small chapel of the larger basilica, when a party of soldiers, ordered to seize it, entered. But instead of carrying out their orders, they laid down their arms and prayed with the Catholics. The people then surged into the adjoining basilica and tore down decorations that had been put up for the emperor's visit. Ambrose refused anything resembling a triumph, and did not himself enter the church until Easter Day, when all were united in joy and thanksgiving.

But Justina did not give up. In January of the following year she had her son issue an edict making religious assemblies of Catholics practically impossible. Ambrose calmly disregarded the edict, yet no official ventured to touch him. "I have said what a bishop ought to say; let the emperor do what an emperor ought to do." On Palm Sunday he preached openly against any surrender of the churches. There were fears for his life, and his people barricaded themselves in the basilica with him. Imperial troops surrounded the church, but those inside did not surrender. On Easter Sunday they were still there. To occupy their time, Ambrose taught them hymns composed by himself, which they sang under his direction, divided into choirs singing alternate stanzas. A tribune now came to Ambrose from the emperor, with an order that he choose laymen to act as judges of his case in a trial court, as Auxentius had already done for his side, so that together they might decide between the two bishops. Ambrose replied that it was his duty to stay with his people, and that laymen could not judge bishops or make laws for the Church. He then ascended the pulpit to tell the people all that had passed between the rulers and himself during the year. In one memorable sentence he defined the principle at stake: "The emperor is in the Church, not over it."

In the meantime, news came that Maximus was on the verge of invading Italy. Valentinian and Justina abjectly begged Ambrose to undertake a second journey to try to stop the aggressor. Ambrose went up to Trier on this embassy, but failed to sway Maximus from his purpose. Justina and her son fled to Thessalonica to throw themselves on the mercy of the Eastern emperor, Theodosius. He received them, declared war on Maximus, defeated and executed him. Valentinian was restored to his own lands as well as to those of his deceased brother Gratian, but Theodosius was now the real ruler of the whole empire. He came to Milan and stayed for a time to prevail on Valentinian to renounce Arianism and accept Ambrose as the true Catholic bishop.

Conflicts between Ambrose and Theodosius were soon to arise. In the first of these the right does not seem to have been wholly on the bishop's side. At Kallinicum, in Mesopotamia, some Christians had pulled down the Jewish synagogue. Theodosius had ordered the local bishop, who was said to be implicated, to rebuild the synagogue. The bishop appealed to Ambrose, who in turn wrote to Theodosius to say that no Christian bishop should pay for the erection of a building to be used for false worship. Ambrose preached against Theodosius to his face; a discussion took place between them in church, and Ambrose refused to go to the altar to sing Mass until he had obtained a promise of pardon for the bishop.

In the year 390 news came to Milan of a shocking massacre at Thessalonica. Botheric, the governor, had had a popular charioteer imprisoned for seducing a slave in his family, and refused to release him when the public wanted to see him in the races. The enraged mob stoned several officers and Botheric himself was killed. Theodosius ordered reprisals of terrible savagery; he is reported to have countermanded his order but too late. When the people were assembled in the circus, soldiers rushed in and put to the sword some seven thousand persons. Ambrose wrote the emperor a letter, exhorting him to penance, and declaring his offering at the altar would not be received, nor would the Divine Mysteries be celebrated in his presence until atonement had been made. "What was done at Thessalonica is unparalleled in the memory of man. . . . You, who so often have been merciful and pardoned the guilty, have now caused many innocent to perish. The devil wished to wrest from you the crown of piety which was your highest glory. Drive him from you while you may. . . . I write this to you with my own hand that you may read it alone."

The appeal had its effect; Theodosius appears to have been sincerely repentant. In his funeral oration, Ambrose said of him: "He, an emperor, was not ashamed to perform the public penance which lesser individuals shrink from, and to the end of his life he never ceased to grieve for his crime." So Christianity was displayed to the world as being no respecter of persons. We have another evidence of Theodosius' humility and Ambrose's moral sway. Once at Milan during Mass on a feast day, Theodosius brought his offering to the altar and then remained standing within the rails. Ambrose asked if he wanted anything; the emperor said that he was staying to assist at the Holy Mysteries and to take Communion. At this Ambrose sent his archdeacon with the message: "My lord, the law is that you go out and stand with the rest. The purple robe makes princes, not priests." Theodosius apologized, saying he thought the custom was the same as at Constantinople, where his place was within the sanctuary.[5] He then took his place among the laity.

In 393 Valentinian II was slain in Gaul by Arbogastes, a pagan officer. Knowing Valentinian was among enemies, Ambrose had set out to rescue him, but on the way met his funeral procession. Ambrose made plain his indignation at the murder, and left Milan before the arrival of Eugenius, whom Arbogastes was putting forward as the new emperor. The bishop went from town to town, strengthening the people against the invaders. On his return, he received a letter from Theodosius, telling of his victory over Arbogastes at Aquileia. A few months later Theodosius died in Ambrose's arms. In his funeral oration, Ambrose spoke with affection of this ruler and praised him for welding the empire together again, declaring that his two sons had come into an inheritance united by law and the Christian faith. The two sons, however, the feeble Arcadius and Honorius, were incapable of carrying on their father's labors. Only a few years later a young cavalry officer named Alaric was to lead the Visigoths south to capture and plunder Rome, while the frightened Honorius remained hidden in Ravenna.

Ambrose survived the emperor two years. When he fell sick, the bishop foretold his own death, saying he would live only until Easter. He busied himself writing a treatise called *The Goodness of Death,* and with an interpretation of the Forty-third Psalm. One day as he was dictating the latter work to Paulinus, his secretary and biographer, he suddenly stopped, and had to take to his bed. When Count Stilicho, guardian of Honorius, heard this, he declared publicly that Italy faced destruction the day the bishop died, and sent messengers begging Ambrose to pray for recovery. "I have not so behaved myself among you," Ambrose answered, "that I should be ashamed to live longer, but I am not afraid to

[5] Later it was part of the design of every Byzantine church to have a mosaic representation of a two-headed eagle set in the floor just outside the sanctuary, to mark the place for the imperial throne. Such eagles may still be seen in Eastern churches.

die, for we have a good Master." On Good Friday, 397, he partook
of the Last Sacrament, and died soon after. He was then about
fifty-seven and had been bishop for twenty-two years. His remains
now rest under the high altar of his basilica, where they were
placed in 835.

Ambrose's varied writings influenced the development of the
Church. He was the first of the Fathers to use Latin effectively,
and as the Roman Empire declined in the West he helped to keep
this great language alive by starting it on its new course in the
service of Christianity. He enriched Church music, and seven of
the hymns he wrote are still a part of the liturgy. His personality
combined firmness where God's law was concerned with warmth,
moderation, and generosity in all else. Trusted by sovereigns, loved
by the people, Ambrose was—to quote Augustine's words after
their first meeting—"a man affectionate and kind."

Letter to Marcellina

Ambrose, to his sister Marcellina.[6]
        . . . 2.   First of all, some great men, counselors of
state, begged me to give up the basilica and see to it that the
people made no disturbance. I replied, of course, that a temple of
God could not be surrendered by a bishop.

3.   The next day my answer was approved by the people in the
church. The prefect came and began to argue with us to give up
at least the Portian basilica, but the people clamored against it.
He then went away, indicating that he would report to the Emperor.

4.   The day following, which was Sunday, after the lessons and
the sermon, when the catechumens had been dismissed,[7] I was

6 The occasion of this letter was the attempt, described above, by the Arian
party at Milan to seize one of the Catholic basilicas.
7 The catechumens, persons under instruction in Catholic doctrine, were not
permitted to remain in the church for the sacred mystery of the Mass but
were required to leave after the reading of the lessons and the sermon.

teaching the creed to some advanced candidates in the baptistery of the church when it was reported to me that they had sent officials from the palace and were putting up hangings [8] around the basilica and a crowd of people were on their way there. I, however, remained at my ministrations, and began to say Mass.

5.   While I was offering the oblation, I was told that a certain Castulus, whom the Arians called a priest, had been seized by the people. On their way they had met him in the streets. I began to weep bitterly and to implore God in the oblation that He would come to our aid and that no one's blood should be shed in the cause of the Church, or at least that it might be my blood, shed not only for my people but for the unbelievers too. In brief then I sent out priests and deacons and rescued the man from violence. . . .

8.   Then counts and tribunes came and urged me to order the basilica surrendered quickly, saying that the Emperor was only exercising his rights, since everything was in his power. I answered that if he asked of me what was mine, that is, my land, my money, or anything of the sort that was my own, I would not refuse it, although all that I have goes to the poor, but that the things which are God's are not subject to the imperial power. "If he wants my patrimony, take it over; if my body, I will go at once. Do you wish to put me in chains or sentence me to death, it will be a joy to me. I will not defend myself behind the crowd of people, nor will I cling to the altars and beg for my life, but will gladly be slain for the altars."

9.   I was indeed struck with horror when I learned that armed men had been sent to take possession of the basilica, lest the people might defend it and there might be some slaughter which would tend to the hurt of the whole city. I prayed that I might not survive the destruction of our great city or—it might be—of all Italy. . . .

10.   Then I was called on to restrain the people. I answered that it was in my power not to excite them but in God's hands to quiet them. And if they thought I was urging the people on, they ought to punish me at once or send me away to any desert place in the world they chose. After I had said this, they departed and I spent

[8] The hangings were evidently banners that marked the basilica as imperial property.

the whole day in the old basilica, but from there I went home to sleep, so that if anyone wanted to carry me off, he might find me ready. . . .

[The next day Ambrose preaches to the people in the "old basilica" on the lesson for the day from the Book of Job and urges them to patience and courage under the trial.]

19. At last the command was given me: "Surrender the basilica." My reply was: "It is not lawful for me to surrender it nor good for you, Emperor, to receive it. By no right can you violate the house of a private person. Do you think that a house of God can be taken away from Him? It is said that for the Emperor everything is lawful, that all things are his. My answer is: 'Do not, O Emperor, impose on yourself the burden of the idea that you have any imperial power over things which belong to God. Exalt not yourself, but if you hope for a long reign, submit yourself to God.' It is written: 'To God the things that are God's; to Caesar the things that are Caesar's. Palaces belong to the emperor, churches to the bishops. Authority is committed to you over public but not over sacred buildings." They said the Emperor had exclaimed: "I too should have one basilica." My answer was: "It is not lawful for you to have one. What have you to do with an adulteress? For she is an adulteress who is not joined to Christ in lawful wedlock."

20. While I was talking on the subject, tidings were brought that the royal hangings were taken down and the basilica filled with people who were calling for my presence. So at once I turned my discourse to that and said: "How high and how deep are the oracles of the Holy Spirit! We said at Matins, as you, brethren, remember and made the response in great grief of mind: 'O God, the heathen are come into thine inheritance.' " . . .

21. Whose gift now, is this, whose work is this but Thine, Lord Jesus? Thou sawest armed men coming to Thy temple; on the one hand, the people wailing and flocking in throngs so as not to seem to abandon the basilica of God; on the other hand, the soldiers ordered to use violence. Death was before my eyes for fear that madness should gain a footing while things stood in suspense. But Thou, O Lord, didst come between and madest of twain one. Thou didst restrain the armed men, saying: "If ye attack them with

arms, if people enclosed in My temple are troubled, what profit was there in My blood?" Thanks to Thee, O Christ. No ambassador, no messenger but Thou, O Lord, hast saved Thy people. Thou hast put off my sackcloth and girded me with gladness.

(Ambrose, *Select Works and Letters. Nicene and Post-Nicene Fathers,* Series II.)

Evening Hymn
(*Deus creator omnium*)

God that all things didst create
And the heavens doth regulate,
Who doth clothe the day with light,
And with gracious sleep the night. . . .

Day sinks; we thank thee for thy gift.
Night comes; to thee again we lift
Our prayers and vows and hymns, that we
Against all ills defended be. . . .

That so, when shadows round us creep
And all is hid in darkness deep,
Faith may not feel the gloom; and night
Borrow from faith's clear gleam new light. . . .

From snares of sense, Lord, keep us free
And let our hearts dream but of thee.
Let not the envious foe draw near
To vex our quiet rest with fear.

Hail we the Father and the Son
And Son's and Father's Spirit, one
Blest Trinity whom all obey;
Guard thou the souls that to thee pray.

Morning Hymn
(*Aeterne rerum conditor*)

Eternal Lord, the world who made,
Who rules the day and night's dark shade
And sets the time to hours, that we
May never faint or weary be.

Hark to the herald of the morn
Who vigil through the dark has borne,
To travelers in the dark a light
That separates the night from night.

The daystar hears and at his call
Loosens the sky from night's black thrall,
While roaming brigands at his word
Their mischief leave and sheathe their sword. . . .

So let us rise in eager haste:
The cock forbids us life to waste.
He stirs the sluggards and doth show
Those who refuse the wrong they do. . . .

O Jesus, aid us where we stray,
Look down and set us on our way.
Beneath thy gaze our faltering cease
And in our tears guilt turns to peace.

Shine on our senses with thy light
And from our minds put sleep to flight.
Let us our first songs raise to thee
And all our hymns be praise to thee.

(F. A. Wright, *Fathers of the Church,* 1928.)

Saint Martin of Tours

Bishop, Confessor

4 0 0

(November 11)

St. Martin, called "the glory of Gaul," was born about the year
316 of pagan parents in Sabaria, Upper Pannonia, a province
comprising northern Jugoslavia and western Hungary. His father
was an officer in the Roman army who had risen from the ranks.
While Martin was still a child, his father was transferred to a new
station in Pavia, north Italy. Here the boy learned of Christianity,
felt drawn to it, and became a catechumen. As the son of a veteran,
at the age of fifteen he was required to begin service in the army.
Though never shirking his military duty, he is said to have lived
more like a monk than a soldier.

Young Martin was stationed at Amiens, in Gaul, when the incident occurred which tradition and art have rendered so famous.
As he rode towards the town one winter day, he noticed near the
gates a poor man, thinly clad, shivering with cold, and begging
alms. Martin saw that none who passed stopped to help the miserable fellow. He had nothing with him but the clothes he wore, but,
drawing his sword from its scabbard, he cut his great woolen cloak
in two pieces, gave one half to the beggar, and wrapped himself
in the other. The following night, the story continues, Martin in
his sleep saw Jesus Christ, surrounded by angels, and dressed in
the half of the cloak he had given away. A voice bade him look at
it well and say whether he knew it. He then heard Jesus say to
the angels, "Martin, as yet only a catechumen, has covered me

with his cloak." [1] Sulpicius Severus, the saint's friend and biographer, says that as a consequence of this vision Martin "flew to be baptized."

When Martin was about twenty, some Teutonic tribes invaded Gaul, and with his comrades he went before the Emperor Julian [2] to receive a war-bounty. Suddenly he was moved to refuse it. "Up to now," he said to Julian, "I have served you as a soldier; allow me henceforth to serve Christ. Give the bounty to these others who are going out to battle. I am a soldier of Christ and it is not lawful for me to fight." Julian, angered, accused Martin of cowardice; the young man replied that he was ready to go into battle the next day unarmed, and advance alone against the enemy in the name of Christ. He was taken off to prison, but discharged as soon as a truce had been made. He then went down to Poitiers, where the renowned Hilary had been bishop for many years. Hilary gladly received this early "conscientious objector" and ordained him deacon.

Having heard in a dream a summons to revisit his home, Martin crossed the Alps, and from Milan went over to Pannonia. There he converted his mother and some other persons; his father he could not win. While in Illyricum he took sides against the Arians with so much zeal that he was publicly scourged and forced to leave. Back in Italy once more, on his way to Gaul, he learned that the Gallic Church was also under attack by the Arians, and that his good friend Hilary had been banished. He remained at Milan, but soon the Arian bishop, Auxentius, drove him away. Martin took refuge with a priest on the island of Gallinaria, in the gulf of Genoa, and stayed there until Hilary returned to Poitiers in 360. It had become Martin's desire to pursue his religious calling in solitude, and Hilary gave him a small piece of land in central France, now called Ligugé. He was joined by other hermits and

[1] The building where St. Martin's cloak was preserved as a precious relic came to be known as the *capella*, from the Latin word for cloak, *cappa*; and from *capella* is derived our word "chapel."
[2] On Julian, see above, *St. Athanasius*, n. 10.

holy men, and the community grew into a monastery, the first, it is said, to be founded in Gaul. It survived until 1607; in 1852 it was rebuilt by the Benedictines of Solesmes.

For ten years Martin lived there, directing the life of his disciples and preaching in outlying places. Many miracles were attributed to him. About the year 371, Lidorius, bishop of Tours, died, and the people demanded Martin in his place. Martin was so reluctant to accept the office that they resorted to stratagem and called him to the city to give his blessing to a sick person, then forcibly conveyed him to the church. When neighboring bishops were summoned to confirm this choice, they thought the monk's poor and unkempt appearance proved him unfit for the office, but they were overruled by the acclamations of the local clergy and the people. Even as a bishop, Martin lived an austere life. Unable to endure the constant interruptions, he retired from Tours to a retreat that was later to become the famous abbey of Marmoutier. The site was enclosed by a steep cliff on one side and by a tributary of the Loire River on the other. Here Martin and some of the monks who followed him built cells of wood; others lived in caves dug out of the rock. In a short time their number grew, with many men of high rank among them. From this time on bishops were frequently chosen from Marmoutier, for the holy Martin took the greatest pains in the training of priests.

Martin's piety and preaching resulted in the decline of paganism in that part of Gaul. He destroyed temples and felled trees which the heathen held sacred. Once when he had demolished a certain temple, he proceeded to the cutting down of a pine tree that stood near. The chief priest and other pagans there offered to cut it down themselves, on condition that he who trusted so strongly in his God would stand under it wherever they would place him. The bishop agreed and allowed himself to be tied and placed on the side towards which the tree was leaning. Just as it seemed about to fall on him, he made the sign of the cross, at which the tree fell in the other direction. Another time, as he was pulling down a temple in the vicinity of Autun, a crowd of pagans fell on him in fury, one brandishing a sword. Martin stood and bared his breast, at sight of which the armed man fell backwards, and in terror begged forgiveness. These marvels are narrated by Sulpicius Severus, who also describes various revelations and visions with which Martin was favored.

Once a year the bishop visited each of his parishes, traveling on foot, or by donkey or boat. He continued to set up monastic communities, and extended the bounds of his episcopate from Touraine to such distant points as Chartres, Paris, Autun, and Vienne. At Vienne, according to his biographer, he cured Paulinus of Nola of a disease of the eyes. When a brutal imperial officer, Avitianus, arrived at Tours with a band of prisoners he planned to torture to death on the following day, Martin, on being informed of this, hurried in from Marmoutier to intercede for them. Reaching the city near midnight, he went straight to the quarters of Avitianus and did not leave until the officer promised mercy to his captives.

The churches of other parts of Gaul and in Spain were being disturbed by the Priscillianists, an ascetic sect, named for its leader, Priscillian, bishop of Avila. A synod held at Bordeaux in 384 had condemned his doctrines, but he had appealed to Emperor Maximus. Meanwhile, Ithacius, the orthodox bishop of Ossanova, had attacked him and urged the emperor to have him put to death. Neither Ambrose at Milan, however, nor Martin at Tours would hold communion with Ithacius or his supporters, because they had appealed to the emperor in a dispute over doctrine, and now were trying to punish a heretic with death. Martin wrote to reprove Ithacius severely. It was sufficient, he said, that Priscillian should be branded as a heretic and excommunicated by the bishops. Maximus, yielding to Martin's remonstrances, ordered the trial deferred and even promised that there should be no bloodshed, but afterwards he was persuaded to turn the case over to his prefect Evodius. He found Priscillian and some others guilty on several charges and had them beheaded. At this news, Martin went to Treves to intercede for the lives of all the Spanish Priscillianists who were threatened with a bloody persecution, and also for two men under suspicion as adherents of the late Emperor Gratian. As a condition before granting this request, Maximus stipulated that Martin should resume communion with the intolerant Ithacius and his party. Since they were not excommunicated, this was no violation of any canon, and he accordingly promised the emperor that he would do so, provided the emperor would pardon the two partisans of Gratian and recall the military tribunes he had sent to Spain. The next day Martin received the Sacrament with the Ithacians in order to save so many people from slaughter; yet he was afterwards troubled in conscience as to whether he had been too yielding. For their part in the affair both the emperor and Ithacius were censured by Pope Siricius. It was the first judicial death sentence for heresy, and it had the effect of spreading Priscillianism in Spain.

Martin had premonitions of his approaching death and predicted it to his disciples, who besought him not to leave them. "Lord," he prayed, "if Thy people still need me, I will not draw back from the work. Thy will be done." When his final sickness came upon him, he was at Candes, in a remote part of his diocese. The monks entreated him to allow them at least to put a sheet under him and make his last hours comfortable. "It becomes not a Christian," said Martin, "to die otherwise than upon ashes. I shall have sinned if I leave you any other example." He lay with eyes and hands raised to Heaven, until the brothers begged him to turn on one side to rest his body a little. "Allow me, my brethren," he answered, "to look towards Heaven rather than to earth, that my soul may be ready to take its flight to the Lord."

On November 8 he died, and three days later was buried at Tours. Two thousand monks and nuns gathered for his funeral. His successor built a chapel over his grave, which was replaced by a fine basilica. A still later church on this site was destroyed during the French Revolution, but a modern one has since been built there. Throughout the Middle Ages, the knightly Martin, who shared his cloak with a beggar, was the subject of innumerable anecdotes, which expressed the love and veneration of the people. His tomb became a national shrine in France, of which country he is patron saint, and one of the most popular pilgrimage places of Europe. St. Martin is patron of the cities of Würtburg and Buenos Aires. Many churches in France and elsewhere have been dedicated to him. His emblems are a tree, armor, a cloak, and a beggar.

Saint Jerome

Confessor, Doctor of the Church

4 2 0

(September 30)

St. Jerome, who was born Eusebius Hieronymous Sophronius, was the most learned of the Fathers of the Western Church. He was born about the year 342 at Stridonius, a small town at the head of the Adriatic, near the episcopal city of Aquileia. His father, a Christian, took care that his son was well instructed at home, then sent him to Rome, where the young man's teachers were the famous pagan grammarian Donatus and Victorinus, a Christian rhetorician. Jerome's native tongue was the Illyrian dialect, but at Rome he became fluent in Latin and Greek, and read the literatures of those languages with great pleasure. His aptitude for oratory was such that he may have considered law as a career. He acquired many worldly ideas, made little effort to check his pleasure-loving instincts, and lost much of the piety that had been instilled in him at home. Yet in spite of the pagan and hedonistic influences around him, Jerome was baptized by Pope Liberius in 360. He tells us that "it was my custom on Sundays to visit, with friends of my own age and tastes, the tombs of the martyrs and Apostles, going down into those subterranean galleries whose walls on both sides preserve the relics of the dead." Here he enjoyed deciphering the inscriptions.

After three years at Rome, Jerome's intellectual curiosity led him to explore other parts of the world. He visited his home and then, accompanied by his boyhood friend Bonosus, went to Aquileia, where he made friends among the monks of the monastery there, notably Rufinus. Then, still accompanied by Bonosus, he traveled to Treves, in Gaul. He now renounced all secular pursuits to dedicate himself wholeheartedly to God. Eager to build up a religious library, the young scholar copied out St. Hilary's books on *Synods* and his Commentaries on the Psalms, and got together other literary and religious treasures. He returned to Stridonius, and later settled in Aquileia. The bishop had cleared the church there of the plague of Arianism and had drawn to it many eminent men. Among those with whom Jerome formed friendships were Chromatius (later canonized), to whom Jerome dedicated several of his works, Heliodorus (also to become a saint), and his nephew Nepotian. The famous theologian Rufinus, at first his close friend, afterward became his bitter opponent. By nature an irascible man with a sharp tongue, Jerome made enemies as well as friends. He spent some years in scholarly studies in Aquileia, then, in search of more perfect solitude, he turned towards the East. With his friends, Innocent, Heliodorus, and Hylas, a freed slave, he started overland for Syria. On the way they visited Athens, Bithynia, Galatia, Pontus, Cappadocia, and Cilicia.

The party arrived at Antioch about the year 373. There Jerome at first attended the lectures of the famous Apollinaris, bishop of Laodicea, who had not yet put forward his heresy.[1] With his companions he left the city for the desert of Chalcis, about fifty miles southeast of Antioch. Innocent and Hylas soon died there, and Heliodorus left to return to the West, but Jerome stayed for four years, which were passed in study and in the practice of austerity. He had many attacks of illness but suffered still more from temptation. "In the remotest part of a wild and stony desert," he wrote years afterwards to his friend Eustochium, "burnt up with the heat of the sun, so scorching that it frightens even the monks who live there, I seemed to myself to be in the midst of the delights and crowds of Rome. . . . In this exile and prison to which through

[1] This heresy was another effort to settle the persistent problem of the nature of the God-man, Christ, by regarding Him as human in body and spirit but never anything but divine in mind.

fear of Hell I had voluntarily condemned myself, with no other company but scorpions and wild beasts, I many times imagined myself watching the dancing of Roman maidens as if I had been in the midst of them. My face was pallid with fasting, yet my will felt the assaults of desire. In my cold body and my parched flesh, which seemed dead before its death, passion was still able to live. Alone with the enemy, I threw myself in spirit at the feet of Jesus, watering them with my tears, and tamed my flesh by fasting whole weeks. I am not ashamed to disclose my temptations, though I grieve that I am not now what I then was."

Jerome added to these trials the study of Hebrew, a discipline which he hoped would help him in winning a victory over himself. "When my soul was on fire with wicked thoughts," he wrote in 411, "as a last resort, I became a pupil to a monk who had been a Jew, in order to learn the Hebrew alphabet. From the judicious precepts of Quintilian, the rich and fluent eloquence of Cicero, the graver style of Fronto, and the smoothness of Pliny, I turned to this language of hissing and broken-winded words. What labor it cost me, what difficulties I went through, how often I despaired and abandoned it and began again to learn, both I, who felt the burden, and they who lived with me, can bear witness. I thank our Lord that I now gather such sweet fruit from the bitter sowing of those studies." He continued to read the pagan classics for pleasure until a vivid dream turned him from them, at least for a time. In a letter he describes how, during an illness, he dreamed he was standing before the tribunal of Christ. "Thou a Christian?" said the judge skeptically. "Thou art a Ciceronian. Where thy treasure is, there thy heart is also."

The church at Antioch was greatly disturbed at this time by party and doctrinal disputes. The anchorites in the desert took sides, and called on Jerome, the most learned of them, to give his opinions on the subjects at issue. He wrote for guidance to Pope Damasus at Rome. Failing to receive an answer, he wrote again. "On one side, the Arian fury rages, supported by the secular power; on the other side, the Church [at Antioch] is being divided into three parts, and each would draw me to itself." No reply from Damasus is extant; but we know that Jerome acknowledged Paulinus, leader of one party, as bishop of Antioch, and that when he left the desert of Chalcis, he received from Paulinus' hands his ordination as priest. Jerome consented to ordination only on condition that he should not be obliged to serve in any church, knowing that his true vocation was to be a monk and recluse.

About 380 Jerome went to Constantinople to study the Scriptures under the Greek, Gregory of Nazianzus, then bishop of that city. Two years later he went back to Rome with Paulinus of Antioch to attend a council which Pope Damasus was holding to deal with the Antioch schism. Appointed secretary of the council, Jerome acquitted himself so well that, when it was over, Damasus kept him there as his own secretary. At the Pope's request he prepared a revised text, based on the Greek, of the Latin New Testament, the current version of which had been disfigured by "wrong copying, clumsy correction, and careless interpolations." He also revised the Latin psalter. That the prestige of Rome and its power to arbitrate between disputants, East as well as West, was recognized as never before at this time, was due in some measure at least to Jerome's diligence and ability. Along with his official duties he was fostering a new movement of Christian asceticism among a group of noble Roman ladies. Several of them were to be canonized, including Albina and her daughters Marcella and Asella, Melania the Elder, who was the first of them to go to the Holy Land, and Paula, with her daughters, Blesilla and Eustochium. The tie between Jerome and the three last-mentioned women was especially close, and to them he addressed many of his famous letters.

When Pope Damasus died in 384, he was succeeded by Siricius, who was less friendly to Jerome. While serving Damasus, Jerome had impressed all by his personal holiness, learning, and integrity. But he had also managed to get himself widely disliked by pagans and evil-doers whom he had condemned, and also by people of taste and tolerance, many of them Christians, who were offended by his biting sarcasm and a certain ruthlessness in attack. An example of his style is the harsh diatribe against the artifices of worldly women, who "paint their cheeks with rouge and their eyelids with antimony, whose plastered faces, too white for human beings, look like idols; and if in a moment of forgetfulness they shed a tear it makes a furrow where it rolls down the painted cheek; women to whom years do not bring the gravity of age, who load their heads with other people's hair, enamel a lost youth upon the wrinkles of age, and affect a maidenly timidity in the midst of a troop of grandchildren." In a letter to Eustochium he writes with scorn of certain members of the Roman clergy. "All their anxiety is about their clothes. . . . You would take them for bridegrooms rather than for clerics; all they think about is knowing the names and houses and doings of rich ladies."

Although Jerome's indignation was usually justified, his manner of expressing it—both verbally and in letters—aroused resentment. His own reputation was attacked; his bluntness, his walk, and even his smile were criticized. And neither the virtue of the ladies under his direction nor his own scrupulous behavior towards them was any protection from scandalous gossip. Affronted at the calumnies that were circulated, Jerome decided to return to the East. Taking with him his brother Paulinian and some others, he embarked in August, 385. At Cyprus, on the way, he was received with joy by Bishop Epiphanius, and at Antioch also he conferred with leading churchmen. It was here, probably, that he was joined by the widow Paula and some other ladies who had left Rome with the aim of settling in the Holy Land.

With what remained of Jerome's own patrimony and with financial help from Paula, a monastery for men was built near the basilica of the Nativity at Bethlehem, and also houses for three communities of women. Paula became head of one of these, and after her death was succeeded by her daughter Eustochium. Jerome himself lived and worked in a large cave near the Saviour's birthplace. He opened a free school there and also a hospice for pilgrims, "so that," as Paula said, "should Mary and Joseph visit Bethlehem again, they would have a place to stay." Now at last Jerome be-

gan to enjoy some years of peaceful activity. He gives us a wonderful description of this fruitful, harmonious, Palestinian life, and
its attraction for all manner of men. "Illustrious Gauls congregate
here, and no sooner has the Briton, so remote from our world,
arrived at religion than he leaves his early-setting sun to seek a
land which he knows only by reputation and from the Scriptures.
Then the Armenians, the Persians, the peoples of India and Ethiopia, of Egypt, and of Pontus, Cappadocia, Syria, and Mesopotamia! . . . They come in throngs and set us examples of every
virtue. The languages differ but the religion is the same; as many
different choirs chant the psalms as there are nations. . . . Here
bread and herbs, planted with our own hands, and milk, all
country fare, furnish us plain and healthy food. In summer the
trees give us shade. In autumn the air is cool and the falling leaves
restful. In spring our psalmody is sweeter for the singing of the
birds. We have plenty of wood when winter snow and cold are
upon us. Let Rome keep its crowds, let its arenas run with blood,
its circuses go mad, its theaters wallow in sensuality. . . ."

But when the Christian faith was threatened Jerome could not
be silent. While at Rome in the time of Pope Damasus, he had
composed a book on the perpetual virginity of the Virgin Mary
against one Helvidius, who had maintained that Mary had not
remained always a virgin but had had other children by St. Joseph,
after the birth of Christ. This and similar ideas were now again put
forward by a certain Jovinian, who had been a monk. Paula's son-
in-law, Pammachius, sent some of this heretical writing to Jerome,
and he, in 393, wrote two books against Jovinian. In the first he
described the excellence of virginity. The books were written in
Jerome's vehement style and there were expressions in them which
seemed lacking in respect for honorable matrimony. Pammachius
informed Jerome of the offense which he and many others at Rome
had taken at them. Thereupon Jerome composed his *Apology to
Pammachius*, sometimes called his third book against Jovinian, in
which he showed by quoting from his own earlier works that he

regarded marriage as a good and honorable state and did not condemn even a second or a third marriage.

A few years later he turned his attention to one Vigilantius, a Gallic priest, who was denouncing both celibacy and the veneration of saints' relics, calling those who revered them idolaters and worshipers of ashes. In defending celibacy Jerome said that a monk should purchase security by flying from temptations and dangers when he distrusted his own strength. As to the veneration of relics, he declared: "We do not worship the relics of the martyrs, but honor them in our worship of Him whose martyrs they are. We honor the servants in order that the respect paid to them may be reflected back to the Lord." Honoring them, he said, was not idolatry because no Christian had ever adored the martyrs as gods; on the other hand, they pray for us. "If the Apostles and martyrs, while still living on earth, could pray for other men, how much more may they do it after their victories? Have they less power now that they are with Jesus Christ?" He told Paula, after the death of her daughter Blesilla, "She now prays to the Lord for you, and obtains for me the pardon of my sins." Jerome was never moderate whether in virtue or against evil. Though swift to anger, he was also swift to feel remorse and was even more severe on his own failings than on those of others.

From 395 to 400 Jerome was engaged in a war against Origenism[2], which unhappily created a breach in his long friendship with Rufinus. Finding that some Eastern monks had been led into error by the authority of Rufinus' name and learning, Jerome attacked him. Rufinus, then living in a monastery at Jerusalem, had translated many of Origen's works into Latin and was an enthusiastic upholder of his scholarship, though it does not appear that he meant to defend the heresies in Origen's writings. Augustine, bishop of Hippo, was one of the churchmen greatly distressed by the quarrel between Jerome and Rufinus, and became unwillingly involved in a controversy with Jerome.

Jerome's passionate controversies were the least important part

[2] On Origen, see above, *St. Athanasius*, n. 5.

of his activities. What has made his name so famous was his critical labor on the text of the Scriptures. The Church regards him as the greatest of all the doctors in clarifying the Divine Word. He had the best available aids for such an undertaking, living where the remains of Biblical places, names, and customs all combined to give him a more vivid view than he could have had at a greater distance. To continue his study of Hebrew he hired a famous Jewish scholar, Bar Ananias, who came to teach him by night, lest other Jews should learn of it. As a man of prayer and purity of heart whose life had been mainly spent in study, penance, and contemplation, Jerome was prepared to be a sensitive interpreter of spiritual things.

We have seen that already while at Rome he had made a revision of the current Latin New Testament, and of the Psalms. Now he undertook to translate most of the books of the Old Testament directly from the Hebrew. The friends and scholars who urged him to this task realized the superiority of a version made directly from the original to any second-hand version, however venerable. It was needed too for argument with the Jews, who recognized no other text as authentic but their own. He began with the Books of Kings, and went on with the rest at different times. When he found that the Book of Tobias and part of Daniel had been composed in Chaldaic, he set himself to learn that difficult language also. More than once he was tempted to give up the whole wearisome task, but a certain scholarly tenacity of purpose kept him at it. The only parts of the Latin Bible, now known as the Vulgate, which were not either translated or worked over by him are the Books of Wisdom, Ecclesiasticus, Baruch, and the two Books of the Maccabees.[3] He revised the Psalms once again, with the aid of Origen's *Hexapla*,[4] and the Hebrew text. This last is the version included now in the

---

[3] These five books, together with the books of Tobias, Judith, and Sophonias, not included in the Protestant Bible, are in the Catholic Bible.

[4] Hexapla, Greek for six-fold, was the name given to Origen's edition of the Old Testament in Hebrew and Greek, because it was arranged in six columns, giving six different versions of the text.

Vulgate and used generally in the Divine Office; his first revision, known as the Roman Psalter, is still used for the opening psalm at Matins and throughout the Missal, and for the Divine Office in the cathedrals of St. Peter at Rome and St. Mark at Venice, and in the Milanese rite.

In the sixteenth century the great Council of Trent pronounced Jerome's Vulgate the authentic and authoritative Latin text of the Catholic Church, without, however, thereby implying a preference for it above the original text or above versions in other languages. In 1907 Pope Pius X entrusted to the Benedictine Order the office of restoring as far as possible the correct text of St. Jerome's Vulgate, which during fifteen centuries of use had naturally become altered in many places. The Bible now ordinarily used by English-speaking Catholics is a translation of the Vulgate, made at Rheims and Douay towards the end of the sixteenth century, and revised by Bishop Challoner in the eighteenth. The Confraternity Edition of the New Testament appearing in 1950 represents a complete revision.

A heavy blow came to Jerome in 404 when his staunch friend, the saintly Paula, died. Six years later he was stunned by news of the sacking of Rome by Alaric the Goth. Of the refugees who fled from Rome to the East at this time he wrote: "Who would have believed that the daughters of that mighty city would one day be wandering as servants and slaves on the shores of Egypt and Africa, or that Bethlehem would daily receive noble Romans, distinguished ladies, brought up in wealth and now reduced to beggary? I cannot help them all, but I grieve and weep with them, and am completely absorbed in the duties which charity imposes on me. I have put aside my commentary on Ezekiel and almost all study. For today we must translate the precepts of the Scriptures into deeds; instead of speaking saintly words, we must act them." A few years later his work was again interrupted by raids of barbarians pushing north through Egypt into Palestine, and later still by a violent onset of Pelagian heretics, who, relying on the protection of Bishop John of Jerusalem, sent a troop of ruffians to Bethlehem to disperse the monks and nuns living there under the direction of Jerome, who had been opposing Pelagianism [5] with his customary truculence. Some of the monks were beaten, a deacon was killed, and monasteries were set on fire. Jerome had to go into hiding for a time.

The following year Paula's daughter Eustochium died. The aged Jerome soon fell ill, and after lingering for two years succumbed. Worn with penance and excessive labor, his sight and voice almost gone, his body like a shadow, he died peacefully on September 30, 420, and was buried under the church of the Nativity at Bethlehem. In the thirteenth century his body was translated and now lies somewhere in the Sistine Chapel of the basilica of Santa Maria Maggiore at Rome. The Church owes much to St. Jerome. While his great work was the Vulgate, his achievements in other fields are valuable; to him we owe the distinction between canonical and apocryphal writings; he was a pioneer in the field of Biblical archeology; his commentaries are important; his letters, published in three volumes, are one of our best sources of knowledge of the times.

St. Jerome has been a popular subject with artists, who have pictured him in the desert, as a scholar in his study, and sometimes in the robes of a cardinal, because of his services for Pope Damasus; often too he is shown with a lion, from whose paw, according to legend, he once drew a thorn. Actually this story was transferred to him from the tradition of St. Gerasimus, but a lion is not an inappropriate symbol for so fearless a champion of the faith.

[5] For an account of the Pelagian heresy, see below, *St. Augustine,* p. 106.

Letter CVII

Let this be said, dear Laeta, most dutiful daughter in Christ, so that you may not despair of your father's salvation. I hope that the same faith which has gained you a daughter as its reward may also win your father, and that you may rejoice over blessings bestowed upon your whole household, knowing God's promise: "The things which are impossible with men are possible with God." It is never too late to be converted. The robber passed from the cross to Paradise. . . .

. . . . Even in Rome now heathenism languishes in solitude. Those who were once the gods of the Gentiles are left beneath their deserted pinnacles to the company of owls and night-birds. The army standards bear the emblem of the cross. The purple robes of kings and the jewels that sparkle on their diadems are adorned with the gibbet sign that has brought to us salvation. Today even the Egyptian Serapis has become a Christian. Marnas [7] mourns in his prison at Gaza, and fears continually that his temple will be overthrown. From India, from Persia and from Ethiopia we welcome crowds of monks every hour. The Armenians have laid aside their quivers, the Huns are learning the psalter, the frosts of Scythia are warmed by the fire of faith. The ruddy flaxen-haired Getae carry tent-churches about with their armies; and perhaps the reason why they fight with us on equal terms is that they believe in the same religion.

[6] This letter, written in 403 to the Roman matron Laeta, who with her family had fled during the barbarian invasion, gave advice on her daughter's education and the winning over of her pagan father, but ends with a vivid report on the advances which Christianity was making.

[7] Serapis was an Egyptian deity; Marnas was one of the chief Syrian gods.

Letter XXII

TO EUSTOCHIUM

. . . Avoid with special care the traps set for you by a desire for vainglory. Jesus says: 'How can ye believe, who receive glory one from another?'[8]. . . . When you are giving alms, let God alone see you. When you are fasting keep a cheerful face. Let your dress be neither elegant nor slovenly, nor conspicuous by any strangeness that might attract the notice of passersby and make people point their fingers at you. . . . Do not try to seem very devout or more humble than necessary. It is possible to seek glory by despising it. . . . When you come into a gathering of brethren and sisters, do not sit in too lowly a place or pretend that you are unworthy of a footstool. . . . If any of your handmaids have taken the vow[9] with you, do not lift yourself up against them or pride yourself on being their mistress. From now on you all have one Bridegroom; you sing psalms together; together you receive the body of Christ. Why then should you sit apart at meals? . . .

Avoid too the sin of avarice. Not merely must you refuse to claim what belongs to another, for that is an offense punished by the laws of the State; you must also give up clinging to your own property, which is no longer yours. . . . But you say: "I am a delicate girl and I cannot work with my hands. If I live to old age and then fall sick, who will take pity on me?" Hear Jesus saying to the Apostles: "Take no thought what ye shall eat; nor yet for your body what ye shall put on. . . ."[10] Let the words be ever on your lips: 'Naked I came out of my mother's womb and naked I shall return thither,'[11] and 'We brought nothing into this world, and certainly we can carry nothing out."[12]

Yet today you see many women packing their wardrobes with dresses, changing their tunics every day, and even so unable to

---

[8] John v, 44.
[9] Of virginity.
[10] Matthew vi, 25.
[11] Job i, 21.
[12] I Timothy vi, 7.

keep ahead of the moth. The more scrupulous wear one dress until it is threadbare, but yet have their boxes full of clothes. Their parchments are dyed purple, gold is melted for the lettering, their books are decorated with jewels, and Christ lies naked and dying at their door. When they stretch out their hands to give anything, they blow a trumpet. Only lately I saw the greatest lady in Rome— I will not tell her name, for this is not a satire—in the church of the Blessed Peter with her eunuchs in front of her, dispensing money to the poor with her own hands so as to be thought the more pious. To each one she gave a penny, and then, as you might easily know by experience would happen, an old woman full of years and rags, ran forward suddenly to get a second penny, but when her turn came, she got not a penny but a blow from the lady's fist and for her terrible crime paid with her blood! . . . .

The Apostle bids us pray without ceasing and to saints their very slumber is a prayer. Yet we should have fixed hours for praying, so that if we happen to be engaged in some business, the time itself will remind us of our duty. Everyone knows that the third, sixth, and ninth hours, dawn, too, and evening, are the right times. And no food should be taken until after a prayer, nor should we leave the table without rendering thanks to the Creator. Twice or three times in the night we should rise from the bed and say over passages of Scripture which we know by heart. . . . Speak evil of no one and slander not your mother's son. "Who art thou who judgest another's servant? To his own lord he standeth or falleth." [13]. . . . If you have fasted for two days, do not think yourself better than one who has not fasted. You fast and are peevish; the other eats and is pleasant. You work off your irritability and hunger by quarreling; the other eats moderately and gives thanks to God. . . .

For our salvation the Son of God became the Son of Man. . . . He held the world in his little hand but he was contained in a narrow manger. I say nothing of the thirty years He lived obscure and content with his parents' poverty. He is scourged and says not a word. He is crucified and prays for his crucifiers. . . . But we are annoyed if our food lacks flavor and imagine we are doing God service when we drink water with our wine. . . .

[13] Romans xiv, 4.

Step out, I beg you, a little from your body and picture above your eyes the reward which "eye hath not seen, nor ear heard, neither hath it entered into the heart of man." [14] What will be the splendor of that day when Mary, the Lord's mother, shall come to meet you, attended by her virgin bands. . . ? . . . Then shall the hundred and forty and four thousand hold their harps before the throne and before the elders and sing a new song. And no man will know that song but the company appointed: "These are they which follow the Lamb whithersoever he goeth." [15] Whenever the world's vain display allures you, whenever you see in the world something glorious, pass over in mind to Paradise. Begin to be now what you will be hereafter. . . .

(St. Jerome, *Select Letters*, translated by
F. A. Wright, Loeb Classical Library.)

[14] I Corinthians ii, 9.
[15] Apocalypse xiv, 4.

Saint Augustine of Hippo
Bishop, Doctor of the Church

4 3 0

(*August 28*)

Pope Leo I, during whose pontificate Augustine was canonized, ordered that the feast of this saint should be observed with the same honors as that of an Apostle. In every succeeding age his memory has been held in the highest veneration and his writings have been an inspiration to Catholics and non-Catholics alike. Augustine was born on November 13, 354, at Tagaste, a small town of Numidia, North Africa, not far from the episcopal city of Hippo. His parents were citizens of good standing, though not wealthy. The father was one Patricius, a hot-tempered man and a pagan, who, under the influence of his Christian wife, the saintly Monica, learned patience and humility and was baptized shortly before his death. Of this union there were three children: Augustine, another son, Navigius, and a daughter, Perpetua, who became an abbess.

Augustine's youth and manhood, up to and including his conversion and the death of his mother, is described fully in his great spiritual autobiography, the *Confessions*. He wrote the book, he says, for "a people curious to know the lives of others, but careless to amend their own," to demonstrate God's mercy as shown in the life of one sinner, and to make sure that no one should think him any better than he really was. With the utmost candor Augustine divulges the sins and follies of his youth, and at the end enumerates the weaknesses which still beset him. With a copy of the book which he sent to a friend, he wrote: "See now what I am from this

SAINT STEPHEN

Memling

Hans Memling (c. 1433-1494) was born in the Rhine city of Mainz and became a master painter in Brussels in 1454. His painting shows a tender sweetness which verges upon mysticism, and gives to his work a lyrical quality rather than being heroic and dramatic.

Saint Stephen, the Protomartyr, wears a deacon's dalmatic and carries three stones, emblematic of his martyrdom by being stoned to death.

SAINT JUDE THADDEUS
Suter

A modern devotional picture, this painting of Saint Jude, also known as Thaddeus, represents him as one of the twelve Apostles, with the Pentecostal flame on his head. The fleur-de-lis in the background are symbols of the Trinity.

Saint Jude is represented by the knotted club. Among his other symbols are an inverted cross, a halberd, or a sailboat.

book; believe me who bear testimony against myself, and regard not what others say of me."

In infancy Augustine was marked with the sign of the cross and enrolled among the catechumens, and later instructed in the tenets of the Christian religion. Once, when ill, the boy asked for baptism, but he suddenly got well and the rite was postponed. At this time it was a common practice for Christians to defer baptism until they were well on in years, for fear of the greater guilt they would incur by sinning after baptism. Augustine himself later condemned this custom, and the Church has long since forbidden it.

When he was barely twelve years old Augustine was sent to a grammar school at Madaura. He writes of this traditionally Roman school: "I had to learn things from which, poor boy, I derived no profit, and yet if I was negligent in learning I was whipped, for this was the method approved by my elders, and the many who had trod that life before us had chalked out for us these wearisome ways." Though the teachers had no other end in view than that their pupils should become military officers or rich merchants, divine Providence, Augustine admits, made good use of their misguided aim; for they forced him to learn, to his later profit and advantage. He accuses himself of avoiding study not for want of aptitude, but out of sheer love of mischief. "We were punished for our play by persons who were doing nothing better than we were, but the boys' play of grown men is called 'business.'" And here is another astute criticism of a teacher, who, "if defeated in some petty argument by a fellow teacher, was more jealous and angry than a boy ever was when beaten by a playmate at a game of ball." Augustine liked Latin very much, for he had learned it in childhood from nurses. Greek was difficult for him and he did not progress far.

At sixteen Augustine returned to Tagaste, where he soon fell into loose company. Patricius wanted his son to be a man of culture, but cared little about the formation of his character. Monica, on the other hand, pleaded with her son to govern his passions. Her words, he writes, "seemed to me but the admonitions of a woman, which I was ashamed to obey, whereas they were Thy admonitions, O God, and I knew it not. Through her Thou didst speak to me, and I despised Thee in her." Patricius died at about this time, and a rich man of the town paid Augustine's expenses to study in the great city of Carthage. Now applying himself in earnest, the young man soon advanced to the first place in the school of rhetoric. His mind was awake and developing rapidly; yet, in retrospect, he writes that his motives for study were the unworthy ones of vanity and ambition. At Carthage he entered into a relationship with a woman whom he kept at his side for more than thirteen years. Before the age of twenty he was the father of a boy who bore the pious name of Adeodatus (Given by God). He read the best of the Latin writers—Vergil, Varro, and Cicero—but in time he grew dissatisfied with them and started to study the Scriptures.

At this point, much troubled by the problem of evil, he came under the influence of the Manichees,[1] according to whom there were two eternal, warring principles, spirit and light, the cause of all good, and matter and darkness, the cause of all evil. These subtle heretics claimed to put everything to the test of reason, and scoffed at those who deferred to the authority of the Church. Writing later to a friend, Augustine said: "You know, my dear Honoratus, that we believed in these men on no other grounds. What else made me reject for almost nine years the religion instilled into me in my childhood, and become their follower and diligent pupil, but their saying that we were overawed by superstition and that faith was imposed on us without reason, whereas they expected no one to believe, except after first examining and clearly seeing the truth? Who would not have been inveigled by such promises? Especially a young man hungry for truth and already proud and talkative, with a reputation among learned men in the schools. They derided the simplicity of the Catholic faith, which commanded men to believe before they were taught by plain reasoning what was the

[1] The Manichees, or Manichaeans, were the successors of the earlier Gnostics, and pushed the principle of dualism to further extremes. The cult had been founded by Manes, a Persian.

truth." Augustine met Faustus, the Manichees' leading exponent, and was disappointed in him.

For nine years he conducted schools of rhetoric and grammar at Tagaste and Carthage. His mother, encouraged by the assurance of the bishop that "the son of so many tears could not perish," never ceased by prayer and exhortation to try to make a Christian of him. In 383 Augustine set out for Rome with his little family, leaving secretly lest his mother should try to prevent him or wish to accompany him. At Rome he opened a school of rhetoric, but the enterprise was not a financial success.

It now happened that orders came to Symmachus, prefect of Rome, from the imperial capital at Milan, to send up a teacher of rhetoric. Augustine applied for the post, gave proof of his ability, and received the appointment. The brilliant young teacher was well received at Milan and soon made the acquaintance of the learned and powerful Bishop Ambrose. Augustine enjoyed the bishop's sermons and little by little the arguments persuaded him. At the same time he was reading the older Greek philosophers, Plato and Plotinus. "Plato," he wrote, "gave me knowledge of the true God, but Jesus showed me the way."

Monica traveled to Milan, for she still had not given up hope of seeing her son a Christian; moreover, she wished to see him properly married to a girl of his own station in life. She persuaded him to send the mother of Adeodatus back to Africa, where, it is supposed, she entered a convent. Augustine's struggle, moral and spiritual, went on. The writings of the Platonic philosophers, he tells us, bred pride and false confidence, instead of teaching him to bewail his condition. Finally turning to the New Testament, especially to the writings of St. Paul, he found the prophecies of the Old Testament fulfilled, the glory of Heaven revealed, and the way thither clearly pointed out. He learned what he had long felt to be true, that the law of his members warred against the law of his mind; and that nothing could free him of the conflict but the grace of Jesus Christ. Although he had now become convinced of the truth of the Catholic faith, he could not surrender. "I sighed and longed," he writes, "to be delivered, but was kept fast bound, not with exterior chains but with my own iron will. The Enemy held my will, and of it he made a chain with which he fettered me fast. Out of a perverse will he created wicked desire or lust, my yielding to lust created habit, and habit unresisted created a kind of necessity, by which, as by links fastened to one another, I was kept close shackled in cruel slavery. I had not the excuse I claimed earlier to have, when I delayed serving Thee because I had not yet certainly discovered Thy truth. Now I knew it, yet I was still fettered."

One day an African Christian employed at court, one Pontitian, came to see Augustine and his friend Alipius. He took occasion to speak of the *Life of St. Antony*,[2] and was astonished that the young men did not even know Antony's name. They listened eagerly to the story of his holy life. The visit affected Augustine deeply; his weakness and vacillation were revealed to him. In his previous state of half wishing for conversion he had begged God for the grace of continence, but at the same time had been a little afraid of being heard too soon. "In the first dawning of my youth," he writes, "I begged of Thee chastity, but by halves, miserable wretch that I am; I said, 'Give me chastity, but not yet,' afraid that Thou mightest hear me too soon, and heal me of the disease which I wished to have satisfied rather than cured."

When Pontitian had departed, Augustine turned to Alipius with the words: "What are we doing to let the unlearned start up and seize Heaven by force, while we, with all our knowledge, linger behind, cowardly and callous, wallowing in our sins? Because they have outstripped us and gone on before, are we ashamed to follow them? Is it not more shameful not to follow them?" He went out into the garden, Alipius following, and they sat down at some distance from the house. Augustine was in the throes of his conflict, torn between the promptings of the Holy Spirit calling him to chastity and the seductive memory of his sins. Advancing farther into the garden alone, he threw himself under a fig-tree, crying out,

[2] For selections from Athanasius' *Life of St. Antony*, see above, p. 55.

"How long, O Lord? Wilt Thou be angry forever? Remember not my past iniquities!" As he lay there despairing, suddenly he heard a childlike voice repeating, *"Tolle lege! Tolle lege!"* (Take, read! Take, read!) He wondered if there was a game in which children said these words, and could not remember that he had ever heard of one. Interpreting the voice as of divine origin, he returned to where Alipius was sitting, opened St. Paul's Epistles at random, and cast his eyes on the words: "Not in revelry and drunkenness, not in debauchery and wantonness, not in strife and jealousy. But put on the Lord Jesus Christ, and as for the flesh, take no thought for its lusts." Augustine felt an immediate sense of release, as if his long struggle was ended. He pointed out the passage to Alipius, who read on, "But him who is weak in faith, receive without disputes about opinions." They then went to relate these happenings to Monica, who rejoiced and praised God, "who is able to do all things more abundantly than we ask or understand." The story of Augustine's conversion has been repeated in some detail here because of its abiding spiritual and psychological interest. It occurred in September, 386, when Augustine was thirty-two.

He gave up his school and retired to spend the winter in a country house near Milan which a friend lent to him. Monica, Navigius, Adeodatus, Alipius, two cousins, and several friends were with him there. Augustine gave himself up to prayer, study, and conversation. He strove to get firm control over his passions and to prepare himself for a new life. From daily discussions with his companions he got ideas for the three *Dialogues* written at this time—*Against the Academicians, On the Happy Life,* and *On Order.*

Returning to Milan, Augustine was baptized by Bishop Ambrose on Easter Eve, 387, with Alipius and the much-loved Adeodatus. Resolving to re-establish himself in Africa, he traveled to the port of Ostia, accompanied by his mother, brother, son, and friends. Monica was taken ill at Ostia and soon died. To her life and final days Augustine devoted some of the most moving chapters of the *Confessions.* He now went back to Rome to speak publicly against the Manichaeans, and a year passed before he took ship for Africa. It was during this period that he wrote his two unfinished books of *Soliloquies*. At Tagaste he settled with friends in his old home, and stayed there for nearly three years, cut off from temporal concerns, serving God by prayer, fasting, and good works. All things in the house were held in common; Augustine even gave up title to the family property. Soon his life was again made desolate by the death of Adeodatus, a brilliant boy of seventeen.

Augustine did not wish to become a priest, but was aware that an attempt might be made to give him a bishopric; by this time he was even more famed for his saintliness than for his learning. He therefore avoided visiting any cities in which sees were vacant. In 391 he was in the city of Hippo, whose bishop, Valerius, had spoken to the people of his need for a priest to assist him. So when Augustine appeared in church, the congregation swept him forward to Valerius, entreating the bishop to ordain him priest. Augustine yielded and was ordained; Valerius gave him some months to prepare for his ministry. When Augustine moved to Hippo, he established a small community in a house adjoining the church, similar to the monastic household at Tagaste. Valerius, who had an impediment in his speech, appointed Augustine to deliver his sermons for him. Augustine also preached his own sermons. He felt that preaching was his most important duty, and this activity continued up to the very end of life. Nearly a hundred of his sermons are extant, many of them not written out by him but taken down in shorthand as he delivered them.

In his sermons Augustine urges meditation on "the last things"; for "even if the Lord's day, the last judgment, be some distance away, is your day of death far off?" He insists on the necessity of penance, "For sin must be punished either by the penitent sinner or by God, his judge; and God, who has promised pardon to the penitent sinner, has nowhere promised to one who delays his conversion a morrow to do penance in." He has much to say of almsgiving, and declares that failure in this duty was the cause of the destruction of most of those who perish, since it is the only sin

Christ mentions in the last judgment. (Matthew xxv, 31-46.) He speaks often of Purgatory, and recommends prayer and the Holy Sacrifice for the repose of the faithful departed. He emphasizes the respect due to holy images and to the sign of the cross, telling of miracles wrought by it, and by martyrs' relics. There are sixty-nine sermons on saints; he refers often to the honor due to martyrs, but says that sacrifices are offered to God alone, not to martyrs, though those "who are with Christ intercede for us." He preached in Latin, but he tried to furnish the rural parts of the diocese, where the Punic tongue was spoken, with priests who could speak this language.

In 395 Augustine was consecrated bishop and coadjutor to Valerius, and on Valerius' death soon after he succeeded him. He now established a regular common life in the episcopal residence, and required all priests, deacons, and sub-deacons who lived with him to renounce their property and accept the rule he set up there. Only those who would bind themselves to such a life were accepted for Holy Orders. His biographer, Possidius, tells us that the furnishings of the house were extremely plain. He would have no silver utensils except spoons; the dishes were of earthenware, wood, and stone; the fare was frugal, and while wine was supplied to guests, the quantity was strictly limited. At meals Augustine preferred reading or literary conversation to secular talk. All clerics who lived with him ate at the same table. Thus, the mode of life instituted by the Apostles and carried out in the early history of the Church was adopted by the good bishop of Hippo. He also founded a community of religious women over whom his sister Perpetua was abbess. Augustine wrote the nuns a letter in which he laid down the broad, ascetic principles of the religious life. This letter, along with two sermons he preached on the subject, comprises the so-called Rule of St. Augustine, which has been the basis for the constitutions of many orders of canons regular, friars, and nuns.[3]

To overseers among his clergy Augustine committed the entire

---

[3] Augustine never drew up a detailed rule, but simply laid down a few general precepts, including poverty, unity, charity, and prayer in common.

care of temporal matters, receiving their accounts at the end of the year. To others he entrusted the building and management of hospitals and churches. He would never accept for the poor any estate or gift when the donation seemed unfair to an heir. But the revenues of his church were freely spent, and Possidius says that sometimes sacred vessels were melted down to raise funds for redeeming captives, an act for which he had the precedent set by Ambrose. He persuaded his people to provide clothing for all the poor of each parish once a year. In times of hardship he was not afraid to contract heavy debts to aid the distressed. His concern for the spiritual welfare of his people was boundless. "I do not wish to be saved without you," he told them. "Why am I in the world? Not only to live in Jesus Christ; but to live in Him with you. This is my passion, my honor, my glory, my joy, and my riches."

Few men have been endowed with a more generous and affectionate nature than Augustine. He talked freely with unbelievers, and often invited them to his table, although he sometimes declined to eat with Christians whose conduct was evil. He was rigorous in subjecting such offenders to canonical penance and the censures of the Church; but in his opposition to wrong-doing he never forgot the precepts of charity, humility, and good manners. He followed Ambrose's example in refusing to persuade men to become soldiers and he took no part in match-making.

St. Augustine's letters show an astonishing breadth of interests. Some are learned treatises on points of Christian doctrine and conduct, others are full of practical counsel. In his letter to Ecdicia he explains the duties of a wife, telling her she ought not wear black clothes, since her husband disliked them; she might be humble in spirit while rich and gay in dress. In all things reasonable, he tells her, she should agree with her husband as to the method of educating their son, and leave the chief care of it to him; he reproves her for having given goods and money to the poor without his consent, and tells her to ask his pardon for it. In like manner, he always impressed on husbands the respect, tender affection, and consideration which they owed their wives.

Augustine's own modesty and restraint is revealed in his exchange with Jerome over the interpretation of a text of Galatians. A private letter from Jerome to him had miscarried, and Jerome, a hot-tempered man, thought himself insulted and retorted angrily. Augustine wrote to him in all gentleness, "I entreat you again and again to correct me firmly when you see me standing in need of it; for though the office of bishop is greater than that of priest, yet in many respects Augustine is inferior to Jerome." He was grieved by the bitterness of the quarrel between Jerome and Rufinus; he saw an element of vanity in such disputes, in which men love their own opinion, he says, "not because it is true, but because it is their own; and they dispute, not for the truth, but for victory."

Throughout his thirty-five years as bishop of Hippo Augustine was continually defending the faith against heresies or paganism. In 404 he debated publicly with a famous Manichaean leader called Felix. The debate ended dramatically, with Felix confessing the Catholic faith and pronouncing an anathema on Manes and his blasphemies. The Priscillianist heresy was similar in some respects to the Manichaean, and had spread through several parts of Spain. Paul Orosius, a Spanish priest, made the voyage to Africa in 415 in order to see Augustine, and was the instigator of the latter's book, *Against the Priscillianists and the Origenists*. In it he condemns the doctrine that the human soul, divine by nature, was imprisoned in the material body as punishment for previous transgressions. In a treatise meant for Jews he maintains that the Mosaic law, good in its time, was destined to come to an end and be replaced by the new law of Christ.

The neighboring town of Madaura, where Augstine had gone to school, had been settled mainly by Roman veterans, many of whom were pagans, and he won their good will by rendering them important public services. Numbers of them became Christians. When Rome was taken and plundered in 410 by Alaric the Goth, there was a new outbreak against the Christian population, the pagans saying that the city's calamities came because the ancient gods had been forsaken. Partially to answer these accusations,

Augustine began in 413 his greatest book, *The City of God,* a survey of human history and justification of Christian philosophy. This work was not finished until 426.

There was also trouble with the Donatists, a faction led by Donatus, bishop of Carthage. They maintained that the Catholic Church, by readmitting to communion penitents who had once apostatized under stress of persecution, and by recognizing the efficacy of sacraments administered by penitent priests, had ceased to be the true Church, and that they were the only true Christians. In Africa, after the cessation of persecution, the feeling against weaklings who had denied Christ ran high. The Donatists had five hundred bishops, and even in Hippo the Catholics were in the minority. In some places the Donatists attacked and murdered Catholics. Augustine's reputation and zeal won followers, but a few Donatists were so exasperated by him as to preach that to kill him would be a great service to their religion and meritorious before God. In 405 he was obliged to invoke the civil power to restrain the Donatist party around Hippo, and the Catholic Emperor Honorius issued severe edicts against it. Augustine himself never countenanced the death penalty for heresy. A conference of Catholics and Donatists at Carthage in 411 marked the beginning of the return of the Donatists to the Church.

Now a new heresy arose, that known as Pelagianism. Pelagius is usually referred to as a Briton; Jerome scornfully called him "a big fat fellow, bloated with Scots porridge." Rejecting the doctrine of original sin, he taught that men had the power of choice and could live good lives of their own free will and win salvation by their own efforts; baptism was simply a sign of their previous admission to God's kingdom. In 411 Pelagius came to Africa from Rome, and the next year his doctrines were condemned by a synod at Carthage. Augustine combatted Pelagianism in treatises, sermons, and letters. Yet when he found it necessary to name Pelagius, it was to speak well of him: "As I hear, he is a holy man, well exercised in Christian virtue, a good man and worthy of praise." He had a loving tolerance for the man, while disliking his ideas. Against a modified doctrine called semi-Pelagianism, Augustine wrote two books, *On the Predestination of Saints* and *On the Gift of Perseverance,* to show that the authors of this doctrine had not retreated from the position of Pelagius. To Augustine, more than to any other man, the Church throughout this troubled period owes the preservation of its doctrine of the dependence of man on God for deliverance and salvation.

In his *Confessions,* as we have said, Augustine retraced his youth and laid bare his sins; in his seventy-second year he did the same for past errors of judgment, and these are summarized in his *Retractations,* which reviews the great body of his writings, and corrects mistakes with candor and severity. The bishop now desired more leisure for writing, and accordingly proposed to his clergy and people that they accept Heraclius, the youngest of his deacons, a man of wisdom and piety, as coadjutor.

The bishop's last years were full of the turmoil brought by the Vandal invasion of North Africa. Count Boniface, formerly imperial general in Africa, had incited Genseric, King of the Vandals, to invade the rich African provinces. Augustine wrote to Boniface, recalling him to his duty, but it was too late to stop the invasion. The Vandals landed in Africa in May, 428, and every contemporary account tells of the horror and desolation they spread as they advanced inland. Flourishing cities were left in ruins and country houses razed, the inhabitants either dead or in flight or seized as slaves. Worship ceased in the churches, most of which were burned. The greater number of clergy who escaped death were stripped and reduced to beggary. Of all the churches in North Africa, there were left hardly more than those in Carthage, Hippo, and Cirta, cities which were too strong for the Vandals to take at first.

In this dire situation another bishop asked Augustine if it was lawful or right for the clergy to flee at the approach of the barbarians. Augustine's prudent reply is deserving of quotation: it was lawful for a bishop or priest to flee and leave his flock when he alone was the object of the attack; or, again, when the people had all fled, and the pastor had no one left; or, yet again, when the ministry might be better performed by others who had no need to flee. Under all other circumstances, he said, pastors were obliged to stay and watch over their flocks, committed to them by Christ. Augustine grieved deeply over the outward calamities of his people, but even more over the damage to souls, for the ruthless Vandals, so far as they professed any religion, were Arians.

Towards the end of May, 430, the Vandals appeared before Hippo, the most strongly fortified city in this region, and settled down for a siege of fourteen months. That first summer Augustine fell ill of a fever, which he felt would be fatal. Death had long been a subject of his meditations, and he now talked of it with serene confidence in God's mercy. He asked for the penitential psalms of David to be written out and hung on the wall by his bed. His mind was sound to the end, and on August 28, 430, at the age of seventy-six, he calmly resigned his spirit to God. This man of tremendous gifts and vital personality, who had piloted the African Church through some of the world's darkest years, never doubted the ultimate victory of that "most glorious City of God."

Excerpts from the Confessions

N, 6. *Not with a doubtful but a sure consciousness, O Lord, do I love Thee.* Thou didst strike on my heart with Thy word and I loved Thee. . . . But what do I love when I love Thee? Not the beauty of bodies nor the loveliness of seasons, nor the radiance of the light around us, so gladsome to our eyes, nor the sweet melodies of songs of every kind, nor the fragrance of flowers and ointments and spices, nor manna and honey, nor limbs delectable for fleshly embraces. I do not love these things when I love my God. And yet I love a light and a voice and a fragrance and a food and an embrace when I love my God, who is a light, a voice, a fragrance, a food, and an embrace to my inner man. . . . This it is that I love when I love my God.

But what is this? I asked the earth [4] and she replied: "It is not I," and all that is in her made the same response. I asked the sea and the deeps and the creeping spirits and they answered: "We are not thy God; look above us." I asked the fleet winds, and the whole air with its inhabitants said: "Anaximenes is mistaken.[5] I am not God." I asked the sky, the sun, the moon and the stars. "Neither are we," said they, "the God whom thou seekest." And I cried to everything that stands about the doors of my flesh: "Tell me of my God, since you art not He. Tell me something of Him!" And they shouted aloud: "He made us." . . .

Then I turned myself to myself and said to myself: "Who art thou?" I replied: "A man. Lo, here are a body and a soul in me, attendant on me, one outside and one within." With which of these should I have sought after my God? With my body I had now searched for Him from the earth to heaven, as far as I could send my messengers, the rays of my eyes. But the inner man is the greater. To him as their superior and judge all my bodily messengers had reported the answers of the heavens and the earth and all that in them is, saying: "We are not God," and "He made us." These things my inner man learned through the services of the outer man. . . .

That same voice speaks indeed to all men, but only they understand it who join that voice, heard from outside, to the truth that is within them. And the truth says to me: "Neither heaven nor earth nor any body is thy God." Their own nature says the same. They see that the substance of a part is less than that of the whole. And now I speak to thee, my soul. Thou art my greater part, since thou quickenest the substance of my body by giving to it life, which no body can give to a body. And thy God is the life of thy life to thee. . . .

27.   Too late have I loved Thee, O Beauty so old and so new! Too late have I loved Thee. And lo, Thou wert inside me and I outside, and I sought for Thee there, and in all my unsightliness

---

[4] It will be remembered that Augustine as a young man had searched for answers to his questionings in the faiths of the time, and that earth, sea, and sky were worshiped in most pagan cults.

[5] Anaximenes, a Greek philosopher of the 6th century B.C., taught that the original source of the entire universe was air.

I flung myself on those beautiful things which Thou hast made. Thou wert with me and I was not with Thee. Those beauties kept me away from Thee, though if they had not been in Thee, they would not have been at all. Thou didst call and cry to me and break down my deafness. Thou didst flash and shine on me and put my blindness to flight. Thou didst blow fragrance upon me and I drew breath, and now I pant after Thee. I tasted of Thee and now I hunger and thirst for Thee. Thou didst touch me and I am aflame for Thy peace. . . .

Excerpts from the City of God

BOOK XII

1.   We said in our earlier books that it was God's pleasure to propagate all mankind from one man, both to keep in human nature a likeness to one society and also to make its original unity a means of concord in heart. Nor would any of mankind have died had not the first two—one of whom was made from the other and the other of nothing—incurred this punishment by their disobedience. For they committed so great a sin that their whole nature was thereby depraved and the same degree of corruption and necessity of death was transmitted to all their offspring. And thereupon death's power by this just punishment became so great over man that all would have been cast headlong into the second death which has no end had not the merciful grace of God acquitted some from it. And hence it comes to pass that although mankind is divided into many nations, distinct in language, training, habit, and fashion, yet there are but two sorts of men, who do properly make the two cities of which we speak. The one is a city of men who live according to the flesh, and the other a city of men who live according to the Spirit, each after his kind. And when they attain their desire, both live in their peculiar peace. . . .

11.   Now God, foreknowing all things, could not but know that man would fall; therefore we must found our city on His prescience and ordinance, not on what we know not and He has not

revealed. For man's sin could not disturb God's decree nor force Him to change His resolve. God foreknew and anticipated both how bad the man He had made would become and what good He meant to produce from him for all his badness. For though God is said to change His intention, as the Scriptures figuratively say He repented, etc., yet this is from the point of view of man's hope or Nature's order, not of His own prescience. So then God made man upright and consequently good in his will; otherwise he could not have been upright. This good will was God's work, man being thus created. The evil will which was in man before his evil deed was rather a falling away from the work of God to its own work than any work in itself. . . . And evil is removed from his nature not by cutting away a nature contrary to it but only by purifying that which was depraved. Then therefore is our will truly free, when it serves neither vice nor sin. Such God gave us, such we lost and can only recover through Him who gave it. . . .

13.   But evil began within them [Adam and Eve], secretly at first, to draw them later into open disobedience. For there would have been no evil deed had there not been an evil will before it. What could beget this evil will but pride, which is the beginning of all sin? And what is pride but a perverse ambition for height, which forsakes Him to whom the soul ought solely to cleave as the source of it, and makes itself seem its one and only source? This is when it likes itself too well or loves itself so that it will abandon that unchangeable Good in which it ought to find more delight than in itself. The defect now is willful, for if the will had remained firm in its love of that loftier and mightier Good which gave it light to see it and zeal to love it, it would not have turned from it to delight in itself and thereat have become so blind of sight and cold of zeal that either Eve would have believed the serpent's words as true or Adam would have dared to prefer his wife's wish to God's command. . . .

15.   Now God had made man in His own image, placed him in Paradise above all creatures, given him all things in abundance and laid no hard or lengthy commands on him but merely that one brief requirement of obedience to show that He Himself was Lord of that creature from whom should come a free service. But when He was thus disregarded, there followed His righteous sentence,

which was that man, who might have kept His commandment and been spiritual in body became thenceforth carnal in mind, and because he had before delighted in his pride, now tasted of God's justice, becoming not, as he had desired, fully his own master but falling even below himself and becoming the slave of him who had taught him sin, exchanging his sweet liberty for a wretched bondage. By his own will he was dead in spirit, though unwilling to die in the flesh. He had lost eternal life and was condemned to eternal death, did not God's good grace deliver him. . . .

(From the translation of John Healey, ed. of 1909.)

SAINT PAUL   Rembrandt

One of the most prolific painters of all time, Rembrandt van Ryn (1606-1669)
painted over 700 pictures and executed over 300 etchings. This
painting of Saint Paul illustrates one of the artist's favorite
devices, the high-lighting of the central figure against a som-
ber background.

Saint Paul is here depicted with a scroll bearing one of his
Epistles although he is more often shown with a book and
sword. When the sword points upward it is symbolic of his
militant preaching; when it points downward it is the attribute of his martyrdom.

SAINT PETER'S RELEASE FROM PRISON   Raphael

In 1508 Raphael (1483-1520) was invited by Pope Julius II to come to Rome
to help in the beautification of the Vatican which had been
started with the rebuilding of St. Peter's. Raphael's assignment was the decoration of a series of rooms in the Vatican
Palace, and this picture of Saint Peter was designed to fit an
awkward window space in one of the rooms.

Saint Peter is here illustrated in the scene of his deliverance
from prison in Jerusalem by an angel. He carries the keys
which are symbolic of Christ's having given him the keys of
the kingdom.

Saint Patrick

Apostle of Ireland

c. 4 6 1

(*March 17*)

The field of St. Patrick's labors was the most remote part of
the then known world. The seed he planted in faraway Ireland, which before his time was largely pagan, bore a rich harvest:
whole colonies of saints and missionaries were to rise up after him
to serve the Irish Church and to carry Christianity to other lands.
Whether his birthplace, a village called Bannavem Taberniae, was
near Dunbarton-on-the-Clyde, or in Cumberland, or at the mouth
of the Severn, or even in Gaul near Boulogne, has never been determined, and indeed the matter is of no great moment. We know
of a certainty that Patrick was of Romano-British origin, and born
about the year 389. His father, Calpurnius, was a deacon, his
grandfather a priest, for at this time no strict law of celibacy had
been imposed on the Christian clergy. Patrick's own full name was
probably Patricius Magonus Sucatus.

His brief *Confession* gives us a few details of his early years. At
the age of fifteen he committed some fault—what it was we are
not told—which caused him much suffering for the rest of his life.
At sixteen, he tells us, he still "knew not the true God." Since he
was born into a Christian family, we may take this to mean that
he gave little heed to religion or to the priests. That same year
Patrick and some others were seized and carried off by sea raiders
to become slaves among the inhabitants of Ireland. Formerly it
was believed that his six years of captivity were spent near Bally-
mena in County Antrim, on the slopes of the mountain now called

Slemish, but later opinion names Fochlad, or Focluth, on the coast of Mayo. If the latter view is correct, then Croachan Aigli or Croag Patrick, the scene of his prolonged fast, was also the mountain on which in his youth he lived alone with God, tending his master's herds of swine or cattle. Wherever it was, he tells us himself that "constantly I used to pray in the daytime. Love of God and His fear increased more and more, and my faith grew and my spirit was stirred up, so that in a single day I said as many as a hundred prayers and at night nearly as many, and I used to stay out in the woods and on the mountain. Before the dawn I used to wake up to prayer, in snow and frost and rain, nor was there any such lukewarmness in me as now I feel, because then my spirit was fervent within."

At length he heard a voice in his sleep bidding him to get back to freedom and the land of his birth. Thus prompted, he ran away from his master and traveled to a harbor where a ship was about to depart. The captain at first refused his request for passage, but after Patrick had silently prayed to God, the pagan sailors called him back, and with them he made an adventurous journey. They were three days at sea, and when they reached land they traveled for a month through an uninhabited tract of country, where food was scarce. Patrick writes:

"And one day the shipmaster said to me: 'How is this, O Christian? Thou sayest that thy God is great and almighty; wherefore then canst thou not pray for us, for we are in danger of starvation? Likely we shall never see a human being again.' Then I said plainly to them: 'Turn in good faith and with all your heart to the Lord my God, to whom nothing is impossible, that this day He may send you food for your journey, until ye be satisfied, for He has abundance everywhere.' And, by the help of God, so it came to pass. Lo, a herd of swine appeared in the way before our eyes, and they killed many of them. And in that place they remained two nights; and they were well refreshed and their dogs were sated, for many of them had fainted and been left half-dead by the way. After this they rendered hearty thanks to God, and I became hon-

orable in their eyes; and from that day they had food in abundance."

At length they arrived at human habitations, whether in Britain
or Gaul we do not know. When Patrick was again restored to his
kinfolk, they gave him a warm welcome and urged him to stay.
But he felt he must leave them. Although there is no certainty as
to the order of events which followed, it seems likely that Patrick
now spent many years in Gaul. Professor Bury, author of the well-
known *Life of St. Patrick,* thinks that the saint stayed for three
years at the monastery of Lerins, on a small islet off the coast of
modern Cannes, France, and that about fifteen years were passed
at the monastery of Auxerre, where he was ordained. Patrick's later
prestige and authority indicate that he was prepared for his task
with great thoroughness.

We now come to Patrick's apostolate. At this time Pelagianism [1]
was spreading among the weak and scattered Christian communities of Britain and Ireland, and Pope Celestine I had sent Bishop
Palladius there to combat it. This missionary was killed among the
Scots in North Britain, and Bishop Germanus of Auxerre recommended the appointment of Patrick to replace him. Patrick was
consecrated in 432, and departed forthwith for Ireland. When we
try to trace the course of his labors in the land of his former captivity, we are confused by the contradictory accounts of his biographers; all are marked by a great deal of vagueness as to geography
and chronology. According to tradition, he landed at Inverdea, at
the mouth of the river Vautry, and immediately proceeded northwards. One chronicler relates that when he was again in the vicinity of the place where he had been a herdboy, the master who had
held him captive, on hearing of Patrick's return, set fire to his
house and perished in the flames. There is historical basis for the
tradition of Patrick's preliminary stay in Ulster, and his founding
of a monastic center there. It was at this time that he set out to
gain the support and favor of the powerful pagan King Laeghaire,
who was holding court at Tara. The stories of Patrick's encounter

[1] For Pelagianism, see above, *St. Augustine,* p. 106.

with the king's Druid priests are probably an accretion of later years; we are told of trials of skill and strength in which the saint gained a great victory over his pagan opponents. The outcome was royal toleration for his preaching. The text of the Senchus More, the old Irish code of laws, though in its existing form it is of later date, mentions an understanding reached at Tara. Patrick was allowed to preach to the gathering, "and when they saw Laeghaire with his Druids overcome by the great signs and miracles wrought in the presence of the men of Erin, they bowed down in obedience to God and Patrick."

King Laeghaire seems not to have become a Christian, but his chief bard and his two daughters were converted, as was a brother, who, we are told, gave his estate to Patrick for the founding of a church. From this time on, Patrick's apostolate, though carried on amid hardships and often at great risk, was favored by many powerful chieftains. The Druids, by and large, opposed him, for they felt their own power and position threatened. They combined many functions; they were prophets, philosophers, and priests; they served as councilors of kings, as judges, and teachers; they knew the courses of the stars and the properties of plants. Now they began to realize that the religion they represented was doomed. Even before the Christian missionaries came in strength, a curious prophecy was current among them. It was written in one of their ancient texts: "Adze-head [a name that the shape of the monk's tonsure might suggest] will come, with his crook-headed staff and his house [the word chasuble means also a little house] holed for his head. He will chant impiety from the table in the east of his house. All his household shall answer: Amen, Amen. When, therefore, all these things come to pass, our kingdom, which is a heathen one, will not stand." As a matter of fact, the Druids continued to exist in Christian Ireland, though with a change of name and a limited scope of activity. They subjected Patrick to imprisonment many times, but he always managed to escape.

In 439 three bishops, Secundinus, Auxilius, and Iserninus, were sent from Gaul to assist Patrick. Benignus, an Irish chieftain who

was converted by Patrick, became his favorite disciple, his coadjutor in the see of Armagh, and, finally, his successor. One of Patrick's legendary victories was his overthrow of the idol of Crom
Cruach in Leitrim, where he forthwith built a church. He traveled
again in Ulster, to preach and found monasteries, then in Leinster
and Munster. These missionary caravans must have impressed the
people, for they gave the appearance of an entire village in motion.
The long line of chariots and carts drawn by oxen conveyed the
appurtenances of Christian worship, as well as foodstuffs, equipment, tools, and weapons required by the band of helpers who
accompanied the leader. There would be the priestly assistants,
singers and musicians, the drivers, hunters, wood-cutters, carpenters, masons, cooks, horsemen, weavers and embroiderers, and
many more. When the caravan stopped at a chosen site, the people
gathered, converts were won, and before many months a chapel or
church and its outlying structures would be built and furnished.
Thus were created new outposts in the struggle against paganism.
The journeys were often dangerous. Once, Odrhan, Patrick's charioteer, as if forewarned, asked leave to take the chief seat in the
chariot himself, while Patrick held the reins; they had proceeded
but a short way in this fashion when the loyal Odrhan was killed
by a spear thrust meant for his master.

About the year 442, tradition tells us, Patrick went to Rome and
met Pope Leo the Great, who, it seemed, took special interest in
the Irish Church. The time had now come for a definite organization. According to the annals of Ulster, the cathedral church of
Armagh was founded as the primatial see of Ireland on Patrick's
return. He brought back with him valuable relics. Latin was established as the language of the Irish Church. There is mention of
a synod held by Patrick, probably at Armagh. The rules then
adopted are still preserved, with, possibly, some later interpolations. It is believed that this synod was called near the close of
Patrick's labors on earth. He was now undoubtedly in more or
less broken health; such austerities and constant journeyings as
his must have weakened the hardiest constitution. The story of his

forty-day fast on Croagh Patrick and the privileges he won from God by his prayers is also associated with the end of his life. Tirechan tells it thus: "Patrick went forth to the summit of Mount Agli, and remained there for forty days and forty nights, and the birds were a trouble to him, and he could not see the face of the heavens, the earth, or the sea, on account of them; for God told all the saints of Erin, past, present, and future, to come to the mountain summit—that mountain which overlooks all others, and is higher than all the mountains of the West—to bless the tribes of Erin, so that Patrick might see the fruit of his labors, for all the choir of the saints came to visit him there, who was the father of them all."

In all the ancient biographies of this saint the marvelous is continuously present. Fortunately, we have three of Patrick's own writings, which help us to see the man himself. His *Confession* is a brief autobiographical sketch; the *Lorica*, also known as *The Song of the Deer*, is a strange chant which we have reproduced in the following pages. *The Letter to Coroticus* is a denunciation of the British king of that name who had raided the Irish coast and killed a number of Christian converts as they were being baptized; Patrick urged the Christian subjects of this king to have no more dealings with him until he had made reparation for the outrage. In his writings Patrick shows his ardent human feelings and his intense love of God. What was most human in the saint, and at the same time most divine, comes out in this passage from his *Confession:*

"It was not any grace in me, but God who conquereth in me, and He resisted them all, so that I came to the heathen of Ireland to preach the Gospel and to bear insults from unbelievers, to hear the reproach of my going abroad and to endure many persecutions even unto bonds, the while that I was surrendering my liberty as a man of free condition for the profit of others. And if I should be found worthy, I am ready to give even my life for His name's sake unfalteringly and gladly, and there [in Ireland] I desire to spend it until I die, if our Lord should grant it to me."

Patrick's marvelous harvest filled him with gratitude. During an apostolate of thirty years he is reported to have consecrated some 350 bishops, and was instrumental in bringing the faith to many thousands. He writes, "Wherefore those in Ireland who never had the knowledge of God, but until now only worshiped idols and abominations, from them has been lately prepared a people of the Lord, and they are called children of God. Sons and daughters of Scottish chieftains are seen becoming monks and virgins of Christ." Yet hostility and violence still existed, for he writes later, "Daily I expect either a violent death, or robbery and a return to slavery, or some other calamity." He adds, like the good Christian he was, "I have cast myself into the hands of Almighty God, for He rules everything."

Patrick died about 461, and was buried near the fortress of Saul, in the vicinity of the future cathedral town of Down. He was intensely spiritual, a magnetic personality with great gifts for action and organization. He brought Ireland into much closer contact with Europe, especially with the Holy See. The building up of the weak Christian communities which he found on arrival and planting the faith in new regions give him his place as the patron of Ireland. His feast day is one of festivity, and widely observed. Patrick's emblems are a serpent, demons, cross, shamrock, harp, and baptismal font. The story of his driving snakes from Ireland has no factual foundation, and the tale of the shamrock, as a symbol used to explain the Trinity, is an accretion of much later date.

Lorica [2]

I arise today
Through a mighty strength, the invocation of the Trinity,
Through a belief in the threeness,

[2] The Latin word *lorica* means a breastplate. Chants like the above, almost in the form of incantations, or invocations of God and Christ, to protect the singer against the wiles of evil men, are not uncommon in early Irish literature.

Through a confession of the oneness
Of the Creator of Creation.

I arise today
Through the strength of Christ's birth with His Baptism,
Through the strength of His crucifixion with His burial,
Through the strength of His resurrection with His ascension,
Through the strength of His descent for the judgment of
    Doom.

I arise today
Through the strength of the love of Cherubim,
In obedience of angels,
In the service of archangels,
In hope of resurrection to meet with reward,
In prayers of patriarchs
In predictions of prophets,
In preachings of apostles,
In faiths of confessors,
In innocence of holy virgins,
In deeds of righteous men.

I arise today
Through the strength of heaven:
Light of sun
Radiance of moon,
Splendor of fire,
Speed of lightning,
Swiftness of wind,
Depth of sea,
Stability of earth,
Firmness of rock.

I arise today
Through God's strength to pilot me:
God's might to uphold me,
God's wisdom to guide me,
God's eye to look before me,
God's ear to hear me,
God's word to speak for me,

God's hand to guard me,
God's way to lie before me,
God's shield to protect me,
God's host to save me
From snares of devils,
From temptations of vices,
From everyone who shall wish me ill,
Afar and anear,
Alone and in a multitude.

I summon today all these powers between me and those evils,
Against every cruel merciless power that may oppose my body
    and soul,
Against incantations of false prophets,
Against black laws of pagandom,
Against false laws of heretics,
Against craft of idolatry,
Against spells of women and smiths and wizards,
Against every knowledge that corrupts man's body and soul.

Christ shield me today
Against poison, against burning,
Against drowning, against wounding,
So that there may come to me abundance of reward,
Christ with me, Christ before me, Christ behind me,
Christ in me, Christ beneath me, Christ above me,
Christ on my right, Christ on my left,
Christ when I lie down, Christ when I sit down, Christ when
    I arise,
Christ in the heart of every man who thinks of me,
Christ in the mouth of everyone who speaks of me,
Christ in every eye that sees me,
Christ in every ear that hears me.

I arise today
Through a mighty strength, the invocation of the Trinity,
Through a belief in the threeness,
Through a confession of the oneness
Of the Creator of Creation.

Saint Leo the Great
Pope, Doctor of the Church
4 6 1
(*April 11*)

During the disintegration of the Western Empire, when
heresy was rife and all moral values were threatened by the
barbarian invasions, Pope Leo I stands out as the resolute champion of the faith. His courage and sagacity lifted the prestige of the
Holy See mightily, and earned for him the title of "The Great," a
distinction bestowed on but one other pope, Gregory I. The Church
honored Leo further with the title of Doctor because of his exposi-
tions of Christian doctrine, extracts from which are now incorporated in the lessons of the Catholic breviary. Of his birth and
early years we have no reliable information; his family was probably Tuscan. We know that he was at Rome as a deacon under
Pope Celestine I and Pope Sixtus III, whose pontificates ran from
422 to 440. Leo must have achieved eminence early, for even then
he corresponded with Archbishop Cyril of Alexandria,[1] and Cassian dedicated his treatise against Nestorius to him.[2] In 440 Leo

---

[1] Cyril, archbishop of Alexandria from 412 to 444, was a zealot for orthodoxy,
who, the pagans said, incited his monks to kill the Platonic philosopher Hy-
patia, when she was lecturing in his city. Cassian, a recluse and theologian,
founded the monastery of St. Victor, near Marseilles.

[2] Nestorius, bishop of Constantinople from 428 to 431, taught a doctrine of
the humanity of Christ, according to which God the divine Son and Jesus the
Man were always two distinct persons; Jesus alone was born of woman, and
as a man of surpassing goodness became the dwelling place of the Word,
which was incarnate in him. The Catholic doctrine is that God and man is
one Christ, one person in two natures.

In 431 Nestorius was deposed and excommunicated by the Council of was sent to Gaul to try to make peace between the imperial generals, Aetius and Albinus. Soon afterward Pope Sixtus died, and a deputation came up from Rome to inform Leo that he had been elected to the chair of St. Peter. His consecration took place in September of that year, and he at once began to show great energy in the performance of the papal duties.

The new pope set himself to make the Roman church a pattern for all other churches. In the ninety-six sermons which have come down to us, we find Leo stressing the virtues of almsgiving, fasting, and prayer, and also expounding Catholic doctrine with clarity and conciseness, in particular the dogma of the Incarnation. He was determined to shield his flock from heresy, and when he discovered that many Manichaeans,[3] who had fled from the Vandals in Africa, had settled in Rome and were spreading their errors, he summoned them before a council of clergy and laymen. Under cross-examination some confessed to immoral practices and some recanted. Against the recalcitrant, Leo invoked the secular authority; their books were burned, and they themselves were banished or else left Rome of their own volition. Meanwhile he was preaching vigorously against the false teaching, as Augustine had done earlier, and writing letters of warning to all the Italian bishops. One hundred and forty-three letters written by him and thirty letters written to him have been preserved; they illustrate the Pope's extraordinary vigilance over the Church in all parts of the Empire. He also encouraged the bishops, especially the Italian ones, to come to Rome to consult him in person.

From Spain Turibius, bishop of Astorga, sent Leo a copy of a letter he had been circulating on the heresy of Priscillianism. The sect had made great headway in Spain and some of the Catholic clergy favored it. As it developed there, it seems to have combined astrology and fatalism with the Manichaean theory of the evil of

---

Ephesus, under the influence of Cyril of Alexandria and Pope Celestine. He and his followers withdrew to the East, where in time they formed many communities, spreading as far as India and the borders of China.

[3] For the Manichaeans, see above, St. Augustine, n. 1.

matter. Leo wrote back a long refutation of this doctrine and described the measures he had taken against the Manichaeans in Rome. Several times he was asked to arbitrate affairs in Gaul. Twice he nullified acts of the saintly Hilary, bishop of Arles, who had exceeded his powers. The Emperor Valentinian III in the famous edict of 445 denounced the Gallic bishop and declared "that nothing should be done in Gaul contrary to ancient usage, without the authority of the bishop of Rome, and that the decree of the apostolic see should henceforth be law." Thus was the primacy of Rome given official recognition. One of Leo's letters to Anastasius, bishop of Thessalonica, reminds him that all bishops had a right to appeal to Rome, "according to ancient tradition." In 446 he writes to the African church in Mauretania, forbidding the appointment of a layman to the episcopate, or of any man who had been twice married or who had married a widow. (I Timothy iii,2.) The rules which he incorporated into Church law regarding admission to the priesthood deserve mention: former slaves and those employed in unlawful or unseemly occupations could not be ordained; to be acceptable, candidates must be mature men who had already proved themselves in the service of the Church.

Leo was now called upon to deal with difficulties in the East far greater than any he had so far encountered in the West. In the year 448, he received a letter from Abbot Eutyches of Constantinople, complaining of a revival of the Nestorian heresy at Antioch. The next year came a second letter, copies of which he sent also to the patriarchs of Alexandria and Jerusalem. In this Eutyches protested against a sentence of excommunication just issued against him by Flavian, patriarch of Constantinople, and asked to be reinstated. His appeal was supported by a letter from the Emperor of the East, Theodosius II. As no official notice of the proceedings at Constantinople had hitherto reached Rome, Leo wrote to Flavian for his version; with his reply, he sent a report of the synod at which Eutyches had been condemned. From this it seemed clear that Eutyches had fallen into the error of denying the human nature of Christ, a heresy which was the opposite of Nestorianism.

A council was summoned at Ephesus by Theodosius, ostensibly to inquire impartially into the matter. Actually it was packed with friends of Eutyches and presided over by one of his strongest supporters, Dioscorus, patriarch of Alexandria. This gathering, which Leo branded as a Robber Council, acquitted Eutyches and condemned Flavian, who was also subjected to physical violence. The Pope's legates refused to subscribe to the unjust sentence; they were not allowed to read to the council a letter from Leo to Flavian, known later as Leo's *Tome*. One legate was imprisoned and the other escaped with difficulty. As soon as the Pope heard of these proceedings, he declared the decisions null and void, and wrote a bold letter to the Emperor, in which he said: "Leave to the bishops the liberty of defending the faith; neither worldly power nor terror will ever succeed in destroying it. Protect the Church and seek to preserve its peace, that Christ in His turn may protect your empire."

Two years later, in 451, under a new emperor, Marcian, a greater council was held at Chalcedon, a city of Bithynia in Asia Minor. At least six hundred bishops were present. Leo sent three legates. Flavian was dead but his memory was vindicated; Dioscorus was convicted of having maliciously suppressed Leo's letters at the Robbers' Council, and of virtually excommunicating the Pope himself. For these and other offenses he was declared excommunicate and deposed. Leo's *Tome* of 449 to Flavian was now read by his legates to the council. In it he concisely defined the Catholic doctrine of the Incarnation and the two natures of Christ, avoiding the pitfalls of Nestorianism on the one hand and of Eutychianism on the other. "Peter has spoken by the mouth of Leo!" exclaimed the bishops. This statement of the two-fold nature of Christ was to be accepted by later ages as the Church's official teaching. Leo, however, refused to confirm the council's canon which recognized the patriarch of Constantinople as primate over the East.

In the meantime, serious events of another kind were happening in the West. Attila, "the scourge of God," after overrunning Greece and Germany with his Huns, had penetrated France, where he had been defeated at Chalons by the imperial general Aetius. Falling back, he gathered fresh forces, and then entered Italy from the northeast, burning Aquileia and leaving destruction in his wake. After sacking Milan and Pavia, he set out to attack the capital. The wretched Emperor Valentinian III shut himself up within the walls of remote Ravenna; panic seized the people of Rome. In the emergency, Leo, upheld by a sense of his sacred office, set out to meet Attila, accompanied by Avienus, the consul, Trigetius, the governor of the city, and a band of priests. Near where the rivers Po and Mincio meet, they came face to face with the enemy. The Pope reasoned with Attila and induced him to turn back.

A few years later the Vandal king, Genseric, appeared from Africa with his army before the walls of Rome, then almost defenseless. This time Leo was able to win from the invader only the promise to restrain his troops from arson and carnage. After ten days of pillaging the city, the Vandals withdrew, taking back to Africa a host of captives and immense booty, but sparing the churches of St. Peter and St. Paul. Leo now set about repairing the damage brought by the invasion. To the Italian captives in Africa he sent priests, alms, and aid in rebuilding their churches. He was apparently never discouraged, maintaining a steady trust in God in the most desperate situations. His pontificate lasted for twenty-one years, and during this time he won the veneration of rich and poor, emperors and barbarians, clergy and laity. He died on November 10, 461, and his body was laid in the Vatican basilica, where his tomb may still be seen.

On the Anniversary of his Elevation to the Pontificate

(SERMON III)

3.   *The covenant of the truth therefore abides and the blessed* Peter, persevering in the strength of the Rock, which he received, has not abandoned the helm of the Church which he accepted. For he was ordained before the rest in such a manner that as he was called the Rock, as he was declared the foundation, as he was constituted doorkeeper of the kingdom of Heaven, as he was appointed judge to bind and loose, whose judgments will retain their validity in Heaven, by all these mystical titles we might perceive the nature of his relationship to Christ.

And today he still more fully and effectually performs the office entrusted to him and carries out every part of his duty and his charge in Him and with Him by whom he was glorified. So if any act or decree of ours is righteous, if we obtain anything by our daily supplications from God's mercy, it is his work and his merits, whose power lives in his see and whose authority is so high. For, dearly beloved, his confession won this reward, his confession inspired by God the Father in the apostle's heart, which transcended all the uncertainty of human judgment and was endowed with the firmness of a rock that no assault could shake. Throughout the Church Peter still says daily: "Thou art the Christ, the Son of the living God," and every tongue which confesses the Lord is inspired by the leadership of his voice. . . .

4. And so, dearly beloved, with reasonable obedience, we celebrate today's festival in such a way that in my humble person he may be recognized and honored, on whom rests the care of all the shepherds, as well as the charge of the sheep commended to him. His dignity is not diminished by even so unworthy an heir. Hence the presence of my venerable brethren and fellow priests, as much desired and valued by me, will be still more sacred and precious if they will transfer the chief honor of this service, in which they have deigned to take part, to him whom they know to be not only the patron of this see but also the primate of all bishops. When therefore we utter our exhortations in your ears, holy brethren, believe that he is speaking whose representative we are, because it is his warning that we give and nothing but his teaching that we preach.

Letter to Flavian, Called the Tome

3. Without detriment, therefore, to the properties of either nature and substance (the divine and the human), which then came together in one person, majesty took on humility, strength

weakness, eternity mortality, and for the payment of the debt belonging to our condition inviolable nature was united with suffering nature, so that, as suited the needs of our case, one and the same Mediator between God and men, the Man Jesus Christ, could both die with the one and not die with the other. Thus in the whole and perfect nature of true man was true God born, complete in what was his own, complete in what was ours. . . .

4.   There enters then these lower parts of the world the Son of God, descending from his heavenly home and yet not quitting His Father's glory, begotten in a new order by a new birthing. In a new order, because being invisible in His own nature, He became visible in ours, and He whom nothing could contain was content to be contained. Abiding before all time, He began to be in time; the Lord of all things He obscured His immeasurable majesty and took on Him the form of a servant. Being God who cannot suffer, He did not disdain to be man that can and, immortal as He is, to subject Himself to the laws of death. The Lord assumed His mother's nature without faultiness, nor in the Lord Jesus Christ, born of the Virgin's womb, does the marvel of His birth make his nature unlike ours. For He who is true God is also true man, and in this union there is no deceit, since the humility of manhood and the loftiness of the Godhead both meet there. For as God is not changed by the showing of pity, so man is not swallowed up in the dignity. . . . To be hungry and thirsty, to be weary and to sleep is clearly human, but to satisfy five thousand men with five loaves, to bestow on the woman of Samaria living water, draughts of which can secure the drinker from thirsting ever again, to walk upon the surface of the water with feet that do not sink and to quell the risings of the waves by rebuking the winds is without any doubt divine. Just as also—to pass over many other instances—it is not part of the same nature to be moved to tears of pity for a dead friend and, when the stone that closed the four-days grave was removed, to raise that same friend to life with a voice of command; or to hang on the cross, and to turn day into night to make all the elements tremble; or to be pierced with nails and then to open the gates of paradise to the robber's faith. So it is not part of the same nature to say: "I and the Father are one," and to say: "The Father is greater than I." For although in the Lord Jesus Christ God and

man is one person, yet the source of the degradation which is shared by both is one, and the source of the glory which is shared by both is another. For his manhood, which is less than the Father, comes from our side; His Godhead, which is equal to the Father, comes from the Father.

(Letters and Sermons of Leo the Great. Select Library of Nicene and Post-Nicene Fathers, Series II.)

Saint Benedict

Abbot, Founder of Western Monasticism

5 5 0

(*March 21*)

O verrun by half-civilized pagan and Arian hordes during the
fifth century, Italy and the entire Mediterranean world was
falling back into barbarism. The Church was torn by conflict, city
and country alike were made desolate by war and pillage, violence
was rampant among Christians as well as heathen. During this
anarchic time appeared one of the noblest of the Fathers of the
Western Church—St. Benedict of Nursia, founder of the great
order which bears his name. We know little of his background, save
that he was born about the year 480 at Nursia, in the province of
Umbria, in north central Italy, and that his family was probably
of noble lineage. We also know that he had a sister called Scholastica, who from childhood vowed herself to God.

Sent to Rome to be educated, young Benedict was quickly re-
volted by the licentiousness of his fellow students. He was not yet
twenty when he decided to go away from Rome to live in some
remote spot. No one knew of his plan except an aged family servant, who loyally insisted on accompanying him to serve his wants.
Benedict and this old woman made their way to a village called
Enfide, in the Sabine Mountains, some thirty miles from Rome. In
the *Dialogues,* St. Gregory gives us a series of remarkable incidents
associated with Benedict's life, one of them occurring at this time.
While staying in the village, Benedict miraculously mended an
earthen sieve which his servant had broken. Wishing to escape the
notice and the talk which this brought upon him, he soon started
out alone in search of complete solitude. Up among the hills he

found a place known as Subiaco or Sublacum (beneath the lake), so named from an artificial lake created there some five centuries earlier. It was near the ruins of one of Nero's palaces. He made the acquaintance of a monk called Romanus, and to him Benedict revealed his desire to become a hermit. Romanus, who lived in a monastery not far away, gave the young man a monastic habit made of skins and led him up to an isolated cave, where he might live completely undisturbed. The roof of the cave was an over-hanging rock over which descent was impossible, and it was approached from below with difficulty. In this desolate cavern Benedict passed the next three years, unknown to all but his friend Romanus, who each day saved for him a part of his own portion of bread and let it down from above in a basket by a rope.

According to Pope Gregory, the first outsider to find his way to the cave was a priest, who while preparing a special dinner for himself on Easter Sunday heard a voice saying to him: "Thou art preparing thyself a savoury dish while my servant Benedict is afflicted with hunger." The priest immediately set out in search of Benedict, and finally discovered his hiding place. Benedict was astonished, but before he would enter into conversation with his visitor he asked that they might pray together. Then, after they had talked for a time on heavenly things, the priest invited Benedict to eat, telling him that it was Easter Day, on which it is not reasonable to fast. Later Benedict was seen by some shepherds, who at first glance took him for a wild animal because he was clothed in the skins of beasts. It did not occur to them that a human being could live among the barren rocks. From that time on, others made their way up the steep cliff, bringing such small offerings of food as the holy man would accept and receiving from him instruction and advice.

Even though he lived thus sequestered from the world, Benedict, like the Desert Fathers, had to struggle with temptations of the flesh and the devil. One of these struggles is described by Gregory. "On a certain day when he was alone the tempter presented him-self. A small dark bird, commonly called a blackbird, began to fly around his face and came so near him that, if he had wished, he could have seized it with his hand. But on his making the sign of the cross, the bird flew away. Then followed a violent temptation of the flesh, such as he had never before experienced. The evil spirit brought before his imagination a woman whom he had formerly seen, and inflamed his heart with such vehement desire at the memory of her that he had very great difficulty in repressing it. He was almost overcome and thought of leaving his solitude. Suddenly, however, with the help of divine grace, he found the strength he needed. Seeing near at hand a thick growth of briars and nettles, he stripped off his habit and cast himself into the midst of them and plunged and tossed about until his whole body was lacerated. Thus, through those bodily wounds, he cured the wounds of his soul." Never again was he troubled in the same way.

Between Tivoli and Subiaco, at Vicovaro, on the summit of a fortified rock overlooking the Anio, there lived at that time a community of monks. Having lost their abbot by death, they now came in a body to ask Benedict to accept the office, no doubt with the idea that his growing fame would attract offerings to their community. He at first refused, assuring the monks that their ways and his would not agree. At length they persuaded him to return with them. It soon became evident that the severe monastic discipline he instituted did not suit their lax habits, and in order to get rid of him they finally poisoned his wine. When, as was his habit, he made the sign of the cross over the cup, it broke as if a stone had fallen on it. "God forgive you, brothers," Benedict said serenely. "Why have you plotted this wicked thing against me? Did I not tell you beforehand that my ways would not accord with yours? Go and find an abbot to your taste, for after what you have done you can no longer keep me with you." Then he bade them farewell and returned to Subiaco.

Disciples now began to gather around Benedict, attracted by his sanctity and by his miraculous powers. At last he found himself in a position to initiate the great work for which God had been preparing him. This was the idea that had slowly been germinating during his years of isolation: to bring together those who wished to share the monastic life, both men of the world who yearned to escape material concerns and the monks who had been living in solitude or in widely scattered communities, to make of them one flock, binding them by fraternal bonds, under one observance, in the permanent worship of God. In short, his scheme was for the establishment in the West of a single great religious order which would end the capricious rule of the various superiors and the vagaries of individual anchorites. Those who agreed to obey Benedict in this enterprise, he settled in twelve monasteries of twelve monks each. Although each monastery had its own prior, Benedict himself exercised general control over all of them from the monastery of St. Clement.

They had no written rule, although they may at first have been guided by the Eastern Rule of St. Basil. According to one old record, they simply followed the example of Benedict's deeds. Romans and barbarians, rich and poor, came to place themselves under a monk who made no distinction of rank or nation. Parents brought their young sons, for, in the prevailing chaos, the safest and happiest way of life seemed to be that of the monk. Gregory tells us of two noble Romans, Tertullus, a patrician, and Equitius, who came with their small sons, Placidus, a child of seven, and Maurus, a lad of twelve. They were the forerunners of the great hosts of boys, in succeeding centuries, who were to be educated in Benedictine schools. On these two aristocratic young Romans, especially on Maurus, who afterwards became his coadjutor, Benedict expended his utmost care.

Gregory tells also of a rough untutored Goth who came to Benedict, was gladly received, and clothed in the monastic habit. As he was working one day with a hedgehook to clear the underbrush from a sloping piece of ground above the lake, the head of the hook flew off and disappeared into the water. When Benedict heard of the accident, he led the man to the water's edge, took from him the shaft, and dipped it into the lake. Immediately from the bottom rose the iron head and fastened itself in the shaft, whereat Benedict returned it to the astonished Goth, saying in a kindly voice, "Take your tool; work and be comforted." One of Benedict's greatest accomplishments was to break down in his monasteries the ancient prejudice against manual work as something in itself degrading and servile. The Romans had for centuries made slaves of conquered peoples, who performed their menial tasks. Now times were changing. Benedict introduced the novel idea that labor was not only dignified and honorable but conducive to sanctity; it was therefore made compulsory for all who joined the order, nobles and plebeians alike. "He who works prays," became the maxim which expressed the Benedictine attitude.

We do not know how long Benedict remained in the neighborhood of Subiaco, but he stayed long enough certainly to establish his monasteries there on a firm and permanent basis. His departure seems to have been unpremeditated. There was living in the neighborhood an unworthy priest called Florentius, who was bitterly envious of the success of Benedict's organization and of the great concourse of people who were flocking to him. Florentius tried to ruin him by slander; then he sent him a poisoned loaf, which failed of its purpose. Finally he set out to corrupt Benedict's monks by introducing into their garden women of evil life. Benedict realized Florentius' malicious schemes were directed at him personally and he resolved to leave Subiaco, lest the souls of his spiritual sons should be further assailed. Having set all things in order, he summoned the monks, or their representatives, from the twelve monasteries, bade them farewell, and withdrew with a few disciples from Subiaco to the more southerly territory of Monte Cassino, a conspicuous elevation where land had been offered him by Placidus' father, the patrician Tertullus.

The town of Cassino, formerly an important place, had been destroyed by the Goths, and the remnant of its inhabitants, left without a priest, were relapsing into paganism; the once-fertile land had fallen out of cultivation. From time to time the inhabitants would climb up through the woods to offer sacrifices in an ancient temple dedicated to Apollo, which stood on the crest of

Monte Cassino. Benedict's first work, after a preliminary forty-day. fast, was to preach to the people and win them back to the faith. With the help of these converts, he proceeded to overthrow the pagan temple and cut down the sacred grove. He built two oratories or chapels on the site; one he dedicated to St. John the Baptist and the other to St. Martin. Round about these sanctuaries new buildings were erected and older ones remodeled, until there rose, little by little, the tremendous pile which was to become the most famous abbey the world has known. The foundation was laid by Benedict probably about the year 520.

Profiting no doubt by his earlier experience, Benedict did not distribute his monks in separate houses, but gathered them together in one great establishment, ruled over by a prior and deans under his own direction. Almost immediately it became necessary to build guest chambers, for Monte Cassino [1] was easily accessible from Rome, Capua, and other points. Among the early visitors were Placidus' father, who came to confirm his donation, and Maurus' father, who bestowed more lands and churches on Benedict. Another generous benefactor was Gregory's father, Gordianus, who in the name of his wife Sylvia gave Benedict the Villa Euchelia in the suburbs of Aquinum, not far away, and other valuable property. Not only laymen but dignitaries of the Church, bishops and abbots, came to consult with the founder, whose reputation for sanctity, wisdom, and miracles was spreading.

It was probably during this period that Benedict composed his famous Rule.[2] Gregory says that in it may be perceived "all his

[1] The monastery of Monte Cassino was destroyed by the Lombards about seventy years later. It was rebuilt and again destroyed, this time by the Saracens in 884; after its second restoration, it enjoyed a period of tranquillity, and in the eleventh century attained its greatest influence. It suffered severely from aerial bombardment during the Allied advance northwards in World War II, but the rebuilding of damaged portions has already begun.

[2] "A monument of legislative art, remarkable alike for its completeness, its simplicity, and its adaptability," wrote H. F. Dudden. The French historian Michelet said that it "gave to a world worn out by slavery the first example of work done by the hands of free men."

own manner of life and discipline, for the holy man could not possibly teach otherwise than as he lived." Although the Rule professes only to lay down a pattern of life for the monks at Monte Cassino, it served as a guide for the monks of the whole Western Empire. It is addressed to all who, renouncing their own will, take upon them "the strong and bright armor of obedience, to fight under our Lord Christ, our true king." It prescribes a diversified routine of liturgical prayer, study, and physical work, in a community under one father. It was written for laymen by one who was not a priest; only after some five hundred years were clerical orders required of Benedictines. Its asceticism was intended to be reasonable; the monks abstained from flesh meat and did not break fast until mid-day. Self-imposed and abnormal austerities damaging to health were not encouraged. When a hermit who lived in a cave near Monte Cassino chained his foot to a rock, Benedict, to whom he looked for direction, sent him the message, "If thou art truly a servant of God, chain thyself not with a chain of iron but with a chain of Christ."

Far from confining his attention to those who accepted his Rule, Benedict extended his solicitude to the people of the countryside. He cured the sick, relieved the distressed, distributed alms and food to the poor, and is said on more than one occasion to have raised the dead. When Campania suffered from a famine, he gave away all the provisions stored in the abbey, with the exception of five loaves. "You have not enough today," he said to his monks, noticing their dismay, "but tomorrow you will have too much." Benedict's faith had its reward. The next morning a large donation of flour was deposited by unknown hands at the monastery gate. Other stories were told of prophetic powers and of an ability to read men's thoughts. A nobleman he had converted once found him in tears and inquired the cause of his grief. Benedict astounded him by replying that the monastery and everything in it would be delivered to the pagans, and the monks would barely escape with their lives. This prophecy came true some forty years later, when the abbey was wrecked by a new wave of invaders, the pagan Lombards.

Meanwhile, Totila, King of the Goths, had defeated the Emperor Justinian's army at Faenza and in 542 was making a triumphal progress through central Italy towards Naples. On the way he wished to visit Benedict, of whom he had heard marvelous tales. He therefore sent word of his coming to the famous abbot, who replied that he would see him. To discover whether Benedict really possessed the supernatural insight attributed to him, Totila ordered Riggo, captain of the guard, to don his own purple robes, and sent him, with the three counts who usually attended him, up to Monte Cassino. The trick did not deceive Benedict, who greeted Riggo with the words, "My son, take off what thou art wearing; it is not thine." Confounded, Riggo threw himself at Benedict's feet and then withdrew in haste to report to his master.

Totila now came himself to the abbey and, we are told, was so awed by Benedict that he fell prostrate. Benedict, raising him from the ground, rebuked him sternly for his cruelties and foretold in a few words all that should befall him. "Much evil," he said, "dost thou do and much wickedness hast thou done. Now, at least, make an end of iniquity. Rome thou shalt enter; thou wilt cross the sea; nine years thou shalt reign, and die the tenth." Totila begged for his prayers and departed, and from that time on, people said, was less cruel. In course of time he advanced on Rome, sailed thence to Sicily, and in the tenth year, lost both his crown and his life.[3] Benedict did not live long enough to see the prophecy fulfilled.

He who had foretold so many things was forewarned of his own death, and six days before the end bade his disciples dig a grave. As soon as this was done, Benedict was stricken with a fever, and on the sixth day, while the brethren supported him, he murmured a few words of prayer and died, standing, with hands uplifted to-

[3] Totila was killed in the battle of Tagina, fighting against the forces of the Emperor Justinian under Narses. With his death all hope of the Goths for a kingdom in Italy ended. For more background on this period, see *St. Gregory,* below.

wards Heaven. He was buried beside his sister Scholastica,[4] on the site of the altar of Apollo which he had thrown down.

In art Benedict is commonly represented with King Totila, or with his finger on his lips, holding the Rule, or with the opening words, *"Ausculta, O fili,"* ("Hearken, O son") proceeding from his mouth. His symbols are reminders of various incidents in his life: we see him with a blackbird, a broken sieve, a rose bush, a scourge, a dove, a globe of fire, or a luminous stairway up which he is proceeding to Heaven; occasionally he is depicted with King Totila at his feet. The order which Benedict founded has spread over the earth. It was mainly responsible for the conversion of the Teutonic races, and has left its mark on the education, art, and literature of Europe. Within its cloisters, always marked by an atmosphere of industry and peace, were copied and recopied the great writings of the past, to be cherished and passed on to succeeding generations.

Excerpts from Benedict's Rule

. . . We are about to found therefore a school for the Lord's service, in the organization of which we trust that we shall ordain nothing severe and nothing burdensome. Yet if, prompted by a desire to attain to righteousness, we prescribe something a little irksome for the correction of vice or the preservation of charity, do you not, therefore, in terror flee from the way of salvation, the entrance to which must needs be narrow. For by continuing in this mode of life and faith the heart is enlarged and in the unutterable sweetness of love, we run in the way of God's commandments. Thus never straying from His guidance but persevering in the mon-

[4] St. Scholastica was abbess of a nunnery about five miles south of Monte Cassino. Once a year she visited her brother and they spent the day in song and prayer and conversation. On the day of her death it is said that Benedict, at prayer in his cell, had a vision of his sister's soul ascending to Heaven. Filled with joy at her happiness, he thanked God, and then went out to announce her passing to his brethren.

astery unto death in His teachings, through patience we become partakers of Christ's passion and worthy heirs of His kingdom. Amen. . . .

2. *What kind of man the abbot should be.* An abbot who is worthy to preside over a monastery should always remember what he is called and justify by his deeds his title as a superior. For in the monastery he is looked upon as the representative of Christ, since he is called by His name, and the Apostle says: "Ye have received the spirit of adoption, whereby we cry Abba, Father." [5] So an abbot ought not to teach, institute, or command anything contrary to the precepts of the Lord, but his orders and teachings should be sprinkled in the minds of his disciples with the leaven of divine justice. . . . He must show no favoritism in the monastery, nor love one more than another, unless it be one whom he finds excelling in good works and obedience. He must not place a man of gentle birth above one lately a serf, except for some other reasonable cause . . . for whether bond or free, we are all one in Christ. . . .

48. *On daily manual labor.* Idleness is the enemy of the soul. At set times, accordingly, the brethren should be occupied with manual work, and again, at set times, with spiritual reading. We believe therefore that the hours for each should be fixed as follows: that is, from Easter to the first of October they should go out early in the morning from Prime [6] and work at what has to be done until about the fourth hour, and from the fourth hour spend their time in reading until about the sixth hour. When they rise from eating, after the sixth hour, they should rest on their beds in complete silence, or if one happens to wish to read let him do so without disturbing anyone else. Let Nones be said in good time, about the middle of the eighth hour; and then let them work again at whatever needs to be done until vespers. And let them not

---

[5] Romans viii, 15. *Abba* (Father) was used by the early Jews as a title of honor, and by Jesus and his contemporaries of the Deity.

[6] Historians differ as to the exact length of the periods of work, rest, and reading, but the office of Prime was said probably between five and six in the morning, and the first hour would be about six, the sixth about noon. In the winter months work did not begin until about an hour later in the morning.

be disturbed if poverty or the necessities of the place compel them
to toil at harvesting the crops with their own hands, as did our
fathers and the Apostles. . . . In Lent they shall each receive a
book from the library and read it entirely through. These books
shall be given out at the beginning of Lent. Above all, have one or
two seniors appointed to go around the monastery during the hours
for reading to see that no restless brother is by chance idle or chattering and not intent on his reading and so of no profit to himself
and a distraction to others. . . . However, if there is anyone so
dull or lazy that he either will not or cannot study or read, let him
have some task assigned him which he can perform, so that he may
not be idle. . . .

   64. *On the ordination of the abbot.* Let him who has been created abbot reflect always on the weighty burden he has assumed
and remember to whom he shall give an account of his stewardship.
Let him understand too that he is to help others rather than command them. . . . He must hate vice but love the brethren. Even
in his corrections he should act wisely lest while he too vigorously
scrubs off the rust the vessel itself is shattered. He shall always
bear in mind his own frailty and remember that the bruised reed
must not be broken. . . . And he shall aim at being loved rather
than feared. . . . Wherefore, adopting these and like principles of
discretion, mother of virtues, let him so temper all things that the
strong man may find scope for action and the weak be not intimidated. And especially let him keep the present Rule in all respects,
so that when he has well administered it, he may hear from our
Lord what that good servant did who gave meat to his fellow
servants in due season.[7] "Verily I say unto you, That he shall make
him ruler over all his goods."

[7] See Matthew xxiv, 45-47.

Saint Columba

Abbot, Confessor

5 9 7

(*June 6*)

Columba, the most famous of the saints associated with Scotland, was actually an Irishman of the O'Neill or O'Donnell clan, born about the year 521 at Garton, County Donegal, in north Ireland. Of royal lineage on both sides, his father, Fedhlimidh, or Phelim, was great-grandson to Niall of the Nine Hostages, Overlord of Ireland, and connected with the Dalriada princes of southwest Scotland; his mother, Eithne, was descended from a king of Leinster. The child was baptized Colum, or Columba.[1] In later life he was given the name of Columcille or Clumkill, that is, Colum of the Cell or Church, an appropriate title for one who became the founder of so many monastic cells and religious establishments.

As soon as he was old enough, Columba was taken from the care of his priest-guardian at Tulach-Dugblaise, or Temple Douglas, to St. Finnian's training school at Moville, at the head of Strangford lough. He was about twenty, and a deacon, when he left to study in the school of Leinster under an aged theologian and bard called Gemman. With their songs of heroes, the bards were the preservers of Irish lore, and Columba himself became a poet. Still later he attended the famous monastic school of Clonard, presided over by another Finnian, who in later times was known as the "tutor of Erin's saints." At one time three thousand students were gathered

[1] Some records say he was baptized Crimthan, meaning the Fox, but that his gentleness and goodness as a child so won all hearts that he was rechristened Colum, or Columba, Latin for dove.

here from all over Ireland, Scotland, and Wales, and even from Gaul and Germany. It was probably at Clonard that Columba was ordained priest, although it may have been later, when he was living with his friends, Comgall, Kieran, and Kenneth, under the most gifted of all his teachers, St. Mobhi, by a ford in the river Tolca, called Dub Linn, the site of the future city of Dublin. In 543 an outbreak of plague compelled Mobhi to close his school, and Columba, now twenty-five years old and fully trained, returned to Ulster. He was a striking figure of great stature and powerful build, with a loud, melodious voice which could be heard from one hilltop to another. For the next fifteen years Columba went about Ireland preaching and founding monasteries, the chief of which were those at Derry, Durrow, and Kells.

The powerful stimulus given to Irish learning by St. Patrick in the previous century was now beginning to burgeon. Columba himself dearly loved books, and spared no pains to obtain or make copies of Psalters, Bibles, and other valuable manuscripts for his monks. His former master Finnian had brought back from Rome the first copy of St. Jerome's Psalter to reach Ireland. Finnian guarded this precious volume jealously, but Columba got permission to look at it, and surreptitiously made a copy for his own use. Finnian, on being told of this, laid claim to the copy. Columba refused to give it up, and the question of ownership was put before King Diarmaid, Overlord of Ireland. His curious decision in this early "copyright" case went against Columba. "To every cow her calf," reasoned the King, "and to every book its son-book. Therefore the copy you made, O Colum Cille, belongs to Finnian." Columba was soon to have a more serious grievance against the King. Prince Curnan of Connaught, who had fatally injured a rival in a hurling match and had taken refuge with Columba, was dragged from his protector's arms and slain by Diarmaid's men, in defiance of the rights of sanctuary.

The war which soon broke out between Columba's clan and the clans loyal to Diarmaid was instigated, it is said, by Columba. At the battle of Cuil Dremne his cause was victorious, but Columba was accused of being morally responsible for driving three thousand unprepared souls into eternity. A church synod was held at Tailltiu (Telltown) in County Meath, which passed a vote of censure and would have followed it by excommunication but for the intervention of St. Brendan. Columba's own conscience was uneasy, and on the advice of an aged hermit, Molaise, he resolved to expiate his offense by exiling himself and trying to win for Christ in another land as many souls as had perished in the terrible battle of Cuil Dremne.

This traditional account of the events which led to Columba's departure from Ireland may well be correct, although missionary zeal and love of Christ are the motives mentioned for his going by the earliest biographers and by Adamnan,[2] our chief authority for his subsequent history. Whatever the impulse that prompted him, in the year 563, Columba embarked with twelve companions in a wicker coracle covered with leather, and on the eve of Pentecost landed on the island of Hi, or Iona.[3] The first thing he did there was to erect a high stone cross; then he built a monastery, which was to be his home for the rest of his life. The island itself was made over to him by his kinsman Conall, king of the British Dalriada, who perhaps had invited him to come to Scotland in the first place. Lying across from the border country between the Picts of the north and the Scots of the south, Iona made an ideal center for missionary work. Columba seems to have first devoted himself to teaching the imperfectly instructed Christians of Dalriada, most of whom were of Irish descent, but after some two years he turned to the work of converting the Scottish Picts. With his old comrades, Comgall and Kenneth, both of them Irish Picts, he made his way

[2] The historian Adamnan was born in Donegal about 624. He became abbot of Iona, being ninth in succession after Columba. His *Life of St. Columba* is a rich mine of anecdote.

[3] The original form of the word was Hy or I, which is Irish for island. Iona is one of the Inner Hebrides, just off the west coast of Scotland. It became known also as Icolmkill, "the island of Columba of the Cell." It had been a sacred place to the Druids before Columba landed there, and was to become the center of Celtic Christianity.

through Loch Ness northward to the castle of the redoubtable King Brude, near modern Inverness.

That pagan monarch had given strict orders that they were not to be admitted, but when Columba raised his arm and made the sign of the cross, it was said that bolts fell out and gates swung open, permitting the strangers to enter. Impressed by such powers, the King listened to them and ever after held Columba in high regard. As Overlord of Scotland he confirmed him in possession of Iona. We know from Adamnan that on several occasions Columba crossed the mountain chain which divides Scotland and that his travels also took him far north, and through the Western Isles. He is said to have planted churches as far east as Aberdeenshire and to have evangelized nearly the whole of the country of the Picts. When the descendants of the Dalriada kings became the rulers of Scotland, they were naturally eager to magnify the achievements of their hero and distant kinsman, Columba, and may have attributed to him victories won by others.

Columba never lost touch with Ireland. In 575 he was at the synod of Drumceatt in County Meath in company with King Conall's successor, Aidan, whom he had helped to place on the throne and had crowned at Iona, in his role as chief ecclesiastical ruler. His immense influence is shown by his veto of a proposal to abolish the order of bards and his securing for women exemption from all military service. When not on missionary journeys, Columba was to be found in his cell on Iona, where persons of all conditions visited him, some in want of spiritual or material help, some drawn by his miracles and sanctity. His biographer gives us a picture of a serene old age. His manner of life was austere; he slept on a bare slab of rock and ate barley or oat cakes, drinking only water. When he became too weak to travel, he spent long hours copying manuscripts, as he had done in his youth. On the day before his death he was at work on a Psalter, and had just traced the words, "They that love the Lord shall lack no good thing," when he paused and said, "Here I must stop; let Baithin do the rest." Baithin was his cousin, whom he had already nominated as

SAINT CECILIA   Dolci

A child prodigy, Carlo Dolci (1616-1686) at the age of eleven painted a whole figure of Saint John, and a head of the infant Christ Child. While he was not a great master, his new and delicate style made him extremely popular in the Florence of his day.

At her wedding banquet, while the pipes were playing, Saint Cecilia sang to the Lord asking that her heart might remain immaculate, that she not be put to shame. This inspired early composers to write elaborate music for the antiphon used on her feast day, and Saint Cecilia became the special patron of musicians. For this reason she is usually shown at the organ, although a harp or lute may be used. Sometimes she wears a wreath of red and white roses.

SAINT CHRISTOPHER   Titian

Titian (1477-1576) painted for 75 of his 99 years, leaving to posterity as

distinguished a collection of work as that of any painter. His style has a quality of pictorial humanism quite different from the style-for-its-own-sake which dominated the other Florentine and Roman painters of his day.

Saint Christopher is shown carrying the Christ Child across the stream. He is sometimes shown with a staff made of a palm tree, or with the palm tree growing beside the river.

his successor. When the monks entered the church for Matins, they found their beloved abbot lying helpless and dying before the altar. As his faithful attendant Diarmaid gently upraised him, he made a feeble effort to bless his brethren and then expired.

Iona was for centuries one of the famous centers of Christian learning. For a long time afterwards, Scotland, Ireland, and Northumbria followed the observances Columba had set for the monastic life, in distinction to those that were brought from Rome by later missionaries. His rule, based on the Eastern Rule of St. Basil, was that of many monasteries of Western Europe until superseded by the milder ordinance of St. Benedict. Adamnan, who must have been brought up on memories and recollections of Columba, writes eloquently of him: "He had the face of an angel; he was of excellent nature, polished in speech, holy in deed, great in council. He never let a single hour pass without engaging in prayer or reading or writing or some other occupation. He endured the hardships of fasting and vigils without intermission by day and night; the burden of a single one of his labors would have seemed beyond the powers of man. And, in the midst of all his toils, he appeared loving unto all, serene and holy, rejoicing in the joy of the Holy Spirit in his inmost heart."

M'Oenuran [4]

Alone am I upon the mountain;
 O Royal Sun, be the way prosperous;
 I have no more fear of aught
 Than if there were six thousand with me.
If there were six thousand with me
 Of people, though they might defend my body,
 When the appointed moment of my death shall come,
 There is no fortress that can resist it.

[4] Columba sang this song as he walked alone; it was thought to be a protection to anyone who sang it on a journey, like the "Lorica" of St. Patrick.

They that are ill-fated are slain even in a church,
　　Even on an island in the middle of a lake;
　　They that are well-fated are preserved in life,
　　Though they were in the first rank of battle, . . .

Whatever God destines for one,
　　He shall not go from the world till it befall him;
　　Though a Prince should seek anything more
　　Not as much as a mite shall he obtain. . . .

O Living God, O Living God!
　　Woe to him who for any reason does evil.
　　What thou seest not come to thee,
　　What thou seest escapes from thy grasp.
Our fortune does not depend on sneezing.
　　Nor on a bird on the point of a twig,
　　Nor on the trunk of a crooked tree,
　　Nor on a sordan hand in hand,
　　Better is He on whom we depend,
　　The Father,—the One,—and the Son. . . .

I reverence not the voices of birds,
　　Nor sneezing, nor any charm in the wide world,
　　Nor a child of chance, nor a woman;
　　My Druid is Christ, the Son of God.

　　Christ the Son of Mary, the great Abbot,
　　The Father, Son, and Holy Ghost;
　　My Possession is the King of Kings;
　　My Order is in Kells and Moone.
　　　　　　　Alone am I.

(D. Macgregor, Saint Columba,
Edinburgh, 1897.)

Saint Gregory the Great
Pope, Doctor of the Church
6 0 4
(*March 12*)

Because of the general breakdown of civil institutions resulting from the great migrations, the Church assumed an important role in the secular life of sixth-century Italy, particularly during the pontificate of Pope Gregory I, called "The Great." It may be useful to dwell briefly on the historical events of the period preceding Gregory's birth. The line of Western emperors had ended in 476, after which Italy was under the German Odoacer, who, at the head of a barbarian army, ruled from Ravenna, subject to the Eastern emperors at Constantinople. Another barbarian, the Ostrogoth Theodoric, at the bidding of the Emperor Zeno, overran Italy, captured Rome, and, in 493, Ravenna also. Theodoric installed himself in this city, and from there dominated the rest of Italy as vice-emperor. After his death in 526, Emperor Justinian, bent on reconquering the West, sent Greek armies under Belisarius. He first retook North Africa from the Vandals, who had captured it in St. Augustine's time, and then gained possession of Italy. During this Italian war, which lasted from 535 to 553, Gregory was born, about the year 540, of one of the few patrician families left in Rome. As a boy he went through the horrors of a siege when Romans were reduced to eating grass and nettles. At this time, according to the historian Procopius, only five hundred persons remained alive in the city. The Goths now advanced into Italy under a strong leader, Totila, who forced the sending of new armies from the East. During these years cities were taken and retaken, the farmlands were laid waste, and the people suffered from pestilence, famine, and looting.

The war was at length ended by Belisarius' successor, Narses, and Italy was again subject to the Emperor, and ruled from Ravenna by an exarch. In addition to their other sufferings, the people were now preyed upon by tax-gatherers, who extorted all they could, with the right of retaining one-twelfth of whatever they collected. Rome, once the proud mistress of the world, was in a lamentable state throughout Gregory's lifetime. Repeatedly besieged and sacked, the city was in ruins; the once fertile hinterland was almost a wilderness. No civil authority was left capable of dealing with the problems created by war and pillage, and to these recurrent evils were added fire, flood, and plague. The destruction of fine old buildings for the sake of their materials was so common that modern archeologists have found no structures erected later than the fourth century which were put up with newly quarried stone.

Gregory's family, famed for its piety, had given two sixth-century popes to the Church. His father, Gordianus, a government official, was a wealthy man, the owner of great estates in Sicily and a fine house on the Coelian Hill; his mother, Sylvia, was later venerated as a saint. Gregory early gave evidence of a brilliant mind and had the best education obtainable. He studied law and prepared to follow his father into public life. Rising steadily in government service, at the age of thirty he was appointed prefect of Rome. In this office, which he filled capably, the importance of law, order, and respect for constituted authority was impressed upon him. These lessons he was soon to apply in the ecclesiastical sphere, for within the year Gregory had abandoned his career to devote himself to the service of God. He went first to Sicily, where he founded six monasteries; then returning to Rome, he made his own home into a Benedictine monastery under the patronage of St. Andrew. By this time his father was dead, and his mother had gone to live at Cella Nova, a conventual retreat outside the city. After giving the remainder of his extensive property to charity, Gregory settled at St. Andrew's, as one of the monks.

He was afflicted now and throughout most of his life by gastric disorders, probably brought on by excessive fasting. Still, the three or four years he spent in the cloister were relatively happy, and it was with regret that he received from Pope Pelagius II an appointment as deacon, which meant a more active life in the world. Rome was under siege by the Lombards, and the Pope decided to send an embassy to Constantinople, to congratulate the new Emperor Tiberias II on his accession and to beg for military aid for the city. Gregory was to accompany this embassy, bearing the title of *apocrisiarius,* or papal ambassador.

Gregory found his position most uncongenial. There was a great contrast between the magnificence of Constantinople and the miseries of Rome. To avoid the intrigues and elaborate etiquette of the court, Gregory passed much of his time in seclusion, writing a commentary on the Book of Job. The embassy itself was a failure; the Emperor claimed that he could render no aid since his armies were busy keeping off the Persians and other enemies. After six years, Gregory was recalled and he settled down in St. Andrew's, where they elected him abbot.

One day, the story goes, Gregory was walking through the Roman slave market when he noticed three fair, golden-haired boys. He asked their nationality and was told that they were Angles. "They are well named," said Gregory, "for they have angelic faces." He asked where they came from, and when told "De Ire," he exclaimed, "De ira [from wrath]—yes, verily, they shall be saved from God's wrath and called to the mercy of Christ. What is the name of the king of that country?" "Aella." "Then must Alleluia be sung in Aella's land." Some modern historians have viewed the tale skeptically, claiming that the serious-minded Gregory would not have descended to punning. However, it seems unlikely that anyone would have taken the trouble to invent this delightful anecdote. Gregory was so touched by the boys' beauty, and by pity for their ignorance, that he resolved to go himself to preach the Gospel in their land. To this end, he obtained the consent of the Pope, and journeyed northwards with several monks. When the Roman people heard of this, they raised such an outcry at the loss of their favorite cleric that Pope Pelagius sent envoys to bring the party back. Later, when Gregory became pope, the evangelization of Britain became one of his most cherished projects.

The custom of offering Thirty Day Masses or Gregorian Masses for the Dead is said to have originated at this time. Justus, one of Gregory's monks, while gravely ill, confessed to having secreted three golden coins, and the abbot forbade his brethren to communicate with the offender or to visit him on his deathbed. His body was denied burial in the monks' burying ground and was interred under a dunghill, along with the gold pieces. Since he died repentant, the abbot had Mass offered for thirty days for the repose of his soul, and Gregory tells us that at the end the dead man's soul appeared to Copiosus, a brother, and assured him that he had been in torment, but by grace of the Masses was now released.

A new outbreak of the plague carried off Pope Pelagius. By general consent Gregory was the candidate best fitted to succeed him, and, pending the arrival from the East of the Emperor's ratification, he carried on the government of the Church. To implore God's mercy he ordered a great processional litany through the streets of Rome. From seven of the more venerable churches streamed out seven columns of people, all to meet at the church of Santa Maria Maggiore. Gregory of Tours, a contemporary historian, heard the report of one who had been present, and gives a vivid picture: "While the plague still raged, the columns marched through the streets chanting *Kyrie Eleison,* and as they walked people were seen falling and dying about them. Gregory inspired these poor people with courage, for he did not cease preaching and asked to have prayers made continually." Following this, there was an abatement of the plague. During the crisis, Gregory devoted himself to the relief of the stricken. Yet his own preference was for the contemplative life, and he wrote privately to Emperor Maurice, begging him not to confirm his election; and to friends at court, asking them to use their influence to the same purpose. His friends ignored his wishes, and the prefect of Rome not only intercepted Gregory's letter to the Emperor, but sent him word that the popular vote for Gregory had been unanimous. The Emperor promptly ratified the election. Dismayed, the pope-elect meditated flight, but was seized and carried off to the basilica of St. Peter, and there consecrated to the pontifical office. This took place on September 3, 590.

From the day he assumed office Gregory applied himself with vigor to his duties. He appointed a *vice-dominus* or overseer to look after the secular affairs and personnel of his household, and gave orders that only clerics should be attached to the service of the pope. He forbade the exaction of fees for ordination, for burial in churches, and for the conferring of the pallium.[1] Deacons were not to conduct the musical part of the Mass lest they be chosen for their voices rather than for their character. As a preacher Gregory liked to make his sermon a part of the sacred solemnity of the Mass, choosing as his subject the Gospel for the day. We possess a number of his homilies, ending always with a moral lesson.

In administering the great Patrimony of St. Peter,[2] Gregory showed a remarkable grasp of detail and administrative capacity. His instructions to his vicars in Sicily and elsewhere specified liberal treatment of tenants and farmers and ordered loans of money to those in need. This Pope was in fact the ideal landlord; tenants were content and revenues flowed into the papal coffers. Yet at his death the treasury was empty because of his huge charities, almost on the scale of state relief. He also spent large sums ransoming captives from the Lombards. Indeed he commended one of the bishops for breaking up and selling church plate for this purpose.

[1] The pallium is a band of white wool ornamented with crosses which is worn by the pope and by archbishops; it is a symbol of archiepiscopal authority.

[2] The Patrimony of St. Peter was the land, revenues, and other property with which the see of Rome was endowed after the Peace of Constantine, in 313, which marked the granting of toleration to Christians. The Peace was followed in the course of years by the bestowal of numberless privileges and possessions on the Church.

In anticipation of a threatened corn shortage, Gregory filled the granaries of Rome with the harvests of Egypt and Sicily; he had regular lists kept of the poor, to whom grants were periodically made. His conscience was so sensitive that once when a beggar died in the street, presumably of starvation, he pronounced an interdiction on himself and refrained for some days from performing his holy functions.

Gregory's sense of justice showed itself in enlightened treatment of the Jews, whom he would not allow to be oppressed or deprived of their synagogues. When the Jews of Cagliari in Sardinia complained that their synagogue had been seized by a converted member of the race, who had turned it into a Christian church and set up in it a cross and an image of Our Lady, he ordered the cross and image to be reverently removed, and the building restored to its former owners.

From the outset Gregory had to face the aggressions of the Lombards, who, from three fortresses they held, made destructive raids on Rome. He organized the city's defenses and even managed to send aid to other cities that were threatened. When in 593 King Agilulph with his Lombard army actually appeared before the walls, it was the Pope who went out to interview the invader. As much by his personality and prestige as by his promise of annual tribute, Gregory induced Agilulph to withdraw his army. For nine years he strove to bring about a political settlement between the Byzantine emperor and the Lombards, but when an agreement was at last arrived at, it was wrecked by the treachery of the Exarch. Then on his own account Gregory negotiated a truce for Rome and the surrounding districts. Agilulph's wife, Theodelinda, a Bavarian princess, was a Catholic, and became Gregory's powerful ally. She finally prevailed on the Lombards to give up the Arian creed which they had been taught and to accept the Catholic faith.

In the confusion and disorder of the times, Gregory must have turned with relief to his writing. Early in his pontificate he wrote the *Regula Pastoralis,* or *Pastoral Rule,* in which he describes the bishop as a physician of souls, with a special duty to preach and to enforce Church discipline. This little work met with tremendous success. Emperor Maurice had it translated into Greek and Bishop Leander gave it circulation in Spain. Licinianus, bishop of Carthage, praised it but feared it set so high a standard that candidates for the priesthood might be discouraged. Augustine took a copy to England, where three hundred years later King Alfred himself translated it into Anglo-Saxon. At a council summoned by Charlemagne all bishops were told to study it, and to give a copy to each new bishop as a part of the ceremony of consecration. For centuries Gregory's ideals were those of the clergy of the West. His *Dialogues,* a collection of contemporary visions, prophecies, and miracles, designed to comfort and hearten the Christian reader by showing him God's mercy, became one of the most popular books of the Middle Ages. The stories in it were obtained from persons still living who in many cases had been eye-witnesses of the events described. However, Gregory's methods were not critical, and the modern reader may often feel misgivings as to the reliability of his informants. In that credulous age any unusual happening was likely to be viewed as supernatural.

Gregory kept in touch with Spain chiefly through Bishop Leander of Seville. The Spanish Church governed itself, and, though loyal, had little to do with Rome. Gregory did much to extirpate the heresy of the Donatists [3] in Africa, while in Istria, a province on the Adriatic, he brought back certain schismatic bishops to the Catholic faith. In Gaul papal influence was not strong outside Provence, but through correspondence with King Childebert and with the Gallic bishops Gregory strove to correct abuses, especially simony and the placing of laymen in ecclesiastical offices.

Of all his work, that which lay nearest his heart was the conversion of England. It is probable that the first move towards the sending of a Roman mission to England was made by Englishmen themselves. News reached Gregory that they had appealed to the bishops of Gaul for preachers, and their appeals had been ignored.

[3] On the Donatists, see above, *St. Augustine of Hippo,* p. 106.

In 596 he began to make far-reaching plans. His first act was to order the purchase of some English slaves, boys of seventeen or eighteen, who might be educated in a monastery in Italy for service in their own land. Since he wished the work of conversion to proceed forthwith, from his own monastery of St. Andrew he chose a band of forty monks to proceed to England under the leadership of their prior, the saintly Augustine. The history of that mission is recounted later, in the life of *St. Augustine of Canterbury*.

During nearly the whole of his thirteen years as pope Gregory was in conflict with Constantinople, either with the Emperor or with the patriarch. He protested against the extortionate tax-collectors and against an imperial edict which forbade soldiers from becoming monks. With John Faster, bishop of Constantinople, he had a correspondence over the title of Ecumenical or Universal Patriarch, which John had assumed. The adjective had previously been applied only to a general council of the church. Gregory charged that the title savored of arrogance. John claimed that he used it in the limited sense of archbishop over many bishops. Gregory himself bore only the proudly humble title of *servus servorum Dei*, servant of the servants of God, which is still retained by his successors.

In 602 Emperor Maurice and his family were killed after a revolt led by the centurion Phocas, who on seizing power sent his portrait and that of his wife to Rome. The people and senate, cowed and abject, received them with acclamations. Gregory himself wrote a tardy and diplomatic letter to the murderous usurper, an act which has exposed him to criticism. In his defense it may be said that the letter consisted largely in hopes for peace; with the people defenseless, Gregory could scarcely risk denunciation. Phocas proved himself incapable of governing and was deposed after a few years.

Gregory never rested and wore himself down almost to a skeleton. Even as death drew near, he directed the affairs of the Church and continued his literary labors. He died in 604, and was buried in St. Peter's Church. The list of his achievements is a long one. He is credited with the compilation of the Antiphonary,[4] the introduction of new styles in church music, the composition of several famous hymns, and the foundation of the Schola Cantorum, the famous training school for singers. Only a small part of so-called Gregorian music dates from his time, but the type of chanting was fixed then for centuries to come. Gregory defined the calendar of festivals and the service of priests and deacons, enforced the celibacy of the clergy, and in general strengthened the papacy. He is venerated as the fourth Doctor of the Latin Church. In his homilies he popularized the great St. Augustine of Hippo, and until the medieval scholars went back to study Augustine himself, Gregory's was the last word on theology; he formulated several doctrines which had not previously been satisfactorily defined. Milman, in his *History of Latin Christianity*, writes: "It is impossible to conceive what would have been the confusion, the lawlessness, the chaotic state of the Middle Ages without the medieval papacy; and of the medieval papacy, the real father is Gregory the Great." In art Gregory is usually represented in a tiara and pontifical robes, carrying a book or musical instrument, or sometimes bearing a staff with a double cross; his symbol is the dove which his deacon Peter said he once saw whispering in his ear.

Excerpts from the Dialogues *on the Lombard Invasion*

*R*edemptus, *bishop of the city of Ferenti, was a man of venerable life who died almost seven years ago. I was well acquainted with him, for he dwelt not far from the abbey in which I lived. He once when I asked him (for the story was very well known thereabouts), told me what he had learned from divine revelation of the end of the world, in the time of John the Younger, my predecessor. He said that on a certain day, when he was, after his custom, out visiting his diocese, he came to the church of the*

---

[4] The antiphonary is a liturgical book for use in the choir; it contains music and texts of all sung portions of the Roman breviary.

blessed martyr Euthicius. And at nightfall he chanced to be lodged near the sepulchre of the martyr, and after his travels lay down there to rest. About midnight he was, as he said, neither fully awake nor yet asleep, but rather heavy with sleep, when he felt his waking soul oppressed with a great sorrow. And in that state he saw the same blessed martyr Euthicius standing before him, who then said to him: "Are you waking, Redemptus?" He answered that he was. Thereat the martyr said: "The end of all flesh is come; the end of all flesh is come!" and after repeating these words three times, he vanished out of his sight.

The man of God rose up and fell to his prayers with many tears, but straightway there followed those fearful signs in heaven, namely, lances of fire and hosts appearing in the North. Straightway too the barbarous and savage nation of the Lombards, drawn like a sword out of its sheath, left their country and invaded ours. Thence the people, who before were like thickly grown cornfields for their great multitude, are now withered and blasted. Cities were laid waste, towns and villages ravaged, churches burned, monasteries of men and women destroyed, farms left desolate, and the land lies solitary, without men to till the soil, and barren of all inhabitants. Beasts possess the regions where before many men had their dwellings. How it goes in other parts of the world I do not know, but here where we live it is not a forecast of the end but rather a spectacle of the end of the world already arrived and come. So that much more jealously should we seek after things of eternity as we find all temporal things suddenly fled and gone.

(*Dialogues,* III, 38.)

Excerpts from a Letter to Recared, King of the Visigoths [5]

I cannot express in words, most excellent son, how gratified I am with your work and your life. On hearing of the power of the new miracle in our days, namely that the whole nation of the Goths has through your Excellency been won over from the error of Arian heresy to the firmness of a right faith, one is ready to exclaim with

[5] Recared, the first Christian king of Spain, had converted his Gothic subjects.

the prophet, This is the change wrought by the right hand of the Most High. . . .

The government of your kingdom in relation to your subjects should be tempered with moderation, lest power unawares corrupt your mind. A kingdom is well ruled when the glory of reigning does not dominate the king's thoughts. Care too should be taken that anger creep not in, lest what is lawful to do be not done too hastily. For anger, even when it punishes the faults of delinquents, ought not to precede reason as its mistress, but attend as a handmaid at the back of reason, to come to the front when bidden. For once it begins to take control of the mind, it calls just what it does cruelly. . . .

We have sent you a small key from the most sacred body of the blessed Apostle Peter to convey his blessings, containing iron from his chains, that what once bound his neck for martyrdom may loosen yours from all sin. We have given also to the bearer of these presents, to deliver to you, a cross in which there is some of the wood of the Lord's cross, and hairs of the Blessed John the Baptist, from which you may ever receive the succor of our Saviour through the intercession of His forerunner. . . .

(*Letters*, IX, *Nicene and Post-Nicene Fathers*, Series II, xiii.)

Letter to Abbot Mellitus, in Britain

When Almighty God shall bring you to the most reverend Bishop Augustine, our brother, tell him what I have, after mature deliberation on the condition of the English, decided upon, namely, that the temples of the idols in that nation should not be destroyed but the idols which are in them should be destroyed. Let holy water be prepared and sprinkled in said temples; then let altars be erected and relics set in place. For if those temples are well built, it is right that they be converted from the worship of devils to the service of the true God, that the nation, seeing that their temples are not destroyed, may abandon the error in their hearts and know and adore the true God, while still resorting familiarly to the places to which they are accustomed.

And since they have been used to slaughtering many oxen in sacrifices to devils, some solemnity should be substituted for that. On the day of dedication, for example, or on the nativities of the holy martyrs whose relics are there deposited,[6] they may build themselves huts of branches of trees around the churches which have been converted to Christian use out of temples, and celebrate the solemnity with religious feasting, offering no more beasts to the devil but killing cattle for eating to the praise of God and returning thanks for their food to the Giver of all things, to the end that while some outward pleasures are permitted them they may more readily accept the inward consolations of the grace of God.

(Bede, *Ecclesiastical History of England,*
ed. by J. A. Giles.)

[6] Bede tells us elsewhere how Gregory sent from Rome to England furnishings for the new churches to be built there, "likewise relics of the holy apostles and martyrs."

Saint Augustine of Canterbury

Confessor, Apostle of the English

c. 6 0 5

(*May 28*)

When Pope Gregory began to plan for the evangelization of England, the land was still largely pagan, although in the southwest there were remnants of earlier missionary efforts. To lead this important mission, Gregory chose Augustine, prior of St. Andrew's monastery in Rome, of which Gregory had been the founder. Nothing is known of Augustine's life until the year 596, when, with a party of Benedictine monks, he set out northwards from Rome. He carried letters of commendation to various Gallic bishops. On reaching Provence, the monks accompanying Augustine grew fearful of the dangers that lay ahead. Alarming stories were told of the ferocity of the pagans and the hazards of the Channel crossing. They persuaded Augustine to return to Rome to ask the Pope's permission to abandon the whole enterprise. Meanwhile the Pope had received word that the common people of England and also some of their chieftains and kings were ready to welcome Christian missionaries. After Pope Gregory had told Augustine this news and had discussed the situation with him further, Augustine rejoined his companions and inspired them with his own courage. Taking with them several Franks to act as interpreters, the party crossed safely over to the Isle of Thanet, in the domain of Ethelbert, King of Kent, whom they formally notified of their arrival and of their purpose in coming.

Ethelbert was still a pagan, but his wife Bertha, daughter of King Charibert of the Franks, had been converted to Christianity.

Sitting under a spreading oak, Ethelbert received the missionaries. After listening carefully to their words, he gave them permission to preach to his subjects. He also made over to them a house in Canterbury, with the use of the little stone church of St. Martin, which had stood there since the period of Roman occupation. This had formerly been the oratory of Queen Bertha and her confessor Liudhard. Ethelbert was converted and baptized at Pentecost, 597. After this promising start, Augustine went back to Provence to be consecrated bishop by Vergilius, metropolitan of Arles and papal legate for Gaul. On his return some ten thousand of Ethelbert's subjects were baptized in the Swale River.

Augustine, greatly heartened by the success of his mission, now sent two of his monks to Rome to report to the Pope, and to ask for more helpers. Also he wished to have the Pope's counsel on various problems. When the monks came back to England with a fresh band of missionaries, they brought the pallium for Augustine. Among the new group were Mellitus, Justus, and Paulinus, who was afterwards archbishop of York. With these "ministers of the Word," wrote the Venerable Bede, "the holy Pope sent all things needed in general for divine worship and the service of the Church, viz. sacred vessels, altar cloths, ornaments for churches, and vestments for priests and clerks, and also many books." The latter item was especially important, for the books helped to inspire the great love of learning which characterized the English Church.

Gregory sent to Augustine a plan for developing an ecclesiastical hierarchy and establishing a working organization for the whole country—a plan which was not fully carried out in Augustine's lifetime. There was to be a northern and a southern province, with twelve suffragan bishops in each. In a letter to Mellitus, which is presented earlier, following the life of *St. Gregory,* he gave instruction on other points, showing his administrative ability as well as considerable psychological insight. Pagan temples were, as far as possible, to be Christianized and retained. Consecration rites and feasts of martyrs were to replace the heathen festivals, for, Gregory

THE COMMUNION OF SAINT LUCY   Tiepolo

Giambattista Tiepolo (1696-1770) was the last and crowning painter in the great tradition of the Italian Renaissance. So great was his fame that he was commissioned to decorate the Archiepiscopal Palace at Würzburg. Subsequently he was asked by the King of Spain to decorate the ceiling of the newly completed Royal Palace in Madrid.

Saint Lucy is symbolized by the dagger and the eyes on a dish.

THE BETROTHAL OF SAINT CATHERINE   Lucas Cranach the Elder

Lucas Cranach the Elder (1472-1553) worked in many media. Besides portraits and altarpieces, he is especially known for some of his copper engravings. He also designed the coins for the state mint of his native Saxony. The

climax of his religious paintings was a series of martyrdoms and scenes from the Passion.

Saint Catherine of Alexandria can almost always be recognized by the inclusion of the spiked wheel with which her pagan persecutors tried to kill her. This painting represents her dream in which she was taken as spouse by Our Lord, the "Mystic Marriage of Saint Catherine."

wisely writes, "he who would climb to a lofty height must go by steps, not leaps."

In 603 Augustine rebuilt and reconsecrated the Canterbury church and the house given him by King Ethelbert. These structures formed the nucleus for his metropolitan cathedral. They were destroyed by fire in 1067, and the present cathedral, begun by the great Lanfranc in 1070, stands on their site. A converted temple outside the walls of Canterbury was made into another religious house, which Augustine dedicated to St. Peter and St. Paul. After his death this abbey became known as St. Augustine's.

With the King's support, the Christianization of Kent proceeded rapidly, but Gregory's charge had stated, "All the bishops of Britain we commend to your Fraternity." The survivors of the ancient British or Celtic Church and their bishops had been driven westward and southward into Wales and Cornwall by the Saxon conquerors of the fifth century. Here they had persisted as Christian communities, cut off from the outside world. Although they were sound in fundamental doctrine, some of their usages were at variance with those of Rome. Now, in virtue of his archiepiscopal jurisdiction, Augustine invited the Celtic bishops to meet with him at a spot outside the confines of Wessex, which has since come to be known as Augustine's Oak. In long conferences with the representatives of the Celtic Church Augustine urged them to comply with the customs of the rest of Western Christendom, in particular in the method of determining the date of Easter, and to aid him in converting the pagans. Loyalty to their own local traditions, however, and bitterness against their Saxon conquerors, made them unwilling to agree, even though Augustine performed a miracle of healing in their presence to prove the supernatural source of his authority. They consented to attend a second conference, held in Flintshire, but it too proved a failure. Augustine did not rise to greet his Celtic brothers when they arrived and they felt that he lacked Christian humility. They refused either to listen to him or acknowledge him as their archbishop. It was not until 664, at the

Synod of Whitby, that their differences were resolved and ecclesiastical uniformity was established.

Augustine's last years were spent in spreading and consolidating the faith in Ethelbert's realm, which comprised large sections of eastern England south of Northumbria. Sees were established in London and Rochester, with Mellitus appointed bishop over one and Justus over the other. Seven years after his arrival Augustine died, leaving the continuation of his work to others.

Correspondence with Pope Gregory I

*O*n his return to Britain he [*Augustine*] sent Laurentius the priest and Peter the monk to Rome to inform Pope Gregory that the English nation had accepted the faith of Christ and that he himself was made their bishop. At the same time he requested his solutions to some problems that had occurred to him. He soon received satisfactory answers to his questions, which we have thought suitable to insert in this history.

First question of Augustine, Bishop of the Church of Canterbury: As regards bishops, how are they to conduct themselves towards their clergy? In how many portions should the gifts of the faithful to the altar be divided? How is the bishop to act in the church?

Answer of Gregory, Pope of the City of Rome: Holy Writ, with which doubtless you are familiar, has instruction for you, in particular, St. Paul's Epistle to Timothy, wherein he endeavors to explain to him how he should behave himself in the house of God. The Apostolic See is accustomed to prescribe rules to bishops newly ordained, that all revenues that accrue should be divided into four portions: one for the bishop and his household for purposes of hospitality and entertainment, another for the clergy, a third for the poor, and a fourth for the upkeep of churches. But since you, my brother, were brought up under monastic rules and should not live apart from your clergy in the English church, which by God's help has lately been brought into the faith, you will follow that course of life which our forefathers led in the time of the primitive church, when no one called anything he possessed his own but all things were common among them. . . .

Augustine's Second Question: Whereas the faith is one and the same, why are there different customs in different churches? And why is one custom at masses observed in the holy Roman church and another in the Gallican church?

Pope Gregory answers: You know, my brother, the custom of the Roman church in which you remember you were trained. But if you have found anything in either the Roman or the Gallican or any other church which may be more acceptable to Almighty God, I am willing that you carefully make choice of the same and diligently teach the English church, which is as yet new in the faith, whatever you can gather from the several churches. For things are not to be loved for the sake of places but places for the sake of good things. Select, therefore, from every church the things that are devout, religious and upright, and when you have, as it were, combined them into one body, let the minds of the English be trained therein.

Augustine's Third Question: I beg you to tell me what punishment to inflict if a man takes anything away by stealth from the church.

Gregory answers: You may judge, my brother, by the person of the thief how he is to be corrected. For there are some who having plenty commit theft, and there are others who sin in this way from poverty. Wherefore it is right that some be punished in their purses, others with stripes, some with more severity, others more mildly. When severity is greater, it must proceed from charity, not from anger, because he who is corrected is thus treated in order that he may not be delivered over to hell-fire. . . . You may add that they are to restore the things they have stolen from the church. But God forbid that the church should make profit from earthly things it seems to lose or seek gain out of such vanities.

Augustine's Fourth Question: Whether two brothers may marry two sisters who are of a family far removed from them?

Gregory answers: This may lawfully be done, for nothing found in Holy Writ appears to forbid it. . . .

(Bede, *Ecclesiastical History of England,*
ed. by J. A. Giles.)

Saint Bede

Confessor, Doctor of the Church

7 3 5

(May 27)

Almost all that is known of the life of Bede is derived from a touching description of his death written by a disciple, the monk Cuthbert, and a short factual account in the final chapter of his famous work, the *Ecclesiastical History of England,* from which we quote: "Thus much of the ecclesiastical history of Britain and especially of the English nation, have I, Bede, a servant of Christ and priest of the monastery of the Blessed Apostles, Peter and Paul, which is at Wearmouth and Jarrow, with the Lord's help composed as far as I could gather it, either from ancient documents or from traditions of the elders or from my own knowledge."

Bede was born on the lands of the monastery of Wearmouth-Jarrow, which stood on the River Tyne in northeastern England. At the age of seven he was given by his relatives to the Abbot Benedict to be educated. From that time he spent his whole life in the monastery devoting himself to the study of the Scriptures. He was a born scholar. "Through all the observance of monastic discipline," Bede wrote, "it has ever been my delight to learn and teach and write." In his nineteenth year he was admitted to the diaconate and in his thirtieth to the priesthood, both by the hands of Bishop John of Beverley and at the bidding of the Abbot Ceolfrid. "From the time of my ordination up till my present fifty-ninth year I have endeavored for my own use and for that of the brethren to make brief notes upon the Holy Scriptures, either out of the works of the venerable fathers or in conformity with their meaning and interpretation." Bede then gives a list of his many writings,— works on science, chronology, poetics, and history, as well as commentaries on the Scriptures. He concludes with these pious words: "And I pray Thee, loving Jesus, that as Thou hast graciously given me to drink in with delight the words of Thy knowledge, so Thou wouldst mercifully grant me to attain one day to Thee, the fountain of all wisdom, and to appear forever before Thy face."

Beyond a few visits to friends in other monasteries, Bede's life was passed at Jarrow in one round of prayer and praise, writing and study. A fortnight before Easter in the year 735, he began to be much troubled by shortness of breath, and his brothers realized that the end was near. Nevertheless his pupils continued to study by his bedside and to read aloud, though their reading was often interrupted by tears. He for his part talked and read to them and sang praises to God. During the Forty Days from Easter to Ascension Day, he took time from his singing and instructing to start dictating two new books, one a translation of St. John's Gospel into Anglo-Saxon, and the other a collection of notes from St. Isidore.[1] On the Tuesday before Ascension Day he began to grow weaker. He passed the day cheerfully and kept on with his dictation, saying occasionally to the scribe: "Go on quickly; I do not know how long I shall hold out and whether my Maker will not soon remove me." After a wakeful night he began to dictate the last chapter of St. John. At three in the afternoon he sent for the priests of the monastery, distributed among them some pepper, incense, and a little linen which he had by him in a chest, and asked for their prayers and Masses. That evening the boy who was taking down his translation of the Book of John said: "There is still one sentence, dear master, that I have not written." That last sentence was supplied, the boy said it was finished, and the dying man murmured: "You have well said . . . all is finished. Now take my head in your hands that I may have the comfort of

[1] Isidore of Seville was a learned Spanish ecclesiastic of the seventh century who wrote copiously on many subjects, including history, theology, grammar, and etymology.

sitting opposite the holy place where I used to pray, and so sitting may call upon my Father." And on the pavement of his cell, the brothers around him singing "Glory be to the Father, and to the Son, and to the Holy Ghost," he peacefully breathed his last.

The title of "Venerable" by which Bede is usually known was a term of respect bestowed in ancient times on highly esteemed members of religious orders. We find it applied to Bede by the Council of Aix-la-Chapelle in 836, and it has clung to him through succeeding centuries. Though in 1899 he was named Saint and Doctor of the Church, "Venerable" remains his special designation to this day.

A Benedictine scholar, the late Cardinal Gasquet, has left a high tribute to Bede's literary work. "When we compare," he writes, "the work done under the inspiration of Bede at Wearmouth and Jarrow with the other literary efforts of the seventh and eighth centuries, one characteristic at once strikes us. The work of that northern school is what may be called 'thorough and scholarly.' . . . It will bear the test of examination; it carries with it evidence of wide reading and full knowledge, utilized with judgment and critical tact, and for this it became a model to subsequent generations. Whether we take Bede's *History* for chronology and the careful determination of dates; or his treatise on meter, which is really philological; or his Scripture commentaries, and compare them with the efforts of a century or two before, or even with those of a century or two later, we can at once detect the difference. . . . Look at his *History*. . . . Reflect how this great record of our own country was composed. Remember that its author was a man who lived his whole life within the narrow circuit of a few miles, remember also the difficulty of obtaining information in those days. Still, to acquire knowledge, accurate knowledge, he went to work precisely as the historian would at the present day, never resting till he had got at the best sources of information available at the cost of whatever time or patience or labor it might involve. It is only now, in this age of minute criticism, that we can realize the full excellence of Bede's historical methods. The chief study of

St. Bede and his fellow monks of Wearmouth and Jarrow was the Bible. It was from this monastery that has come to us the most correct manuscript of the Vulgate, a scientific achievement of the highest quality."

Bede's writings include works on natural phenomena, chronology, and grammar, also commentaries on the Latin Fathers, and a *History of the Abbots*. He summed up and gave to the English people of his day the learning of Western Europe as well as an invaluable history of their own land. In all that he wrote he had the artist's instinct for proportion, and a literary feeling for interesting and picturesque detail. Yet, above all, Bede was the Christian thinker and student.

Preface to the Ecclesiastical History

. . . *To the end that I may remove from yourself* [2] *and other* readers or hearers of this history all occasion of doubting what I have written, I will now tell you briefly from what authors chiefly I have gleaned the same.

My principal authority and aid in the work was the learned and revered Abbot Albinus who was educated in the church at Canterbury by those venerable and learned men, Archbishop Theodore [3] of blessed memory and the Abbot Adrian, and transmitted to me by Nothelm, the godly priest of the Church of London, either in writing or by word of mouth of the same Nothelm, all that he thought worthy of memory that had been done in the province of Kent and adjacent parts by the disciples of the blessed Pope Gregory, as he had learned the same either from written records or the traditions of his predecessors. The same Nothelm afterwards went to Rome, where by leave of the present Pope Gregory [4] he searched into the archives of the holy Roman Church and found some letters of the blessed Pope Gregory and other popes. Return-

---

[2] Bede is addressing Ceolwulph, king of Northumbria, to whom he is sending a copy of his history for the king's approval.

[3] Theodore of Tarsus.

[4] Gregory III.

ing home, by the advice of the aforesaid most reverend father Albinus, he brought them to me to be inserted in my history.

Thus the writings of our predecessors from the beginning of this volume to the time when the English nation received the faith of Christ we have collected and from them gathered the material of our history. From that time until the present what was transacted in the church of Canterbury by the disciples of St. Gregory and their successors and under what kings these things took place has been conveyed to us by Nothelm through the industry of the aforesaid Abbot Albinus. They also partly informed me by what bishops and under what kings the provinces of the East and West Saxons, as also of the East Angles and the Northumbrians received the faith of Christ. In short I was encouraged to undertake this work chiefly by the persuasions of Albinus.

In like manner, Daniel, the most reverend bishop of the West Saxons, who is still living, communicated to me in writing some facts regarding the ecclesiastical history of that province and the next adjoining it of the South Saxons, as also the Isle of Wight. And how through the pious ministry of Cedd and Ceadda the province of the Mercians was brought to the faith of Christ, which they had not known before, and how the East Saxons recovered it after having rejected it, and how those fathers lived and died, we learned from the brethren of the monastery which was built by them and is called Lastingham. . . . And what took place in the church of the province of the Northumbrians from the time they received the faith of Christ until this present, I learned not from any particular writer but from the faithful testimony of innumerable witnesses who might know or remember the same, besides what I had of my own knowledge. . . .

And I humbly entreat the reader that if he find anything in this that we have written not recounted according to the truth, he will not impute the fault to me, who, as the true rule of history requires, have labored sincerely to commit to writing what I could gather from the general report for the instruction of posterity. Moreover, I beseech all men who shall hear or read this history of our nation that for my manifold infirmities of both mind and body they will offer up frequent supplications to the throne of Grace. And I further pray that as reward for the labor wherewith I have recorded for the several countries the events which were most worthy of note and most grateful to the ears of their inhabitants I may have in recompense the benefit of their godly prayers.

The Conversion of King Edwin of Northumbria

The king, hearing these words, answered that he was both willing and bound to receive the faith which he taught; but that he would confer about it with his principal friends and counsellors, to the end that if they also were of his opinion, they might all together be cleansed in Christ the Fountain of Life. Paulinus [5] consenting, the king did as he said; for, holding a council with the wise men, he asked of everyone in particular what he thought of the new doctrine, and the new worship that was preached? To which the chief of his own priests, Coifi, immediately answered, "O King, consider what this is which is now preached to us; for I verily declare to you, that the religion which we have hitherto professed has, as far as I can learn, no virtue in it. For none of your people has applied himself more delightedly to the worship of our own gods than I; and yet there are many who receive greater favors from you, and are more preferred than I, and are more prosperous in all their undertakings. Now if the gods were good for anything, they would rather forward me, who have been more careful to serve them. It remains, therefore, that if upon examination you find those new doctrines which are now preached to us better and more efficacious, we immediately receive them without delay."

Another of the king's chief men, approving of his words and exhortations, presently added, "The present life of man, O King, seems to be, in comparison with that time which is unknown to us, like the swift flight of a sparrow through the room wherein you sit at supper in winter, with your commanders and ministers, and a good fire in the midst, whilst the storms of rain and snow prevail abroad; the sparrow, I say, flying in at one door, and immediately out at another, whilst he is within, is safe from the wintry storm; but after a short space of fair weather, he imme-

[5] Paulinus had been sent to preach Christianity in Northumbria.

diately vanishes out of your sight, into the dark winter from which he had emerged. So this life of man appears for a short space, but of what went before, or what is to follow, we are entirely ignorant. If, therefore, this new doctrine contains something more certain, it seems justly to deserve to be followed."

(Bede, *Ecclesiastical History of England*, ed. by J. A. Giles.)

Saint Boniface
Martyr, Apostle of Germany
7 5 4
(June 5)

I solated missionary groups had penetrated central Germany in earlier times, but not until the eighth century was there a systematic effort to Christianize the vast pagan wilderness. To the English monk Boniface belongs the honor of opening up this region and creating a hierarchy under direct commission from the Holy See. Thirty-six years of missionary labor under difficult and dangerous conditions, ending at last in martyrdom, entitle this good and courageous man to the designation, "Apostle of Germany."

Boniface, or Winfrid, to give him his baptismal name, was born into a Christian family of noble rank, probably at Crediton in Devonshire, about the year 680. The reorganized English Church, still under the inspiration brought to it from Rome two generations earlier by Augustine of Canterbury, was full of fervor and vitality. Winfrid was a very small boy when he found himself listening to the conversation of some monks who were visiting his home. He resolved then to enter the Church, and this resolution never weakened. Winfrid's father had other plans for his clever son, but a serious illness altered his attitude, and he sent the boy to the neighboring abbey of Exeter to be educated. Some years later, Winfrid went to the abbey of Bursling, in the diocese of Winchester. After completing his studies there, he was appointed head of the school. His teaching skill attracted many students, and for their use he wrote a grammar which is still extant. The pupils diligently took notes at his classes, and these were copied and circulated in other monasteries, where they were eagerly studied. At the age of thirty he was ordained priest, and now added preaching to teaching and administrative work.

Winfrid was assured of rapid advancement in the English Church, but God revealed to him that his work was to be in foreign lands, where need was greater. Northern Europe and most of Central Europe were still in pagan darkness. In Friesland, which then included modern Netherlands and lands to the east, the Northumbrian missionary Willibrord had long been striving to bring the Gospel to the people. It was to this region that Winfrid felt himself called. Having obtained the consent of his abbot, he and two companions set out in the spring of 716. Soon after landing at Doerstadt they learned that Duke Radbold of Friesland, an enemy of Christianity, was warring with Charles Martel, the Frankish duke, and that Willibrord had been obliged to retire to his monastery at Echternacht. Realizing that the time was inauspicious, the missionaries prudently returned to England in the autumn. Winfrid's monks at Bursling tried to keep him there, and wished to elect him abbot, but he was not to be turned from his purpose.

This first attempt had shown him that to be effective as a missionary he must have a direct commission from the Pope, so in 718, with commendatory letters from the bishop of Winchester, he presented himself in Rome before Gregory II. The Pope welcomed him warmly, kept him in Rome until spring of the following year, when traveling conditions were favorable, and then sent him forth with a general commission to preach the word of God to the heathen. At this time Winfrid's name was changed to Boniface (from the Latin, *bonifatus*, fortunate). Crossing the lower Alps, the missionary traveled through Bavaria into Hesse. Duke Radbold had died and his successor was more friendly. Going into Friesland, Boniface labored for three years under Willibrord, who was now very old. Boniface declined to become Willibrord's coadjutor and successor as bishop of Utrecht, saying that his commission had been general, "to the heathen," and he could not be limited to any one diocese. He now returned to work in Hesse.

Boniface had little difficulty in making himself understood as a preacher, since the dialects of the various Teutonic tribes closely resembled his native Anglo-Saxon. He won the interest of two powerful local chieftains, Dettic and Deorulf, who at some previous time had been baptized. For lack of instruction they had remained little better than pagans; now they became zealous Christians and influenced many others to be baptized. They also gave Boniface a grant of land on which he later founded the monastery of Amoeneburg. Boniface was able to report such remarkable gains that the Pope summoned him back to Rome to be ordained bishop.

In Rome on St. Andrew's Day, November 30, 722, Pope Gregory II consecrated him as regionary bishop with a general jurisdiction over "the races in the parts of Germany and east of the Rhine who live in error, in the shadow of death." The Pope also gave him a letter to the powerful Charles Martel, "The Hammer." When Boniface delivered it to the Frankish duke on his way back to Germany, he received the valuable gift of a sealed pledge of Frankish protection. Armed thus with authority from both the Church and the civil power, the prestige of Boniface was vastly enhanced. On his return to Hesse, he decided to try to root out the pagan superstitions which seriously affected the stability of his converts. On a day publicly announced, and in the midst of an awe-struck crowd, Boniface and one or two of his followers attacked with axes Thor's sacred oak. These German tribes, along with many other primitive peoples, were tree-worshipers. Thor, god of thunder, was one of the principal Teutonic deities, and this ancient oak, which stood on the summit of Mt. Gudenberg, was sacred to him. After a few blows, the huge tree crashed to earth, splitting into four parts. The terrified tribesmen, who had expected a punishment to fall instantly on the perpetrators of such an outrage, now saw that their god was powerless to protect even his own sanctuary. To signalize the victory, Boniface built a chapel on the spot. From that time the work of evangelization in Hesse proceeded steadily.

Moving east into Thuringia, Boniface continued his crusade. He found a few undisciplined Celtic and Irish priests, who tended to be a hindrance; many of them held heretical beliefs and others lived immoral lives. Boniface restored order among them, although his chief aim was to win over the pagan tribes. At Ohrdruff, near Gotha, he established a second monastery, dedicated to St. Michael, as a missionary center. Everywhere the people were ready to listen, but there was a critical lack of teachers. Boniface appealed to the English monasteries and convents, and their response was so whole-hearted that for several years bands of monks, schoolmasters, and nuns came over to place themselves under his direction. The two monasteries already built were enlarged and new ones founded. Among the new English missionaries were Lullus, who was to succeed Boniface at Mainz, Eoban, who was to share his martyrdom, Burchard, and Wigbert; the nuns included Thecla, Chunitrude, and Boniface's beautiful and learned young cousin, Lioba, later to become abbess of Bischofsheim and friend of Hildegarde, Charlemagne's wife.

Pope Gregory III sent Boniface the pallium in 731, appointing him archbishop and metropolitan of all Germany beyond the Rhine, with authority to found new bishoprics. A few years later Boniface made his third trip to Rome to confer about the churches he had founded, and at this time he was appointed apostolic legate. Stopping at Monte Cassino, he enlisted more missionaries. In his capacity as legate he traveled into Bavaria to organize the Church there into the four bishoprics of Regensburg, Freising, Salzburg, and Passau. From Bavaria he returned to his own field and founded new bishoprics at Erfurt for Thuringia, Buraburg for Hesse, Wurzburg for Franconia, and Eichstadt for the Nordgau. An English monk was placed at the head of each new diocese. In 741 the great Benedictine abbey at Fulda was founded in Prussia to serve as the fountainhead of German monastic culture. Its first abbot was Boniface's young Bavarian disciple, Sturm or Sturmio. In the early

Middle Ages Fulda produced a host of scholars and teachers, and became known as the Monte Cassino of Germany.

While the evangelization of Germany was proceeding steadily, the Church in Gaul, under the Merovingian kings, was disintegrating. High ecclesiastical offices were either kept vacant, sold to the highest bidder, or bestowed on unworthy favorites. Pluralism, the holding by one man of many offices, each of which should demand his full time, was common. The great mass of the clergy was ignorant and undisciplined. No synod or church council had been held for eighty-four years. Charles Martel had been conquering and consolidating the regions of western Europe, and now regarded himself as an ally of the papacy and the chief champion of the Church, yet he had persistently plundered it to obtain funds for his wars and did nothing to help the work of reform. His death, however, in 741, and the accession of his sons, Carloman and Pepin the Short, provided an opportunity which Boniface quickly seized. Carloman, the elder, was very devout and held Boniface in great veneration; Boniface had no trouble in persuading him to call a synod to deal with errors and abuses in the Church in Austrasia, Alemannia, and Thuringia.

The first assembly was followed by several others. Boniface presided over them all, and was able to carry through many important reforms. The vacant bishoprics and parishes were filled, discipline reestablished, and fresh vigor infused into the Frankish Church. A heretic who had been creating much disturbance, one Adalbert of Neustria, was condemned by the synod of Soissons in 744. In 747 another general council of the Frankish clergy drew up a profession of faith and fidelity which was sent to Rome and laid upon the altar in the crypt of St. Peter's. After five years' labor Boniface had succeeded in restoring the Church of Gaul to its former greatness.

Now Boniface desired that Britain too should share in this reform movement. At his request and that of Pope Zacharias, the archbishop of Canterbury held a council at Clovesho, in 747, which adopted many of the resolutions passed in Gaul. This was also the year when Boniface was given a metropolitan see. Cologne was at first proposed as his cathedral city, but Mainz was finally chosen. Even when Cologne and other cities became archiepiscopal sees, Mainz retained the primacy. The Pope also made Boniface primate of Germany as well as apostolic legate for both Germany and Gaul.

Carloman now retired to a monastery, but his successor, Pepin, who brought all Gaul under his control, gave Boniface his support. "Without the patronage of the Frankish chiefs," Boniface wrote in a letter to England, "I cannot govern the people or exercise discipline over the clergy and monks, or check the practice of paganism." As apostolic legate, Boniface crowned Pepin at Soissons in 751, thus giving papal sanction to the assumption of royal power by the father of Charlemagne. Boniface, beginning to feel the weight of his years, made Lullus his coadjutor. Yet even now, when he was past seventy, his missionary zeal burned ardently. He wished to spend his last years laboring among those first converts in Friesland, who, since Willibrord's death, were relapsing once more into paganism. Leaving all things in order for Lullus, who was to become his successor, he embarked with some fifty companions and sailed down the Rhine. At Utrecht the party was joined by Eoban, bishop of that diocese. They set to work reclaiming the relapsed Christians, and during the following months made fruitful contact with the hitherto untouched tribes to the northeast. Boniface arranged to hold a great confirmation service on Whitsun Eve on the plain of Dokkum, near the banks of the little river Borne.

While awaiting the arrival of the converts, Boniface was quietly reading in his tent. Suddenly a band of armed pagans appeared in the center of the encampment. His companions would have tried to defend their leader, but Boniface would not allow them to do so. Even as he was telling them to trust in God and welcome the prospect of dying for Him, the Germans attacked. Boniface was one of the first to fall; his companions shared his fate. The pagans, expecting to carry away rich booty, were disgusted when they found, besides provisions, only a box of holy relics and a few books.

SAINT AGNES   Dolci

Carlo Dolci (1616-1686) is best known for the perfection of finish in his work.
The painstaking attention which he gave to his painting overcame the somewhat mediocre talent with which he was endowed.

Saint Agnes is usually represented by a lamb—sometimes
lying on a book—the symbol of meekness and purity. It is
especially attributed to this saint as a kind of pun on her
name, the Latin word for lamb being "agnus."

SAINT BLAISE   XVth Century Wood Block

This most interesting representation of one of the Fourteen Holy Helpers is

taken from a sheet representing all fourteen printed in the
fifteenth century. It was apparently intended for the use of
pilgrims; the individual pictures were probably cut apart to
form one of the earliest instances of holy cards.

Saint Blaise carries a lighted taper, emblematic of the candles
brought to dispel the gloom of his cell. Often a pig, or a pig's
head, identifies him.

They did not bother to carry away these objects, which were later collected by the Christians who came to avenge the martyrs and rescue their remains. The body of Boniface was carried to Fulda for burial, and there it still rests. The book the bishop was reading and which he is said to have lifted above his head to save it when the blow fell is also one of Fulda's treasures.

Boniface has been called the pro-consul of the papacy. His administrative and organizing genius left its mark on the German Church throughout the Middle Ages. Though Boniface was primarily a man of action, his literary remains are extensive. Especially interesting and important from the point of view of Church dogma and history are his letters. Among the emblems of Boniface are an oak, an axe, a sword, a book.

Letter XXVI

*T*o his most reverend and beloved sister, the abbess Ead-burga,[1] Boniface, humble servant of the servants of God, sends heartfelt greetings of love in Christ.

I pray Almighty God, the rewarder of all good works, that he repay you in the heavenly mansions and eternal tabernacles and choir of the blessed angels for all the kindnesses you have shown me, the solace of the books and the comfort of the garments with which you have relieved my distress. And now I ask you to do still more for me and write out in gold the Epistles of my lord, St. Peter the Apostle, that I may visibly impress honor and reverence for the sacred Scriptures on the carnal minds to whom I preach. I should like to have with me always the words of him who is my guide on this road. I am sending materials for your writing by the priest Eoban.

Do then, dearest sister, with this petition of mine as you have always done with all my requests, that here also your works may shine in letters of gold to the glory of our heavenly Father. I pray for your well-being in Christ, and may you go on to still greater heights of holy virtue.

[1] Eadburga was abbess of a convent on the island of Thanet.

Letter LXXV

To his friend in the embrace of loving arms, his brother in the bonds of spiritual brotherhood, Archbishop Egbert [2] clothed with the garment of supreme prelacy, abundant greeting of unfailing love in Christ from Boniface, humble bishop, legate in Germany of the Roman Catholic and Apostolic Church.

We have received with joyful and grateful heart the gifts and books you sent us. . . . Meantime we greatly need your advice and counsel. When I find a priest who long since fell into carnal sin and after doing penance was restored to his office by the Franks, and now dwells in a large district with no other priests and is administering baptism and celebrating Mass for a population who are believers but are prone to error—if now I withdraw him, according to the most approved canons, then, because of the scarcity of priests, infants will die without the sacred water of birth, unless I have some better man to replace him. Judge therefore between me and the erring people, whether it is better, or at least the lesser evil, that such a man should perform the service of the sacred altar or that the mass of the people should die as pagans because they have no way of securing a better minister.

Or when in the multitude of priests, I find one who has fallen into that same sin and with penitence has been reinstated in his former rank, so that the whole body of priests and people have confidence in his good character, if I should now degrade him, his secret sin would be revealed, the mass of the people would be shocked, many souls would be lost through the scandal and there would be great hatred of priests and distrust of the ministers of the Church, so that all would be despised as faithless and unbelieving. Therefore we have boldly ventured to bear with this man and allow him to remain in the sacred ministry, thinking the danger from one man's offense would be less evil than the perdition of the souls of almost the entire people. On this whole subject I earnestly desire your holy advice in writing.

(Emerton, *Letters of St. Boniface,* Records of Civilization, 1940.)

[2] Egbert was archbishop of York.

Saint Stephen

Confessor, King of Hungary

1 0 3 8

(*September 2*)

Coming from the east under a chief called Arpad, a fierce, marauding people called Magyars invaded and conquered the central part of the Danube valley during the last years of the ninth century. King Stephen was of this race. The Magyars first learned of Christianity on sporadic raids into north Italy and France. In the middle of the ninth century the Thessalonian priests, SS. Cyril and Methodius, had planted the faith in Pannonia, to the south, and had translated the Bible into the native tongue. It was not for a hundred years, however, that the Magyars gave serious attention to the Church. This was in the time of Geza, the third duke after Arpad. He was shrewd enough to see the practical desirability of Christianity as a protection against the inroads of his Christian neighbors on either side. He had the choice of turning to the Eastern Church at Constantinople or to the Church of Rome. Although Rome was more distant, he chose the Western Church, in fear that if he accepted Christianity from the east his domain would be incorporated in the recently revived Eastern Empire, the boundaries of which extended to the Danube.

Geza's first wife was Sarolta, one of the few Magyar women who was truly Christian. Of this union was born, about the year 975, a son named Vaik, the future king and saint. His mother took great care of his early training, and he had excellent Italian and Czech tutors. Geza married as his second wife a Christian princess, Adelaide, sister of the duke of Poland; at her behest, Adalbert, archbishop of Prague, came on a preaching mission to Hungary. Geza and his young son were baptized in 986, Vaik being given the name of the first martyr, Stephen; a number of the Hungarian nobles were baptized at the same time. For most of them it was a conversion of expediency, and their Christianity was, at the outset, merely nominal. The young prince, on the contrary, became a Christian in a true sense, and his mature life was spent spreading the faith and trying to live according to its disciplines and tenets.

At the age of twenty Stephen married Gisela, sister of the duke of Bavaria, the future Emperor Henry II. Since Hungary was then at peace with its neighbors, Stephen devoted himself to rooting out idolatry among his people. In the guise of a missionary, he often accompanied the Christian preachers; sometimes he had to check their tendency to impose the faith forcibly. There had recently been a migration of German Christian knights into the rich and fertile plains of Hungary. These newcomers took up land and they also labored to make converts of the peasantry. Many Magyars not unnaturally resented this infiltration, which they thought jeopardized their territorial rights and their ancient pagan customs. They rose in revolt under the leadership of Koppany, a man of great valor. Stephen met the insurgents himself, having prepared for battle by fasting, almsdeeds, and prayer, and invoking the aid of St. Martin of Tours, whom he had chosen as his patron. The historic meeting took place at Veszprem in 998, and though Stephen's forces were inferior in size to those of the rebels, with the help of the German knights he won a famous victory. Koppany was slain.

To give God the glory for his success, Stephen built near the site of the battle a monastery dedicated to St. Martin, called the Holy Hill, and bestowed on it extensive lands, as well as one third of the spoils of victory. Known since that time as the archabbey of Martinsberg, or Pannonhalma, it flourished down to modern times. It is the mother house of all Benedictine congregations in Hungary. Stephen now followed up his plans by inviting priests and monks to come from Germany, France, and Italy. They continued the work of taming the savage nation by teaching it the Gospel; they built churches and monasteries to serve as centers of religion, industry, and education. Some of them died as martyrs.

Hungary was still without ecclesiastical organization, and Stephen now founded the archbishopric of Gran, with five dioceses under it, and later the archbishopric of Kalocsa, with three dioceses. He then sent Abbot Astricius to Rome to obtain from Pope Sylvester II the confirmation of these foundations as well as of other things he had done for the honor of God and the exaltation of His Church. At the same time he begged the Pope to confer on him the title of king, that he might have more authority to accomplish his designs for promoting God's glory and the good of the people. It happened that Boleslaus, duke of Poland, at this same time had sent an embassy to Rome to get the title of king confirmed to him by papal ordinance. Pope Sylvester, persuaded to grant the request, had prepared a royal crown to send him with his blessing. But the special zeal, piety, and wisdom of Stephen of Hungary seemed to deserve priority. The Pope too may have been moved by political considerations, since the powerful German Emperor Otto II was at that moment in Rome. At any rate, he delivered this famous crown [1] to Stephen's ambassador, Astricius, and at the same time by a bull confirmed all the religious foundations Stephen had erected and the ordination of the Hungarian bishops. On his envoy's return, Stephen went out to meet him, and listened with reverence to the reading of the Pope's bull, bowing as often as the Pope's name was mentioned. It was this same Abbot Astricius who anointed and crowned him king with solemnity and pomp at Gran, in the year 1001.

To plant Christianity firmly in his kingdom and provide for its continued growth after his death, King Stephen filled Hungary

---

[1] The upper part of this crown, decorated with jewels and enameled figures of Christ and the Apostles, was later fitted on to the lower part of a crown given to King Geza I by the Eastern Emperor Michael VII, to form what is known as the Holy Crown of Hungary. It was recovered from the Nazis after World War II and placed in the custody of the United States Government.

with religious foundations. At Stuhlweissenburg he built a stately church in honor of the Mother of God, in which the kings of Hungary were afterwards crowned and buried. In Buda he founded the monastery of SS. Peter and Paul, and in Rome, Ravenna, and Constantinople hospices for pilgrims. He filled Martinsberg with Benedictines, who, as we have seen, were notable for practical works, and founded four other monasteries of the order, as well as convents for nuns. At Veszprem there was a convent for nuns of the Byzantine rite. One effect of the conversion of Hungary was that the road used by pilgrims and crusaders going to the Holy Land was made safer, since the valley of the Danube formed a natural highway for at least a part of the long, difficult journey. To support churches and pastors and to relieve the poor, Stephen started the collection of tithes, and every tenth town was required to maintain a church and support a priest. Stephen himself built the churches and the bishops appointed the priests. He passed edicts for the severe punishment of blasphemy, murder, theft, and adultery. He commanded his subjects to marry, with the exception of monks, nuns, and clergy; he forbade marriages between Christians and pagans. Easy of access to persons of all ranks, Stephen was always ready to listen to the complaints of the poor, knowing that in helping them he honored Christ. Widows and orphans he took under his special protection.

This democratic King would often go about in disguise in order to find out the needs of humble persons whom his officials might overlook. Once, while dealing out alms thus, a rough band of beggars crowded around him, pulled at his beard and hair, knocked him down, and snatched away his purse. The King took this indignity in good humor, without making known who he was. When his nobles heard of the incident, they insisted that he should not again expose himself to such danger. Yet he renewed his vow never to refuse an alms to anyone who begged of him.

The code of laws which King Stephen put into effect was well suited to control a hot-tempered people, newly converted to Christianity; but it was not at all pleasing to those who still opposed the new religion, and the wars which Stephen now undertook were religious as well as political. Stephen undertook the political reorganization of Hungary. He abolished the old tribal divisions and partitioned the land into counties, under a system of governors and magistrates, similar to that of the Western Empire. He also developed a kind of feudalism, turning the independent nobles into vassals of the crown, thus welding them into a political unity. He retained direct control over the common people. In 1025 there was a revolt led by a noble called Ajton, who was moving to transfer his allegiance to the Eastern emperor. Stephen mobilized his forces at Kalocsa and gained an overwhelming victory. After he had repulsed an invasion of Bulgarians, some of the Bulgarians returned, hoping to settle peaceably in Hungary. They were set upon by vengeful Magyars. Stephen straightway had a number of the Magyars hanged along the frontier, as a warning that well-intentioned strangers must not be molested. When Stephen's saintly brother-in-law, Emperor Henry II, died, he was succeeded by his cousin, Conrad II. Fearing Stephen's growing power, Conrad marched against him. A parley was arranged, and Conrad retired. This settlement, according to Stephen's subjects, showed the peace-loving disposition of their king.

The death of Stephen's son Emeric left him without a direct heir, and the last years of the king's life were embittered by family disputes and dark intrigues over the succession. Of the four or five claimants, the successful one was Peter, son of Stephen's sister, a ruthless woman who stopped at nothing to gain her end. Two of Stephen's cousins were no better and even conspired to have him killed. A hired assassin entered his bedroom one night, but the King awakened and calmly called out, "If God be for me, who shall be against me?" The King pardoned the assassin and his cousins as well. It is not surprising that "a time of troubles" followed the death of this great statesman and king; it lasted until the reign of St. Ladislas, some forty years later.

Stephen died on the feast of the Assumption, 1038. His tomb at Stuhlweissenburg became the scene of miracles, and forty-five years after his death Pope Gregory VII, at the request of Ladislas, ordered his relics enshrined and placed in the rich chapel which bears his name in the church of Our Lady at Buda. King Stephen was canonized in 1083. In 1696 Pope Innocent XI appointed his festival for September 2, the day on which Emperor Leopold won Buda back from the Turks. In Hungary his feast is still kept on August 20, the day of the translation of his relics. This saint merits the highest veneration for his accomplishments in both secular and religious matters, and, most especially, for having been an exemplar of justice, mercy, charity, and peace in a cruel age.

Saint Anselm of Canterbury
Archbishop, Doctor of the Church
1 1 0 9
(April 21)

I f William the Conqueror in 1066 [1] deprived the English nation of its liberty and of many of its possessions, he was responsible also for bringing into England from various parts of Europe eminent men who were to serve the country well as leaders in church and state. Among the great churchmen were the two archbishops of Canterbury, Lanfranc [2] and his successor, St. Anselm. The latter was born about the year 1033 of noble parents at Aosta, in northern Italy. Under the influence of a pious mother, at fifteen Anselm asked to be admitted to a monastery, but the abbot, fearing the father's displeasure, refused to accept him. Thus thwarted, the young man for a time lost his interest in religion and lived the usual carefree life of a young nobleman. There was never any sympathy between him and his stern father, whose harshness was mainly the cause of his leaving home after his mother's death. He studied for a time in Burgundy, then went on to the school of Bec in Normandy, which was under the direction of the renowned Lanfranc.

On his father's death Anselm consulted his superior as to whether he should return to Italy and manage the estates he had inherited,

1 William the Conqueror had the sanction of Pope Alexander II for his invasion of England, as a crusade against schism and corruption.
2 Lanfranc, one of the greatest churchmen of the Middle Ages, was an Italian, like Anselm. After serving as abbot at Bec and Caen in Normandy, he became archbishop of Canterbury and rose to a position of great power in both political and ecclesiastical affairs.

or remain in France and enter the Church. Lanfranc, fearing to influence unduly his young disciple and friend, referred him to Maurillus, archbishop of Rouen, and on his advice Anselm, then twenty-seven, became a monk. Three years later, when Lanfranc was appointed abbot of St. Stephen's at nearby Caen, Anselm succeeded him as prior at Bec. There was some criticism of this rapid promotion, but he soon won the allegiance of the other monks, including that of his bitterest rival. This was an undisciplined young man named Osbern, whom Anselm gradually persuaded to lead a more serious life and whom he nursed tenderly in his last illness.

Always an independent thinker, Anselm also became the most learned theologian of his generation, and as a metaphysician and a mystic surpassed all Latin Christian writers since St. Augustine. Not content with collecting and rewording the books of earlier Church Fathers, he pursued an independent line of reasoning. His predecessors for the most part had assumed without argument the fundamental principle that the God whom they loved and worshiped had real existence. Although Anselm never doubted, he nevertheless wished to satisfy his mind by rational proof that what he already believed was true. "I do not seek to understand in order that I may believe, but I believe in order to understand." While prior at Bec, he wrote his *Monologium*, in which he restated all such logical arguments as he could find in earlier writings to prove that God *is*. Then, still unsatisfied, he devised an original proof of his own, and explained it in his *Proslogium*. To some of his successors it was convincing, to others not, but these and other of his works gave a great stimulus to fresh, logical thinking and arguing in the theological schools of the period, the movement known as medieval scholasticism.

With regard to the education of the young, Anselm held very liberal views. To an abbot who was lamenting the poor success of his efforts, he said: "If you planted a tree in your garden, and bound it down on all sides, so that it could not spread out its branches, what kind of a tree would it prove when in after years you gave it room to spread? Would it not be useless, with its boughs all twisted and tangled? . . . But that is how you treat your boys . . . cramping them with fears and blows and debarring them from the enjoyment of any freedom."

In 1078, after serving as prior for fifteen years, Anselm was chosen abbot of Bec. The office entailed visits to England, where the abbey owned a great deal of property and where his old teacher Lanfranc, now archbishop of Canterbury, was upholding the rights of the Church against the successful and arrogant King William I. Anselm was received in England with honor, even by the King himself. The English monk Eadmer, Anselm's biographer, writes that he had a winning way of giving instruction, pointed with homely illustrations which even the simplest could understand.

Anselm accepted an invitation to go to England in 1092 to advise Hugh, Earl of Chester, about a monastery he proposed building. He had hesitated to go, for there was a rumor that he himself was to succeed Lanfranc, who had died three years before. The business affairs of Bec and of the proposed new monastery detained him in England for five months. Meanwhile the see of Canterbury was being kept vacant by King William Rufus. It was his custom to refuse to nominate or to give permission to elect new bishops, in order to retain the episcopal revenues for himself. In reply to requests for a nomination to Canterbury, he swore that neither Anselm nor anyone else should be archbishop there so long as he lived. A violent illness which brought him to death's door frightened Rufus into changing his mind. When he recovered, he nominated Anselm archbishop of Canterbury, issued a proclamation against various abuses, and promised that in future he would govern according to law.

Anselm was reluctant to accept the honor, pleading ill-health, age, and unfitness for the management of affairs. The bishops declared that if he declined, all that was wrong in Church and State might not unfairly be laid to his account. In William's presence they forced the pastoral staff into his unwilling hands, and then bore him away to the church, where they sang a solemn *Te Deum*. Even then he refused to undertake the charge, unless in a dispute then current over the papacy William would acknowledge Urban II as legitimate Pope and would promise to return to the see of Canterbury all the lands which had been taken from it since the days of Lanfranc. Matters were at length adjusted, and Anselm was consecrated at Canterbury on December 4, 1093.

But the heart of William Rufus had not really changed. Soon after the new archbishop had been installed, the king, plotting to wrest the duchy of Normandy from his brother Robert, began making demands on his subjects for money and supplies. Not content with Anselm's offer of five hundred marks, a large sum in those days, William, at the instigation of some of his courtiers, called for a thousand, as the price of the nomination to the see. Naturally Anselm refused absolutely to yield to such an extortionate demand. Instead, he urged the King to fill vacant offices in the abbeys and to sanction the convening of church synods to correct flagrant abuses among the clergy and laity. The king replied angrily that his abbeys were no more to be wrenched away from him than his crown, and from then on he worked to deprive Anselm of his see.

He succeeded in detaching from obedience to Canterbury a number of time-serving bishops, but when he bade his lay barons condemn their archbishop's behavior, he was met with a flat refusal. The unscrupulous king even tried to inveigle Pope Urban II into deposing Anselm by a promise of annual tribute. The legate from Rome who came charged to tell William that his request could not be granted brought the pallium for Anselm, which made his position unassailable. Convinced, however, that the king was resolved to oppress the Church unless the clergy would surrender its treasures, Anselm asked permission to leave the country to consult the Holy See. Twice refused, he was finally told that he might go if he liked, but that if he did his revenues would be confiscated and he would never be allowed to return.

Nevertheless, Anselm, now about sixty-three years old, set out from Canterbury on the long, hard trip to Rome in October, 1097. He was dressed as a pilgrim, and was accompanied by Eadmer and another monk. At Rome the Pope not only assured him of his protection but wrote to King William to demand that he reinstate Anselm in all his rights and possessions. Meanwhile Anselm had found a quiet retreat in a sunny Calabrian monastery, and there he remained to complete his book, *Cur Deus Homo*, or *Why God Became Man*, in which he explains the wisdom, justice, and necessity of the Incarnation. Despairing of doing any good at Canterbury and convinced that he could serve God better in a private capacity, he now asked the Pope to relieve him of his office. The Pope refused, but as it was obviously impossible at the moment for him to return to England, he allowed Anselm to remain in southern Italy.

A council had been summoned to meet at Bari in 1098, for the purpose of bringing about a reconciliation between the Greek and Roman Churches. Urban invited Anselm to attend this gathering. The Greeks, as expected, raised the question of the Procession of the Holy Ghost,[3] and there followed a protracted discussion that was bitter on both sides. Suddenly the Pope cried out, "Anselm, our father and master, where are you?" Anselm went to the Pope's side at once, and the next day he delivered a convincing discourse which put an end to the dispute. The council then proceeded to denounce the king for simony, for the persecution of Anselm, oppression of the Church, and personal depravity. An anathema was prevented only by the entreaties of Anselm, who persuaded the Pope to confine himself to a threat of excommunication to be made against William at an impending synod at Rome, unless he

---

[3] In several creeds of the late fourth century, following the mention of the Third Person of the Trinity, there was inserted the explanatory clause, "who proceedeth from the Father." This addition was accepted by both Greek and Latin Churches, but later the Latin Church added to this clause the words "and the Son," which the Greeks denounced as an innovation and refused to accept. The doctrine in dispute was known as the Procession of the Holy Ghost.

first made satisfaction. The execution of the sentence of excommunication was postponed.

Back in France, Anselm stayed for a time in Lyons, writing his
treatise *On Original Sin*. At the death of William Rufus he returned
to England, to be welcomed by the new king, Henry I, and the
people. But difficulties arose when Henry desired that Anselm
should receive a fresh investiture from him and perform the customary act of homage for his see. Since the recent synod had
forbidden lay investiture to cathedral posts and abbeys, Anselm
would not comply. This matter was therefore referred to the Pope.

In the meanwhile England was stirred by rumors that Duke
Robert of Normandy was about to invade the island, to contest
his younger brother's claim to the crown. Many of the barons, who
had sworn allegiance to Henry, now joined Robert when he landed
with an army at Portsmouth. Eager to obtain the support of the
Church, Henry made lavish promises, while Anselm on his side did
his utmost to prevent an English rebellion. Not content to supply
his own required quota of armed men for Henry's forces, he denounced the barons for their treachery, and finally launched an
excommunication against Robert as an invader, thus compelling
him to come to terms with the king and leave England. Henry owed
this victory in no small part to Anselm, yet when the danger was
past he renewed his claim to the right of nominating and in-
vesting English bishops. Anselm steadily refused to consecrate
bishops nominated by the king unless they were canonically
elected; the divergence between them grew ever wider. Anselm set
out once more to lay these questions before the Pope, while the
king sent a deputy to present his own case. Pope Paschal II confirmed his predecessor's rulings; at this the king sent word to
Anselm forbidding his return as long as he continued recalcitrant,
and informing him of the confiscation of his revenues. After a
rumor reached the king that he was about to be excommunicated,
there was some kind of reconciliation in Normandy, at which
Henry restored to Anselm the revenues of his see. Later, in England, at a royal council of clergy and barons in 1107, the king for-

mally renounced the right of investiture to bishoprics and abbeys, while Anselm, with the Pope's approval, agreed that no man should be debarred from consecration for having done homage to the king, and that English bishops should be free to do homage for their temporal possessions. Henry kept this pact, and now came to regard the archbishop so highly that in the following year he appointed Anselm regent during his own absence in France.

Anselm's health had long been failing. He died the next year, 1109, on Wednesday of Holy Week, among his monks at Canterbury. His body, it is said, still lies in the Cathedral church there, in the chapel now known as St. Anselm's, on the southwest side of the high altar. Throughout his life he displayed a sympathy and sincerity which won the affection of persons of all classes. He was among the first to take a public stand against the slave trade: in 1102, at a church council in St. Peter's church, Westminster, he obtained the passage of a resolution against the practice of selling men like cattle. In Dante's *Divine Comedy,* this noble churchman appears as one of the spirits of light and power in the lofty sphere of the Sun. For his scholarship and vision Anselm has been declared a Doctor of the Church.

Proslogium

Come now, little man! flee for a while from your tasks, hide yourself for a little space from the turmoil of your thoughts. Come, cast aside your burdensome cares, and put away your laborious pursuits. For a little while give your time to God, and rest in Him for a little. Enter the inner chamber of your mind, shut out all things save God and whatever may aid you in seeking God; and having barred the door of your chamber, seek Him. Speak now, O my heart, O my whole heart, speak now and say to your God: My face hath sought Thee: Thy face, O Lord, will I seek. . . .

Be it mine to look up to Thy light, even from afar, even from the depths. Teach me to seek Thee and reveal Thyself to me when I seek Thee, for I cannot seek Thee except Thou teach me, nor find

Thee, except Thou reveal Thyself. Let me seek Thee in longing, let me long for Thee in seeking; let me find Thee in love and love Thee in finding. Lord I acknowledge and thank Thee that Thou hast created me in this Thine image, in order that I may be mindful of Thee, conceive of Thee and love Thee. But that image has been so consumed and wasted away by vices, and obscured by the smoke of wrongdoing that it cannot achieve that for which it was created except Thou renew it and create it anew.

I do not endeavor, Lord, to penetrate Thy heights, for in no wise do I compare my understanding with Thine; but I long to understand in some degree Thy truth which my heart believes and loves. For I do not seek to understand in order that I may believe, but I believe in order to understand. For this also I believe—that unless I believe I shall not understand.

II. And so, Lord, do Thou, who dost give understanding to faith, give me, so far as Thou knowest it to be profitable, to understand that Thou art as we believe, and that Thou art what we believe. And we believe that Thou art a being than whom nothing greater can be conceived. Or is there no such being, since the fool hath said in his heart, there is no God? (Psalms xiii,1.) But at least this same fool, when he hears of this being of whom I speak—a being than whom nothing greater can be conceived—understands what he hears and what he understands is in his understanding, although he does not understand it to exist.

For it is one thing to conceive an object as in the understanding, and another to understand that the object exists. When a painter first conceives what he will afterwards paint he has it in his understanding but does not yet understand it to exist, because he has not yet painted it. But after he has finished the picture, he both has it in his understanding and understands that it exists, because he has painted it.

Hence even the fool knows that something exists in the understanding, at least, than which nothing greater can be conceived. For when he hears of it, he understands it, and whatever is understood exists in the understanding. But assuredly that than which nothing greater can be conceived cannot exist in the understanding alone. For suppose it exists in the understanding alone, then it can be conceived to exist in reality, which is greater. . . .

SAINT NICHOLAS BESTOWING A DOWRY   David

Gerard David (c. 1450-1523) was the last great master of the Bruges school
of painting in the Netherlands. His fame was built on several great altarpieces
which are remarkable for their coloring, and for the realism
of the human figures.

The beloved legend of Saint Nicholas of Myra is illustrated
in this picture of the saint reaching through the window to
bestow a bag of gold on the three sleeping daughters of an
impoverished noble man. The three golden balls, representing
three bags of gold, are his most frequent symbol.

THE MEETING OF SAINT ANTHONY AND SAINT PAUL   Sassetta

Stephano di Giovanni Sassetta (1392-1450) was a noted painter of Siena. This

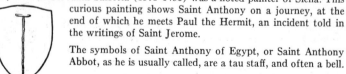

curious painting shows Saint Anthony on a journey, at the end of which he meets Paul the Hermit, an incident told in the writings of Saint Jerome.

The symbols of Saint Anthony of Egypt, or Saint Anthony Abbot, as he is usually called, are a tau staff, and often a bell.

III. And assuredly it exists so truly that it cannot be conceived not to exist. For it is possible to conceive of a being which cannot be conceived as non-existing; and it is greater than one which can be conceived as non-existing. Hence if that than which nothing greater can be conceived can be conceived as non-existing, it is not that than which nothing greater can be conceived. But this is an irreconcilable contradiction. There is then so truly a being than which nothing greater can be conceived to exist that it cannot even be conceived as non-existent. And this being Thou art, O Lord.

So truly, therefore, dost Thou exist, O Lord my God, that Thou canst not be conceived as non-existent, and rightly. For if a mind could conceive of a being better than Thou, the creature would rise above its Creator, which is utterly absurd.

XVI. . . . O supreme and unapproachable light, O holy and blessed Trinity, how far Thou art from me who am so near to Thee! How far art Thou removed from my vision, although I am so near to Thine! Everywhere Thou art wholly present and I see Thee not. In Thee I move and in Thee I have my being and cannot come to Thee. Thou art within me and about me and I feel Thee not. . . .

XXIV. But now, my soul, arouse and lift up all Thy understanding and conceive so far as Thou canst what is the character and how great is that good. For if individual goods are delectable, conceive earnestly how delectable is that good which contains the pleasantness of all goods; not such as we have known in created objects but as different as the Creator from the creature. For if created life is good, how good is the creative life! If salvation given us is a joy, how joyful is the salvation which has given all salvation! If wisdom in knowledge of the created world is lovely, how lovely is the wisdom that created all things from nothing! Finally, if there are many great delights in delectable things, what and how great is the delight in Him who made these delectable things! . . .

XXVI. . . . I long, O God, to know Thee, to love Thee, that I may rejoice in Thee. And if I cannot attain to full joy in this life, may I at least advance from day to day until that joy shall come to me in full. . . .

(*Proslogium, Monologium,* trans. by S.N. Deane. 1910.)

Saint Bernard of Clairvaux

Abbot, Doctor of the Church

1 1 5 3

(*August 20*)

Bernard, son of Tescelin Sorrel, and Aleth, daughter of the lord of Montbard, was born in the family castle of Fontaines, near Dijon, in Burgundy. His pious French mother offered all her seven children—six sons and one daughter—to God at birth and devoted herself to their upbringing. According to the standards of that day, they were very well educated, the sons learning Latin and verse-making even before being trained in the profession of arms. Bernard was sent to Chatillon-on-the-Seine, to study in a college of secular canons. At school he gave evidence of a strong intellect as well as of a genuinely religious nature. During this period the death of his mother, to whom he was deeply attached, threw him into a state of prolonged and acute depression.

When Bernard finished his schooling at nineteen or thereabouts, he had, in addition to the advantages of noble birth and natural talent, the sweetness of temper, wit, and personal charm that make for popularity. Subject to strong temptations of the flesh, he often considered giving up the world, and even forsaking the study of literature, which was one of his greatest pleasures. He felt attracted to the Benedictine monastery at Cîteaux,[1] founded fifteen years

[1] Cîteaux or Cistertium was some sixteen miles from Dijon. Cistercians have subsequently been divided into two Observances, the Common and the Strict. The latter, popularly known as the Trappists, requires perpetual silence, except in cases of necessity, and abstinence from flesh, fish, and eggs, except in illness. Both Observances are rigidly cloistered and engage in manual labor, chiefly agricultural.

before by Robert of Molesme, Alberic, and Stephen Harding. One day Bernard knelt in prayer in a wayside church, to ask God's guidance as to his future. On arising all doubt had vanished and he was resolved to follow the strict Cistercian way of life. His uncle, Gaudry, a valiant fighting man, and Bernard's younger brothers, Bartholomew and Andrew, declared they would accompany him, and an appeal was made to their eldest brother, Guy. He, however, had a wife and two children; but when his wife soon after entered a convent, he also joined them. Gerard, another brother, was a soldier, engrossed in his calling; still, after being wounded and taken prisoner, he also heard God's call, and on his release followed the others. Hugh of Macon was also won over, and others who had previously given no thought to the religious life. Such was Bernard's eloquence that within a few weeks he had succeeded in persuading thirty-one Burgundian nobles to go with him to Cîteaux. Bernard and his brothers gathered to bid their father farewell and ask his blessing. Only one son was left behind, Nivard, the youngest, and as the party rode away, Guy called to him, "Farewell, little Nivard! You will have all our lands and estates for yourself." "Oh," answered the boy, "then you are taking Heaven and leaving me only the earth! The division is too unequal!" Such was the pervasive spiritual atmosphere of this age of faith.

When they at length arrived at Cîteaux near Easter, 1112, there had been no new novices for several years, and Stephen Harding, the abbot, received them with open arms. Bernard, now twenty-two, wished to live hidden and forgotten, concerned only with God. From the start, he trained himself to obey the command he later gave to all postulants, "If you desire to live in this house, leave your body behind; only spirits can enter here." At the end of a year, he and his companions—all save one—made their profession and continued their cloistered life. When Bernard was unable to reap the grain as fast as the others, he was assigned to lighter work, but he prayed God to give him strength to use a scythe properly, and soon did as well as the best. He used to say, "Our fathers built their monasteries in damp, unwholesome places, so that monks might have the uncertainty of life more sharply before their eyes." The Cistercians had in fact chosen swampy, unproductive lands, but their diligence was rapidly transforming them into fertile fields, gardens, and pastures. In 1113 Stephen founded the monastery of La Ferté, and in 1114 that of Pontigny. The Count of Troyes offered a site on his great estates for a third new monastery. Stephen, aware of Bernard's exceptional abilities, appointed him abbot, and ordered him to take twelve monks, including his own brothers, and found a house in the diocese of Langres, in Champagne. They settled in the Valley of Wormwood, which had once been a retreat for robbers. Here they cleared a piece of land, and, with the help of the people round about, built themselves a plain dwelling.

The land was poor and the monks lived through a period of extreme hardship. Their bread was of the coarsest barley; wild herbs or boiled beech leaves sometimes served as vegetables. Also, Bernard was at first so severe in his discipline that the monks, though obedient, began to be discouraged. Their apathy made him realize his fault, and as a penalty he condemned himself to a long silence. At length he was bidden by a vision to start preaching again. He now took care that food should be more plentiful, though it was still coarse and simple. The fame of the house and its holy abbot soon spread through that part of France. The number of monks grew to one hundred and thirty. The monastery was given the name of Clairvaux.

Bernard, a prey to many anxieties, suffered from stomach trouble, but he never complained or took advantage of an indulgence for the sick. In 1118 he became so ill that his life was in danger. One of the powerful ecclesiastics of the time, William of Champeaux, bishop of Chalons, recognized in the ailing abbot a predestined leader. He obtained from the Cistercian chapter held in that year at Cîteaux the authority to govern him for twelve months as his superior. Knowing that Bernard required rest and quiet, he placed him in a little house outside the monastic enclosure at Clairvaux, with orders not to follow the rule and to free his mind from all concerns of the community. Bernard, after living on a special diet and under a physician's care for this period, returned to the monastery in improved health. His old father and young Nivard had by then followed him there, and received their habits at his hands.

The four first daughter houses of Cîteaux, namely, La Ferté, Pontigny, Clairvaux, and Morimond, founded in their turn other houses, Clairvaux having the most numerous offshoots. In 1121 Bernard performed his first miracle. While singing Mass he restored to Josbert de la Ferté, a relative of his who had been stricken dumb, the power of speech. The man was enabled to confess before he died, three days later, and to make retribution for many acts of injustice. There are also accounts of sick persons whom Bernard cured by making the sign of the cross over them, all attested to by truthful eyewitnesses. Another story has to do with the church at Foigny which was infested with pestilential flies; Bernard pronounced an excommunication upon them, at which all died. This occurrence gave rise to the old French saying, "the curse of the flies of Foigny."

Because of his continued poor health, the general chapter relieved Bernard of work in the fields and directed him to devote himself to preaching and writing. The change gave him an opportunity to produce a treatise on *Degrees of Humility and Pride,* which contains an excellent analysis of human character. In 1122, at the request of the archbishop of Paris, he went up and preached to the university students who were candidates for Holy Orders. Some of them were so deeply impressed by his preaching that they accompanied him back to Clairvaux. A band of German knights who stopped to visit at Clairvaux returned later to ask admission to the order. Their conversion was the more remarkable as their main interest in life up to that time had been wars and tournaments. Centuries later, in his *Art of Preaching,* Erasmus wrote, "Bernard is an eloquent preacher, much more by nature than by art; he is full of charm and vivacity, and knows how to reach and move the affections." Bernard was always willing to receive monks who came from other orders or to release any of his who wished to transfer to another religious institution in the hope of attaining greater perfection.

Notwithstanding his longing for a retired life, for years on end Bernard was traveling about Europe on missions connected with the Church. His reputation for learning and sanctity and his talent as a mediator became so famous that princes called on him to decide their disputes, bishops asked his opinion on problems involving their churches, and popes accepted his counsel. It was said that he governed the churches of the West from his isolated monastery at Cîteaux. Once he wrote that his life was "overrun everywhere by anxieties, suspicions, cares. There is scarcely an hour free from the crowd of discordant applicants, and the troubles and cares of their business. I have no power to stop their coming and cannot refuse to see them, and they do not leave me even time to pray."

The election of unworthy men to the episcopacy and to other Church offices troubled Bernard deeply, and he fought it with all his might. A monk, his enemies said, should stay in his cloister and not bother himself with such matters. A monk, he replied, was as much a soldier of Christ as other Christians were, and had a special duty to defend the honor of God's sanctuary. Bernard's outspoken censures had their effect in changing the way of life of several high churchmen. Henry, archbishop of Sens, and Stephen, bishop of Paris, renounced their attendance at court and their secular style of living. Abbot Suger of St. Denis,[2] who as regent of France lived for a time in great state, now gave up his worldly habits, resigned his secular posts, and busied himself reestablishing discipline in his own abbey. Bernard wrote to the dean of Languedoc: "You may imagine that what belongs to the Church belongs to you, while you

[2] Suger and his abbey are both famous in French history. The abbey was founded by Dagobert I on the spot where St. Denis, the Apostle of Paris, was interred, a few miles north of Paris. As the burial place of kings and princes, it became one of the most powerful abbeys in France. Suger was an able and trusted adviser of the King. He began the rebuilding of the abbey in the then new Gothic style.

officiate there. But you are mistaken; for though it is reasonable that one who serves the altar should live by the altar, yet it must not be to promote either his luxury or his pride. Whatever is taken beyond what is needed for bare nourishment and simple plain clothing is sacrilege and theft." Bernard also had a sharp exchange with Peter the Venerable, archabbot of Cluny, in which he criticized Peter's way of life and that of the Cluniacs.[3]

Bernard was obliged to assist at many important synods. He also helped to found the celebrated order of the Knights Templars.[4] A serious schism followed the death of Pope Honorius II in 1130. Innocent II was chosen pope by a majority of the cardinals, but simultaneously a minority faction elected one of their number, Cardinal Peter de Leone, who took the name of Anacletus. An ambitious and worldly man, Anacletus succeeded in getting the strongholds of Rome into his hands, and Pope Innocent fled to Pisa. A council of bishops was held soon afterwards at Etampes. Bernard attended and as a result of his vigorous defense, Innocent

[3] Peter the Venerable of the monastery of Cluny was a reformer of the Cluniac Order, but his zeal did not halt its decline, which proceeded rapidly after his time. It had been founded in 910 at Cluny, in eastern France, and by Bernard's time had spread to all parts of Europe and the Holy Land. During the two and a half centuries when it flourished, its influence was potent, and the authority of its abbot stood next to that of the pope. It was organized on the principle that performance of the Divine Office should be well-nigh the sole occupation of its monks, and all services were carried out with impressive ritual and splendor.

[4] The Knights Templars, or Poor Knights of Christ and of the Temple of Solomon, was one of the three great military and religious orders founded in the twelfth century for the defense of the Christian kingdom of Jerusalem and the protection of pilgrims to the Holy Land. The others were the Teutonic Knights and the Hospitallers of St. John of Jerusalem, later called the Knights of Malta. The Templars were an order of warrior monks of the Rule of St. Benedict, much praised at the outset for disciplining and converting the rabble of "rogues and impious men, robbers and committers of sacrilege, perjurors and adulterers" who streamed eastward more for gain and adventure than for any religious purpose. Before Bernard's death the Templars were established in all parts of Latin Christendom and had grown fabulously rich.

was recognized by the council. The new Pope soon went to France, where he was splendidly received by King Louis VI. Bernard went with him to Chartres, and there he met King Henry of England, who was also persuaded to acknowledge Innocent; then the party continued on to Germany, and Bernard was present at Innocent's meeting with the Emperor Lothaire II, who offered recognition if he were given the right to invest new bishops. Bernard's remonstrances caused Lothaire to withdraw his condition, which, indeed, Innocent had already promptly rejected.

In 1131 Pope Innocent visited Clairvaux. He was received by a simple procession of monks. At table the food consisted of coarse bread, vegetables and herbs, with one small fish for the Pope, which the others, writes the chronicler, had to view from a distance. The following year Bernard accompanied the Pope back to Italy, reconciled him with several cities, and went on with him to Rome. Innocent then made him legate to Germany, and along the way north Bernard preached in the Pope's behalf and converted sinners. Having brought more harmony to the Church in Germany, Bernard returned to Italy to assist at the council of Pisa. There it was voted to excommunicate schismatics. Later he went to Milan and persuaded the people to become reconciled with both Innocent and the emperor. The citizens helped him to establish at nearby Chiaravalle the first Cistercian monastery in Italy. Returning to Clairvaux, he took with him a number of postulants for admission, among them a young canon of Pisa, Peter Bernard, later to become Pope Eugenius III. As his first task after arriving at the monastery, the future pontiff was asked to stoke the fire in the calefactory.[5]

A year before Bernard had been called into Aquitaine, where William, the duke of that province, was persecuting the adherents of Pope Innocent, and had expelled the bishops of Poitiers and

[5] The calefactory was a room with a fire in it for warming oneself in winter. The only other fires in most medieval monasteries were in the kitchen (generally out of bounds for the community), the infirmary, and, perhaps, the guest house. The cells, church, corridors, library, scriptorium, etc., were unheated.

Limoges. William was a prince of great wealth, gigantic stature, and exceptional ability, who from his youth on had been irreverent and aggressive. Bernard's prayers and persuasion having failed to prevail on William to restore the bishops, he used a more powerful weapon. He went to the church to say Mass, while the duke and other schismatics stood at the door, as under excommunication. The kiss of peace before the Communion had been given, when suddenly Bernard laid the wafer of the Host on the paten, turned, and holding it high advanced with it to the door, his eyes flashing and his countenance all on fire. "Hitherto," he said, "I have entreated and besought you, and you have despised me. Other servants of God have joined their prayers to mine, and you have not regarded them. Now the Son of the Virgin, the Lord and Head of that Church which you persecute, comes in person to see if you will repent. He is your judge, at whose name every knee bows, in Heaven, in Earth, and in Hell. Into His hands your obstinate soul will one day fall. Will you despise Him? Will you scorn Him as you have done His servants?" Unable to bear more, the terrified duke fell on his face. Bernard lifted him up, and bade him salute the bishop of Poitiers. The duke did as bidden, abandoned the schism, and restored the bishop to his see. William afterwards founded a new Cistercian monastery and went on pilgrimage to Compostella,[6] in the course of which he died.

Through Bernard's efforts other schisms were healed. The death of Anacletus in 1138 opened the way to peace, for though his adherents elected a successor, Bernard's preaching in Rome won them over to Innocent. After these valiant labors, Bernard returned to Clairvaux. He refused five bishoprics which were offered to him in order to concentrate on preaching to his own monks; his sermons on the Song of Songs became particularly famous.

---

[6] Compostella was the site of a famous pilgrimage church in the province of Galicia in northwestern Spain. According to legend, the Apostle James the Great preached the Gospel there and the church contained his bones. With Toledo it remained a stronghold of Christian faith when most of Spain was ruled by Mohammedans.

We now come to one of the famous controversies of medieval times. Bernard was recognized as the most eloquent and influential man of his age. Next to him in stature was the brilliant and unfortunate teacher, Peter Abelard,[7] who was a far greater scholar than Bernard. It was perhaps inevitable that the two should clash, for they represented opposite currents of thought. Bernard was a defender of traditional authority, of "faith not as an opinion but as a certitude"; Abelard spoke for the new rationalism, represented by Anselm, and for the free exercise of human reason. In 1121 Abelard's orthodoxy had been questioned, and a synod had condemned him to burn his book on the Trinity. Forced to keep away from Paris, where he enjoyed great popularity as a teacher, he had lived as a hermit for many years. He had returned to resume his lectures, and in 1139 William of St. Thierry, a Cistercian, denounced him as a heretic to the legate of the Holy See, and also to Bernard, saying they were the only men powerful enough to crush the error. Bernard had three private talks with Abelard, in which the latter promised to withdraw what was dangerous in his views, but he remained defiant. In 1141 at a council at Sens, Abelard was formally arraigned, charged with heresy on a number of counts. Bernard was at first unwilling to appear; but when Abelard's supporters claimed that he was afraid to meet the recalcitrant teacher face to face, he felt obliged to attend. Abelard listened to the charges drawn up by Bernard, and refused to make a defense, though told he might do so. He felt that the bishops were solidly massed against him, so with an appeal to the Pope he left the assemblage. The bishops then condemned as heretical seventeen propositions taken from Abelard's writings, sentenced him to silence, and wrote an account of the proceedings for Pope Innocent, who confirmed the sentence. Stopping off at the monastery of Cluny on his way to Rome, Abelard heard of the Pope's confirmation. By this time he was completely broken in health and spirit; his

---

[7] Of the many accounts of Abelard's life, Helen Waddell's novel, *Peter Abelard,* is one of the best for the clarity of its treatment of the theological controversies of the time.

death followed in April, 1142. Bernard has been severely criticized for his uncompromising attitude, but he felt that Abelard's brilliance made him extremely dangerous. He wrote to the Pope that Abelard was "trying to reduce to nothing the merits of Christian faith, since he seems himself able by human reason to comprehend God altogether."

One of Bernard's great friends was the Irish bishop, Malachy (Maelmhaedhoc l'Morgair), a zealous reformer of monasticism in his native isle. After retiring from the see of Armagh, Malachy came to Clairvaux, and died there some years later in Bernard's arms. He had brought a number of young men with him from Ireland to be trained under Bernard, and in 1142 the first Cistercian monastery was established in Ireland. In 1145 that same Peter Bernard of Pisa who had followed Bernard to Clairvaux in 1138 was elected Pope, taking the name of Eugenius III. Bernard felt a fatherly concern for Eugenius, a shy and retiring man, unaccustomed to public life. For his guidance he wrote the most important of his works, *On Consideration*. In it he impressed on Eugenius the varied obligations of his office, but reminded him to reserve time every day for self-examination and contemplation, a duty more vital than any official business. There was danger, he wrote, of becoming so preoccupied as to fall into forgetfulness of God; the reformation of the Church must begin at the very top, for if the Pope fails, the whole Church is dragged down. This book has been in high repute with the clergy ever since Bernard's time.

Arnold of Brescia, a pupil of Abelard, now attracted Bernard's notice—and his flaming opposition. Arnold had been condemned with Abelard by the council of Sens, but four years later, in Rome, he led a movement of the commune of citizens to overthrow the Pope and set up a government on the model of the ancient Roman republic. His stirring up of the populace compelled Eugenius to flee the city for a time. There were uprisings elsewhere against the temporal authority of the bishops, but the whole movement was confused and badly organized. Arnold was tried and condemned by the Church, and later executed by Emperor Frederick Barbarossa.

During this time the Albigensian heresy,[8] with all its startling social and moral implications, had been making alarming progress in the south of France. In 1145 the papal legate to France, Cardinal Alberic, asked Bernard to go down to Languedoc. Ill and weak though he was, Bernard obeyed, stopping to preach along the way. Geoffrey, his secretary, accompanied him, and relates various miracles to which he was an eyewitness. At a village in Perigord Bernard blessed with the sign of the cross some loaves of bread, saying, "By this you shall know the truth of our doctrines and the falsehood of what the heretics teach, if such as are sick among you recover their health on eating these loaves." The bishop of Chartres, who stood near Bernard, afraid of the possible outcome, added, "That is, if they eat with a right faith, they will be cured." But Bernard insisted on his own statement, "whoever tastes will be cured." And a number of sick persons were, in fact, made well after eating the bread. Although the supporters of the heresy were stubborn and violent, especially at Toulouse and Albi, in a short time he had apparently restored orthodoxy. Twenty-five years later, however, the Albigensians had a stronger hold on the country than ever. The great St. Dominic, whose story appears later in this volume, then came to win back the country once more.

On Christmas Day, 1144, the Seljuk Turks captured Edessa, chief city of one of the Christian principalities set up by the First Crusade. Appeals for help went at once to Europe, for the position of all Christians in Syria was jeopardized. King Louis VII of France announced his intention of leading a new crusade, and the Pope commissioned Bernard to preach the Holy War. Bernard began at Vezelay on Palm Sunday, 1146. Queen Eleanor and a company of nobles, the first to take the cross, were followed by

[8] This heresy, a revival of the Manichaeism of Augustine's day, flourished in the twelfth and thirteenth centuries. The Albigensians taught a dualistic doctrine, namely, that there were two opposing spirits in the universe, good and evil, and that all matter was evil and all spirit good. They denied the resurrection of the body. Their name was derived from the district of Albi in Languedoc. For a further account of this heresy, see below, *St. Dominic*, p. 225.

such a throng that the supply of cloth badges [9] was exhausted and Bernard tore strips from his own habit to make more. Having roused France, he wrote to the rulers and peoples of England, Italy, Sicily, Spain, Poland, Denmark, Moravia, Bohemia, and Bavaria, and went in person to Germany. Bernard had to deal there with a half-crazy monk, who in his name was inciting the populace to massacre Jews. He then made a triumphant tour through the Rhineland. The Emperor Conrad III took the cross, and set out in May, 1147; Louis of France soon followed.

This Second Crusade was a miserable failure. Conrad's army was cut to pieces crossing the mountains of Asia Minor. Louis was diverted to the East and his forces were exhausted by a futile siege of Damascus. The chief reason for the collapse of the great enterprise lay within the crusaders themselves. Many were led by sordid motives; they committed every kind of lawless act on their march. Bernard, because he had seemed to promise success, was bitterly criticized. In reply he declared that he had trusted the Divine mercy to bless a crusade undertaken for the honor of His Name, but that the army's sins had brought catastrophe; yet who could judge of its true success or failure? "How is it," he asked, "that the rashness of mortals dares condemn what they cannot understand?"

Soon after the return of the defeated crusaders, Bernard started to organize a third expedition to deliver the Holy Land from the Turks, working this time with Abbot Suger, who had opposed the previous venture. But early in 1151 Suger died; France was again on the verge of civil war and the project was dropped. Pope Eugenius died in 1153, and that same year Bernard was taken with his last illness. He had long dwelt in Heaven in desire, though he had ascribed his desire to weakness rather than piety. "The saints," he said, "were moved to pray for death out of a longing to see Christ, but I am driven hence by scandals and evil." In the spring of 1153 the archbishop of Trier implored him to go to Metz and try to make peace between the citizens of Metz and the duke of

[9] Crusaders were distinguished by cloth badges in the shape of a cross worn on their shoulders.

Lorraine, who had subjugated them. Forgetting his infirmities, Bernard set out for Lorraine, and there prevailed on both sides to lay down their arms and later to accept the treaty he drew up for them.

Back at Clairvaux after performing this final work of mediation, the abbot's health failed rapidly. With his spiritual sons gathered round him, he received the Last Sacraments. He comforted them, saying that the unprofitable servant should not occupy a place uselessly, that the barren tree should be rooted up. On August 20 God took him. Bernard was sixty-three years old, had been abbot for thirty-eight years, and had seen sixty-eight monasteries established by his men from Clairvaux. According to one historian, he had "carried the twelfth century on his shoulders." *Doctor Mellifluus*, the Honey-Sweet Doctor, as he was called for his eloquence, had been the counselor of prelates and the reformer of disciplines; his writings have continued to inspire the faithful. Although he lived after Anselm of Canterbury, the great scholastic who used reason as a means to clarify faith, Bernard was on the side of the ancient doctors who trusted wholly to Scripture and faith and mystical experience. For the outstanding excellence of his life and works he is reckoned the last of the Church Fathers. He was canonized in 1174, twenty-one years after his death. His relics are at Clairvaux, his skull in the cathedral of Troyes; his emblems are a pen, bees, and instruments of the Passion.

Jesus, Thou Joy of Loving Hearts

Jesus, thou joy of loving hearts,
  Thou fount of life, thou Light of men,
From the poor bliss that earth imparts,
  We turn unfilled to thee again.

Thy truth unchanged hath ever stood;
  Thou savest those who on thee call;
To them that seek thee, thou art good,
  To them that find thee, all in all.

We taste thee, O thou living Bread,
  And long to feast upon thee still;
We drink of thee the Fountain-head,
  And thirst our souls from thee to fill.

Our restless spirits yearn for thee,
  Where'er our changeful lot is cast;
Glad, when thy gracious smile we see,
  Blest, when our faith can hold thee fast.

O Jesus, ever with us stay;
  Make all our moments calm and bright;
Chase the dark night of sin away;
  Shed o'er the world thy holy light.

Excerpts from The Steps of Humility

iii, 6. . . . *We seek truth in ourselves, in our neighbors,* and in its own nature: in ourselves, judging ourselves; in our neighbors, sympathizing with their ills; in its own nature, contemplating it with a pure heart. First, let the Truth itself teach you that you should seek it in your neighbors before seeking it in its own nature. Later, you will see why you should seek it in yourself before seeking it in your neighbors. For in the list of the Beatitudes which He enumerated in his sermon, He placed the merciful before the pure in heart. The merciful quickly grasp the truth in their neighbors, extending their own feelings to them and conforming themselves to them through love, so that they feel their joys and troubles as their own. They are weak with the weak; they burn with the offended. "They rejoice with them that do rejoice and weep with them that weep." After the spiritual vision has been purified by this brotherly love, they enjoy the contemplation of truth in its own nature, and then bear others' ills for love of it. But those who do not unite themselves with their brethren in this way, but on the contrary either revile those who weep or disparage those who rejoice, not feeling in themselves that which is in others, because they are not similarly situated—how can they grasp the truth in their neighbors? For the popular proverb well applies to them: "The healthy do not know how the sick feel, nor the full how the hungry suffer." But sick sympathize with sick, and hungry with hungry, the more closely the more they are alike. For just as pure truth is seen only with a pure heart, so a brother's misery is truly felt only with a miserable heart.

But in order to have a miserable heart because of another's misery, you must first know your own; so that you may find your neighbor's mind in your own and know from yourself how to help him, after the example of our Saviour, who willed His passion in order to learn compassion, his misery to learn commiseration. For just as it is written of him, *Yet learned he obedience by the things which he suffered,* so also he learned mercy in the same way. Not that he did not know how to be merciful before, he whose mercy is from everlasting to everlasting; he knew it by nature from eternity, but learned it in time by experience. . . .

9. I do not say he became any wiser through this experience, but he seemed to be nearer, so that the feeble sons of Adam, whom he was not ashamed to make and call his brethren, should not hesitate to commit their infirmities to him who could cure them, having suffered the same things. Wherefore Isaiah calls him *a man of sorrows,* and *acquainted with grief,* And the Apostle says, *For we have not an high priest which cannot be touched with the feeling of our infirmities,* and explains this by adding, *but was in all points tempted like as we are, yet without sin.*

For the blessed God, Son of the blessed God, in that form in which he thought it not robbery to be equal with the Father, that is, passionless, before he had made himself of no reputation and taken upon him the form of a servant, since he had not undergone misery or submission, did not know mercy or obedience by experience. He knew them intuitively, but not empirically. But when he had made himself not only lower than his own dignity but even a little lower than the angels, who are themselves passionless by grace, not by nature, even to that form in which he could undergo suffering and submission, which he could not do in his own form, as was said; then he learned mercy in suffering and obedience in submission. Through this experience, however, not his knowledge, as I said, but our boldness was increased, when he from whom we had long been astray was brought nearer to us by this sort of unhappy wisdom. For when should we have dared to approach him, remaining in his impassivity? But now we are urged by the Apostle *to come boldly into the throne of grace* of him who, we know from another verse, *hath borne our griefs and carried our sorrows;* and because of his own passion we are sure of his compassion for us. . . .

12. Since then you see that Christ in one person has two natures, one by which he always was, the other by which he began to be, and always knew everything in his eternal essence but temporally experienced many things in his temporal essence; why do you hesitate to grant that, as he began in time to be in the flesh, so also he began to know the ills of the flesh by that kind of knowledge which the weakness of the flesh teaches? Our first parents would have been wiser and happier to have remained ignorant of that kind of knowledge, since they could only attain it by folly and misery. But God, their maker, seeking again what had perished, accompanied his creatures in pity. There whither they had fallen so pathetically, he also came down sympathetically, willing to experience in himself what they justly suffered for defying him, not because of a similar curiosity, but because of marvelous love, not to remain miserable with the miserable but to become pitiful and free the pitiable. Become pitiful, I say, not with that pity which he, ever blessed, had from eternity, but with that which he learned through sorrow, when in our form. And the labor of love which he began through the former, he finished in the latter, not because he could not finish it in the one, but because he could not fulfill our needs without the other. Each one was necessary, but the latter was more human. Device of ineffable love! How could we conceive that marvelous pity produced by no previous pain? How could we imagine that superhuman compassion not preceded by passion but coexistent with impassivity? Yet if that pity free from pain had not come first, he would never have thought of this pity which is born of pain.

(*The Steps of Humility,* trans. by G. B.
Burch, Loeb Classical Library.)

Saint Thomas Becket

Bishop, Martyr

1 1 7 0

(*December 29*)

There is a romantic legend that the mother of Thomas Becket was a Saracen princess who followed his father, a pilgrim or crusader, back from the Holy Land, and wandered about Europe repeating the only English words she knew, "London" and "Becket," until she found him. There is no foundation for the story. According to a contemporary writer, Thomas Becket was the son of Gilbert Becket, sheriff of London; another relates that both parents were of Norman blood. Whatever his parentage, we know with certainty that the future chancellor and archbishop of Canterbury was born on St. Thomas day, 1118, of a good family, and that he was educated at a school of canons regular at Merton Priory in Sussex, and later at the University of Paris. When Thomas returned from France, his parents had died. Obliged to make his way unaided, he obtained an appointment as clerk to the sheriff's court, where he showed great ability. All accounts describe him as a strongly built, spirited youth, a lover of field sports, who seems to have spent his leisure time in hawking and hunting. One day when he was out hunting with his falcon, the bird swooped down at a duck, and as the duck dived, plunged after it into the river. Thomas himself leapt in to save the valuable hawk, and the rapid stream swept him along to a mill, where only the accidental stopping of the wheel saved his life. The episode serves to illustrate the impetuous daring which characterized Becket all through his life.

At the age of twenty-four Thomas was given a post in the household of Theobald, archbishop of Canterbury, and while there he apparently resolved on a career in the Church, for he took minor orders. To prepare himself further, he obtained the archbishop's permission to study canon law at the University of Bologna, continuing his studies at Auxerre, France. On coming back to England, he became provost of Beverley, and canon at Lincoln and St. Paul's cathedrals. His ordination as deacon occurred in 1154. Theobald appointed him archdeacon of Canterbury, the highest ecclesiastical office in England after a bishopric or an abbacy, and began to entrust him with the most intricate affairs; several times he was sent on important missions to Rome. It was Thomas' diplomacy that dissuaded Pope Eugenius III from sanctioning the coronation of Eustace, eldest son of Stephen, and when Henry of Anjou, great grandson of William the Conqueror, asserted his claim to the English crown and became King Henry II, it was not long before he appointed this gifted churchman as chancellor, that is, chief minister. An old chronicle describes Thomas as "slim of growth, and pale of hue, with dark hair, a long nose, and a straightly featured face. Blithe of countenance was he, winning and lovable in conversation, frank of speech in his discourses but slightly stuttering in his talk, so keen of discernment that he could always make difficult questions plain after a wise manner." Thomas discharged his duties as chancellor conscientiously and well.

Like the later chancellor of the realm, Thomas Moore, who also became a martyr and a saint, Thomas Becket was the close personal friend as well as the loyal servant of his young sovereign. They were said to have one heart and one mind between them, and it seems possible that to Becket's influence were due, in part, those reforms for which Henry is justly praised, that is, his measures to secure equitable dealing for all his subjects by a more uniform and efficient system of law. But it was not only their common interest in matters of state that bound them together. They were also boon companions and spent merry hours together. It was almost the only relaxation Thomas allowed himself, for he was an ambitious man. He had a taste for magnificence, and his household was as fine—if not finer—than the King's. When he was sent to France to negotiate a royal marriage, he took a personal retinue of two hundred men, with a train of several hundred more, knights and squires, clerics and servants, eight fine wagons, music and singers, hawks and hounds, monkeys and mastiffs. Little wonder that the French gaped in wonder and asked, "If this is the chancellor's state, what can the King's be like?" His entertainments, his gifts, and his liberality to the poor were also on a very lavish scale.

In 1159 King Henry raised an army of mercenaries in France to regain the province of Toulouse, a part of the inheritance of his wife, the famous Eleanor of Aquitaine. Thomas served Henry in this war with a company of seven hundred knights of his own. Wearing armor like any other fighting man, he led assaults and engaged in single combat. Another churchman, meeting him, exclaimed: "What do you mean by wearing such a dress? You look more like a falconer than a cleric. Yet you are a cleric in person, and many times over in office—archdeacon of Canterbury, dean of Hastings, provost of Beverley, canon of this church and that, procurator of the archbishop, and like to be archbishop, too, the rumor goes!" Thomas received the rebuke with good humor.

Although he was proud, strong-willed, and irascible, and remained so all his life, he did not neglect to make seasonal retreats at Merton and took the discipline imposed on him there. His confessor during this time testified later to the blamelessness of his private life, under conditions of extreme temptation. If he sometimes went too far in those schemes of the King which tended to infringe on the ancient prerogatives and rights of the Church, at other times he opposed Henry with vigor.

In 1161 Archbishop Theobald died. King Henry was then in Normandy with Thomas, whom he resolved to make the next primate of England. When Henry announced his intention, Thomas, demurring, told him: "Should God permit me to be the archbishop of Canterbury, I would soon lose your Majesty's favor, and the affection with which you honor me would be changed into hatred.

For there are several things you do now in prejudice of the rights of the Church which make me fear you would require of me what I could not agree to; and envious persons would not fail to make it the occasion of endless strife between us." The King paid no heed to this remonstrance, and sent bishops and noblemen to the monks of Canterbury, ordering them to labor with the same zeal to set his chancellor in the see as they would to set the crown on the young prince's head. Thomas continued to refuse the promotion until the legate of the Holy See, Cardinal Henry of Pisa, overrode his scruples. The election took place in May, 1162. Young Prince Henry, then in London, gave the necessary consent in his father's name. Thomas, now forty-four years old, rode to Canterbury and was first ordained priest by Walter, bishop of Rochester, and then on the octave of Pentecost was consecrated archbishop by the bishop of Winchester. Shortly afterwards he received the pallium sent by Pope Alexander III.

From this day worldly grandeur no longer marked Thomas' way of life. Next his skin he wore a hairshirt, and his customary dress was a plain black cassock, a linen surplice, and a sacerdotal stole about his neck. He lived ascetically, spent much time in the distribution of alms, in reading and discussing the Scriptures with Herbert of Bosham, in visiting the infirmary, and supervising the monks at their work. He took special care in selecting candidates for Holy Orders. As ecclesiastical judge, he was rigorously just.

Although as archbishop Thomas had resigned the chancellorship, against the King's wish, the relations between the two men seemed to be unchanged for a time. But a host of troubles was brewing, and the crux of all of them was the relationship between Church and state. In the past the landowners, among which the Church was one of the largest, for each hide [1] of land they held, had paid annually two shillings to the King's officers, who in return undertook to protect them from the rapacity of minor tax-gatherers. This was actually a flagrant form of graft and the King now ordered

[1] A hide of land was the amount considered necessary for the support of one household; it varied from eighty to a hundred acres, according to location.

the money paid into his own exchequer. The archbishop protested, and there were hot words between him and the King. Thenceforth the King's demands were directed solely against the clergy, with no mention of other landholders who were equally involved.

Then came the affair of Philip de Brois, a canon accused of murdering a soldier. According to a long-established law, as a cleric he was tried in an ecclesiastical court, where he was acquitted by the judge, the bishop of Lincoln, but ordered to pay a fine to the deceased man's relations. A king's justice then made an effort to bring him before his civil court, but he could not be tried again upon that indictment and told the king's justice so in insulting terms. Thereat Henry ordered him tried again both for the original murder charge and for his later misdemeanor. Thomas now pressed to have the case referred to his own archiepiscopal court; the King reluctantly agreed, and appointed both lay and clerical assessors. Philip's plea of a previous acquittal was accepted as far as the murder was concerned, but he was punished for his contempt of a royal court. The King thought the sentence too mild and remained dissatisfied. In October, 1163, the King called the bishops of his realm to a council at Westminster, at which he demanded their assent to an edict that thenceforth clergy proved guilty of crimes against the civil law should be handed over to the civil courts for punishment. Thomas stiffened the bishops against yielding. But finally, at the council of Westminster they assented reluctantly to the instrument known as the Constitutions of Clarendon, which embodied the royal "customs" in Church matters, and including some additional points, making sixteen in all. It was a revolutionary document: it provided that no prelate should leave the kingdom without royal permission, which would serve to prevent appeals to the Pope; that no tenant-in-chief should be excommunicated against the King's will; that the royal court was to decide in which court clerics accused of civil offenses should be tried; that the custody of vacant Church benefices and their revenues should go to the King. Other provisions were equally damaging to the authority and prestige of the Church. The bishops gave their assent only with a reservation, "saving their order," which was tantamount to a refusal.

Thomas was now full of remorse for having weakened, thus setting a bad example to the bishops, but at the same time he did not wish to widen the breach between himself and the King. He made a futile effort to cross the Channel and put the case before the Pope. On his part, the King was bent on vengeance for what he considered the disloyalty and ingratitude of the archbishop. He ordered Thomas to give up certain castles and honors which he held from him, and began a campaign to persecute and discredit him. Various charges of chicanery and financial dishonesty were brought against Thomas, dating from the time he was chancellor. The bishop of Winchester pleaded the archbishop's discharge. The plea was disallowed; Thomas offered a voluntary payment of his own money, and that was refused.

The affair was building up to a crisis, when, on October 13, 1164, the King called another great council at Northampton. Thomas went, after celebrating Mass, carrying his archbishop's cross in his hand. The Earl of Leicester came out with a message from the King: "The King commands you to render your accounts. Otherwise you must hear his judgment." "Judgment?" exclaimed Thomas. "I was given the church of Canterbury free from temporal obligations. I am therefore not liable and will not plead with regard to them. Neither law nor reason allows children to judge and condemn their fathers. Wherefore I refuse the King's judgment and yours and everyone's. Under God, I will be judged by the Pope alone."

Determined to stand out against the King, Thomas left Northampton that night, and soon thereafter embarked secretly for Flanders. Louis VII, King of France, invited Thomas into his dominions. Meanwhile King Henry forbade anyone to give him aid. Gilbert, abbot of Sempringham, was accused of having sent him some relief. Although the abbot had done nothing, he refused to swear he had not, because, he said, it would have been a good deed and he would say nothing that might seem to brand it as a criminal act. Henry quickly dispatched several bishops and others to put his case before Pope Alexander, who was then at Sens. Thomas also presented himself to the Pope and showed him the Constitutions of Clarendon, some of which Alexander pronounced intolerable, others impossible. He rebuked Thomas for ever having considered accepting them. The next day Thomas confessed that he had, though unwillingly, received the see of Canterbury by an election somewhat irregular and uncanonical, and had acquitted himself badly in it. He resigned his office, returned the episcopal ring to the Pope, and withdrew. After deliberation, the Pope called him back and reinstated him, with orders not to abandon his office, for to do so would be to abandon the cause of God. He then recommended Thomas to the Cistercian abbot at Pontigny.

Thomas then put on a monk's habit, and submitted himself to the strict rule of the monastery. Over in England King Henry was busy confiscating the goods of all the friends, relations, and servants of the archbishop, and banishing them, first binding them by oath to go to Thomas at Pontigny, that the sight of their distress might move him. Troops of these exiles soon appeared at the abbey. Then Henry notified the Cistercians that if they continued to harbor his enemy he would sequestrate all their houses in his dominions. After this, the abbot hinted that Thomas was no longer welcome in his abbey. The archbishop found refuge as the guest of King Louis at the royal abbey of St. Columba, near Sens.

This historic quarrel dragged on for three years. Thomas was named by the Pope as his legate for all England except York, whereupon Thomas excommunicated several of his adversaries; yet at times he showed himself conciliatory towards the King. The French king was also drawn into the struggle, and the two kings had a conference in 1169 at Montmirail. King Louis was inclined to take Thomas' side. A reconciliation was finally effected between Thomas and Henry, although the lines of power were not too clearly drawn. The archbishop now made preparations to return to his see. With a premonition of his fate, he remarked to the bishop of Paris in parting, "I am going to England to die." On

December 1, 1172, he disembarked at Sandwich, and on the journey to Canterbury the way was lined with cheering people, welcoming him home. As he rode into the cathedral city at the head of a triumphal procession, every bell was ringing. Yet in spite of the public demonstration, there was an atmosphere of foreboding.

At the reconciliation in France, Henry had agreed to the punishment of Roger, archbishop of York, and the bishops of London and Salisbury, who had assisted at the coronation of Henry's son, despite the long-established right of the archbishop of Canterbury to perform this ceremony and in defiance of the Pope's explicit instructions. It had been another attempt to lower the prestige of the primate's see. Thomas had sent on in advance of his return the papal letters suspending Roger and confirming the excommunication of the two bishops involved. On the eve of his arrival a deputation waited on him to ask for the withdrawal of these sentences. He agreed on condition that the three would swear thenceforth to obey the Pope. This they refused to do, and together went to rejoin King Henry, who was visiting his domains in France.

At Canterbury Thomas was subjected to insult by one Ranulf de Broc, from whom he had demanded the restoration of Saltwood Castle, a manor previously belonging to the archbishop's see. After a week's stay there he went up to London, where Henry's son, "the young King," refused to see him. He arrived back in Canterbury on or about his fifty-second birthday. Meanwhile the three bishops had laid their complaints before the King at Bur, near Bayeux, and someone had exclaimed aloud that there would be no peace for the realm while Becket lived. At this, the King, in a fit of rage, pronounced some words which several of his hearers took as a rebuke to them for allowing Becket to continue to live and thereby disturb him. Four of his knights at once set off for England and made their way to the irate family at Saltwood. Their names were Reginald Fitzurse, William de Tracy, Hugh de Morville, and Richard le Bret.

On St. John's day Thomas received a letter warning him of

danger, and all southeast Kent was in a state of ferment. On the afternoon of December 29, the four knights came to see him in his episcopal palace. During the interview they made several demands, in particular that Thomas remove the censures on the three bishops. The knights withdrew, uttering threats and oaths. A few minutes later there were loud outcries, a shattering of doors and clashing of arms, and the archbishop, urged on by his attendants, began moving slowly through the cloister passage to the cathedral. It was now twilight and vespers were being sung. At the door of the north transept he was met by some terrified monks, whom he commanded to get back to the choir. They withdrew a little and he entered the church, but the knights were seen behind him in the dim light. The monks slammed the door on them and bolted it. In their confusion they shut out several of their own brethren, who began beating loudly on the door. Becket turned and cried, "Away, you cowards! A church is not a castle." He reopened the door himself, then went towards the choir, accompanied by Robert de Merton, his aged teacher and confessor, William Fitzstephen, a cleric in his household, and a monk, Edward Grim. The others fled to the crypt and other hiding places, and Grim alone remained. At this point the knights broke in shouting, "Where is Thomas the traitor?" "Where is the archbishop?" "Here I am," he replied, "no traitor, but archbishop and priest of God!" He came down the steps to stand between the altars of Our Lady and St. Benedict.

The knights clamored at him to absolve the bishops, and Thomas answered firmly, "I cannot do other than I have done. Reginald, you have received many favors from me. Why do you come into my church armed?" Fitzurse made a threatening gesture with his axe. "I am ready to die," said Thomas, "but God's curse on you if you harm my people." There was some scuffling as they tried to carry Thomas outside bodily. Fitzurse flung down his axe and drew his sword. "You pander, you owe me fealty and submission!" exclaimed the archbishop. Fitzurse shouted back, "I owe no fealty contrary to the King!" and knocked off Thomas' cap. At this, Thomas covered his face and called aloud on God and the saints. Tracy struck a blow, which Grim intercepted with his own arm, but it grazed Thomas' skull and blood ran down into his eyes. He wiped the stain away and cried, "Into Thy hands, O Lord, I commend my spirit!" Another blow from Tracy beat him to his knees, and he pitched forward onto his face, murmuring, "For the name of Jesus and in defense of the Church I am willing to die." With a vigorous thrust Le Bret struck deep into his head, breaking his sword against the pavement, and Hugh of Horsea added a blow, although the archbishop was now dying. Hugh de Morville stood by but struck no blow. The murderers, brandishing their swords, now dashed away through the cloisters, shouting "The King's men! The King's men!" The cathedral itself was filling with people unaware of the catastrophe, and a thunderstorm was breaking overhead.[2] The archbishop's body lay in the middle of the transept, and for a time no one dared approach it. A deed of such sacrilege was bound to be regarded with horror and indignation. When the news was brought to the King, he shut himself up and fasted for forty days, for he knew that his chance remark had sped the courtiers to England bent on vengeance. He later performed public penance in Canterbury Cathedral and in 1172 received absolution from the papal delegates.

Within three years of his death the archbishop had been canonized as a martyr. Though far from a faultless character, Thomas Becket, when his time of testing came, had the courage to lay down his life to defend the ancient rights of the Church against an aggressive state. The discovery of his hairshirt and other evidences of austerity, and the many miracles which were reported at his tomb, increased the veneration in which he was held. The shrine of the "holy blessed martyr," as Chaucer called him, soon became famous, and the old Roman road running from London to Canterbury known as "Pilgrim's Way." His tomb was magnificently adorned with gold, silver, and jewels, only to be despoiled by Henry VIII; the fate of his relics is uncertain. They may have

[2] T. S. Eliot's play, "The Murder in the Cathedral," gives us the dramatic sequence of events with high artistry.

been destroyed as a part of Henry's policy to subordinate the English Church to the civil authority. Mementoes of this saint are preserved at the cathedral of Sens. The feast of St. Thomas of Canterbury is now kept throughout the Roman Catholic Church, and in England he is regarded as the protector of the secular clergy.

Letter to All the Clergy of England [3]

*T*homas, *by the grace of God humble minister of the church* of Canterbury, to his reverend brothers, all the bishops, by God's grace, of the province of Canterbury,—if, indeed, they all wrote me,—greeting and a will to do what as yet they do not.

. . . One thing I say to you, to speak out, saving your peace. For a long time I have been silent, waiting if perchance the Lord would inspire you to pluck up your strength again; if perchance one, at least, of you all would arise and take his stand as a wall to defend the house of Israel, would put on at least the appearance of entering the battle against those who never cease daily to attack the army of the Lord. I have waited; not one has arisen. I have endured; not one has taken a stand. I have been silent; not one has spoken. I have dissimulated; not one has fought even in appearance. . . .

May God lift the veil from your hearts that you may know what you ought to do. Let any man of you say who knows if ever since my promotion I have taken from anyone of you his ox or his ass or his money, if I have judged anyone's cause unjustly, if out of anyone's loss I have won gain for myself, and I will return it fourfold. If I have done nothing to offend you, why leave me alone to defend the cause of God? . . .

Let us then, all together, make haste to act so that God's wrath descend not on us as on negligent and idle shepherds, that we be not counted dumb dogs, too feeble to bark, that passersby speak

[3] This letter was written in 1166, while Thomas was in exile in France, in reply to a letter from the bishops and other clergy of England, deploring his hostile and implacable attitude towards King Henry and urging him for the sake of the Church to be more conciliatory and forgiving.

not scorn of us. . . . In truth, if you hear me, be assured that God will be with you and with us all, in all our ways, to uphold peace and defend the liberty of the Church. If you will not hear, let God be judge between me and you and from your hands demand account for the confusion of the Church. . . . But this hope I have stored in my breast, that he is not alone who has the Lord with him. If he fall, he shall not be destroyed for the Lord himself upholds him with his hand. . . .

My lord knows with what intent he chose to have us exalted. Let his purpose reply to him and we will reply to him, as our office requires of us, that by God's mercy we are more faithful in our severity than are those who flatter him with lies. For better are the blows of a friend than the false kisses of an enemy. By implication you charge us with ingratitude. We believe that no criminal act brings with it disgrace unless it comes from the soul. So if a man unintentionally commits murder, although he is called a murderer and is one, still he does not bear the guilt of murder. So we say that even if by right of lordship we owe our lord king service, if we are bound by the law of kings to show him reverence, if we have upheld him as lord, if we have treated him as our own son with fatherly affection, and if then in council, to our grief, he has not listened to us and we, as our office compels us, are severe in our censure of him, we believe we are doing more for him and with him than against him, and more deserve gratitude from him than a charge of ingratitude or punishment. . . .

You remind us of the danger to the Roman Church, of loss of temporal possessions. There is danger indeed to us and ours, without mentioning the danger to souls. You imply a threat of the lord king's withdrawal (which God forbid!) from fealty and devotion to the Roman Church. God forbid, I say, that our lord king's fealty and devotion should ever for some temporal advantage or disadvantage swerve from fealty and devotion to the Roman Church. Such conduct, which would be wicked and reprehensible in a private man, would be far more so in a prince, who draws many along with him and after him. . . . Do you in your discretion look to it that the words of your mouths do not infect some other man or men, to the loss and damnation of their souls, like the golden cup, called the cup of Babylon, which is smeared within and without with poison, but from which one may drink and not fear the poison because he sees the gold. Even such may be the effect of your conduct on the people. . . .

In the midst of tribulation and bloodshed the Church from of old has increased and multiplied. It is the way of the Church to win her victories when men are persecuting her, to arrive at understanding when men are refuting her, to gain strength when men are forsaking her. Do not, my brothers, weep for her but for yourselves who are making by your acts and words a name, and not a great one, for yourselves in everyone's mouth, who are calling down on yourselves the hatred of God and of the world, preparing a snare for the innocent, and fashioning new and ingenious reasons for overthrowing the liberty of the Church. By God's mercy, brothers, you are laboring in vain, for the Church, although often shaken, will stand in the courage and steadfastness on which she was steadfastly founded, until the Son of perdition arises. As for him, we do not believe he will arise in the West, unless the order of events and the sequence of history is wrongfully altered.

But if your concern is for the temporal things, we should fear more a danger to the soul than to them. For the Scripture says: "What doth it profit a man to gain the whole world and lose his own soul?" Hence the peril to us and to ours we utterly scorn. He is not to be feared who kills the body, but He who kills both body and soul. . . .

Pray for us that our faith fail not in tribulation and that we may safely say with the Apostle that neither death nor life nor angels nor any creature shall be able to separate us from the love of God, which has subjected us to affliction until He come Who will come, and will do with us according to his mercy, and will lead us into the land of promise, the land flowing with milk and honey. . . .

(*Materials for the History of Thomas Becket, Archbishop of Canterbury*, ed. J. C. Robertson, 1881. Vol. v, Epistle **cxxiii.**)

Saint Dominic
Founder of the Friars Preachers, Confessor

1 2 2 1

(August 4)

Dominic, founder of the great order of preaching friars which bears his name, was born in the year 1170 at Calaruega, Castile, Spain, of a noble family with illustrious connections. His father, Don Felix de Guzman, held the post of royal warden of the village; his mother, a woman of unusual sanctity, was to become Blessed Joan of Aza. Very early it was decided that Dominic should have a career in the Church. His call was so evident that while he was still a student, Martin de Bazan, bishop of Osma, appointed him canon of the cathedral, and the stipend he received helped him to continue his studies. Dominic's love of learning and his charity are both exemplified in a story of his student days. He had gathered a collection of religious books inscribed on parchment; these he greatly treasured, but one day he sold the whole lot that he might give the money thus obtained to some poor people. "I could not bear to prize dead skins," he said, "when living skins were starving and in need."

At the age of twenty-five he was ordained and took up his duties. The chapter lived under the rule of St. Augustine, and the strict observance gave the young priest the discipline that he was to practice and teach to others all his life. Someone who knew Dominic at this time wrote that he was first of all the monks in holiness, frequenting the church day and night, and scarcely venturing beyond the walls of the cloister. He was soon made subprior, and when the prior, Diego d'Azevado, became bishop of Osma, about

1201, Dominic succeeded to his office. He had then been leading the contemplative life for six or seven years.

When, two years later, the bishop was appointed by the King to go on an embassy to negotiate a marriage for the King's son, he chose Dominic to accompany him. On the way, they passed through Languedoc, in southern France, where the Albigensian heresy was winning many adherents.[1] The host at an inn where they stopped was an Albigensian, and Dominic spent a whole night in discussion with him. By morning he had convinced the man of his error. From that day, it appears, Dominic knew with certainty that the work God required of him was an active life of teaching in the world. The ambassadors returned to Castile after their mission was accomplished, then were sent back to escort the young woman to her future home, but they arrived only to assist at her funeral. Their retinue returned to Castile, while they went to Rome to ask leave of Pope Innocent III to preach the Gospel to the infidels in the East. The Pope urged them to stay and fight against the heresy which was threatening the Church in France. Bishop Diego begged to be allowed to resign his episcopal see, but to this the Pope would not consent, though he gave him permission to stay two years in Languedoc. They paid a visit to St. Bernard's monastery at Cîteaux, whose monks had been appointed to go on a mission to convert the Albigensians. Don Diego put on the Cistercian habit and almost at once set out with Dominic and a band of preachers.

Albigensian doctrine was based on a dualism of two eternally opposing principles, good and evil, all matter being regarded as evil and the creator of the material world as a devil. Hence the doctrine of the Incarnation was denied, and the Old Testament and the Sacrament rejected. To be perfect or "pure" a person must refrain from sexual relations and be extremely abstemious in eating and drinking. Suicide by starvation was by some regarded as a noble act. In its more extreme form Albigensianism thus threatened the very existence of human society. The rank and file did

---

[1] For more on the Albigensian heresy, called thus because it flourished in the town of Albi, see *St. Bernard of Clairvaux*, n. 8.

SAINT MARTIN   Vivarini

Bartolommeo Vivarini (c. 1432-c. 1499) was one of a family of uncles and
nephews who painted in fifteenth century Murano. Bartolommeo soon outstripped his elder brother and became the head
of the school of Murano. His works are notable for their stat-
uesque qualities.

Saint Martin of Tours is most often painted in his meeting
with the beggar with whom he divided his cloak. The horse,
and the sword cutting the garment in half, are his usual symbols.

SAINT JEROME IN HIS STUDY   Marinus

Marinus Roejmerswaele (or Reymerswaele) was born in Zeeland, Holland, about 1493 and died about 1567. He is noted for the realism with which he painted the Dutch people of his day. One of his religious masterpieces is this painting of Saint Jerome.

Saint Jerome's symbols are a skull and an open Bible. The small church which can be seen through the window also is emblematic of this saint because of his great work in support of the Faith.

not attempt such austerity, of course, but the leaders maintained high standards of asceticism, in contrast with which the easy-going observance of the Cistercian preachers away from home looked far from saintly. Dominic and Diego now advised those who had been in charge of the mission to give up their horses, retinues, and servants. Also, as soon as they won a hearing, they were to use the method of peaceful persuasion instead of threats. The way of life Dominic enjoined on others he was the first to follow himself. He rarely ate anything but bread and soup; if he drank wine it was two thirds water; his bed was the floor, unless—as sometimes happened—he was so exhausted that he lay down at the side of the road to sleep.

The missionaries' first meeting with the heretics took place at Servian in 1206, where they made several conversions; afterwards they preached at Carcassone and neighboring towns, but nowhere did they meet with unusual success. At one public debate the judges submitted Dominic's statement of the Catholic faith to the ordeal by fire, and three times, it is recorded, the parchment was left unharmed by the flames. The heresy, supported as it was by the great spiritual and temporal lords of the country, had a strong hold on the populace, who seemed unmoved either by preaching or miracles. Diego, disappointed with the results, returned to Osma, leaving Dominic in France.

Women often exerted great influence in the Middle Ages, and Dominic was struck by their share in the propagation of Albigensianism. He also observed that many Catholic girls of good family were exposed to wrong examples in their own homes or else were sent to Albigensian convents to be educated. On the feast of St. Mary Magdalen in 1206 he had a vision which led him to found a convent at Prouille, in the diocese of Toulouse, to shelter nine nuns, who had been converted from heresy. He wrote for them a rule of strict enclosure, penance, and contemplation, with the spinning of wool for their manual occupation. A house was founded a little later, in the same locality, for his preaching friars, whom he placed under a strict rule of poverty, study, and prayer.

In 1208, after the murder of a papal legate, Pope Innocent called on the Christian princes to suppress the heresy by force of arms. The Catholic forces were led by Simon de Montfort, the Albigensian by the Count of Toulouse. Everywhere Montfort was victorious, but he left behind him destruction and death. Dominic had no part in this terrible civil war. Courageously he continued to preach, going wherever he was called, seeking only the good of those who hated him. Many attempts were made on his life, and when he was asked what he would do if caught by his enemies, he answered, "I would tell them to kill me slowly and painfully, a little at a time, so that I might have a more glorious crown in Heaven." When Montfort's armies approached where he was preaching, he did all he could to save human life. Among the crusaders themselves, many of whom had joined the Catholic side for the sake of plunder, he discovered disorder, vice, and ignorance. Dominic labored among them with as much diligence and compassion as among the heretics. The Albigensian military forces were finally crushed in the battle of Muret, in 1213, a victory which Montfort attributed to Dominic's prayers. The victor was not satisfied, however, and, to Dominic's great distress, kept up for five years longer a campaign of devastation, until at last he was killed in battle.

Dominic had no illusions as to the righteousness or efficacy of establishing orthodoxy by armed force, nor had he himself anything to do with the episcopal courts of the Inquisition which were set up in southern France to work with the civil power. He never appears to have approved of the execution of those unfortunate persons whom the courts condemned as obdurate. His biographers say that he saved the life of a young man on his way to the stake, by assuring the judges that, if released, the man would die a good Catholic. The prophecy was fulfilled some years later, when the man entered the Dominican Order. Dominic rebuked the bishop of Toulouse for traveling with soldiers, servants, and pack-mules. "The enemies of the faith cannot be overcome like that," he said.

"Arm yourself with prayer instead of a sword; be clothed with humility instead of fine raiment." Offered a bishopric three times, Dominic each time declined, knowing well that his work lay elsewhere.

He thus spent nearly ten years in Languedoc, with headquarters at Prouille, leading the mission and directing the work of his special band of preachers. His great desire was to revive a true apostolic spirit in the ministers of the altar, for too many of the Catholic clergy lived for their own pleasure, without scruple. He dreamed of a new religious order, not like the older ones, whose members led lives of contemplation and prayer in isolated groups, and who were not necessarily priests. His men would join to their prayers and meditation a thorough training in theology and the duties of a popular pastor and preacher; like the earlier monks, they would practice perpetual abstinence from meat and live in poverty, depending on alms for subsistence. They would be directed from a central authority, so that they could be moved about according to the need of the time. Dominic hoped thus to provide the Church with expert and zealous preachers, whose spirit and example would spread the light. In 1214 Bishop Foulques conferred on him a benefice at Fanjeaux, and gave his episcopal approval to the new order. A few months later he took Dominic with him to Rome to attend the Fourth Lateran Council, as his theologian.

Pope Innocent III approved the convent at Prouille. He also issued a decree, which was counted as the tenth canon of the council, reminding all parish clergy of their obligation to preach, and stressing the need of choosing pastors who were powerful in both words and works. The current neglect of preaching, said the Pope, was one cause of the ignorance, disorders, and heresies then rampant. Yet Dominic did not find it easy to get formal approval for his preaching order; it contained too many innovations for sanction to be granted hastily; moreover, the council had already voted against the multiplication of religious orders.[2] It is said that In-

[2] The Franciscan Order had been orally confirmed only seven years before.

nocent had decided to withhold his consent, but on the next night dreamed he saw the Lateran Church [3] tottering as if on the verge of collapse; Dominic stepped forward to support it. Be that as it may, the Pope finally gave oral approval to Dominic's plan, bidding him return to his brothers and select one of the rules already approved.

The little company which met at Prouille in August, 1216, consisted of eight Frenchmen, eight Spaniards, and one Englishman. After some discussion, they chose the rule of St. Augustine, the oldest and least detailed of the existing rules, which had been written for priests by a priest who was himself an eminent preacher. He added certain special provisions, some borrowed from the more austere order of Prémontré. Meanwhile Pope Innocent died, in July of 1216, and Honorius III was elected in his place. In October of that year, after Dominic had set up a friary in Toulouse, he went to Rome. Honorius formally confirmed his order and its constitutions in December. The brothers were to be, in the words of the Pope's bull, "the champions of the faith and the true lights of the world."

Instead of returning at once to France, Dominic stayed in Rome until the following Easter in order to preach. He suggested to the Pope that since many of the clerics attached to his court could not attend lectures and courses outside, a master of sacred studies in residence would be very useful. Honorius then created the office of Master of the Sacred Palace, who ex-officio serves as the Pope's personal canonist and theologian, nominates his preachers, and assists at consistories. He ordered Dominic to assume the office temporarily, and ever since it has been held by a member of the order. While at Rome, too, Dominic composed a commentary on

[3] The church of St. John Lateran has the highest rank of any church in the Catholic world. The palace of the Laterani family was bestowed by the Emperor Constantine on the pope, and the church built beside it is the cathedral church of the pope as bishop of Rome. The palace was the residence of the popes from the fourth century to the fourteenth, when it was destroyed by fire.

the Epistles of St. Paul, much commended in his day, but, like his sermons and letters, it has not survived.

During this time Dominic formed friendships with Cardinal Ugolino and Francis of Assisi. The story goes that in a dream Dominic saw the sinful world threatened by the divine anger but saved by the intercession of the Virgin, who pointed out to her Son two figures, one of whom Dominic recognized as himself, while the other was a stranger. The next day in church he saw a poorly dressed fellow whom he recognized at once as the man in his dream. It was Francis of Assisi. He went up to him and embraced him, exclaiming, "You are my companion and must walk with me. For if we hold together no earthly power can withstand us." This meeting of the founders of the two great orders of friars, whose special mission was to go out into the world to save it, is still commemorated twice a year, when on their respective feast days the brothers of both orders sing Mass together, and afterwards sit at the same table. Dominic's character was in marked contrast to that of Francis, but they stood united on the common ground of faith and charity.

On August 13, 1217, the Friars Preachers, popularly known in later times as the Dominicans, first met as an order at Prouille. Dominic spoke to them on methods of preaching and urged them to unremitting study and training. He reminded them too that their primary duty was their own sanctification, for they were to be successors of the Apostles. They must be humble, putting their whole confidence in God alone; only thus might they be invincible against evil. Two days later, Dominic abruptly broke up his little band, dispersing them in different directions. Four he sent to Spain, seven to Paris, two returned to Toulouse, and two stayed at Prouille. Dominic himself went back to Rome. He had hopes that he might resign his post and set off to preach to the Tartars, but Pope Honorius would not give his consent.

The four remaining years of Dominic's life were spent in developing the order. Honorius gave him the church of St. Sixtus in Rome as a center for his activities. He preached in many of the city's churches, including St. Peter's. An old chronicle tells us that a woman named Gutadona, on coming home one day from hearing him preach, found her little child dead. In her grief she lifted him out of the cradle, and carried him to the church of St. Sixtus to lay him at Dominic's feet. He uttered a few words of fervent prayer, made the sign of the cross, and the child was straightway restored to life. The Pope would have had this miracle proclaimed from the pulpit, but the entreaties of Dominic checked him.

Large numbers of nuns were living in Rome at this time, un-cloistered and almost unregulated, some scattered about in small convents, others staying in the houses of parents or friends. Honorius now asked Dominic to assemble these nuns into one enclosed house. Dominic gave to the nuns his own monastery of St. Sixtus, which was then completed. For his friars he was given a house on the Aventine Hill, with the adjacent church of St. Sabina.

A house of the order had been founded at the University of Paris, and Dominic had sent a contingent to the University of Bologna, there to set up one of the most famous of his establishments. In 1218 he journeyed through Languedoc to his native Spain, and founded a friary at Segovia, another at Madrid, and a convent of nuns, directed by his brother. In April, 1219, he returned to Toulouse, and from there went to Paris, the first and only visit he paid to the city. On his way back he stopped to found houses at Avignon, Asti and at Bergamo in Lombardy. Towards the end of the summer Dominic reached Bologna, there to live until his death. In 1220 Pope Honorius confirmed his title as Master General of the Order of Brothers Preachers, and the first general chapter was held at Bologna. The final constitutions were then drawn up which made the order what it has since been called, "the most perfect of all the monastic organizations produced by the Middle Ages." That same year the Pope charged them, along with the monks of other orders, to undertake a preaching crusade in Lombardy. Under Dominic's leadership, a hundred thousand heretics are said to have been brought back to the Church.

Although Dominic had hoped to journey to barbarous lands to preach and eventually to achieve martyrdom, this was denied him. The ministry of the Word, however, was to be the chief aim of his great order. Those members who had a talent for preaching were never to rest, except during the intervals assigned to them for retirement. They must prepare for their high calling by prayer, self-denial, and obedience. Dominic frequently quoted the saying: "A man who governs his passions is master of the world. We must either rule them, or be ruled by them. It is better to be the hammer than the anvil." He taught his friars the art of reaching the hearts of their hearers by animating them with a love of men. Once, after delivering a stirring sermon, he was asked in what book he had studied it. "In none," he answered, "but that of love."

Dominic never altered the severe discipline he had established at the start. When he came back to Bologna in 1220, he was shocked to find a stately monastery being built for his friars; he would not allow it to be completed. This strong discipline helped the rapid spread of the order. By the time of the second general chapter at Bologna in 1221, it numbered some sixty houses, divided into eight provinces. Already there were black-robed brothers in Poland, Scandinavia, and Palestine, and Brother Gilbert, with twelve to aid him, had set up monasteries in Canterbury, London, and Oxford. The Order of Preachers is world-wide and noted especially for its intellectual achievement; it has become the mouthpiece of scholastic theology and philosophy today. There are Dominican establishments adjacent to almost all the chief seats of learning, and the founder has sometimes been called "the first minister of public instruction in Europe." The Dominicans are cloistered, but there is also a Third Order for active workers in the world, religious and lay.

At the close of the second general chapter, Dominic visited Cardinal Ugolino in Venice. Afterwards he fell ill and was taken to the country. He knew the end was near, and made his last testament in a few simple, loving words: "These, my much loved ones, are the bequests which I leave to you as my sons; have charity

among yourselves; hold fast to humility; keep a willing poverty."
He asked to be carried back to Bologna, that he might be buried
"under the feet of his brethren." Gathered about him on an August
evening, they said the prayers for the dying; at the *Subvenite,* he
repeated the words and died; he was only fifty-six years old. The
saint died "in Brother Moneta's bed, because he had none of his
own, in Brother Moneta's habit, because he had not another to
replace the one he had long been wearing."

Jordan of Saxony, Dominic's successor as master-general of the
order, wrote of him: "Nothing disturbed the even temper of his
soul except his quick sympathy with every sort of suffering. And as
a man's face shows whether he is happy or not, it was easy to see
from his friendly and joyous countenance that he was at peace
inwardly." When in 1234 Pope Gregory IX, formerly Cardinal
Ugolino, signed the decree of canonization, he remarked that he no
more doubted the sanctity of Dominic than he doubted that of
St. Peter or St. Paul.

Saint Francis of Assisi

Founder of the Friars Minor, Confessor

1 2 2 6

(October 4)

We know more of St. Francis than of any other medieval saint. Not only have we his own words, his Rule, Testament, letters, poems, and liturgical writings, but also the intimate accounts of several of his disciples, written down within twenty years after his death. These first biographies, by Brothers Thomas of Celano, Leo, Angelo, and Rufino, were soon revised and added to by other friars who wanted to call attention to one phase or another of Francis' work and teachings. From this great store of authentic material a clear picture of the man emerges. St. Francis is one saint whom both Catholics and non-Catholics have united in honoring. Certainly no other has so appealed to Protestants and even to non-Christians. And the appeal is timeless: Francis captured the imagination of his contemporaries as well as that of modern men by his unique simplicity and a pure grace of spirit. A classic collection of popular legends, the *Little Flowers of St. Francis,* first printed in 1476, contains charming and beautiful stories of Francis' love of the poor, of animals, of all nature. In action he was original, in speech picturesque and poetic, yet he was a man utterly inspired by faith in and devotion to the risen Christ.

Francis was born in the stony hill-town of Assisi in Umbria, in the year 1181 or 1182. His father, Peter Bernadone, was a wealthy merchant. His mother, Pica, by some accounts was gently born and of Provençal blood. Much of Bernadone's trade was with France, and his son was born while he was absent in that country.

Perhaps for this reason the child was called Francesco, "the French-man," though his baptismal name was John. As a youth he was ardent in his amusements and seemed carried away by the mere joy of living, taking no interest at all in his father's business or in formal learning. Bernadone, proud to have his son finely dressed and associating with young noblemen, gave him plenty of money, which Francis spent carelessly. Though Francis was high-spirited, he was too fastidious to lead a dissolute life. It was the age of chivalry, and he was thrilled by the songs of the troubadours and the deeds of knights. At the age of twenty or thereabouts, during a petty war between the towns of Assisi and Perugia, he was taken prisoner. During a year of captivity he remained cheerful and kept up the spirits of his companions. Soon after his release he suffered a long illness. This he bore with patience.

After his recovery Francis joined the troop of a knight of Assisi who was riding south to fight under Walter de Brienne for the Pope against the Germans. Having equipped himself with sumptuous apparel and fine armor, he fared forth. On the way he met a knight shabbily clad, and was so touched with compassion that he ex-changed clothes with him. That night he dreamed he saw his father's house transformed into a castle, its walls hung with armor, all marked with the sign of the cross; and he heard a voice saying that the armor belonged to Francis and his soldiers. Confident now that he would win glory as a knight, he set out again, but on the first day fell ill. While lying helpless, a voice seemed to tell him to turn back, and "to serve the Master rather than the man." Francis obeyed. At home he began to take long rambles in the country and to spend many hours by himself; he felt contempt for a life wasted on trivial and transitory things. It was a time of spiritual crisis during which he was quietly searching for something worthy of his complete devotion. A deep compassion was growing within him. Riding one day in the plains below Assisi, he met a leper whose loathsome sores filled Francis with horror. Overcoming his revulsion, he leapt from his horse and pressed into the leper's hand all the money he had with him, then kissed the hand. This was a turning point in his life. He started visiting hospitals, especially the refuge for lepers, which most persons avoided. On a pilgrimage to Rome, he emptied his purse at St. Peter's tomb, then went out to the swarm of beggars at the door, gave his clothes to the one that looked poorest, dressed himself in the fellow's rags, and stood there all day with hand outstretched. The rich young man would experience for himself the bitterness and humiliation of poverty.

One day, after his return from Rome, as he prayed in the humble little church of St. Damian outside the walls of Assisi, he felt the eyes of the Christ on the crucifix gazing at him and heard a voice saying three times, "Francis, go and repair My house, which you see is falling down." The building, he observed, was old and ready to fall. Assured that he had now found the right path, Francis went home and in the singleness and simplicity of his heart took a horseload of cloth out of his father's warehouse and sold it, together with the horse that carried it, in the market at the neighboring town of Foligno. He then brought the money to the poor priest of St. Damian's church, and asked if he might stay there. Although the priest accepted Francis' companionship, he refused the money, which Francis left lying on a window sill. Bernadone, furious at his son's waywardness, came to St. Damian's to bring him home, but Francis hid himself and could not be found.

He spent some days in prayer, and then went bravely to see his father. He was now so thin and ill-clad that boys in the streets pelted him and called him mad. The exasperated Bernadone beat Francis, fettered his feet, and locked him up. A little later his mother set him free and Francis returned to St. Damian's. His father pursued him there and angrily declared that he must either return home or renounce his share in his inheritance—and pay the purchase price of the horse and the goods he had taken as well. Francis made no objection to being disinherited, but protested that the other money now belonged to God and the poor. Bernadone had him summoned for trial before Guido, the bishop of Assisi, who heard the story and told the young man to restore the money and trust in God. "He does not wish," the bishop said, "to have His church profit by goods which may have been unjustly acquired." Francis not only gave back the money but went even further. "My clothing is also his," he said, and stripped off his garments. "Hitherto I have called Peter Bernadone father. . . . From now on I say only, 'Our Father, who art in Heaven.' " Bernadone left the court in sorrow and rage, while the bishop covered the young man with his own cloak until a gardener's smock was brought. Francis marked a cross on the shoulder of the garment with chalk, and put it on.

Henceforth he was completely cut off from his family, and began a strange new life. He roamed the highways, singing God's praise. In a wood some robbers stopped him and asked who he was. When he answered soberly, "I am the herald of the Great King," they jeered and threw him into a ditch. He picked himself up and continued on his way singing. At a monastery, Francis was given alms and a job of work, as a poor traveler. Trudging on to the town of Gubbio, he was recognized by a friend, who took him to his house and gave him a proper tunic, belt, and shoes. These he wore for nearly two years as he walked about the countryside. When he returned to St. Damian's the priest welcomed him, and Francis now began in earnest to repair the church, begging for building stones in the streets of Assisi and carrying off those that were given him. He labored with the masons in the actual reconstruction, and, by the spring of 1208, the church was once more in good condition. Next he repaired an old chapel dedicated to St. Peter. By this time many people, impressed by his sincerity and enthusiasm, were willing to contribute to the work. Francis was now attracted to a tiny chapel known as St. Mary of the Portiuncula, belonging to a Benedictine monastery on Monte Subasio. It stood in the wooded plain, some two miles below Assisi, forsaken and in ruins. Francis rebuilt it as he had done the others, and seems to have thought of spending his life there as a hermit, in peace and seclusion. Here on the feast of St. Matthias, in 1209, the way of life he was to follow was revealed to him. The Gospel of the Mass for this day was Matthew x,7-19: "And going, preach, saying The Kingdom of Heaven is at

hand. . . . Freely have you received, freely give. Take neither
gold nor silver nor brass in your purses . . . nor two coats nor
shoes nor a staff. . . . Behold I send you forth as sheep in the
midst of wolves. . . ." These words suddenly became Christ's
direct charge to him. His doubts over, he cast off shoes, staff, and
leathern girdle, but kept his rough woolen coat, which he tied
about him with a rope. This was the habit he gave his friars the
following year. In this garb he went to Assisi the next morning and,
with a moving warmth and sincerity, began to speak to the people
he met on the shortness of life, the need of repentence, and the
love of God. His salutation to those he passed on the road was,
"Our Lord give you peace."

An early disciple was Bernard Quintavalle, a rich and prudent
merchant of the city, who invited Francis to stay at his house. At
night they had long talks, and there was no mistaking Francis'
passionate dedication. Bernard soon informed Francis that he
would sell all his goods and give the proceeds to the poor and join
him. Shortly afterward, a canon of the cathedral, Peter de Cattaneo,
asked to come with them. The three then went down to the Portiuncula, where, on April 16, Francis "gave his habit" to these two
companions and they built themselves simple huts. Brother Giles,
a man of great gentleness and purity of spirit, was the next to
come, and others soon followed.

For a year Francis and his now numerous companions preached
among the peasants and helped them in the fields. A brief rule
which has not been preserved was drawn up. Apparently it consisted of little more than the passages from the Gospel which Francis had read to his first followers, with brief injunctions to manual
labor, simplicity, and poverty. In the summer of 1210 he and some
of the others carried it to Rome to obtain the Pope's approbation.
Innocent III, the great ruler of Catholic Europe, listened but hesitated. Most of the cardinals he consulted thought that the existing
orders should be reformed before their number was increased and
that the proposed rule for the new organization, taken though it
was from Christ's own command, was impractical. Cardinal John

Colonna, who pleaded for Francis, was deputed to examine him as to his orthodoxy, while Innocent considered the matter. Later the Pope dreamed he saw Francis propping up the Lateran Church with his shoulder. He was to see Dominic in a similar position five years later. Summoning Francis and his companions, he orally approved their mission of preaching penitence, only requiring that they always get the consent of the local bishop; also they must choose a leader with whom the ecclesiastical authorities might communicate. Francis was thereupon elected head, and Cardinal Colonna gave them the monk's tonsure.

Francis and his little band returned to Umbria rejoicing. A temporary shelter was found near the foot of Monte Subasio, and from there they went out in all directions preaching repentance, and the blessedness of doing God's will. The cathedral of Assisi was the only church large enough to hold the crowds that flocked to hear them, especially after it was known that their rule had papal approval. Soon the abbot of the Benedictine monastery gave them in perpetuity their beloved Portiuncula chapel and the ground on which it stood. Francis would accept only the use of the property. The spirit of holy poverty must govern their order, if they were to be disciples of Him who had not where to lay His head. In token of this arrangement, the friars sent to the Benedictines every year as rent a basket of fish caught in a neighboring river. In return, the monks gave the friars a barrel of oil. This annual exchange of gifts still goes on between the Benedictines of St. Peter's in Assisi and the Franciscans of the Portiuncula. On the ground around the chapel the friars quickly built themselves some huts of wood and clay, enclosing them by a hedge. This was the first Franciscan monastery.

Because the body was meant to carry burdens, to eat scantily and coarsely, and to be beaten when sluggish or refractory, Francis called it Brother Ass. When, early in his new life, he was violently tempted, he threw himself naked into a ditch full of snow. Again when tempted, like Benedict he plunged into a briar patch and rolled about until he was torn and bleeding. Yet before he died he asked pardon of his body for having treated it so cruelly; by that time he considered excessive austerities wrong, especially if they decreased the power to labor. He had no use for eccentricity for its own sake. Once when he was told that a friar so loved silence that he would confess only by signs, his comment was, "That is not the spirit of God but of the Devil, a temptation, not a virtue."

Francis was reverently in love with all natural phenomena— sun, moon, air, water, fire, flowers; his quick warm sympathies responded to all that lived. His tenderness for and his power over animals were noted again and again. From his companions we have the story of his rebuke to the noisy swallows who were disturbing his preaching at Alviano: "Little sister swallows, it is now my turn to speak; you have been talking enough all this time." We hear also of the birds that perched attentively around when he told them to sing their Creator's praises, of the rabbit that would not leave him at Lake Trasymene, and of the tamed wolf of Gubbio—all incidents that have inspired innumerable artists and story tellers.

The early years were a time of training in poverty, mutual help, and brotherly love. The friars worked at their various trades and in the fields of neighboring farmers to earn their bread. When work was lacking, they begged, though they were forbidden to take money. They were especially at the service of lepers, and those who were helpless and suffering. Among the recruits soon to present themselves were the "Three Companions," Angelo, Leo, and Rufino, who were in time to write of their beloved leader; and the "renowned jester of the Lord," Brother Juniper, of whom Francis said, "I would I had a forest of such junipers." It was he who, while a crowd was waiting to receive him at Rome, was found playing seesaw with some children outside the city.

In the spring of 1212, an eighteen-year-old girl of Assisi named Clara [1] heard Francis preach in the cathedral and left her father's castle to take the vow of poverty and become a disciple. The monks of Monte Subasio again aided Francis by giving him a place where Clara and her earliest followers could be lodged; to them he

[1] For *St. Clara,* see p. 259.

gave the same rules as the brothers had. In the autumn of that year Francis resolved to go as a crusader of peace to the Mohammedans of the East. With a companion he embarked for Syria, only to suffer shipwreck off the Dalmatian coast. Having no money for the return passage, they got back to Ancona as stowaways. The following year Francis preached up and down central Italy. In 1214 he made another attempt to reach the Mohammedans, this time by the land route through Spain. So eager was he to arrive that his companion could scarcely keep up with him on the road. But once more Francis was disappointed, for in Spain he was taken ill and had to return to Italy.

There, on his recovery, he resumed direction of the order and his tours of preaching. To the order he gave the name of Friars Minor, Little Brothers, to express his wish that they should never be in positions above their fellows. Many cities were now anxious to have the brothers in their midst to act as peace-makers in periods of civil strife, and small communities of them sprang up rapidly throughout Umbria, Tuscany, and Lombardy. In 1215 Francis went to Rome for the great Council of the Lateran, which was also attended by the future St. Dominic, who had begun his missionary work in Languedoc while Francis was still a youth.

At Pentecost in 1217 a general chapter of all Friars Minor was held at Assisi. They had now become so numerous and so widely dispersed that some more systematic organization was necessary. Italy was divided into provinces, each in charge of a responsible minister provincial. "Should anyone be lost through the minister's fault and bad example, that minister will have to give an account before our Lord Jesus Christ." Missions were sent to Spain, Germany, and Hungary, and Francis himself made plans to go to France, of which he had heard so much in childhood from his father. He was dissuaded by Cardinal Ugolino, who after the death of Cardinal John Colonna began to serve as advisor to the new convent. He sent instead Brother Pacifico and Brother Agnello; the latter was afterwards to establish the order in England.

Although still the head, Francis was prevailed on at times to

THE VISION OF SAINT AUGUSTINE
Botticelli

Sandro Botticelli (1445-1510) worked under the patronage of the Medici family, and was the supervisor of the painting of the side walls of the Sistine Chapel in Rome. The strong feeling which permeates his religious pictures often overwhelmed his ability to express it, but he was one of the great painters of the late fifteenth century.

This picture illustrates Saint Augustine's vision: while walking along the shore, he saw a child spooning water into a hole in the sand. The child explained that he was going to empty the sea into the hole. Saint Augustine explained that it was impossible; the child answered that it was no more impossible than the effort of the saint to explain the Triune God. His usual symbol in art is an eagle, or a flaming heart pierced with arrows.

SAINT PATRICK   Suter

In this modern devotional picture, Saint Patrick is shown as Primate of the Irish Church. Often he is depicted as a missionary, in the habit of the Augustinian order, and carrying a pilgrim's staff.

Saint Patrick is almost always shown crushing the snakes with the staff of his crozier. His symbols also include the shamrock and sometimes a dragon.

submit to the prudent Ugolino. The cardinal actually presided at the general chapter of 1219, called, like its predecessor, a "mat chapter" because of the huts of wattles and straw hastily put up to shelter the five thousand friars present. The more learned and worldly-wise of the brothers were critical of the free and venturesome spirit of their founder, who, they claimed, was improvident and naïve. They wanted more material security and a more elaborate rule, similar to that of the older orders. Francis defended his position with spirit: "My brothers, the Lord called me into the way of simplicity and humility, and this way He has pointed out to me for myself and for those who will believe and follow me. . . . The Lord told me he would have me poor and foolish in this world, . . . God will confound you by your own wisdom and learning, and, for all your fault-finding, bring you repentance whether you will or no."

From this chapter Francis sent some of his friars on missions to the infidels in Tunisia, Morocco, and Spain, while he himself undertook one to the Saracens of Egypt and Syria, embarking with eleven friars from Ancona in June, 1219. At the city of Damietta on the Nila Delta, which the crusaders were besieging, Francis was deeply shocked at the profligacy, the cynicism, and the lack of discipline of the soldiers of the cross. When in August the leaders prepared to attack, he predicted failure and tried to dissuade them from the attempt. The Christians were driven back with the slaughter of six thousand men, yet they continued the siege, and at last took the city. Meanwhile, a number of the soldiers had pledged themselves to live by Francis' rule. He also paid several visits to the Saracen leader, Melek-el-Kamil, Sultan of Egypt. There is a story to the effect that he first went among the enemy with only Brother Illuminato, calling out, "Sultan! Sultan!" When he was brought before the Sultan and asked his errand, Francis replied boldly, "I am sent by the Most High God, to show you and your people the way of salvation by announcing to you the truths of the Gospel." Discussion followed, and other audiences. The Sultan, somewhat moved, invited Francis to stay with him. "If

you and your people," said Francis, "will accept the word of God,
I will with joy stay with you. If you yet waver between Christ
and Mohammed, order a fire kindled and I will go into it with your
priests that you may see which is the true faith." The Sultan replied that he did not think any of his *imams* would dare to enter
the fire, and he would not accept Francis' condition for fear of
upsetting the people. He offered him many presents, which Francis
refused. Fearing finally that some of his Moslems might desert to
the Christians, he sent Francis, under guard, back to the camp.

Sickened by the senseless slaughter and brutality that marked
the taking of the city, Francis went on to visit the Holy Places of
Palestine. When he returned to Italy he found that in his absence
his vicars, Matthew of Narni and Gregory of Naples, had held a
general chapter and introduced certain innovations, tending to
bring the Franciscans a little more into line with other orders and
to confine them in a more rigid framework. At several of the
women's convents, regular constitutions, drawn up on the Benedictine model, had been imposed by Cardinal Ugolino. In Bologna
Francis found his brothers housed in a fine new monastery. He
refused to enter it, and went for lodging to Dominic's Friars
Preachers. Sending for his provincial minister, he upbraided him,
and ordered the friars to leave the building. He felt that his fundamental idea was being betrayed. It was a serious crisis, but it ended
in Francis' acceptance of some measure of change. Ugolino convinced him that he himself, not the order, was the owner of the
new building; also that systematic supervision and regulation were
necessary for such a far-flung organization. Francis' profound humility made him ready to blame himself for anything that went
wrong. He would not give up his faith in the way of life that
Christ had shown him, but he became less confident. He finally
went to Pope Honorius III and asked that the cardinal be made
official protector and counselor of the order. At the chapter meeting of 1220 he resigned his position as minister general; in May,
1221, he offered his draft for a revised rule, a long and confused
document, containing a new requirement, a year's novitiate before

a candidate could be admitted; there were long extracts from the New Testament, and passionate appeals to the brothers to preserve the old life of poverty and love. The jurists of the order, those who knew the problems of administration, and the provincial ministers all wanted something more precise, a rule which could be understood and followed anywhere in the world by men who had never seen Francis, and which would also keep Franciscans from diverging too widely from the established usages of the historic Church.

Once at least during the two years that followed, Francis broke away to the solitude of a mountain near Rieti, and worked over the rule alone. The final result he delivered to Brother Elias of Cortona, then minister general, but the copy was somehow lost, and Francis patiently dictated the substance of it to Brother Leo. In the form in which it was at last presented to the chapter general in 1223 and solemnly approved by Pope Honorius it has remained ever since. The words of Christ which made up almost all of the original rule of 1210 are omitted. It is explicit on a number of points which in 1210 had been left indefinite—methods of admission, times of fasting, government by ministers and triennial general chapters, requirements for preaching, obedience to superiors; at the head of all is a cardinal governor appointed by the pope. The early simplicity is gone, though now and again the fervor of Franciscan idealism breaks through the sober text. The brothers are still to receive no money, to labor as far as they are able, to own no house "nor anything." They are not to be ashamed to beg, since "the Lord made himself poor for us in this world." They are not to trouble to educate illiterate brothers but to strive instead for pure hearts, humility, and patience. The contrast, however, between the old rule and the new shocked and pained some of the members. Yet it seemed true that such a great institution could not be run without a system of uniform control or let its members wander as they pleased over the earth, with no churches of their own where they could preach regularly, and no house where they could live together. To Brother Elias, the able and masterful friar who with Cardinal Ugolino became the directing force, there was still too much of the unworkable Franciscan dream in the new rule and in later years he refused to be bound by it. In 1230 the car-dinal, then Pope Gregory IX, issued an official interpretation of it.

Somewhat earlier Francis and the cardinal had drawn up a rule for the fraternity of lay men and women who wished to associate themselves with the Friars Minor and followed as best they could the rules of humility, labor, charity, and voluntary poverty, without withdrawing from the world: the Franciscan tertiaries or Third Order of today.[2] These congregations of lay penitents became a power in the religious life of the late Middle Ages.

The Christmas season of 1223 Francis spent near the village of Greccio in the valley of Rieti, weary in mind and body. There he remarked to his friend, the knight, Giovanni di Vellita, "I would make a memorial of that Child who was born in Bethlehem, and in some sort behold with bodily eyes the hardships of His infant state, lying on hay in a manger, with the ox and the ass standing by." So a rude stable was set up at the hermitage, with a live ox and ass, and a child lying on straw, and the people crowded to the midnight Mass, at which Francis as deacon read the Gospel story and then preached. His use of the *crèche* gave impetus to its later popularity. Having become extremely frail, he remained at Greccio for some months longer.

In June, 1224, Francis attended his last chapter meeting, at which the new rule was formally delivered to the provincial ministers. In August, with a few of the brothers closest to him, he made his way through the Apennine forest to the peak of Alvernia, a place of retreat put at his disposal years earlier by the lord of Chiusi. A hut of branches was built for him, a little way from his companions. Brother Leo daily brought him food. His fears for the future of the order now increased and reached a climax. And here it was, on or about Holy Cross Day, September 14, that at sunrise, after a night of prayer, he had a vision of a winged seraph, nailed

[2] The name of Second Order was given to the nuns who under Clara's leadership based their lives on the principles of St. Francis.

to a cross, flying towards him; he also felt keen stabs of pain in hands, feet, and sides. The vision vanished, and he discovered on his body the stigmata of the crucified Christ. During his lifetime, few persons saw the stigmata, called by Dante, "the ultimate seal." Thenceforth he kept his hands covered with the sleeves of his habit, and wore shoes and stockings. To those who were there with him, he disclosed what had happened, and within a few days composed the poem, "Praise of the Most High God."

After celebrating the feast of St. Michael on September 29, the now enfeebled friar rode down the mountain on a borrowed horse, and healed several persons who were brought to him in the plain below. Weak as he was, he insisted on preaching, riding from village to village on an ass. Young and ambitious members of the order, already set on rivaling the Dominicans as brilliant and popular preachers in the towns, were eager to outshine them in the schools as well. Francis realized that learning had its uses, but to fulfill their special mission, he knew that his brothers needed much time for prayer, meditation, and helpful labor. He feared the prescribed scholastic training, thinking it tended to feed conceit and extinguish charity and piety. Above all, Lady Learning was dangerous as a rival to Lady Poverty. Yet under pressure he yielded so far as to consent to the appointment of Antony of Padua as reader and teacher.

Francis' health was growing worse, the stigmata were a source of pain, and his eyes were failing. In the summer of 1225 Cardinal Ugolino and the vicar-general, Elias, made him consent to put himself in the hands of the Pope's physician at Rieti. On his way there he stopped to pay a final visit to Abbess Clara and the nuns of St. Damian. He stayed for over a month, and seemed depressed by his apparent failure to accomplish his mission in life. For two weeks he lost his sight, but finally triumphed over suffering and gloom, and in a sudden ecstasy one day composed the beautiful, triumphant "Canticle of the Sun," and set it to music. The brothers might sing it as they went about their preaching. He went on to Rieti to undergo the agonizing treatment prescribed—cauterization of the forehead by white-hot iron, and plasters to keep the wound open. Strangely enough, he obtained some relief. During the winter he preached a little, and dictated a long letter to his brothers, which he hoped would be read at the opening of future general chapters. They were to love one another, to love and follow Lady Poverty, to love and reverence the Eucharist, and to love and honor the clergy. He also composed a still longer letter to all Christians, repeating his message of love and harmony.

Yearning to be at home, when spring came he was carried north to Assisi and lodged in the bishop's palace, but these fine surroundings depressed Francis, and he begged to be taken to the Portiuncula. As they bore him down the hill, he asked to have the stretcher set down, and turning back for a moment towards the city he blessed it and bade it farewell. At the Portiuncula he was able to dictate his Will, a final, firm defense of all he had been and done. No one coming after him must introduce glosses to explain away any part of the rule or of this Will, for he had written it "in a clear and simple manner" and it should be understood in the same way and practiced "until the end." Four years later Ugolino, then Pope Gregory IX, at the same time that he gave an official interpretation of the rule, announced that the brothers were not bound to observe the Will.

As the end drew near, Francis asked his brothers to send to Rome for the Lady Giacoma di Settesoli, who had often befriended him. Even before the messenger started, the lady arrived at his bedside. Francis also sent a last message to Clara and her nuns. While the brothers stood about him singing the "Canticle of the Sun," with the new stanza he had lately given them, in praise of Sister Death, he repeated the one hundred and forty-first Psalm, "I cried to the Lord with my voice; with my voice I made supplication to the Lord." At his request he was stripped of his clothing and laid for a while on the ground that dying he might rest in the arms of Lady Poverty. Back upon his pallet once more, he called for bread and broke it and to each one present gave a piece in token of their love. The Gospel for Holy Thursday, the story of the

Lord's Passion as told by St. John, was read aloud. And as darkness fell on Saturday, October 3, 1226, Francis died.

He had asked to be buried in the criminals' cemetery in the Colle d'Inferno, but early the next morning a crowd of his fellow citizens came down and bore his body to the church of St. George in Assisi. Here it remained for two years, during which time a process of canonization was being carried through. In 1228 the first stone was laid for the beautiful basilica built in Francis' honor, under the direction of Brother Elias. In 1230 his body was secretly removed to it and, in fear that the Perugians might send a raiding party to steal it, buried so deep that not until 1818, after a fifty-two days' search, was it discovered beneath the high altar of the lower church.

The order which Francis founded divided early into three branches, the Brothers Minor of the Observance, who follow the rule of 1223, preach, perform works of charity, and go as missionaries abroad, the Brothers Minor Conventual, who live by the later, less stringent rule, which permits the corporate holding of property, and the Brothers Minor Capuchin, for whom Francis' rule is not ascetic enough, and who live strictly cloistered, under a regimen of silence.

Canticle of the Sun

O most high, almighty, good Lord God, to Thee belong praise, glory, honor, and all blessing!

By Thee alone, Most High, were all things made and no man is worthy to speak Thy name.

Praised be my Lord with all his creatures, especially Messer Brother Sun, who brings us the day and brings us the light; fair is he and shining with a very great splendor; Most High, he signifies to us Thee!

Praised be my Lord for Sister Moon, and for the stars, the which He has set in heaven clear and precious and lovely.

Praised be my Lord for Brother Wind, and for air and cloud, calms and all weather, by the which Thou upholdest life in Thy creatures.

Praised be my Lord for Sister Water, who is very serviceable unto us, and humble, and precious, and clean.

Praised be my Lord for Brother Fire, through whom Thou givest us light in the night; and he is beautiful and joyous, and very mighty, and strong.

Praised be my Lord for our Sister, Mother Earth, who doth sustain us and keep us, and bring forth divers fruits, and flowers of many colors, and grass.

Praised be my Lord for those who pardon one another for His love's sake, and who endure weakness and tribulation; blessed are they who peaceably endure, for by Thee, Most Highest, shall they be crowned.

Praised be my Lord for our sister the death of the body, from whom no man living can escape. Woe unto them who die in mortal sin. Blessed are they who are found walking by Thy most holy will, for the second death shall do them no harm.

Praise ye and bless my Lord, and give thanks unto Him and serve Him with great humility.

Will

See in what manner God gave it to me, to me, Brother Francis, to begin to do penitence; when I lived in sin, it was very painful to me to see lepers, but God himself led me into their midst, and I remained there a little while. When I left them, that which had seemed to me bitter had become sweet and easy.

A little while after I quitted the world, and God gave me such a faith in his churches that I would kneel down with simplicity and I would say: "We adore thee, Lord Jesus Christ, here and in all thy churches which are in the world, and we bless thee that by thy holy cross thou hast ransomed the world."

Besides, the Lord gave me and still gives me so great a faith in priests who live according to the form of the holy Roman Church, because of their sacerdotal character, that even if they persecuted me I would have recourse to them. And even though I had all the wisdom of Solomon, if I should find poor secular priests, I would not preach in their parishes without their consent. I desire to respect them like all the others, to love them and honor them as my lords. I will not consider their sins, for in them I see the Son of God, and they are my lords. I do this because here below I see nothing corporally of the most high Son of God if not his most holy Body and Blood, which they receive and they alone distribute to others. I desire above all things to honor and venerate all these most holy mysteries and to keep them precious. Whenever I find the sacred name of Jesus or his words in indecent places, I desire to take them away, and I pray that others take them away and put them in some decent place. We ought to honor and revere all the theologians and those who preach the most holy word of God, as dispensing to us spirit and life.

When the Lord gave me some brothers no one showed me what I ought to do, but the Most High himself revealed to me that I ought to live according to the model of the holy Gospel. I caused a short and simple formula to be written, and the lord pope confirmed it for me.

Those who presented themselves to observe this kind of life distributed all that they might have to the poor. They contented themselves with a tunic, patched within and without, with the cord and breeches, and we desired to have nothing more.

The clerks said the office like other clerks, and the laymen *Pater Noster.*

We loved to live in poor and abandoned churches, and we were ignorant and submissive to all. I worked with my hands and would continue to do so, and I will that all other friars work at some honorable trade. Let those who have none learn one, not for the purpose of receiving the price of their toil, but for their good example and to flee idleness. And when they do not give us the price of the work, let us resort to the table of the Lord, begging our bread from door to door. The Lord revealed to me the salutation which we ought to give: "God give you peace!"

Let the Brothers take great care not to receive churches, habitations, and all that men build for them, except as all is in accordance with the holy poverty which we have vowed in the Rule, and let them not receive hospitality in them except as strangers and pilgrims.

I absolutely interdict all the brothers, in whatever place they may be found, from asking any bull from the court of Rome, whether directly or indirectly, under pretext of church or convent or under pretext of preachings, or even for their personal protection. If they are not received anywhere, let them go elsewhere, thus doing penance with the benediction of God. . . .

And let the Brothers not say: "This is a new Rule"; for this is a reminder, a warning, an exhortation; it is my Will, that I, little Brother Francis, make for you, my blessed Brothers, in order that we may observe in a more Catholic way the Rule which we promised the Lord to keep.

Let the minsters-general, all the other ministers, and the guardians be held by obedience to add nothing to and take nothing from these words. Let them always keep this writing near them, beside the Rule; and in all the chapters which shall be held, when the Rule is read, let these words be read also.

I interdict absolutely, by obedience, all the Brothers, clerics and laymen, to introduce glosses in the Rule or in this Will, under pretext of explaining it. But since the Lord has given me to speak and to write the Rule and these words in a clear and simple manner, without commentary, understand them in the same way, and put them in practice until the end. . . .

And I, little brother Francis, your servitor, confirm to you so far as I am able this most holy benediction. Amen.

(Sabatier, *Life of St. Francis of Assisi.*)

Saint Antony of Padua

Confessor, Doctor of the Church

1 2 3 1

(*June 13*)

Although he was a native of Lisbon, Antony derived his surname from the Italian city of Padua, where his mature years were passed and where his relics are still venerated in the basilica, Il Santo. He was born in 1195 of a noble Portuguese family, and was baptized Ferdinand. His parents sent him to be educated by the clergy of the cathedral of Lisbon. At the age of fifteen he joined the canons regular [1] of St. Augustine, and at seventeen, in order to have more seclusion, asked for and obtained leave to transfer to the priory of St. Cross, of the same order, at Coimbra, then the capital of Portugal. There, for a period of eight years, he devoted himself to study and prayer. With the help of a remarkable memory he acquired a thorough knowledge of the Scriptures.

In the year 1220, Don Pedro, crown prince of Portugal, brought back from Morocco the relics of some Franciscan missionaries who had recently suffered martyrdom. The young student conceived an ardent desire to die for his faith, a hope he had little chance of realizing while he lived in a monastic enclosure. He spoke of this to some mendicant Franciscans who came to St. Cross, and was encouraged by them to apply for admission to their order. Although he met with some obstacles, he at length obtained his release and received the Franciscan habit in the chapel of St. Antony of Olivares, near Coimbra, early in 1221. He changed

---

[1] The canons, or clergy, attached to a church or cathedral for the conduct of its services, are called regular when they live under a monastic rule. The Canons Regular of St. Augustine was a popular order at this time.

251

his name to Antony in honor of St. Antony of Egypt, to whom this chapel was dedicated.

Almost at once he was permitted to embark for Morocco on a mission to preach Christianity to the Moors. He had scarcely arrived when he was prostrated by a severe illness, which obliged him to return to Europe. The ship in which he sailed for home was driven out of its course by contrary winds and he found himself landed at Messina, Sicily. From there he made his way to Assisi, where, he had learned from his Sicilian brethren, a chapter general was about to be held. It was the great gathering of 1221, the last chapter, as it proved, open to all members of the order, and presided over by Brother Elias, the new vicar-general, with the saintly Francis seated at his feet. The whole spectacle seems to have deeply impressed the young Portuguese friar.

At the close of the proceedings the friars set out for the posts assigned to them by their respective provincial ministers. In the absence of any Portuguese provincial, Antony was allowed to attach himself to Brother Gratian, the provincial of Romagna, who sent him to the lonely hermitage of San Paolo, near Forli, either at his own request, that he might live for a time in retirement, or as chaplain to the lay friars of the community. We do not know whether Antony was already a priest at the time. What is certain is that no one then suspected the brilliant intellectual gifts latent in the sickly young brother. When he was not praying in the chapel or in a little grotto, he was serving the other friars by washing their cooking pots and dishes after the common meal.

His talents were not to remain hidden long. It happened that an ordination service of both Franciscans and Dominicans was to be held at Forli, on which occasion all the candidates for consecration were to be entertained at the Franciscan Convent there. Through some misunderstanding, not one of the Dominicans had come prepared to deliver the expected address at the ceremony and no one among the Franciscans seemed ready to fill the breach. Antony, who was present, perhaps in attendance on his superior, was told by him to go forward and speak whatever the Holy

Ghost put into his mouth. Diffidently, he obeyed. Once having begun he delivered an address which astonished all who heard it by
its eloquence, fervor, and learning. Brother Gratian promptly sent
the brilliant young friar out to preach in the cities of the province.
As a preacher Antony was an immediate success. He proved particularly effective in converting heretics, of whom there were many
in northern Italy. They were often men of education and open to
conviction by Antony's keen and resourceful methods of argument.

In addition to his work as an itinerant preacher, he was appointed reader in theology to the Franciscans, the first to fill such
a post. In a letter, generally considered authentic, and character-
istically guarded in its approval of book learning, Francis himself
confirmed the appointment. "To my dearest brother Antony,
brother Francis sends greetings in Jesus Christ. I am well pleased
that you should read sacred theology to the friars, provided that
such study does not quench the spirit of holy prayer and devotion according to our rule."

Antony spent two years in northern Italy, after which he taught
theology in the universities of Montpellier and Toulouse and held
the offices of guardian or prior of a monastery at Puy and of
custodian at Limoges. For his ability in formulating arguments
against the heresies of the Albigensians, he became widely known
under the sobriquet of "Hammer of Heretics." It became more and
more plain that his career lay in the pulpit. Antony had not Francis' sweetness and simplicity, and he was no poet, but he had learning, eloquence, marked powers of logical analysis and reasoning, a
burning zeal for souls, a magnetic personality, and a sonorous voice
that carried far. The mere sight of him sometimes brought sinners
to their knees, for he appeared to radiate spiritual force. Crowds
flocked to hear him, and hardened criminals, careless Catholics,
heretics, all alike were converted and brought to Confession. Men
locked up their shops and offices to go and attend his sermons;
women rose early or stayed overnight in church to secure their
places. When churches could not hold the congregations, he
preached to them in public squares and market places.

In 1226, shortly after the death of St. Francis, Antony was re-called to Italy, apparently to become a provincial minister. It is not clear what his attitude was towards the dissensions which were rising everywhere in the order over the nature of the obedience to be paid to the rule and testament of Francis. Antony, it seems, acted as envoy from the discordant chapter general of 1226 to the innovating Pope Gregory IX, to lay before him the various con-flicts that had arisen. On that same occasion he obtained from Gregory his release from office-holding, so that he might devote himself to preaching. The Pope had a high respect for him, and because of his extraordinary familiarity with the Scriptures once called him "the Ark of the Testament."

Thereafter Antony made his home in Padua, a city which he already knew and where he was highly revered. There, more than anywhere else, he could see the results of his ministry. Not only were his sermons listened to by enormous congregations, but they led to a widespread reformation of morals and conduct in the city. Long standing quarrels were amicably settled, hopeless prisoners were liberated, owners of ill-gotten goods made restitution, often in public at Antony's feet. In the name of the poor he denounced the prevailing vice of extortionate usury and induced the city magistrates to pass a law exempting from prison debtors willing to surrender all their possessions to satisfy their creditors. He is said to have ventured boldly into the presence of the truculent and dangerous Duke Eccelino III, the Emperor's son-in-law, to plead for the liberation of some citizens of Verona whom the duke was holding captive. The attempt was unsuccessful, but due to the respect he inspired he was listened to with tolerance and allowed to depart unmolested.

In the spring of 1231, after preaching a powerful course of sermons, Antony's strength gave out and he retired with two of the brothers to a woodland retreat. It was soon clear that his days were numbered, and he asked to be taken back to Padua. He never got beyond the outskirts of the city. On June 13, in the apartment reserved for the chaplain of the sisterhood of Poor Clares of Arcella, he received the last rites and died. He was only in his thirty-sixth year. Within a year of his death he was canonized, and the Paduans have always regarded his relics as their most precious possession. They built a basilica to their saint in 1263.

The innumerable benefits he has won for those who prayed at his altars have obtained for Antony the name of the "Wonder-working Saint." Since the seventeenth century he has often been painted with the Infant Saviour on his arm because of a late legend to the effect that once, when stopping with a friend, his host, glancing through a window, had a glimpse of him gazing with rapture on the Holy Child, whom he was holding in his arms. In the earlier portraits he usually carries a book, symbolic of his knowledge of the Bible, or a lily. Occasionally he is accompanied by a mule which, legend says, fell on its knees before the Sacrament when upheld in the hands of the saint, and by so doing converted its heretical owner to a belief in the Real Presence. Antony is the special patron of barren and pregnant women, of the poor, and of travelers; alms given to obtain his intercession are called "St. Antony's Bread." How he came to be invoked, as he now is, as the finder of lost articles has not been satisfactorily explained. The only story that bears on the subject at all is contained in the so-called *Chronicles of the Twenty-four Generals,* number 21. A novice ran away from his monastery carrying with him a valuable psalter which Antony had been using. He prayed for its recovery and the novice was frightened by a startling apparition into bringing it back.

Sermons for the Liturgical Year

CHRISTMAS

*U*nto us a child is born, unto us a son is given; he bears his kingship on his shoulders and his name is called Wonderful, Counsellor, . . . the Prince of Peace. (Isaiah, ix,6)." A little above, Isaiah says: "Behold, a virgin shall conceive and bear a son and his name shall be Emmanuel, that is to say, God-with-us."

God made himself for us a little child; he was born for us. Among his many titles Christ is called a little child; I shall use but this one. You have hurt a child, you have struck him, but you show him a kindness, you give him a flower, a rose, or some other object he likes. Instantly he forgets the hurt you did him, his anger is gone and he runs to embrace you. Thus it is with Christ. You have offended him by a mortal sin or wounded him by some fault, but you offer him the flower of contrition or the rose of a confession steeped in tears. Tears are the blood of the soul. At once he forgets your offense, he forgives your sin, he runs, he takes you in his arms and gives you his kiss of peace. . . .

His name is called Wonderful, Counsellor . . . the Prince of Peace. In the moral sense, these words indicate the qualities of any penitent or good man. The good man is wonderful in his keen and frequent examination of his own conscience, for he sees strange things in the depths of his heart. "The anguish of his spirit" and "the bitterness of his soul," as Job says (vii,11) let nothing pass by him but he scrutinizes and examines everything down to the least detail.

The good man is a Counsellor in the spiritual and bodily necessities of his neighbor. Like Job (xxix,15) he says: "I am eye to the blind and foot to the lame." Blind is he who sees not his own conscience; lame is he who wanders from the right way. The good man comes to the help of each. He makes himself eye to the blind by leading him to recognize the sad state of his conscience. He makes himself foot to the lame by supporting him and guiding him into the way of righteousness and goodness. . . .

Prince of Peace, the good man lives in a perfect tranquillity of soul and body. As Job says (v,23), "the beasts of the field," that is, the stirrings of the flesh, "leave him in peace." Unknown, dead to the world in contemplation, "he sleeps in safety and no one disturbs his rest." (Job xi,19.)

Third Sunday after Epiphany

THE HAND OF JESUS

"Jesus stretched forth his hand and touched the leper and said to him: I will: be thou clean." (Matthew viii,3; Mark i,41; Luke v,13.)

O, how I marvel at that hand! "That hand carved of gold, set with precious stones (Canticles v,14)"; that hand whose touch looses the tongue of the dumb man, brings back to life the daughter of Jairus, and cleanses the leper; that hand of which the prophet Isaiah (lxvi,2) speaks to us: "it alone has done all these wondrous things." To stretch forth the hand is to bestow a gift. O Lord, stretch forth thine hand, that hand which the executioner will stretch out on the cross; touch the leper and give him of thy bounty! All that thy hand shall touch shall be purified and healed. "He touched," says St. Luke (xxii,51), "Malchus' ear and healed it." He stretched forth his hand to bestow on the leper the gift of health; he said: "I will: be thou clean," and immediately the leprosy was cleansed. "He does whatsoever he wills (Psalm cxiv, 3)." In him nothing separates willing from accomplishment.

Now this instant healing God performs daily in the soul of the sinner through the ministry of the priest. The priest has a three-fold office: he must stretch forth his hand, that is, pray for the sinner and take pity on him; he must touch him, console him, promise him pardon; he must will that pardon, and grant it and his absolution. Such is the threefold pastoral ministry which the Lord committed to Peter, when he said to him thrice: "Feed my sheep (John xxi,15-17)."

First Sunday after Pentecost

LOVE

"God is love," we read today at the beginning of the Epistle. (I John iv,8.) As love is the chief of all the virtues, we shall treat of it here at some length in a special way. . . .

If God loved us to the point that he gave us his well-beloved Son, by whom he made all things, we too should ourselves love one another. "I give you," he says, "a new commandment, that ye love one another (John xiii,34)." . . . We have, says St. Augustine, four objects to love. The first is above us: it is God. The second is ourselves. The third is round about us: it is our neighbor. The fourth is beneath us: it is our body. The rich man loved his body first and above everything. Of God, of his neighbor, of his soul, he had not a thought; that was why he was damned.

Our body, says St. Bernard, should be to us like a sick person entrusted to our care. We must refuse it many of the worthless things it wants; on the other hand, we must forcefully compel it to take the helpful remedies repugnant to it. We should treat it not as something belonging to us but as belonging to Him who bought it at so high a price, and whom we must glorify in our body (I Corinthians vi,20). We should love our body in the fourth and last place, not as the goal of our life but as an indispensable instrument of it.

(Les Sermons de St. Antoine de Padoue pour L'année Liturgique. Translated by Abbé Paul Bayart. Paris, n.d.)

Saint Clara

Virgin, Foundress of the Poor Clares

1 2 5 3

(August 12)

The Lady Clara, "shining in name, more shining in life," was born in the town of Assisi about the year 1193. Her mother was to become Blessed Ortolana di Fiumi. Her father is said to have been Favorino Scifi, Count of Sasso-Rosso, though whether he came of that noble branch of the Scifi family is not certain. Concerning Clara's childhood we have no reliable information. She was eighteen years old when St. Francis, preaching the Lenten sermons at the church of St. George in Assisi, influenced her to change the whole course of her life. It is likely that a marriage not to her liking had been proposed; at any rate, she went secretly to see Friar Francis and asked him to help her to live "after the manner of the Holy Gospel." Talking with him strengthened her desire to leave all worldly things behind and live for Christ. On Palm Sunday of that year, 1212, she came to the cathedral of Assisi for the blessing of palms, but when the others went up to the altar-rails to receive their branch of green, a sudden shyness kept Clara back. The bishop saw it and came down from the altar and gave her a branch.

The following evening she slipped away from her home and hurried through the woods to the chapel of the Portiuncula, where Francis was then living with his small community. He and his brethren had been at prayers before the altar and met her at the door with lighted tapers in their hands. Before the Blessed Virgin's altar Clara laid off her fine cloak, Francis sheared her hair, and gave her his own penitential habit, a tunic of coarse cloth tied

259

with a cord. Then, since as yet he had no nunnery, he took her at once for safety to the Benedictine convent of St. Paul, where she was affectionately welcomed.

When it was known at home what Clara had done, relatives and friends came to rescue her. She resisted valiantly when they tried to drag her away, clinging to the convent altar so firmly as to pull the cloths half off. Baring her shorn head, she declared that Christ had called her to His service, she would have no other spouse, and the more they continued their persecutions the more steadfast she would become. Francis had her removed to the nunnery of Sant' Angelo di Panzo, where her sister Agnes, a child of fourteen, joined her. This meant more difficulty for them both, but Agnes' constancy too was victorious, and in spite of her youth Francis gave her the habit. Later he placed them in a small and humble house, adjacent to his beloved church of St. Damian, on the outskirts of Assisi, and in 1215, when Clara was about twenty-two, he appointed her superior and gave her his rule to live by. She was soon joined by her mother and several other women, to the number of sixteen. They had all felt the strong appeal of poverty and sackcloth, and without regret gave up their titles and estates to become Clara's humble disciples. Within a few years similar convents were founded in the Italian cities of Perugia, Padua, Rome, Venice, Mantua, Bologna, Milan, Siena, and Pisa, and also in various parts of France and Germany. Agnes, daughter of the King of Bohemia, established a nunnery of this order in Prague, and took the habit herself.

The "Poor Clares," as they came to be known, practiced austerities which until then were unusual among women. They went barefoot, slept on the ground, observed a perpetual abstinence from meat, and spoke only when obliged to do so by necessity or charity. Clara herself considered this silence desirable as a means of avoiding the innumerable sins of the tongue, and for keeping the mind steadily fixed on God. Not content with the fasts and other mortifications required by the rule, she wore next her skin a rough shirt of hair, fasted on vigils and every day in Lent on bread and water,

and on some days ate nothing. Francis or the bishop of Assisi sometimes had to command her to lie on a mattress and to take a little
nourishment every day.

Discretion came with years, and much later Clara wrote this
sound advice to Agnes of Bohemia: "Since our bodies are not of
brass and our strength is not the strength of stone, but instead we
are weak and subject to corporal infirmities, I implore you vehe-
mently in the Lord to refrain from the exceeding rigor of abstinence
which I know you practice, so that living and hoping in the Lord
you may offer Him a reasonable service and a sacrifice seasoned
with the salt of prudence."

Francis, as we know, had forbidden his order ever to possess
revenues or lands or other property, even when held in common.
The brothers were to subsist on daily contributions from the people
about them. Clara also followed this way of life. When she left
home she had given what she had to the poor, retaining nothing
for her own needs or those of the convent. Pope Gregory IX proposed to mitigate the requirement of absolute poverty and offered
to settle a yearly income on the Poor Ladies of St. Damien. Clara,
eloquent in her determination never to break her vows to Christ
and Francis, got permission to continue as they had begun. "I
need," she said, "to be absolved from my sins, but I do not wish to
be absolved from my obligation to follow Jesus Christ." In 1228,
therefore, two years after Francis' death, the Pope granted the
Assisi sisterhood a *Privilegium paupertatis,* or Privilege of Poverty,
that they might not be constrained by anyone to accept possessions.
"He who feeds the birds of the air and gives raiment and nourishment to the lilies of the field will not leave you in want of clothing
or of food until He come Himself to minister to you for eternity."
The convents in Perugia and Florence asked for and received this
privilege; other convents thought it more prudent to moderate their
poverty. Thus began the two observances which have ever since
been perpetuated among the Poor Clares, as they later came to be
called. The houses of the mitigated rule are called Urbanist, from
the concession granted them in 1263 by Pope Urban IV. But as

early as 1247 Pope Innocent IV had published a revised form of
the rule, providing for the holding of community property. Clara,
the very embodiment of the spirit and tradition of Francis, drew
up another rule stating that the sisters should possess no property,
whether as individuals or as a community. Two days before she
died this was approved by Pope Innocent for the convent of St.
Damian.

Clara governed the convent continuously from the day when
Francis appointed her abbess until her death, a period of nearly
forty years. Yet it was her desire always to be beneath all the rest,
serving at table, tending the sick, washing and kissing the feet of
the lay sisters when they returned footsore from begging. Her
modesty and humility were such that after caring for the sick and
praying for them, she often had other sisters give them further
care, that their recovery might not be imputed to any prayers
or merits of hers. Clara's hands were forever willing to do whatever
there was of woman's work that could help Francis and his friars.
"Dispose of me as you please," she would say. "I am yours, since
I have given my will to God. It is no longer my own." She would be
the first to rise, ring the bell in the choir, and light the candles;
she would come away from prayer with radiant face.

The power and efficacy of her prayers are illustrated by a story
told by Thomas of Celano, a contemporary. In 1244, Emperor
Frederick II, then at war with the Pope, was ravaging the valley of
Spoleto, which was part of the patrimony of the Holy See. He employed many Saracens in his army, and a troop of these infidels
came in a body to plunder Assisi. St. Damien's church, standing
outside the city walls, was one of the first objectives. While the
marauders were scaling the convent walls, Clara, ill as she was, had
herself carried out to the gate and there the Sacrament was set up
in sight of the enemy. Prostrating herself before it, she prayed
aloud: "Does it please Thee, O God, to deliver into the hands of
these beasts the defenseless children whom I have nourished with
Thy love? I beseech Thee, good Lord, protect these whom now I
am not able to protect." Whereupon she heard a voice like the

voice of a little child saying, "I will have them always in My care." She prayed again, for the city, and again the voice came, reassuring her. She then turned to the trembling nuns and said, "Have no fear, little daughters; trust in Jesus." At this, a sudden terror seized their assailants and they fled in haste. Shortly afterward one of Frederick's generals laid siege to Assisi itself for many days. Clara told her nuns that they, who had received their bodily necessities from the city, now owed it all the assistance in their power. She bade them cover their heads with ashes and beseeech Christ as suppliants for its deliverance. For a whole day and night they prayed with all their might and with many tears, and then "God in his mercy so made issue with temptation that the besiegers melted away and their proud leader with them, for all he had sworn an oath to take the city."

Another story, which became very popular in later times, told how Clara and one of her nuns once left their cloister and went down to the Portiuncula to sup with Francis, and how a marvelous light radiated from the room where they sat together. However, no contemporary mentions this story, nor any other writer for at least one hundred and fifty years, whereas Thomas of Celano says that he often heard Francis warning his followers to avoid injudicious association with the sisters, and he states flatly that Clara never left the enclosure of St. Damian.

During her life and after her death there was disagreement at intervals between the Poor Clares and the Brothers Minor as to their correct relations. The nuns maintained that the friars were under obligation to serve their needs in things both spiritual and temporal. When in 1230 Pope Gregory IX forbade the friars to visit the convents of the nuns without special license, Clara feared the edict might lead to a complete severing of the ties established by Francis. She thereupon dismissed every man attached to her convent, those who served their material needs as well as those who served them spiritually; if she could not have the one, she would not have the other. The Pope wisely referred the matter to the minister general of the Brothers Minor to adjust.

After long years of sickness borne with sublime patience, Clara's life neared its end in the summer of 1253. Pope Innocent IV came to Assisi to give her absolution, remarking, "Would to God I had so little need of it!" To her nuns she said, "Praise the Lord, beloved daughters, for on this most blessed day both Jesus Christ and his vicar have deigned to visit me." Prelates and cardinals gathered round, and many people were convinced that the dying woman was truly a saint. Her sister Agnes was with her, as well as three of the early companions of Francis—Leo, Angelo, and Juniper. They read aloud the Passion according to St. John, as they had read it at the death-bed of Francis twenty-seven years before. Someone exhorted Clara to patience and she replied, "Dear brother, ever since through His servant Francis I have known the grace of our Lord Jesus Christ, I have never in my whole life found any pain or sickness that could trouble me." To herself she was heard to say, "Go forth without fear, Christian soul, for you have a good guide for your journey. Go forth without fear, for He that created you has sanctified you, has always protected you, and loves you as a mother."

Pope Innocent IV and his cardinals assisted at the funeral of the abbess. The Pope would have had her canonized immediately had not the cardinals present advised against it. His successor, Alexander IV, canonized her after two years, in 1255, at Anagni. Her body, which lay first in the church of St. George in Assisi, was translated to a stately church built to receive it in 1260. Nearly six hundred years later, in 1850, it was discovered, embalmed and intact, deep down beneath the high altar, and subsequently removed to a new shrine in the crypt, where, lying in a glass case, it may still be seen. In 1804 a change was made in the rule of the Poor Clares, originally a contemplative order, permitting these religious to take part in active work. Today there are houses of the order in North and South America, Palestine, Ireland, England, as well as on the Continent. The emblem of St. Clara is a monstrance, and in art she is frequently represented with a ciborium.

Saint Louis

Confessor, King of France

1 2 7 0

(*August 25*)

In Louis IX of France were united the qualities of a just and upright sovereign, a fearless warrior, and a saint. This crusading king was a living embodiment of the Christianity of the time: he lived for the welfare of his subjects and the glory of God. His father was Louis VIII, of the Capet line, and his mother was the redoubtable Queen Blanche, daughter of King Alfonso of Castile and Eleanor of England. Louis, the oldest son, was born at Poissy on the Seine, a little below Paris, on April 25, 1214, and there was christened. Much of his virtue is attributed to his mother's care, for the Queen devoted herself to her children's education. Louis had tutors who made him a master of Latin, taught him to speak easily in public and write with dignity and grace. He was instructed in the arts of war and government and all other kingly accomplishments. But Blanche's primary concern was to implant in him a deep regard and awe for everything related to religion. She used often to say to him as he was growing up, "I love you, my dear son, as much as a mother can love her child; but I would rather see you dead at my feet than that you should commit a mortal sin."

Louis never forgot his upbringing. His friend and biographer, the Sieur de Joinville,[1] who accompanied him on his first crusade to the Holy Land, relates that the King once asked him, "What is God?" Joinville replied, "Sire, it is that which is so good that there can be

[1] The best contemporary account of Louis is contained in the *Memoirs of Sieur de Joinville.*

nothing better." "Well," said the King, "now tell me, would you rather be a leper or commit a mortal sin?" The spectacle of the wretched lepers who wandered along the highways of medieval Europe might well have prompted a sensitive conscience to ask such a question. "I would rather commit thirty mortal sins," answered Joinville, in all candor, "than be a leper." Louis expostulated with him earnestly for making such a reply. "When a man dies," he said, "he is healed of leprosy in his body; but when a man who has committed a mortal sin dies he cannot know of a certainty that he has in his lifetime repented in such sort that God has forgiven him; wherefore he must stand in great fear lest that leprosy of sin last as long as God is in Paradise."

After a reign of only three years, Louis VIII died, and Queen Blanche was declared regent for her eleven-year-old son. To forestall an uprising of restless nobles, she hastened the ceremony of Louis' coronation, which took place at Rheims on the first Sunday of Advent, 1226. The boy was tall, and mature for his age, yet he trembled as he took the solemn oath; he asked of God courage, light, and strength to use his authority well, to uphold the divine honor, defend the Church, and serve the good of his people. The ambitious barons, who were not present at the coronation, were soon making extravagant demands for more privileges and lands, thinking to take advantage of the King's youth. But they reckoned without the Queen; by making clever alliances, she succeeded in overcoming them on the battlefield, so that when Louis assumed control some years later, his position was strong.

In May, 1234, Louis, then twenty, married Margaret, the oldest daughter of Raymond Beranger, Count of Provence. They had eleven children, five sons and six daughters. This line continued in power in France for five hundred years. In 1703, as the guillotine fell on Louis XVI, it will be recalled that the Abbé Edgeworth murmured: "Son of St. Louis, ascend to Heaven!"

After taking the government of the realm into his hands, one of the young King's first acts was to build the famous monastery of Royaumont, with funds left for the purpose by his father. Louis gave encouragement to the religious orders, installing the Carthusians in the palace of Vauvert in Paris, and assisting his mother in founding the convent of Maubuisson. Ambitious to make France foremost among Christian nations, Louis was overjoyed at the opportunity to buy the Crown of Thorns and other holy relics from the Eastern Emperor at Constantinople. He sent two Dominican friars to bring these sacred objects to France, and, attended by an impressive train, he met them at Sens on their return. To house the relics, he built on the island in the Seine named for him, the shrine of Sainte-Chapelle, one of the most beautiful examples of Gothic architecture in existence. Since the French Revolution it stands empty of its treasure.

Louis loved sermons, heard two Masses daily, and was surrounded, even while traveling, with priests chanting the hours. Though he was happy in the company of priests and other men of wisdom and experience, he did not hesitate to oppose churchmen when they proved unworthy. The usual tourneys and festivities at the creation of new knights were magnificently celebrated, but Louis forbade at his court any diversion dangerous to morals. He allowed no obscenity or profanity. "I was a good twenty-two years in the King's company," writes Joinville, "and never once did I hear him swear, either by God, or His Mother, or His saints. I did not even hear him name the Devil, except if he met the word when reading aloud, or when discussing what had been read." A Dominican who knew Louis well declared that he had never heard him speak ill of anyone. When urged to put to death the rebel son of Hugh de la Marche, he would not do so, saying, "A son cannot refuse to obey his father's orders."

In 1230 the King forbade all forms of usury, in accordance with the teachings of the Christian religion. Where the profits of the Jewish and Lombard money-lenders had been exorbitant, and the original borrowers could not be found, Louis exacted from the usurers a contribution towards the crusade which Pope Gregory was then trying to launch. He issued an edict that any man guilty of blasphemy should be branded. Even the clergy objected to the harshness of this penalty, and later, on the advice of Pope Clement IV, it was reduced to a fine, or flogging, or imprisonment, depending on circumstances. Louis protected vassals and tenants from cruel lords. When a Flemish count hanged three children for hunting rabbits in his woods, he had the man imprisoned, and tried, not by his peers, as was the custom, but by ordinary civil judges, who condemned him to death. Louis spared the count's life, but fined him heavily and ordered the money spent on religious and charitable works. He forbade private wars between his feudal vassals. In his dealings with other great princes, he was careful not to be drawn into their quarrels. If, when putting down a rebellion, he heard of damage inflicted on innocent people, by his or the enemy's forces, he invariably had the matter examined and full restitution paid. Barons, prelates, and foreign princes often chose him to arbitrate their disputes. A rising of the nobles in the southwest occurred in 1242, but the King's armies quickly put it down, although Henry III of England had come to their aid.

After recovering from a violent fever in 1244, Louis announced his long-cherished intention of undertaking a crusade to the East. Although his advisers urged him to abandon the idea, he was not to be moved from his decision. Elaborate preparations for the journey and settling certain disturbances in the kingdom caused him to postpone his departure for three and a half years. All benefices in Christendom were ordered taxed a twentieth of their income for three years for the relief of the Holy Land. Blanche was to be regent during the King's absence. On June 12, 1248, Louis left Paris, accompanied by his wife and three brothers. Their immediate objective was Egypt, whose Sultan, Melek Selah, had been overrunning Palestine. Damietta, at the mouth of one of the branches of the Nile, was easily taken. Louis and the Queen, accompanied by his brothers, the nobles, and prelates, made a solemn entry into the city, singing *Te Deum*. The King issued orders that all acts of violence committed by his soldiers should be punished and restitution made to the persons injured. He forbade the killing of any infidel taken prisoner, and gave directions that all who might desire to embrace the Christian faith should be given instruction, and, if they wished it, baptized. Yet as long as the army was quartered around Damietta, many of his soldiers fell into debauchery and lawlessness. The rising of the Nile and the summer heat made it impossible for them to advance and follow up their success. After six months they moved forward to attack the Saracens on the opposite side of the river, in Mansourah. The ranks of the crusaders were thinned more by disease than by combat. In April, 1250, Louis himself, weakened by dysentery, was taken prisoner, and his army was routed.

During his captivity the King recited the Divine Office every day with two chaplains and had the prayers of the Mass read to him. He met insults with an air of majesty which awed his guards. In the course of negotiations for his liberation, the Sultan was murdered by his emirs. The King and his fellow prisoners were released, though the sick and wounded crusaders left in Damietta were slain. With the remnant of his army Louis then sailed to the Syrian coast and remained in that region until 1254, fortifying the cities of Acre, Jaffa, Caesarea, and Tyre, which as yet remained in Christian hands. He visited the Holy Places that were in the possession of Christians, encouraging their garrisons, and doing what he could to strengthen their defenses. Not until news was brought him of the death of his mother did he feel that he must return to France. He had now been away almost six years, and even after his return, he continued to wear the cross on his shoulder to show his intention of going back to succor the Eastern Christians. Their position worsened, and within a few years Nazareth, Caesarea, Jaffa, and Antioch had been captured.

The foundations for the famous college of theology which was later known as the Sorbonne were laid in Paris about the year 1257. Its head, Master Robert de Sorbon, a learned canon and doctor, was the King's friend and sometimes his confessor. Louis helped to endow the college and obtained for it the approval of Pope Clement IV. It was perhaps the most famous theological school of Europe. The King himself founded in Paris the hospital of Quinze-vingt, so named because it had beds for three hundred patients. He also received indigent persons daily and saw that they were fed; in Lent and Advent he cared for all who came, often waiting on them in person. He had, as we have said, a passion for justice, and changed the "King's court" of his ancestors into a popular court, where, seated in his palace or under a spreading oak in the forest of Vincennes, he listened to any of his subjects who came with grievances and gave what seemed to them wise and impartial judgments. The feudal method of settling disputes by combat he tried to replace by peaceful arbitration or the judicial process of trial, with the presentation of testimony. In later times, whenever the French complained of oppression, their cry was for justice to be meted out impartially, as it had been in the reign of St. Louis.

In 1258 Louis concluded the Peace of Paris with his old enemy Henry III of England. Though Louis had been victorious in most of the battles, he now voluntarily surrendered to England the provinces of Limousin, Quercy, and Perigord, while Henry renounced all claim to recover Normandy, Anjou, Maine, Touraine, and Poitou. The French nobility were outraged by their King's concessions, but Louis explained that he hoped thus to cement a lasting friendship between the two nations. Unfortunately, peace did not ensue; the Hundred Years' War was still to come. A similar compromise was made with the King of Aragon, by which France secured Provence and most of Languedoc, and gave up claims to Roussillon and Barcelona.

One day, after standing godfather to a Jewish convert who had been baptized at St. Denis, Louis remarked to an ambassador from the emir of Tunis that to see the emir baptized he would himself joyfully spend the rest of his life in Saracen chains. The King was determined to go on another crusade, and in 1267 he announced his intention. His people objected, fearing they would lose their excellent and revered ruler, who, though only fifty-two years old, was worn with toil, illness, and austerities. The Pope supported the crusade, and granted Louis one-tenth of all Church

revenues to help meet the expense. A toll-tax was also levied on the
French people. Louis appointed the abbot of St. Denis and Simon
de Clermont as regents. His three eldest sons, Philip, John, and
Peter, accompanied him. The worthy Joinville disapproved the
enterprise and stayed at home.

Louis sailed with his forces from Aigues-Mortes, at the mouth
of the Rhone, on July 1, 1270, heading for Tunis, where, he had
been told, the emir was ready to be converted and join the expedition to win back the Holy Places. The crusade was a dismal failure.
On landing at Carthage, Louis learned to his dismay that the
information about the emir was false. He decided to wait there
for reinforcements from the King of Sicily. Dysentery and other
diseases broke out among the crusaders, and Louis' second son,
who had been born at Damietta during the earlier crusade, died.
That same day the King and his eldest son, Philip, sickened, and
it was soon apparent that Louis would not recover. He was
speechless all the next morning, but at three in the afternoon he
said, "Into Thy hands I commend my spirit," and quickly breathed
his last. His bones and heart were taken back to France and kept
enshrined in the abbey-church of St. Denis, until they were scattered at the time of the Revolution. Louis was strong, idealistic,
austere, just; his charities and foundations were notable, and he
went on two crusades. Little wonder that a quarter of a century
after his death the process of canonization was started and quickly
completed: the man who was "every inch a king" became a saint
of the Church in 1297, twenty-seven years after his death.

Last Instructions to his Eldest Son

*T*hen he [*Louis*] *called my Lord Philip, his son, and commanded him,* as if by testament, to observe all the teachings
he had left him, which are hereinafter set down in French, and
were, so it is said, written with the king's own saintly hand:

"Fair son, the first thing I would teach thee is to set thine heart
to love God; for unless he love God none can be saved. Keep thy-

self from doing aught that is displeasing to God, that is to say, from mortal sin. Contrariwise thou shouldst suffer every manner of torment rather than commit a mortal sin.

"If God send thee adversity, receive it in patience and give thanks to our Saviour and bethink thee that thou hast deserved it, and that He will make it turn to thine advantage. If He send thee prosperity, then thank Him humbly, so that thou becomest not worse from pride or any other cause, when thou oughtest to be better. For we should not fight against God with his own gifts.

"Confess thyself often and choose for thy confessor a right worthy man who knows how to teach thee what to do, and what not to do; and bear thyself in such sort that thy confessor and thy friends shall dare to reprove thee for thy misdoings. Listen to the services of Holy Church devoutly, and without chattering; and pray to God with thy heart and with thy lips, and especially at Mass when the consecration takes place. Let thy heart be tender and full of pity toward those who are poor, miserable, and afflicted, and comfort and help them to the utmost of thy power.

"Maintain the good customs of thy realm and abolish the bad. Be not covetous against thy people and do not burden them with taxes and imposts save when thou art in great need.

"If thou hast any great burden weighing upon thy heart, tell it to thy confessor or to some right worthy man who is not full of vain words. Thou shalt be able to bear it more easily.

"See that thou hast in thy company men, whether religious or lay, who are right worthy and loyal and not full of covetousness, and confer with them oft; and fly and eschew the company of the wicked. Hearken willingly to the Word of God and keep it in thine heart, and seek diligently after prayers and indulgences. Love all that is good and profitable and hate all that is evil, wheresoever it may be.

"Let none be so bold as to say before thee any word that would draw or move to sin, or so bold as to speak evil behind another's back for pleasure's sake; nor do thou suffer any word in disparagement of God and of His saints to be spoken in thy presence. Give often thanks to God for all the good things he has bestowed on thee, so that thou be accounted worthy to receive more.

"In order to do justice and right to thy subjects, be upright and

POPE GREGORY AND DEACON PETER   Unknown

Nothing is known about the artist who did this interesting illustration of
Pope Gregory the Great in Trier, Germany, about the year
983. It is a primitive form of drawing showing no knowledge
of perspective. The important figure—the Pope—is large; the
less important deacon is very much smaller.

Saint Gregory is shown dictating his famous "Homilies" with
the dove of inspiration on his shoulder. The dove, and the
book on a desk, are his usual symbols.

SAINT AUGUSTINE OF CANTERBURY
Unknown

Not an example of great art, nevertheless this picture of Saint Augustine represents a form of church art which can be quite good, as here, or sometimes quite bad. It is a devotional picture, as distinguished from a narrative picture, and shows the saint with his various attributes and symbols.

Saint Augustine bears his pastoral staff surmounted by a cross fitchée, and a book. Sometimes he carries the banner of the crucifixion, and sometimes King Ethelbert is shown in a baptismal font.

firm, turning neither to the right hand nor to the left, but always to what is just; and do thou maintain the cause of the poor until such a time as the truth is made clear. And if anyone has an action against thee, make full inquiry until thou knowest the truth; for thus shall thy counsellors judge the more boldly according to the truth, whether for thee or against.

"If thou holdest aught that belongeth to another, whether by thine own act or the act of thy predecessors, and the matter be certain, make restitution without delay. If the matter be doubtful, cause inquiry to be made by wise men diligently and promptly.

"Give heed that thy servants and thy subjects live under thee in peace and uprightness. Especially maintain the good cities and commons of thy realm in the same estate and with the same franchises as they enjoyed under thy predecessors; and if there be aught to amend, amend and set it right, and keep them in thy favor and love. For because of the power and wealth of the great cities, thine own subjects, and especially thy peers and thy barons and foreigners also will fear to undertake aught against thee.

"Love and honor all persons belonging to Holy Church, and see that no one take away or diminish the gifts and alms paid to them by thy predecessors. It is related of King Philip, my grandfather, that one of his counsellors once told him that those of Holy Church did him much harm and damage in that they deprived him of his rights, and diminished his jurisdiction, and that it was a great marvel that he suffered it; and the good king replied that he believed this might well be so, but he had regard to the benefits and courtesies that God had bestowed on him, and so thought it better to abandon some of his rights than to have any contention with the people of Holy Church.

"To thy father and mother thou shalt give honor and reverence, and thou shalt obey their commandments. Bestow the benefices of Holy Church on persons who are righteous and of a clean life, and do it on the advice of men of worth and uprightness.

"Beware of undertaking a war against any Christian prince without great deliberation; and if it has to be undertaken, see that thou do no hurt to Holy Church and to those that have done thee no injury. If wars and dissensions arise among thy subjects, see that thou appease them as soon as thou art able.

"Use diligence to have good provosts and bailiffs, and inquire often of them and of those of thy household how they conduct themselves, and if there be found in them any vice of inordinate covetousness or falsehood or trickery. Labor to free thy land from all vile iniquity, and especially strike down with all thy power evil swearing and heresy. See to it that the expense of thy household be reasonable.

"Finally, my very dear son, cause Masses to be sung for my soul, and prayers to be said throughout thy realm; and give to me a special share and full part in all the good thou doest. Fair, dear son, I give thee all the blessings that a good father can give to his son. And may the blessed Trinity and all the saints keep and defend thee from all evils; and God give thee grace to do His will always, so that He be honored in thee, and that thou and I may both, after this mortal life is ended, be with Him together and praise Him everlastingly. Amen."

(Joinville, *Chronicle of the Crusade of St. Lewis,* contained in *Memoirs of the Crusades,* Everyman Edition.)

Saint Thomas Aquinas

Confessor, Doctor of the Church

1 2 7 4

(March 7)

The Italian family of Aquino traced its ancestry back to the Lombard kings and was linked with several of the royal houses of Europe. Landulph, father of Thomas Aquinas, held the titles of Count of Aquino and Lord of Loreto, Acerro, and Belcastro; he was nephew of Emperor Frederick Barbarossa and also connected to the family of King Louis IX of France, whose life precedes this; his wife, Theodora, Countess of Teano, was descended from the Norman barons who had conquered Sicily some two centuries earlier. Thomas himself, at maturity, was a man of imposing stature, massive build, and fair complexion, and appeared more of a Norseman than a south Italian. The place and date of his birth are not definitely known, but it is assumed that he was born in 1226 at his father's castle of Roccasecca, whose craggy ruins are still visible on a mountain which rises above the plain lying between Rome and Naples. He was the sixth son in the family. While Thomas was still a child, his little sister, who slept in the same room with him and their nurse, was instantly killed one night by a bolt of lightning. This shocking experience caused Thomas to be extremely nervous during thunderstorms all his life long, and while a storm raged he often took refuge in a church. After his death, there arose a popular devotion to him as a protector from thunderstorms and sudden death.

A few miles to the south of Roccasecca, on a high plateau, stands the most famous of Italian monasteries, Monte Cassino,[1] the abbot

[1] On Monte Cassino, see above, *St. Benedict*, p. 134.

of which, at the time, was Thomas' uncle. When he was about nine years old the boy was sent to Cassino, in care of a tutor, to be educated in the Benedictine school which adjoined the cloister. In later years, when Thomas had achieved renown, the aged monks liked to recall the grave and studious child who had pored over their manuscripts, and who would ask them questions that revealed his lively intelligence and his deeply religious bent. Thomas was popular too with his companions, though he seldom took part in their games. He spent five happy years in the school at Cassino, returning home now and again to see his parents.

On the advice of the abbot, when Thomas had reached the age of fourteen, he went to the University of Naples to begin the seven years' undergraduate course prescribed in all European universities. He lived with his tutor, who continued to supervise his life. Under a famous teacher, Peter Martin, Thomas went through the Trivium, the three-year preliminary training in logic, rhetoric, and grammar, which also included the study of Latin literature and Aristotle's logic.[2] This was followed by four years of the Quadrivium, which comprised advanced work in mathematics, music, geometry, and astronomy or astrology. In addition to these subjects, there was also some study of physics under a celebrated scholar, Peter of Ireland, and extensive reading in philosophy. It was then the custom for pupils to recapitulate to the class a lecture they had just heard. Thomas' fellow students observed that, when his turn came, the summary he gave was usually clearer and better reasoned than the original discourse had been.

All this time Thomas was becoming more and more attracted to the youthful Dominican Order, with its stress on intellectual train-

[2] Aristotle's treatise on logic, the *Organon,* was known in Latin translation in Western Europe from the twelfth century and formed the basis of the teaching of logic in the schools. At the end of that century and through the thirteenth more of his important works became known, as new manuscripts and their translations were brought to the Universities of Paris, Oxford, and Cambridge from Spain, where the Mohammedan and Jewish scholars had them, and from Constantinople. From this time on Aristotle ranks as the authority on most branches of knowledge through the later Middle Ages.

ing. He attended its church and became friendly with some of the friars. To the prior of the Benedictine house in Naples Thomas confided his desire to become a Dominican. In view, however, of the almost certain opposition of his family, the prior advised him to foster his vocation, and wait for three years before taking any decisive step. The passage of time only strengthened Thomas' determination, and early in 1244, at the age of nineteen, he was received as a novice and clothed in the habit of the Brothers Preachers.

News of the ceremony, which took place before a large assemblage, was soon carried to Roccasecca. The members of his family were indignant, not that Thomas had joined a religious community, but that he, scion of a noble family, had chosen one of the humble, socially scorned, mendicant orders. His mother, especially, had expected that he would become a great churchman, possibly abbot of Monte Cassino. Appeals were sent to the Pope and to the archbishop of Naples; the Countess Theodora herself set out for Naples to persuade her son to return home. The friars hurried Thomas off to their convent in Rome, then sent him on to join the Father General of the Dominicans, who was leaving for Paris. The countess now sent word to her other sons, who were serving with the army in Tuscany, to waylay the fugitive. Thomas was overtaken as he was resting at the roadside, and was forcibly brought back. He was kept in confinement in the castle of San Giovanni. His sisters were allowed to visit him, and although they tried to undermine his resolution, before long they were won over to his side, and secretly got books for him from the friars at Naples. During his captivity Thomas studied Aristotle's *Metaphysics*, Peter Lombard's *Sentences*,[3] and learned by heart long passages of the Bible. His brothers tried to break his resistance by introducing into his room a woman of loose character. Thomas

[3] This famous work by an Italian-born bishop of Paris, known as the *Sentences* (*Sententiae*) was the most popular theological handbook of the period. It was a collection of opinions of the Church Fathers on well-nigh every crucial point of doctrine.

seized a burning brand from the hearth and drove her out, then knelt and implored God to grant him the gift of perpetual chastity. His early biographers write that he at once fell into a deep sleep, during which he was visited by two angels, who girded him around the waist with a cord so tight that it waked him. Thomas himself did not reveal this vision, until, on his deathbed, he described it to his old friend and confessor, Brother Reginald, adding that from this time on he was never again troubled by temptations of the flesh.

At last, influenced by the remonstrances that came from both the Pope and the Emperor, his family began to yield. A band of Dominicans hurried in disguise to the prison, where, we are told, with the help of his sisters, Thomas was let down by a cord into their arms, and they took him joyfully to Naples. The following year he made his full profession there, before the prior who had first clothed him with the habit of St. Dominic. Somewhat later, the powerful Aquino family obtained from Pope Innocent IV permission to have Thomas appointed abbot of Monte Cassino without resigning his Dominican habit. When Thomas declined this honor, the Pope expressed a willingness to promote him to the archiepiscopal see of Naples, but the young man made clear his determination to refuse all offices.

The Dominicans now decided to send Thomas to Paris to complete his studies under their great teacher, Albertus Magnus,[4] and he set out on foot with the Father General, who was again on his way northward. Carrying only their breviaries and their satchels, they made their way over the Alps in midwinter, and trudged first to Paris, and then, it is thought, on to Cologne, where Albertus was lecturing. The schools there were full of young clerics from all corners of Europe, eager to learn and discuss. The humble,

---

[4] Albertus Magnus (c. 1200-1280) was a scientist and scholastic philosopher, called *Doctor Universalis* because of his vast knowledge in all fields. Born in Swabia, he joined the Dominican Order and taught in various German cities before coming to Paris. He is famous for his interest in experimental and biological science and for his popularization of Aristotle.

reserved newcomer was not immediately appreciated by students or professors. In fact, his silence at disputations and his bulky figure won him the name of "the dumb Sicilian ox." A fellow student, out of pity for his apparent dullness, offered to explain the daily lessons, and Thomas thankfully accepted. But when they came to a difficult passage which baffled the would-be teacher, he was amazed when his pupil explained it clearly. Albertus once asked his pupils for their views on an obscure passage in the mystical treatise, *The Book of Divine Names,* by the ancient author known as Dionysius the Areopagite. Albertus was struck by the brilliance of Thomas' explanation. The next day he questioned Thomas in public and at the close exclaimed, "We have called Thomas 'dumb ox,' but I tell you his bellowing will yet be heard to the uttermost parts of the earth." He forthwith had the young man moved to a cell beside his own, took him on walks, and invited him to draw on his own stores of knowledge. It was at this period that Thomas began his commentary on the *Ethics* of Aristotle.

The general chapter, which decreed that Albertus should go to Paris to take the degree of Doctor and occupy a chair in the university, arranged that Thomas should accompany him. They set out, on foot, as always; they ate by the roadside the food given them in charity, and slept wherever they found shelter, or even under the stars. At the Dominican convent in Paris Thomas proved himself an exemplary friar, excelling in humility as he did in learning. Albertus drew such crowds to his lectures that he had to deliver them in a public square. It is likely that Thomas was always present. He made one intimate friend in Paris, a Franciscan student, later to be known to the world as St. Bonaventura,[5] the "Seraphic Doctor," as Thomas was to be the "Angelic Doctor." The two seemed to complement each other perfectly. Bonaventura was the elder by four years, but they were at the same stage in

---

[5] St. Bonaventura, cardinal-bishop of Albano, is considered the greatest mystical theologian of the Middle Ages and one of its eminent scholars. He wrote commentaries on the Scriptures as well as a life of St. Francis. He is the intellectual light of the Franciscan Order as Thomas is of the Dominican.

their studies, and both received the degree of Bachelor of Theology in 1248.

That same year Albertus went back to Cologne, accompanied by Thomas, who lectured under him, and, as a Bachelor, supervised the students' work, corrected their essays, and read with them. Thomas exhibited a marvelous talent for imparting knowledge. After he had received Holy Orders from the archbishop of Cologne, his religious fervor became more marked. One of his biographers writes, "When consecrating at Mass, he would be overcome by such intensity of devotion as to be dissolved in tears, utterly absorbed in its mysteries and nourished with its fruits." It was at this period that he became celebrated as a preacher, and his sermons in the German vernacular attracted enormous congregations. He was also occupied writing Aristotelian treatises and commentaries on the Scriptures. In the autumn of 1252, Thomas returned to Paris to study for his doctorate. On the way he preached at the court of the Duchess of Brabant, who had requested his advice on how to treat the Jews in her dominion. He wrote for her a dissertation urging humanity and tolerance.

Academic degrees were then conferred for the most part only on men actually intending to teach. To become a Bachelor a man must have studied at least six years and attained the age of twenty-one; to be a Master or a Doctor, he must have studied eight more years and be thirty-five years of age. But when Thomas in 1252 began lecturing publicly in Paris, he was not yet twenty-eight.

The popularity of the lectures of the young Dominican inflamed a situation which was already acute. The secular or non-monastic clergy, who from the early years of the universities had furnished the bulk of the teaching staffs, saw dangerous rivals in the eloquent and popular young friar preachers, who were often less conventional in their methods and approach. They appealed to Rome to forbid the intrusion of either Franciscans or Dominicans into what they regarded as their particular preserve, and Innocent IV in 1254 withdrew all favor from the two orders. However, he died at about this time and his successor, Alexander IV, was to prove friendly to the friars. The opposition to their admission to teaching posts in the universities grew even more bitter with the publication of a libellous tract, *On the Dangers of These Last Times,* by William de Saint-Armour, in which both the ideas and the organization of the mendicant orders were denounced. Representatives of the two orders were now summoned to Rome, Thomas being chosen as one of the Dominican delegates. He pleaded with such success that the decision was given in their favor. The Pope now compelled the university authorities to admit Thomas and Bonaventura to positions as teachers and to the degree of Doctor of Theology. This was in October, 1257, when Thomas was thirty-two years old.

From 1259 to 1269 Thomas was in Italy teaching in the school for select students attached to the papal court, which accompanied the Pope through all his changes of residence. As a consequence, he lectured and preached in many Italian towns. In 1263 he probably visited London as representative from the Roman province at the general chapter of the Dominican Order. In 1269 he was back again for a year or two in Paris. By then King Louis IX held him in such esteem that he consulted him on important matters of state.

The university referred to him a question on which the older theologians were themselves divided, namely, whether, in the Sacrament of the altar, the accidents [6] remained in reality in the consecrated Host, or only in appearance. After much fervent prayer, Thomas wrote his answer in the form of a treatise, still preserved, and laid it on the altar before offering it to the public. His decision was accepted by the university and afterwards by the whole Church. On this occasion we first hear of his receiving the Lord's approval of what he had written. Appearing in a vision, the Saviour said to him, "Thou hast written well of the Sacrament of My body," whereupon, it is reported, Thomas passed into an ecstasy and remained so long raised in the air that there was time to sum-

---

[6] The accidents in the case of the sacrament were the qualities perceived by our senses, the taste, color, shape, and feeling of the bread. The substance of bread, it was agreed, was changed by the act of consecration into the substance of Christ's body.

mon many of the brothers to behold the spectacle. Again, towards the end of his life, when at Salerno he was laboring over the third part of his great treatise, *Against the Pagans (Summa Contra Gentiles)*, dealing with Christ's Passion and Resurrection, a sacristan saw him late one night kneeling before the altar and heard a voice, coming, it seemed, from the crucifix, which said, "Thou hast written well of Me, Thomas; what reward wouldst thou have?" To which Thomas replied, "Nothing but Thyself, Lord."

After his second period of teaching in Paris he was recalled to Rome, and from there was sent, in 1272, to lecture at the University of Naples, in his home city. On the feast of St. Nicholas the following year, as he said Mass in the convent, he received a revelation which so overwhelmed him that he never again wrote or dictated. He put aside his chief work, the *Summary of Theology (Summa Theologica)*, still incomplete. To Brother Reginald's anxious query, he replied, "The end of my labors is come. All that I have written seems to me so much straw after the things that have been revealed to me."

He was already ill when he was commissioned by the Pope to attend the general council at Lyons, which had for its business the discussion of the reunion of the Greek and Latin Churches. He was to bring with him his treatise, *Against the Errors of the Greeks*. On the way he became so much worse that he was taken to the Cistercian abbey of Fossa Nuova near Terracina. Yielding to the entreaties of the monks, he began to expound the "Song of Songs," but was unable to finish the interpretation. He made his confession to Brother Reginald, received the Viaticum from the abbot, repeated aloud his own beautiful hymn, "With all my soul I worship Thee, Thou hidden Deity," and in the early hours of March 7, 1274, gave up his spirit. He was only forty-eight years of age. On that day his old master, Albertus Magnus, then in Cologne, burst suddenly into tears in the midst of the community, and exclaimed: "Brother Thomas Aquinas, my son in Christ, the light of the Church, is dead! God has revealed it to me."

Thomas was canonized by Pope John XXII at Avignon, in 1323.

In 1367 the Dominicans got possession of his body and translated it with great pomp to Toulouse, where it still lies in the Church of St. Sernin. Pope Pius V conferred on Thomas the title of Doctor of the Church, and Leo XIII, in 1880, declared him the patron of all Catholic universities, academies, colleges, and schools. Among his emblems are the following: ox, chalice, dove, and monstrance.

Of his writings, which fill twenty volumes, we cannot here speak at length. As a philosopher, the great contribution of Aquinas was his use of the works of Aristotle to build up a rational and ordered system of Christian doctrine, his method of exposition and proof being scientific and lucid. He would first state the problem or question under consideration, next, one by one, fairly and objectively, the arguments against his own point of view, often citing the authorities on which they rested. Then came a statement of his own position with the arguments to support it, and, finally, one by one, the answers to his opponents. The general tone of his arguments was invariably judicial and serene. To him faith and reason could never be contradictory, for they both came from the one source of all truth, God, the Absolute One. The most important of his books were the *Summa Theologica* and the *Summa Contra Gentiles,* which were written between 1265 and 1272. Together they form the fullest and most exact exposition of Catholic dogma yet given to the world. Over the former he labored for five years, and left it, as we have said, unfinished. Almost at once it was recognized as the greatest intellectual achievement of the period. Three centuries later, at the momentous Council of Trent, this work was one of the three authoritative sources of Catholic faith laid down before the assembly, the other two being the Bible and the Decretals of the Popes. No theologian save Augustine has had so much influence on the Western Church as the "Angelic Doctor."

His work was not confined to the fields of dogma, apologetics, and philosophy. When Pope Urban IV decided to institute the Feast of Corpus Christi, he asked Thomas to compose a liturgical office and Mass for the day. These are remarkable both for their doctrinal accuracy and their tenderness of feeling. Two of his hymns, the *"Verbum Supernum"* ("Word on High") and *"Pange Lingua"* ("Sing my Tongue") are familiar to all Catholics, because their final verses are regularly sung at Benediction; but there are others, notably the *"Lauda Sion"* ("Praise Zion") and the *"Adoro Te Devote"* ("With all my Soul I Worship Thee"), hardly less popular.

About his attainments Thomas was singularly modest. Asked if he were never tempted to pride, he replied, "No." If any such thoughts occurred to him, he said, his common sense immediately dispelled them by showing him their absurdity. He was always apt to think others better than himself, and never was he known to lose his temper in argument, or to say anything unkind. As a young friar in Paris, he was once mistakenly corrected, by the official corrector, while reading aloud the Latin text for the day in the refectory. He accepted the emendation and pronounced what he knew to be a false quantity. On being asked afterwards how he could consent to make so obvious a blunder, he replied, "It matters little whether a syllable be long or short, but it matters much to practice humility and obedience."

During a stay in Bologna, a lay brother who did not know him ordered him to accompany him to the town where he had business to transact. The prior, it seemed, had told him to take as companion any brother he found disengaged. Thomas was lame and although he was aware that the brother was making a mistake, he followed him at once, and took several scoldings for walking so slowly. Later the lay brother discovered his identity, and was overcome with self-reproach. To his abject apologies Thomas replied simply, "Do not worry, dear brother. . . . I am the one to blame. . . . I am only sorry I could not be more useful." When others asked him why he had not explained who he was, he answered: "Obedience is the perfection of the religious life; for by it a man submits to man for the love of God, even as God made Himself obedient to men for their salvation."

The Goodness of God

(QUESTION 6)

*F*irst Article. *Whether goodness belongs to God?*
We proceed thus to the First Article:—

Objection 1. It seems that goodness does not belong to God. For goodness consists in limit, species and order. But these do not seem to belong to God, since God is vast and not in the order of anything. Therefore goodness does not belong to God.

Obj. 2. Further, the good is what all things desire. But all things do not desire God, because all things do not know Him; and nothing is desired unless it is known. Therefore goodness does not belong to God.

On the contrary, It is written (Lamentations iii,25): The Lord is good to them that hope in Him, to the soul that seeketh Him.

I answer that, Goodness belongs pre-eminently to God. For a thing is good according to its desirableness. And everything seeks after its own perfection, and the perfection and form of an effect consist in a certain likeness to its cause, since every cause creates its like. Hence the cause itself is desirable and has the nature of a good. The thing desirable in it is a participation in its likeness. Therefore, since God is the first producing cause of all things, it is plain that the aspect of good and of desirableness belong to Him; and hence Dionysius attributes goodness to God as to the first efficient cause, saying that "God is called good as the One by Whom all things subsist."

Reply Obj. 1. To have limit, species, and order belongs to the essence of a caused good; but goodness is in God as in its cause; hence it belongs to Him to impose limit, species, and order on others; wherefore these three things are in God as in their cause.

Reply Obj. 2. All things, by desiring their own perfection, desire God Himself, inasmuch as the perfections of all things are so many approaches to the divine being, as appears from what is said above. Of those beings that desire God, some know Him as He is in Himself, and this is true of the rational creature; others know some participation in His goodness, and this belongs to sense knowledge; and others have a natural desire, but without knowledge, and are directed to their ends by a higher knower.

The Cause of Evil (QUESTION 49)

Second Article. Whether the Highest Good, God, is the Cause of Evil?

We proceed thus to the Second Article:—

Objection 1. It would seem that the highest good, God, is the cause of evil. For it is said (Isaiah xlv,5,7): I am the Lord, and there is no other God, forming the light and creating the darkness, making peace and creating evil. It is also said (Amos iii,6), Shall there be evil in a city which the Lord hath not done?

Obj. 2. Further, the effect of a secondary cause is attributable to its first cause. But good is the cause of evil, as was said above. Therefore, since God is the cause of every good, as was shown above, it follows that every evil also is from God.

Obj. 3. Further, as the Philosopher [7] says, the cause of both the safety and the danger of a ship is the same.[8] But God is the cause of the safety of all things. Therefore He is the cause of all destruction and of all evil.

On the contrary, Augustine says that, "God is not the author of evil, because He is not the cause of the tendency to cease from being." [9]

[7] "The Philosopher" to Thomas Aquinas and his contemporaries was always Aristotle.

[8] "That which by its presence brings about one result is sometimes blamed for bringing about the contrary by its absence. Thus we ascribe the wreck of a ship to the absence of the pilot, whose presence was the cause of its safety." Aristotle, *Physics,* II, 3.

[9] In Augustine's, as in Thomas' philosophy, evil was a form of negation of life and power to act, whereas goodness was affirmative, life-bringing, and active. As a thing became evil, it gradually lost its hold on the being with which God had originally endowed it and lapsed into nothingness.

I answer that, As appears from what has been said, the evil which consists in defective action is caused always by the defect of the agent. But in God there is no defect but the highest perfection, as was shown above. Hence the evil which consists in defective action, or which is caused by defect in the agent, is not attributable to God as its cause.

But the evil which consists in the corruption of things is attributable to God as its cause. And this seems true as regards both things of nature and creatures with will. For we have said that whenever an agent produces by its power a form which is followed by corruption and decay, it causes by its power that corruption and decay. Now clearly the form which God chiefly intends in created things is the good of the order of the universe. But the order of the universe requires, as was said above, that there should be some things that can, and sometimes do, fail. Thus God, by causing in things the good of the order of the universe, consequently, and as it were incidentally, causes corruptions in things, in accordance with I Kings ii,6: [10] The Lord killeth and maketh alive.

And when we read that God hath not made death (Wisdom i,13), the meaning is that God does not will death for its own sake. Yet the order of justice too belongs to the order of the universe; and this requires that penalty should be dealt out to sinners. Thus God is the author of the evil which is penalty, but not of the evil which is fault, by reason of what we have said.

Reply Obj. 1. These passages refer to the evil of penalty, and not to the evil of fault.

Reply Obj. 2. The effect of a defective secondary cause is attributable to its first non-defective cause as regards what it contains of being and perfection, but not as regards what it contains of defect; just as whatever there is of movement in the act of limping is caused by a motive energy, whereas whatever is unbalanced in it does not come from the motive energy but from the curvature of the leg. So whatever there is of being and action in a bad act is attributable to God as the cause; and whatever there is

[10] I Kings in the modern Protestant versions of the Bible is called I Samuel.

of defect is not caused by God but by the defective secondary cause.

Reply Obj. 3. The sinking of a ship is attributed to the pilot as its cause since he does not perform what the safety of the ship requires; but God does not fail to do what is necessary for our safety. Hence there is no comparison.

(*Summa Theologica,* I.)

THE VISION OF SAINT BERNARD   Filippo Lippi

Filippo Lippi (1406-1469), notorious even in the dissolute morality of Florence under the Medici, nevertheless painted some great religious paintings. His was a completely worldly art, yet his sensitive use of tone and value and his highly developed sense of color lent inspiration to his themes.

Saint Bernard is shown writing his homilies on the Annunciation (Luke 1, 2), "Missus est" under the guidance of the Blessed Virgin, using the inkhorn and pen which are two of his symbols.

SAINT DOMINIC MEDITATING   Fra Angelico

For the home of the Dominican order in Florence, the Monastery of San
Marco, Fra Angelico (1387-1455) and his assistants painted the walls with
scenes from the life of Christ and other religious subjects as
an aid to prayer and meditation. Such a painting is this study
of the founder of the order.

Saint Dominic wears the habit of his order, of white wool,
with a black cloak. The open book is one of his symbols. He
usually has a star in his nimbus or on his shoulder.

Saint Catherine of Siena

Virgin

1 3 8 0

(*April 30*)

The Middle Ages were drawing to a close and the brave new world of the Renaissance was springing to life when Catherine Benincasa was born. The place was Siena, and the day was the feast of the Annunciation, 1347. Catherine and a twin sister who did not long survive were the youngest of twenty-five children. The father, Giacomo or Jacopo Benincasa, a prosperous wool dyer, lived with his wife Lapa and their family, sometimes comprising married couples and grandchildren, in a spacious house which the Sienese have preserved to the present day. As a child Catherine was so merry that the family gave her the pet name of Euphrosyne, which is Greek for Joy and also the name of an early Christian saint. At the age of six she had the remarkable experience which may be said to have determined her vocation. With her brother she was on the way home from a visit to a married sister, when suddenly she stopped still in the road, gazing up into the sky. She did not hear the repeated calls of the boy, who had walked on ahead. Only after he had gone back and seized her by the hand did she wake as from a dream. She burst into tears. Her vision of Christ seated in glory with the Apostles Peter, Paul, and John had faded. A year later the little girl made a secret vow to give her whole life to God. She loved prayer and solitude, and when she mingled with other children it was to teach them to do what gave her so much happiness.

When Catherine was twelve, her mother, with marriage in mind, began to urge her to pay more attention to her appearance. To please her mother and sister, she dressed in the bright gowns and jewels that were fashionable for young girls. Soon she repented of this vanity, and declared with finality that she would never marry. When her parents persisted in their talk about finding her a husband, she cut off the golden-brown hair that was her chief beauty. As punishment, she was now made to do menial work in the household, and the family, knowing she craved solitude, never allowed her to be alone. Catherine bore all this with sweetness and patience. Long afterwards, in *The Dialogue,* she wrote that God had shown her how to build in her soul a private cell where no tribulation could enter.

Catherine's father at last came to the realization that further pressure was useless, and his daughter was permitted to do as she pleased. In the small, dimly-lighted room now set apart for her use, a cell nine feet by three, she gave herself up to prayers and fasting; she scourged herself three times daily with an iron chain, and slept on a board. At first she wore a hair shirt, subsequently replacing it by an iron-spiked girdle. Soon she obtained what she ardently desired, permission to assume the black habit of a Dominican tertiary, which was customarily granted only to matrons or widows. She now increased her asceticism, eating and sleeping very little. For three years she spoke only to her confessor and never went out except to the neighboring church of St. Dominic, where the pillar against which she used to lean is still pointed out to visitors.

At times now she was enraptured by celestial visions, but often too she was subjected to severe trials. Loathsome forms and enticing figures would present themselves to her imagination, and the most degrading temptations assailed her. There would be long intervals during which she felt abandoned by God. "O Lord, where wert Thou when my heart was so sorely vexed with foul and hateful temptations?" she asked, when after such a time of agonizing He had once more manifested Himself. She heard a voice saying, "Daughter, I was in thy heart, fortifying thee by grace," and the voice then said that God would now be with her more openly, for the period of probation was nearing an end.

On Shrove Tuesday, 1366, while the citizens of Siena were keeping carnival, and Catherine was praying in her room, a vision of Christ appeared, accompanied by His mother and the heavenly host. Taking the girl's hand, Our Lady held it up to Christ, who placed a ring upon it and espoused her to Himself, bidding her to be of good courage, for now she was armed with a faith that could overcome all temptations. To Catherine the ring was always visible, though invisible to others. The years of solitude and preparation were ended and soon afterwards she began to mix with her fellow men and learn to serve them. Like other Dominican tertiaries, she volunteered to nurse the sick in the city hospitals, choosing those afflicted with loathsome diseases—cases from which others were apt to shrink.

There gathered around this strong personality a band of earnest associates. Prominent among them were her two Dominican confessors, Thomas della Fonte and Bartholomew Dominici, the Augustinian Father Tantucci, Matthew Cenni, rector of the Misericordia Hospital, the artist Vanni, to whom we are indebted for a famous portrait of Catherine, the poet Neri di Landoccio dei Pagliaresi, her own sister-in-law Lisa, a noble young widow, Alessia Saracini, and William Flete, the English hermit. Father Santi, an aged hermit, abandoned his solitude to be near her, because, he said, he found greater peace of mind and progress in virtue by following her than he ever found in his cell. A warm affection bound her to these whom she called her spiritual family, children given her by God that she might help them along the way to perfection. She read their thoughts and frequently knew their temptations when they were away from her. Many of her early letters were written to one or another of them. At this time public opinion about Catherine was divided; many Sienese revered her as a saint, while others called her a fanatic or denounced her as a hypocrite. Perhaps as a result of charges made against her, she was summoned to Florence to appear before the general chapter of the Dominicans. Whatever the charges were, they were completely disproved, and shortly afterwards the new lector for the order in Siena, Raymund de

Capua, was appointed her confessor. In this happy association, Father Raymund was in many things of the spirit her disciple. Later he became the saint's biographer.

After Catherine's return to Siena there was a terrible outbreak of the plague, during which she and her circle worked incessantly to relieve the sufferers. "Never did she appear more admirable than at this time," wrote a priest who had known her from girlhood. "She was always with the plague-stricken; she prepared them for death and buried them with her own hands. I myself witnessed the joy with which she nursed them and the wonderful efficacy of her words, which brought about many conversions." Among those who owed their recovery directly to her were Raymund of Capua himself, Matthew Cenni, Father Santi, and Father Bartholomew, all of whom contracted the disease through tending others. Her pity for dying men was not confined to those who were sick. She made it a practice to visit condemned persons in prison, hoping to persuade them to make their peace with God. On one occasion she walked to the scaffold with a young Perugian knight, sentenced to death for using seditious language against the government of Siena. His last words were: "Jesus and Catherine!"

Her deeds of mercy, coupled with a growing reputation as a worker of miracles, now caused the Sienese to turn to Catherine in all kinds of difficulties. Three Dominican priests were especially deputed to hear the confessions of those whom she had prevailed on to amend their lives. In settling disputes and healing old feuds she was so successful that she was constantly called upon to arbitrate at a time when all through Italy every man's hand seemed to be against his neighbor. It was partly, perhaps, with a view to turning the energies of Christendom away from civil wars that Catherine threw herself into Pope Gregory's campaign for another crusade to wrest the Holy Sepulchre from the Turks. This brought her into correspondence with Gregory himself.

In February, 1375, she accepted an invitation to visit Pisa, where she was welcomed with enthusiasm. She had been there only a few days when she had another of the spiritual experiences which seem to have presaged each new step in her career. She had made her Communion in the little church of St. Christina, and had been gazing at the crucifix, when suddenly there descended from it five blood-red rays which pierced her hands, feet and heart, causing such acute pain that she swooned. The wounds remained as stigmata, visible to herself alone during her life, but clearly to be seen after her death.

She was still in Pisa when she received word that the people of Florence and Perugia had entered into a league against the Holy See and the French legates. The disturbance had begun in Florence, where the Guelphs and the Ghibellines [1] united to raise a large army under the banner of freedom from the Pope's control, and Bologna, Viterbo, and Ancona, together with other strongholds in the papal domain, rallied to the insurgents. Through Catherine's untiring efforts, the cities of Lucca, Pisa, and Siena held back. From Avignon, meanwhile, after an unsuccessful appeal to the Florentines, the Pope, Gregory XI, sent Cardinal Robert of Geneva with an army to put down the uprising, and laid Florence under an interdict. The effects of the ban on the life and prosperity of the city were so serious that its rulers sent to Siena, to ask Catherine to mediate with the Pope. Always ready to act as a peacemaker, she promptly set out for Florence. The city's magistrates met her as she drew near the gates, and placed the negotiations entirely in her hands, saying that their ambassadors would follow her to Avignon and confirm whatever she did there. Catherine arrived in Avignon on June 18, 1376, and was graciously received by the Pope. "I desire nothing but peace," he said; "I place the affair entirely in your hands, only I recommend to you the honor of the

[1] It is impossible to explain here in detail the complex political and religious currents of this troubled time. The two great powers, the Holy Roman Empire and the Papacy, were engaged in an intermittent struggle for power throughout the late Middle Ages. Ghibelline was the name given to the imperial party in Italy and Guelph to the supporters of the Papacy. Florence was traditionally a Guelph city, but Italians as a whole resented the long absence of the popes from Rome and the excessive influence of France in papal administration.

Church." As it happened, the Florentines proved untrustworthy and continued their intrigues to draw the rest of Italy away from allegiance to the Holy See. When their ambassadors arrived, they disclaimed all connection with Catherine, making it clear by their demands that they did not desire a reconciliation.

Although she had failed in this matter, her efforts in another direction were successful. Many of the troubles which then afflicted Europe were, to some degree at least, due to the seventy-four-year residence of the popes at Avignon, where the Curia [2] was now largely French. Gregory had been ready to go back to Rome with his court, but the opposition of the French cardinals had deterred him. Since in her letters Catherine had urged his return so strongly, it was natural that they should discuss the subject now that they were face to face. "Fulfill what you have promised," she said, reminding him of a vow he had once taken and had never disclosed to any human being. Greatly impressed by what he regarded as a supernatural sign, Gregory resolved to act upon it at once.

On September 13, 1376, he set out from Avignon to travel by water to Rome, while Catherine and her friends left the city on the same day to return overland to Siena. On reaching Genoa she was detained by the illness of two of her secretaries, Neri di Landoccio and Stephen Maconi. The latter was a young Sienese nobleman, recently converted, who had become an ardent follower. When Catherine got back to Siena, she kept on writing the Pope, entreating him to labor for peace. At his request she went again to Florence, still rent by factions, and stayed there for some time, frequently in danger of her life. She did finally establish peace between the city governors and the papacy, but this was in the reign of Gregory's successor.

After Catherine returned to Siena, Raymund of Capua tells us, "she occupied herself actively in the composition of a book which she dictated under the inspiration of the Holy Ghost." This was

[2] The papal Curia consists of all organized bodies, congregations, tribunals, curial offices, and certain permanent commissions, which assist the pope in the government and administration of the Church.

the mystical work, in four treatises, called *The Dialogue of St. Catherine*.[3]

Her health was now so impaired by austerities that she was never free from pain; yet her thin face was usually smiling. She was grieved by any sort of scandal in the Church, especially that of the Great Schism [4] which followed the death of Gregory XI. Urban VI was elected as his successor by the cardinals of Rome and Clement VII by the rebellious cardinals of Avignon. Western Christendom was divided; Clement was recognized by France, Spain, Scotland, and Naples; Urban by most of North Italy, England, Flanders, and Hungary. Catherine wore herself out trying to heal this terrible breach in Christian unity and to obtain for Urban the obedience due to the legitimate head. Letter after letter was dispatched to the princes and leaders of Europe. To Urban himself she wrote to warn him to control his harsh and arrogant temper. This was the second pope she had counseled, chided, even commanded. Far from resenting reproof, Urban summoned her to Rome that he might profit by her advice. Reluctantly she left Siena to live in the Holy City. She had achieved a remarkable position for a woman of her time. On various occasions at Siena, Avignon, and Genoa, learned theologians had questioned her and had been humbled by the wisdom of her replies.

Although Catherine was only thirty-three, her life was now nearing its close. On April 21, 1380, a paralytic stroke made her helpless from the waist downwards, and eight days later she passed away in the arms of her cherished friend, Alessia Saracini. The Dominicans at Rome still treasure the body of Catherine in the Minerva Church, but Siena has her head enshrined in St. Dominic's Church. Pope Pius II canonized Catherine in 1461. The saint's talents as a writer caused her to be compared with her countrymen,

---

[3] It is also known as *The Book of Divine Doctrine*. With the *Divine Comedy* of Dante it has stood as one of the supreme attempts in Italian literature to express the eternal in the symbols of the day.

[4] The Schism lasted from 1378 to 1418, when Church unity was restored with the election of Pope Martin V.

Dante and Petrarch. Among her literary remains are the *Dialogue* and some four hundred letters, many of them of great literary beauty, and showing warmth, insight, and aspiration. One of the important women of Europe, Catherine's gifts of heart and mind were used in the furtherance of the Christian ideal.

Letter to Gregory XI

In the name of Jesus Christ crucified and of sweet Mary: Most holy and most reverend my father in Christ Jesus: I Catherine your poor unworthy daughter, servant and slave of the servants of Christ, write to you in His precious blood; with desire to see you a good shepherd. For I reflect, sweet my father, that the wolf is carrying away your sheep, and there is no one found to succor them. So I hasten to you, our father and our shepherd, begging you on behalf of Christ crucified to learn from Him, who with such fire of love gave Himself to the shameful death of the most holy cross, how to rescue that lost sheep, the human race, from the hands of the demons; because through man's rebellion against God they were holding him for their own possession.

Then comes the Infinite Goodness of God, and sees the evil state and the loss and the ruin of these sheep, and sees that they cannot be won back to Him by wrath or war. So, notwithstanding they have wronged Him—for man deserves an infinite penalty for his disobedient rebellion against God—the Highest and Eternal Wisdom will not do this, but finds an attractive way, the gentlest and most loving possible to find. For it sees that the heart of man is in no way so drawn as by love, because he was created by love. This seems to be the reason why he loves so much: he was created by nothing but love, both his soul and his body. For by love God created him in His Image and Likeness, and by love his father and mother gave him substance, conceiving and bearing a son.

God, therefore, seeing that man is so ready to love, throws the book of love straight at him, giving him the Word, His Only-Begotten Son, who takes our humanity to make a great peace. But

justice wills that vengeance should be wrought for the wrong that
has been done to God: so comes Divine Mercy and unspeakable
Charity, and to satisfy justice and mercy condemns His Son to
death, having clothed him in our humanity, that is, in the clay of
Adam who sinned. So by His death the wrath of the Father is
pacified, having wrought justice on the person of His son: so He
has satisfied justice and has satisfied mercy, releasing the human
race from the hands of demons. This sweet Word jousted with His
arms upon the wood of the most holy Cross, death fighting a tour-
nament with life and life with death: so that by His death He destroyed our death, and to give us life He sacrificed the life of His
body. So then with love He has drawn us to Him, and has overcome
our malice with His benignity, in so much that every heart should
be drawn to Him: since greater love one cannot show—and this
He himself said—than to give one's life for one's friend. And if He
commended the love which gives one's life for one's friend, what
then shall we say of that most burning and perfect love which gave
its life for its foe? For we through sin had become foes of God. Oh,
sweet and loving Word, who with love hast found Thy flock once
more, and with love hast given Thy life for them, and hast brought
them back to Thy fold, restoring to them the Grace which they
had lost!

Holiest sweet father of mine, I see no other way for us and no
other aid to winning back your sheep, which have left the fold of
Holy Church in rebellion, not obedient nor submissive to you, their
father. I pray you therefore, in the name of Christ crucified, and I
will that you do me this grace, to overcome their malice with your
benignity. Yours we are, father! I know and realize that they all
feel that they have done wrong; but although they have no excuse
for their crimes, nevertheless it seemed to them that they could not
do differently, because of the many sufferings and injustices and
iniquitous things they have endured from bad shepherds and governors. For they have breathed the stench of the lives of many
rulers whom you know yourself to be incarnate demons, and fallen
into terrible fears, so that they did like Pilate, who not to lose his

authority killed Christ; so did they, for not to lose their state, they maltreated you. I ask you then, father, to show them mercy. Do not regard the ignorance and pride of your sons, but with the food of love and your benignity inflict such mild discipline and benign reproof as shall satisfy your Holiness and restore peace to us miserable children who have done wrong.

I tell you, sweet Christ on earth, on behalf of Christ in Heaven, that if you do this, without strife or tempest, they will all come grieving for the wrong they have done, and lay their heads on your bosom. Then you will rejoice, and we shall rejoice, because by love you have restored the sheep to the fold of Holy Church. And then, sweet my father, you will fulfill your holy desire and the will of God by starting the holy Crusade, which I summon you in his name to do swiftly and without negligence. They will turn to it with great eagerness; they are ready to give their lives for Christ. Ah me, God, sweet Love! Raise swiftly, father, the banner of the most holy Cross and you will see the wolves become lambs. Peace, peace, peace, that war may not delay that happy time!

But if you will wreak vengeance and justice, inflict them on me, poor wretch, and assign me any pain and torment that may please you, even death. I believe that through the foulness of my iniquities many evils have occurred, and many misfortunes and discords. On me then, your poor daughter, take any vengeance that you will. Ah me, father, I die of grief and cannot die! Come, come, and resist no more the will of God that calls you; the hungry sheep await your coming to hold and possess the place of your predecessor and Champion, Apostle Peter. For you, as the Vicar of Christ, should abide in your own place. Come, then, come, and delay no more; and comfort you, and fear not anything that might happen, since God will be with you. I ask humbly your benediction for me and all my sons; and I beg you to pardon my presumption. I say no more. Remain in the holy and sweet grace of God—Sweet Jesus, Jesus Love.

(*Letters of Saint Catherine of Siena*,
translated by Vida D. Scudder. 1906.)

Saint Joan of Arc

Virgin

1 4 3 1

(*May 8*)

Savior of France and the national heroine of that country, Joan of Arc lives on in the imagination of the world as a symbol of that integrity of purpose that makes one die for what one believes. Jeanne la Pucelle, the Maid, is the shining example of what a brave spirit can accomplish in the world of men and events. The saint was born on the feast of the Epiphany, January 6, 1412, at Domremy, a village in the rich province of Champagne, on the Meuse River in northeast France. She came of sound peasant stock. Her father, Jacques d'Arc, was a good man, though rather morose; his wife was a gentle, affectionate mother to their five children. From her the two daughters of the family received careful training in all household duties. "In sewing and spinning," Joan declared towards the end of her short life, "I fear no woman." She whose destiny it was to save France was a well-brought-up country girl who, in common with most people of the time, never had an opportunity to learn to read or write. The little we know of her childhood is contained in the impressive and often touching testimony to her piety and dutiful conduct in the depositions presented during the process for her rehabilitation in 1456, twenty-five years after her death. Priests and former playmates then recalled her love of prayer and faithful attendance at church, her frequent use of the Sacraments, kindness to sick people, and sympathy for poor wayfarers, to whom she sometimes gave up her own bed. "She was so good," the neighbors said, "that all the village loved her."

Joan's early life, however, must have been disturbed by the confusion of the period and the disasters befalling her beloved land. The Hundred Years War between England and France was still running its dismal course. Whole provinces were being lost to the English and the Burgundians, while the weak and irresolute government of France offered no real resistance. A frontier village like Domremy, bordering on Lorraine, was especially exposed to the invaders. On one occasion, at least, Joan fled with her parents to Neufchâtel, eight miles distant, to escape a raid of Burgundians who sacked Domremy and set fire to the church, which was near Joan's home.

The child had been three years old when in 1415 King Henry V of England had started the latest chain of troubles by invading Normandy and claiming the crown of the insane king, Charles VI. France, already in the throes of civil war between the supporters of the Dukes of Burgundy and Orleans, had been in no condition to resist, and when the Duke of Burgundy was treacherously killed by the Dauphin's servants, most of his faction joined the British forces. King Henry and King Charles both died in 1422, but the war continued. The Duke of Bedford, as regent for the infant king of England, pushed the campaign vigorously, one town after another falling to him or to his Burgundian allies. Most of the country north of the Loire was in English hands. Charles VII, the Dauphin, as he was still called, considered his position hopeless, for the enemy even occupied the city of Rheims, where he should have been crowned. He spent his time away from the fighting lines in frivolous pastimes with his court.

Joan was in her fourteenth year when she heard the first of the unearthly voices, which, she felt sure, brought her messages from God. One day while she was at work in the garden, she heard a voice, accompanied by a blaze of light; after this, she vowed to remain a virgin and to lead a godly life. Afterwards, for a period of two years, the voices increased in number, and she was able to see her heavenly visitors, whom she identified as St. Michael, St. Catherine of Alexandria, and St. Margaret, the three saints whose

images stood in the church at Domremy. Gradually they revealed
to her the purpose of their visits: she, an ignorant peasant girl, was
given the high mission of saving her country; she was to take
Charles to Rheims to be crowned, and then drive out the English!
We do not know just when Joan decided to obey the voices; she
spoke little of them at home, fearing her stern father's disapproval.
But by May, 1428, the voices had become insistent and explicit.
Joan, now sixteen, must first go quickly to Robert de Baudricourt,
who commanded the Dauphin's forces in the neighboring town of
Vaucouleurs and say that she was appointed to lead the Dauphin
to his crowning. An uncle accompanied Joan, but the errand proved
fruitless; Baudricourt laughed and said that her father should give
her a whipping. Thus rebuffed, Joan went back to Domremy, but
the voices gave her no rest. When she protested that she was a poor
girl who could neither ride nor fight, they answered, "It is God who
commands it."

At last, she was impelled to return secretly to Baudricourt, whose
skepticism was shaken, for news had reached him of just the sort of
serious French defeat that Joan had predicted. The military position was now desperate, for Orleans, the last remaining French
stronghold on the Loire, was invested by the English and seemed
likely to fall. Baudricourt now agreed to send Joan to the Dauphin,
and gave her an escort of three soldiers. It was her own idea to put
on male attire, as a protection. On March 6, 1429, the party
reached Chinon, where the Dauphin was staying, and two days
later Joan was admitted to the royal presence. To test her, Charles
had disguised himself as one of his courtiers, but she identified him
without hesitation and, by a sign which only she and he understood, convinced him that her mission was authentic.

The ministers were less easy to convince. When Joan asked for
soldiers to lead to the relief of Orleans, she was opposed by La
Tremouille, one of Charles' favorites, and by others, who regarded
the girl either as a crazy visionary or a scheming impostor. To
settle the question, they sent her to Poitiers, to be questioned by a
commission of theologians. After an exhaustive examination lasting

for three weeks, the learned ecclesiastics pronounced Joan honest, good, and virtuous; they counseled Charles to make prudent use of her services. Thus vindicated, Joan returned full of courage to Chinon, and plans went forward to equip her with a small force. A banner was made, bearing at her request, the words, "Jesus, Maria," along with a figure of God the Father, to whom two kneeling angels were presenting a fleur-de-lis, the royal emblem of France. On April 27 the army left Blois with Joan, now known to her troops as "La Pucelle," the Maid, clad in dazzling white armor. Joan was a handsome, healthy, well-built girl, with a smiling face, and dark hair which had been cut short. She had now learned to ride well, but, naturally, she had no knowledge of military tactics. Yet her gallantry and valor kindled the soldiers and with them she broke through the English line and entered Orleans on April 29. Her presence in the city greatly heartened the French garrison. By May 8 the English fort outside Orleans had been captured and the siege raised. Conspicuous in her white armor, Joan had led the attack and had been slightly wounded in the shoulder by an arrow.

Her desire was to follow up these first successes with even more daring assaults, for the voices had told her that she would not live long, but La Tremouille and the archbishop of Rheims were in favor of negotiating. However, the Maid was allowed to join in a short campaign along the Loire with the Duc d'Alençon, one of her devoted supporters. It ended with a victory at Patay, in which the English forces under Sir John Falstolf suffered a crushing defeat. She now urged the immediate coronation of the Dauphin, since the road to Rheims had been practically cleared. The French leaders argued and dallied, and finally consented to follow her to Rheims. There, on July 17, 1429, Charles VII was duly crowned, Joan standing proudly behind him with her banner.

The mission entrusted to her by the heavenly voices was now only half fulfilled, for the English were still in France. Charles, weak and irresolute, did not follow up these auspicious happenings, and an attack on Paris failed, mainly for lack of his promised support and presence. During the action Joan was again wounded and had to be dragged to safety by the Duc d'Alençon. There followed a winter's truce, which Joan spent for the most part in the company of the court, where she was regarded with ill-concealed suspicion. When hostilities were renewed in the spring, she hurried off to the relief of Compiègne, which was besieged by the Burgundians. Entering the city at sunrise on May 23, 1430, she led a sortie against the enemy later in the day. It failed, and through miscalculation on the part of the governor, the drawbridge over which her forces were retiring was lifted too soon, leaving her and a number of soldiers outside, at the mercy of the enemy. Joan was dragged from her horse and led to the quarters of John of Luxembourg, one of whose soldiers had been her captor. From then until the late autumn she remained the prisoner of the Duke of Burgundy, incarcerated in a high tower of the castle of the Luxembourgs. In a desperate attempt to escape, the girl leapt from the tower, landing on soft turf, stunned and bruised. It was thought a miracle that she had not been killed.

Never, during that period or afterwards, was any effort made to secure Joan's release by King Charles or his ministers. She had been a strange and disturbing ally, and they seemed content to leave her to her fate. But the English were eager to have her, and on November 21, the Burgundians accepted a large indemnity and gave her into English hands. They could not take her life for defeating them in war, but they could have her condemned as a sorceress and a heretic. Had she not been able to inspire the French with the Devil's own courage? In an age when belief in witchcraft and demons was general, the charge did not seem too preposterous. Already the English and Burgundian soldiers had been attributing their reverses to her spells.

In a cell in the castle of Rouen to which Joan was moved two days before Christmas, she was chained to a plank bed, and watched over night and day. On February 21, 1431, she appeared for the first time before a court of the Inquisition. It was presided over by Pierre Cauchon, bishop of Beauvais, a ruthless, ambitious man who apparently hoped through English influence to become archbishop of Rouen. The other judges were lawyers and theologians who had been carefully selected by Cauchon. In the course of six public and nine private sessions, covering a period of ten weeks, the prisoner was cross-examined as to her visions and voices, her assumption of male attire, her faith, and her willingness to submit to the Church. Alone and undefended, the nineteen-year-old girl bore herself fearlessly, her shrewd answers, honesty, piety, and accurate memory often proving embarrassing to these severe inquisitors. Through her ignorance of theological terms, on a few occasions she was betrayed into making damaging statements. At the end of the hearings, a set of articles was drawn up by the clerks and submitted to the judges, who thereupon pronounced her revelations the work of the Devil and Joan herself a heretic. The theological faculty of the University of Paris approved the court's verdict.

In final deliberations the tribunal voted to hand Joan over to the secular arm for burning if she still refused to confess she had been a witch and had lied about hearing voices. This she steadfastly refused to do, though physically exhausted and threatened with torture. Only when she was led out into the churchyard of St. Ouen before a great crowd, to hear the sentence committing her to the flames, did she kneel down and admit she had testified falsely. She was then taken back to prison. Under pressure from her jailers, she had some time earlier put off the male attire, which her accusers seemed to find particularly objectionable. Now, either by her own choice or as the result of a trick played upon her by those who wanted her death, she resumed it. When Bishop Cauchon, with some witnesses, visited her in her cell to question her further, she had recovered from her weakness, and once more she claimed that God had truly sent her and that the voices had come from Him. Cauchon was well pleased with this turn of events.

On Tuesday, May 29, 1431, the judges, after hearing Cauchon's report, condemned Joan as a relapsed heretic and delivered her to the English. The next morning at eight o'clock she was led out into the market place of Rouen to be burned at the stake. As the faggots were lighted, a Dominican friar, at her request, held up a cross before her eyes and, while the flames leapt higher and higher, she was heard to call on the name of Jesus. John Tressart, one of King Henry's secretaries, viewed the scene with horror and was probably joined in spirit by others when he exclaimed remorsefully, "We are lost! We have burned a saint!" Joan's ashes were cast into the Seine.

Twenty-five years later, when the English had been driven out, the Pope at Avignon ordered a rehearing of the case. By that time Joan was being hailed as the savior of France. Witnesses were heard and depositions made, and in consequence the trial was pronounced irregular. She was formally rehabilitated as a true and faithful daughter of the Church. From a short time after her death up to the French Revolution, a local festival in honor of the Maid was held at Orleans on May 8, commemorating the day the siege was raised. The festival was reestablished by Napoleon I. In 1920 the French Republic declared May 8 a day of national celebration. Joan was beatified in 1909 and canonized by Benedict XV in 1919.

Excerpts from the Trial of Jeanne d'Arc

THURSDAY, FEBRUARY 22, SECOND SESSION

. . . *"Then she declared that at the age of thirteen she had a* voice from God to help her and guide her. And the first time she was much afraid. And this voice came towards noon, in summer, in her father's garden; and the said Jeanne had not fasted on the preceding day. She heard the voice on her right, in the direction of the Church; and she seldom heard it without a light. The light came from the same side as the voice, and generally was a great light. When she came to France, she often heard the voice.

Asked how she could see the light of which she spoke, since it was at the side, she made no reply, and went on to other things. She said that if she was in a wood, she easily heard the voices come to her. It seemed to her a worthy voice and she believed it was sent from God; when she heard the voice a third time, she knew

that it was the voice of an angel. She said also that this voice
always protected her well and that she understood it well.

Asked what instruction this voice gave her for the salvation of
her soul, she said it taught her to be good and to go to church
often; and it told her she must come to France. . . . She further
said that this voice told her once or twice a week that she should
leave and come to France, and that her father should know nothing
of her leaving. She said that the voice told her to come, and she
could no longer stay where she was; and the voice told her again
that she should raise the siege of the city of Orleans. . . .

After this the said Jeanne told that she went without hindrance
to him whom she calls her king. And when she had arrived at
Ste. Catherine de Fierbois, then she went first to Chinon, where
he whom she calls her king was. She reached Chinon towards noon
and lodged at an inn; and after dinner she went to him whom she
calls king. She said that when she entered her king's room she recognized him among many others by the counsel of her voice, which
revealed him to her. She told him she wanted to make war on the
English. . . .

Then Jeanne said that there is not a day when she does not hear
this voice; and she has much need of it. She said she never asked
of it any final reward but the salvation of her soul. The voice told
her to remain at St. Denis in France, and the said Jeanne had to
remain; but against her will the lords took her away.

SATURDAY, FEBRUARY 24, THIRD SESSION

. . . Asked if she knows she is in God's grace, she answered:
"If I am not, may God put me there; and if I am, may God so
keep me. I should be the saddest creature in the world if I knew
I were not in His grace." She added that if she were in a state of
sin, she did not think that the voice would come to her; and she
wished everyone could hear the voice as well as she did. . . .

TUESDAY, FEBRUARY 27, FOURTH SESSION

. . . Asked whether the voice which spoke to her was that of
an angel, or of a saint, male or female, or straight from God, she
answered that the voice was the voice of St. Catherine and of St.

Margaret. And their heads were crowned in a rich and precious fashion with beautiful crowns. "And to tell this," she said, "I have God's permission. If you doubt it, send to Poitiers where I was examined before." . . .

Asked how she knew one from the other, she answered she knew them by the greeting they gave her. She said further that a good seven years have passed since they undertook to guide her. She said also she knew the saints because they tell her their names. . . . She added that she had received comfort from St. Michael.

Asked which of the apparitions came to her first, she answered that St. Michael came first. . . .

Asked which was the first voice which came to her when she was about thirteen, she answered that it was St. Michael whom she saw before her eyes; and he was not alone, but accompanied by many angels from heaven. She said also that she came into France only by the instruction of God.

Asked if she saw St. Michael and these angels corporeally and in reality, she answered: "I saw them with my bodily eyes as well as I see you; and when they left me, I wept; and I fain would have had them take me with them too."

SATURDAY, MARCH 17, IN PRISON

. . . Asked if she would submit [her deeds and words] to the decision of the Church, she answered: "I commit myself to Our Lord Who sent me, to Our Lady, and to all the Blessed Saints of Paradise." And she thought that our Lord and the Church were all one, and therein they ought not to make difficulties for her. "Why do you make difficulties when it is all one?"

Then she was told that there is the Church Triumphant, where God is with the saints and the souls who are already saved; and also the Church Militant, that is, our Holy Father the Pope, vicar of God on earth, the Cardinals, the prelates of the Church, and the clergy and all the good Christians and Catholics: and the Church in good assembly cannot err and is governed by the Holy Spirit. Therefore she was asked if she would submit to the Church Militant, namely the Church on earth which is so called. She answered that she came to the King of France in God's name, and in the names of the Blessed Virgin and of all the Blessed Saints of

Paradise, and of the Church Victorious above, and at their command; to that Church she submitted all her good deeds and all she had done or should do. And concerning her submission to the Church Militant she would answer nothing more. . . .

THE TRIAL FOR RELAPSE, MONDAY, MAY 28

. . . As we her judges had heard from certain people that she had not yet cut herself off from her illusions and pretended revelations, which she had previously renounced, we asked her whether she had since Thursday [the day of her abjuration] heard the voices of St. Catherine and St. Margaret. She answered yes.

Asked what they told her, she answered that they told her God had sent her word through St. Catherine and St. Margaret of the great pity of this treason, by which she had consented to abjure and recant in order to save her life; that she had damned herself to save her life. . . . She said that if she declared God had not sent her she would damn herself, for in truth she was sent from God. She said that her voices had since told her that she had done very wrong to say what she did. She said that what she had recanted on Thursday she had done only for fear of the fire. . . . She said she did not deny or intend to deny her visions, that is, that they were St. Catherine and St. Margaret; all that she said she said for fear of the fire.

(*Trial of Jeanne d'Arc,* translated by W. P. Barrett. 1932.)

Saint Rita

Widow

1 4 5 7

(*May 22*)

In 1381 in a humble peasant home at Rocca Porena, central
Italy, there was born a little girl who was to attain a reputation for great holiness on account of her mystical transports, her
austerities, and her long-suffering patience in meeting affliction.
Rita, the child of her parents' old age, in youth demonstrated a
strong religious sense. When the time came for marriage, her
parents forced her to marry an unsuitable person, in spite of her
desire to enter a convent. Rita submitted sorrowfully, and the
marriage proved to be one long torment. Rita's husband was brutal,
dissolute, and uncontrolled; for eighteen years she bore his insults
and infidelities. With anguish she watched the two sons of this
union grow up in the likeness of their father. She wept and prayed
for them all three without ceasing. At last her husband came to a
realization of his sinful life, and begged Rita to forgive him for
what he had made her suffer. Soon after this he was killed in a
brawl, and the sons vowed to avenge their father's death. Rita
prayed that they might die rather than commit murder. Then
they both fell ill, and their mother nursed them and brought them
to a more forgiving state before they too died.

Left alone, Rita now began to practice unusual austerities. She
finally gained admission to the Augustinian convent of Cascia,
persuading the prioress to overlook the rule that allowed her to
accept only virgins. In 1413 Rita received the habit of the order.
She became quite pitiless in her self-mortifications, scourging her-

309

self three times daily. Her charity found an outlet in caring tenderly for other nuns in times of illness. The contemplation of Christ's sufferings would send her into ecstatic transports. A suppurating wound on her forehead seemed to be connected with her intense response to a sermon on the Crown of Thorns, an emblem which had especial significance for her. During her later years Rita suffered from a wasting disease, which was the cause of her death, on May 22, 1457. The first life of this saint was written in 1600. She was canonized in 1900. Rita is joint patroness of a sodality which exists to venerate the crown of thorns.

The old tradition that associates roses and figs with Rita has the following origin. Shortly before her death she asked a friend to bring her a rose from her garden at home. It was not the season for roses to bloom, but to gratify the whim of a woman who was desperately ill, the friend went there and was amazed to find a rose bush in full bloom. Picking a rose and taking it back to the convent, she asked Rita if she could get her something else. "Yes," was the answer; "bring me back two figs from the garden." The friend hastened away to the garden once more and discovered two ripe figs on a leafless fig tree. Rita is sometimes represented in art as holding these emblems. St. Rita of Cascia is especially venerated in Spain, and there and elsewhere she has been called "the saint of the impossible." In all countries persons who have especially heavy burdens to bear have been comforted and helped by meditating on the example of this saint, and praying to her.

Saint Thomas More
Martyr, Chancellor of England
1 5 3 5
(July 9)

Twice in the history of England there appears the figure of a great martyr who was also chancellor of the realm. Thomas Becket, whose story appears earlier in this volume, gave his life to keep the English Church safe from royal aggression; Thomas More gave his in a vain effort to preserve it from further aggression. Each was a royal favorite who loved God more than his king. The coincidence is striking, although on closer comparison the differences are also striking; first, those of time and status, between the high ecclesiastic of the late twelfth century and the layman of the Renaissance; and, more importantly, the differences in character and way of life.

Thomas More's father was a highly-esteemed citizen of London, Sir John More, lawyer and judge; his mother was Agnes, daughter of Thomas Grainger. He was born on Milk Street, Cheapside, on February 7, 1478. As a child he was sent to St. Anthony's School in Threadneedle Street, whose director, Nicholas Holt, a fine Latin scholar, taught boys of good family their classics. At the age of thirteen Thomas was taken into the household of John Morton, archbishop of Canterbury and Lord Chancellor, who was soon to become a cardinal. It had long been a custom for promising youths to be placed in the homes of noblemen and ranking churchmen to learn the ways of great gentlefolk. Thomas admired Morton and he, fortunately, liked the boy, and was instrumental in having him sent on to Canterbury College, Oxford. Sir John More was very

strict with his son, allowing him money only for necessities. Later
in life Thomas admitted that his father's parsimony during this
period had the good effect of keeping him at the studies which he
really loved. Linacre, the finest Greek scholar in England, was his
tutor and inspired him with such a zest for Greek literature that
his father feared for the legal career he had planned for his son,
and called him home after only two years at the university. By this
time Thomas knew Greek, French, and mathematics, spoke Latin
as well as English, and could play the lute and the viol—all proper
accomplishments for a young gentleman of that day.

In February, 1496, he was admitted as a student to Lincoln's
Inn; in 1501, at twenty-three, he was called to the bar, and for
three years thereafter was reader in law at Furnival's Inn; then he
entered Parliament. He was already a close friend of the eminent
Dutch humanist, Desiderius Erasmus, who had been teaching
Greek at Cambridge and Oxford. Among other friends were Colet,
the scholarly dean of St. Paul's, and William Lilly, with whom he
composed epigrams in Latin from the Greek Anthology. He lectured on St. Augustine's *City of God* at the church of St. Lawrence
Jewry, of which William Grocyn was rector. All in all, Thomas
More was a versatile, brilliant, and successful young man, as well
as extremely popular and charming. Of his sense of humor, Erasmus
wrote, "From childhood he had such a love for witty jests that he
seemed to have been sent into the world for the sole purpose of
coining them; he never descends to buffoonery, but gravity and
dignity were never made for him. He is always amiable and good-
tempered, and puts everyone who meets him in a happy frame
of mind."

More was seriously perplexed as to his vocation. He was strongly
attracted by the austere life of the Carthusian monks, and had
some leaning too towards the Friars Minor of the Observance; but
there seemed to be no real call to either the monastic life or the
secular priesthood. Though he remained a man of the world, he
kept throughout life certain ascetic practices; for many years
he wore a hair shirt next his skin, and followed the rules of Church

discipline for Fridays and vigils; every day he assisted at a Mass and recited the Little Office of Our Lady.

At about this time More met a certain John Colt of Essex, and became acquainted with his family, which included three daughters. More now took the decisive step of marriage, choosing the eldest daughter, Jane. According to his son-in-law, William Roper,[1] he thought the second daughter fairest, "yet when he considered it would be both great grief and some shame also to the eldest to see her younger sister preferred before her in marriage, he then, of a certain pity, framed his fancy towards her, and soon after married her." He and Jane were nevertheless very happy together; he set himself to teach her the literary and musical accomplishments which the wife of a man in More's position needed to have.

Four children were born to them, Margaret, Elizabeth, Cecily, and John. In addition, several children of friends were reared in their household, and here More tried out his original ideas in education. The house was for years a center of learning and culture, and of high good spirits as well. The girls were taught as carefully as the boys, a practice for which More had the authority of "prudent and holy ancients," such as St. Jerome and St. Augustine. At mealtime a passage from the Scriptures, with a short commentary, was read aloud by one of the children; afterwards there was singing and merry conversation; cards and dicing were forbidden. Family and servants met together for evening prayers. More himself built and endowed a chapel in his parish church of Chelsea, and even when he had attained the rank of Lord Chancellor he sang in the choir, dressed in the ordinary surplice.

He was extremely sensitive to the sufferings of others. "More was used," wrote a friend, "whenever in his house or in the village he lived in there was a woman in labor, to begin praying, and so continue until news was brought him that the delivery had come happily to pass. . . . His charity was without bounds, as is proved

[1] Roper was the husband of More's beloved eldest daughter, Margaret. As a boy he was one of those brought into the More home to be educated, and later he wrote an admiring life of his father-in-law.

by the frequent and abundant alms he poured without distinction among all unfortunate persons. He used himself to go through the back lanes and inquire into the state of poor families. . . . He often invited to his table his poorer neighbors, receiving them . . . familiarly and joyously; he rarely invited the rich, and scarcely ever the nobility. . . . In his parish of Chelsea he hired a house in which he gathered many infirm, poor, and old people, and maintained them at his own expense." But if the rich were rarely seen at his house, his friends Grocyn, Linacre, Colet, Lilly, and Fisher, all distinguished for scholarship and virtue, were frequent visitors; and famous men from across the Channel sought him out—Erasmus, whom we have spoken of, and Holbein, who has left us a fine portrait of More as well as a beautiful drawing of the More family group.

The first years of his married life were spent in Bucklersbury. Here in spare time More translated from Latin into English the life of the Italian humanist, Pico della Mirandola, and, with Erasmus, some *Dialogues* of the second-century satirist, Lucian of Samosata, from Greek into Latin. In 1508 he was abroad visiting the Universities of Louvain and Paris. He may also have had a hand in Erasmus' most popular work, *The Praise of Folly*, written in More's house that same year. More had led the opposition in Parliament to excessive royal taxation, and brought the king's ire down on himself and his father, old Sir John More, who was imprisoned in the Tower for a time and fined a hundred pounds. In 1509 King Henry VII died, and the accession of the youthful Henry VIII meant a rise in worldly favor and fortune for the More family. The following year Thomas was elected a bencher of Lincoln's Inn and appointed undersheriff for the city of London, an office of considerable importance.

At almost the same time, his "little Utopia," as More called the family group, was sadly shaken by the death of his dutiful young wife. Since More was preoccupied with many diverse interests and duties, he needed someone to care for the four children. Within a short time, therefore, he married Alice Middleton, a widow seven years his senior, a practical and kindly woman. Erasmus wrote of this marriage: "A few months after his wife's death, he married a widow. . . . She was neither young nor fair, as he would say laughingly, but an active and vigilant housewife, with whom he lived as pleasantly and sweetly as if she had all the charms of youth. You will scarcely find a husband who by authority or severity has gained such ready compliance as More by playful flattery."

Some years later More bought a new house and garden in Chelsea, then a small country village. It was his home until his death. In 1515 he was away for six months in Flanders, as a member of an English delegation to negotiate new trade agreements with the merchants of the Hanseatic League. In the intervals of leisure between business trips to Antwerp, he now worked on the famous *Utopia*, which he published the following year. There is no space here to discuss fully the significance of this remarkable book. It is proof both of More's thoughtful reading of Plato and of his profound interest in the social, economic, and political problems of his own time. As undersheriff since 1510, he had been brought into contact with much suffering, destitution, injustice, and unemployment. His picture of a commonwealth that was happier and radically different from the realm of England, one that was free from poverty and inequality, was both a challenge to constructive political thinking on the part of the statesmen of Europe and a plea for a better life for people in general. He wrote the book in Latin, that it might be read by the educated everywhere, and since it was both brilliant and provocative, it produced strong reactions— amusement, horror, or admiration. Within three years after its first appearance in Louvain it was published in Paris, Basle, Florence, Vienna, and Venice. It is *Utopia* that gives More his high place in the fields of social philosophy and letters.

The king and Cardinal Wolsey were now set on having More's services at the court. More had no illusions about Henry or court life, and knew that he could do little to remedy the vices which prevailed in the royal circle. Yet his conscience told him that that was no reason for "forsaking the commonwealth," and that which he could not turn to good, he must "so order that it be not very bad." In the year *Utopia* was published he was obliged to accept from the king an annual pension of a hundred pounds; in 1517 he became a member of the King's Council and a judge in the Court of Requests. As a member of the Council he accompanied Henry to the "Field of the Cloth of Gold," where the kings of England and France vied with one another in magnificence and in making promises that were soon broken. He was taken as Wolsey's confidant on a diplomatic mission to Calais and Bruges. In 1521 he was appointed under-treasurer, and privy-councilor, and raised to knighthood. His awards and honors make a long catalogue: grants of land in Oxfordshire and Kent; Latin orator in 1523, when the Emperor Charles V paid a state visit to London; speaker of the House of Commons, and author of the answer to Martin Luther's attack on the king's book, *Defense of the Seven Sacraments;* [2] steward of Oxford University in 1524 and of Cambridge University in 1525, and chancellor of the Duchy of Lancaster; again, in 1527, with Wolsey to France, and two years later with Bishop Tunstal of London to Cambrai to sign the treaty which meant a temporary pause in the wars of Europe. In October, 1529, Henry chose him as chancellor to succeed Wolsey, who had roused the king's wrath by opposing his scheme for nullifying his marriage. Thomas More was the first layman to hold the office.

Erasmus gives us a picture of More at this period: "In serious matters no man's advice is more prized, while if the king wishes to recreate himself, no man's conversation is gayer. Often there are deep and intricate matters that demand a grave and prudent judge. More unravels them in such a way that he satisfies both

---

[2] Martin Luther, the German monk who became leader of the Protestant movement in Europe, had published in 1520 three tracts in which he denounced the current corruption of the clergy, papal government in general, and the sacramental system of the Church. The following year Henry VIII, with advice from More, brought out an answer to Luther's argument, the *Defense of the Seven Sacraments*. Luther in turn replied to King Henry.

sides. No one, however, has ever prevailed on him to receive a gift for his decision. Happy the commonwealth where kings appoint such officials! His elevation has brought with it no pride. . . . You would say that he had been appointed public guardian of those in need." Another tribute from More's confessor speaks of his remarkable purity and devotion. But in spite of his many honors and achievements, the public esteem which he enjoyed, and the many tokens of the royal regard, More knew well that there was no security in his position. "Son Roper," he once said to his son-in-law, "I may tell thee I have no cause to be proud thereof, for if my head would win him a castle in France, it should not fail to go."

Although Henry's relations with the Pope had by this time become strained, More's time and thought were largely taken up with the general movement against Church authority in England. He composed answers to Protestant attacks and dealt with problems of heresy. Tyndale, then the leading English Protestant, was his ablest opponent. This scholar and reformer had left England for the Continent, in order to find freedom for the work he wished to do. At Worms he published the first Protestant translation of the New Testament from the Greek text, and at Marburg a translation of the Pentateuch. Tyndale was a better popular debater than More; the Chancellor was moderate and fair, and could top off his scholarly arguments with a shaft of wit, but his style was less vigorous and trenchant. As a controversial writer his chief work was *A Dialogue . . . Wherein he treated Divers Matters, as of the Veneration and Worship of Images and Relics, Praying to Saints, and Going on Pilgrimage. With many other things touching the pestilent sect of Luther and Tyndale . . .* (London, 1529.) Tyndale replied in 1531, and two years later More published a *Confutation,* a discursive treatise in which he touched incidentally on the doctrine of the Pope's infallibility.

In his *Apology* and again in *The Debellation of Salem and Bizance* (both in 1533) he defended the principle of punishment of heresy by secular power on the ground that it threatened the peace and safety of the commonwealth. As Chancellor it was his duty to administer the civil laws of England, which prescribed the death penalty for obstinate heretics. Nevertheless, during his term of office only four, it seems, were burned, and these were relapsed persons, whom he had no power to reprieve. Actually, it was heresy and not the heretics that More tried to get rid of.

One of Tyndale's vehement charges against the Catholics was what he called their failure to give the complete Bible to the people in a language they understood. His own translations were being smuggled into England from the Continent and avidly read. More favored the dissemination of selected books of Scripture in the vernacular; the reading of other books, he thought, should be at the discretion of every man's bishop, who would probably "suffer some to read the Acts of the Apostles whom he would not suffer to meddle with the Apocalypse." More added that some of the best minds among the Catholic clergy were also of this opinion.

When at length the break between King Henry and the Pope became open and the English clergy were commanded by Henry to acknowledge him as "Protector and Supreme Head of the Church of England, . . . so far as the law of Christ allows," More wished to resign his office, but was persuaded to retain it and turn his attention to Henry's "great matter"—his petition for a nullification of his marriage with Catherine of Aragon, on the ground that she had previously been the wife of his dead brother Arthur. The actual reason behind the petition was Henry's desire for a male heir and his infatuation with a young woman of the court, Anne Boleyn. The idea had been mooted first in 1527, and the failure in 1529 of a papal commission under Cardinal Campeggio to grant Henry's request, had been the cause of the downfall of Wolsey, who, the King thought, might have persuaded Campeggio to decide in his favor.

This drawn-out affair, which shook Christendom to its very foundations, was indeed so involved, both as to fact and law, that men of good will might well disagree on it. More, after much study of Church authorities, had become convinced of the validity of

Henry's marriage to Catherine, but, as a layman, had been allowed to refrain from taking sides publicly. When, in March, 1531, he reported to Parliament on the state of the case, he was asked for his opinion and refused to give it. In 1532 came the "submission of the clergy," who were now forced to promise to make no new laws without the King's consent and to submit the laws they had to a commission for revision. Later in the year an Act of Parliament prohibited the payment of annates, or first year's income from Church appointments, to the Holy See. At this More could no longer stand by in silence. To Henry's exasperation, he opposed the measure openly, and on May 16 offered his resignation as chancellor. He had held the office for less than three years.

The loss of his office and its perquisites reduced More to comparative poverty. Gathering his family around him he cheerfully explained the situation, adding, "Then we may yet with bags and wallets go a-begging together, and hoping that for pity some good folk will give us their charity, at every man's door to sing *Salve Regina*, and so keep company and be merry together." For the next eighteen months he lived very quietly, occupied with writing. He declined to attend the coronation of Anne Boleyn, though by the King's order three bishops wrote asking him to come and sent him money to pay for the necessary robes. He kept the money and stayed at home, explaining to the bishops that his honor would not allow him to grant their request, but that he accepted the money with gratitude and without scruple, since they were rich and he was poor.

More was not permitted to escape the royal displeasure. The case of the so-called "Holy Maid of Kent" served as a means of incriminating him. This woman, a Benedictine nun by the name of Elizabeth Barton, had for some time been creating a sensation by falling into trances and seeing visions, on the strength of which she warned evildoers of terrors to come. Eventually she was prevailed upon to condemn Henry's treatment of Catherine and prophesy his early death. In consequence she was seized, imprisoned in the Tower, and in April, 1534, executed for treason. In the bill of attainder drawn up against her were included, as sharers in her guilt, the saintly bishop of Rochester, John Fisher, and Thomas More. Fisher had been impressed by the nun's revelations, and More had seen and spoken to her, and at first given some countenance to her claims, though he ended by calling her a "false, deceiving hypocrite." The Lords expressed a wish to hear More for themselves in his own defense. Henry, knowing well that More had many stanch friends in Parliament, had the charge against him withdrawn.

In March Pope Clement VII formally pronounced the marriage of Henry and Catherine valid and therefore not to be annulled. A week later an Act of Succession was pushed through Parliament, requiring all the king's subjects to take oath to the effect that his union with Catherine had been no lawful marriage, that his union with Anne Boleyn was a true marriage, and that their offspring would be legitimate heirs to the throne, regardless of the objections of "any foreign authority, prince, or potentate." Opposition to this Act was declared high treason. On April 13 More and Fisher were offered the oath before a royal commission at Lambeth; they accepted the new line of royal succession established by the Act but refused to subscribe to it as a whole, since it was a clear defiance of the Pope's authority to decide a question involving a sacrament of the Church. Thereupon Thomas More was committed to the custody of one of the commissioners, William Benson, abbot of Westminster. Henry's new favorite, Thomas Cranmer, urged the King to compromise, but he would not. The oath was again tendered and again refused, and More was imprisoned in the Tower.

The fifteen months that he spent in prison were borne with a serene spirit; the tender love of his wife and children, especially that of his daughter Margaret, comforted him. He rejected all efforts of wife and friends to induce him to take the oath and so pacify Henry. Visitors were forbidden towards the end, and in his solitude he wrote the noblest of his religious works, the *Dialogue of Comfort against Tribulation.*

In November he was formally charged with the crime of treason,

SAINT FRANCIS' SERMON TO THE BIRDS   Giotto

The earliest of Giotto's known works (c. 1266-1336) is a series of frescoes in the Upper Church of Assisi dealing with the life of Saint Francis. The best known is "The Sermon to the Birds" which portrays the incident in the saint's life when he promised to preach to the birds if they would be silent while he was preaching to a group of people.

Saint Francis is dressed in the habit of his order, with the bare feet which are characteristic of the Franciscans. His special symbols are birds and animals and the stigmata.

THE VISION OF SAINT ANTHONY   C. Bosseron Chambers

A contemporary American painter, Chambers devotes himself to liturgical art.
Saint Anthony of Padua is dressed in the brown habit of a Franciscan monk.

The symbol of the Christ Child on an open book—as used here—is that most
often associated with Saint Anthony. The lilies are a secondary symbol.

and all the lands and honors granted him by the Crown were forfeited. Save for a small pension from the Order of St. John of Jerusalem, his family was almost penniless; Lady More sold her fine clothing to buy necessaries for him, and twice she petitioned the king for his release on the plea of sickness and poverty. In February, 1535, the Act of Supremacy came into operation; this conferred the title of Supreme Head of the Church of England, without qualification, on the king, and made it treason to refuse it. In April, Thomas Cromwell, Henry's hardfisted new secretary and councilor, called on More to elicit from him his opinion of this Act, but he would not give it. Margaret visited him on May 4 for the last time, and from the window of his cell they watched three Carthusian priors and one Bridgittine, who would not acknowledge a civil supremacy over the Church, go to their execution. "Lo, dost thou not see, Meg," he said, "that these blessed fathers be now as cheerfully going to their deaths as bridegrooms to their marriage? . . . Whereas thy silly father, Meg, that like a most wicked caitiff hath passed the whole course of his miserable life most sinfully, God, thinking him not worthy so soon to come to that eternal felicity, leaving him here yet still in the world, further to be plagued and turmoiled with misery." A few days later Cromwell with other officials questioned him again and taunted him for his silence. "I have not," he said gently, "been a man of such holy living as I might be bold to offer myself to death, lest God for my presumption might suffer me to fall."

On June 22 Bishop John Fisher was beheaded on Tower Hill. Nine days later More himself was formally indicted and tried in Westminster Hall. By this time he was so weak that he was permitted to sit during the proceedings. He was charged with having opposed the Act of Supremacy, both in conversation with members of the Council who had visited him in prison, and in an alleged discussion with Rich, the solicitor-general. More maintained that he had always refrained from talking with anyone on the subject and that Rich was swearing falsely. However, he was found guilty and condemned to death. Then at last he spoke out his mind firmly.

No temporal lord, he said, could or ought to be head of the spirituality. But even as St. Paul persecuted St. Stephen "and yet be they now both twain holy saints in Heaven, and shall continue there friends for ever, so I verily trust, and shall therefore right heartily pray, that though your lordships have now here in earth been judges of my condemnation, we may yet hereafter in Heaven merrily all meet together to everlasting salvation."

On his way back to the Tower he said farewell to Margaret, who broke through the guard to reach him, and four days later, now deprived of pen and ink, he wrote her his last letter with a piece of coal, sending with it his hair shirt, a relic now in care of the Canonesses Regular of Newton Abbot. Early in the morning of July 7, Sir Thomas Pope, a friend, came to inform him that he was to die that day at nine o'clock. More thanked him, said he would pray for the king, and with talk of a joyful meeting in Heaven strove to cheer up his weeping friend. When the hour came he walked out to Tower Hill, and mounted the scaffold, with a jest for the lieutenant who helped him climb it. To the bystanders he spoke briefly, asking for their prayers and their witness that he died in faith of the Holy Catholic Church and as the king's loyal subject. He then knelt and repeated the psalm *Miserere;* after which he encouraged the executioner, though warning him that his neck was very short and he must take heed to "strike not awry." So saying, he laid down his head and was beheaded at one stroke. His body was buried in the church of St. Peter-ad-Vincula within the Tower; his head, after being exposed on London Bridge, was given to Margaret and laid in the Roper vault in the church of St. Dunstan, outside the West Gate of Canterbury. There, presumably, it still is, beneath the floor under the organ, at the east end of the south aisle.

More was beatified by Pope Leo XIII in 1886, along with other English martyrs, and canonized in 1935. Had he never met death for the faith he still would have been a candidate for canonization as a confessor. From first to last his life was singularly pure, lived in the spirit of his own prayer: "Give me, good Lord, a longing to be with Thee; not for the avoiding of the calamities of this wicked world, nor so much for the avoiding of the pains of purgatory, nor the pains of Hell neither, nor so much for the attaining of the joys of Heaven in respect of mine own commodity, as even for a very love of Thee."

Excerpts from Dialogue of Comfort against Tribulation [3]

iii, 27. . . . *The devil it is therefore that, if we for fear of* men will fall, is ready to run upon us and devour us. . . . Therefore when he roareth out upon us in the threats of mortal men, let us tell him that with our inward eye we see him well enough and intend to stand and fight with him, even hand to hand. If he threaten us that we be too weak, let us tell him that our captain Christ is with us and that we shall fight with his strength which hath vanquished him already. And let us fence us in with faith and comfort us with hope and smite the devil in the face with a firebrand of charity. For surely if we be of the tender loving mind that our master was and do not hate them that kill us, but pity them and pray for them, with sorrow for the peril that they make for themselves, that fire of charity, thrown in his face, striketh the devil suddenly so blind that he cannot see where to fasten a stroke on us.

When we feel us too bold, remember our own feebleness. When we feel us too faint, remember Christ's strength. In our fear, let us remember Christ's painful agony that himself would for our comfort suffer before his passion to the intent that no fear should

---

[3] *The Dialogue of Comfort* was written by More during the last few months of his life, when already he envisaged what was before him. It is in the form of a conversation between two Hungarian Christians, an old man and his nephew, preparing themselves to face the invasion of the Turkish army, which then threatened Eastern Europe. None who read the little book could fail to see in the Moslem Grand Turk ordering Christian captives to abjure their faith on pain of death the figure of the English king ordering his subjects to betray what they felt was Christ's church. It was published in 1553, the year in which Henry VIII's Catholic daughter Mary came to the throne.

make us despair. And ever call for his help such as himself wills to send us. And then need we never to doubt but that either he shall keep us from the painful death, or shall not fail so to strengthen us in it that he shall joyously bring us to heaven by it. And then doeth he much more for us than if he kept us from it. For as God did more for poor Lazarus in helping him patiently to die of hunger at the rich man's door than if he had brought to him at the door all the rich glutton's dinner, so, though he be gracious to a man whom he delivereth out of painful trouble, yet doeth he much more for a man if through right painful death he deliver him from this wretched world into eternal bliss. From which whosoever shrink away, forsaking his faith, and falleth in the peril of ever-lasting fire, he shall be very sure to repent it ere it be long after. For I ween that whensoever he falleth sick next, he will wish that he had been killed for Christ's sake before. . . .

But to fear while the pain is coming, there is all our trouble. But then if we would remember hell pain on the other side, into which we fall while we flee from this, then should this short pain be no hindrance at all. And we should be still more pricked forward, if we were faithful, by deep considering of the joys of heaven, of which the Apostle saith: ". . . The passions of this time are not worthy of the glory that is to come which shall be shown in us." [4] We should not, I ween, cousin, need much more on all this whole matter than that one text of St. Paul, if we would consider it well. For surely, mine own good cousin, remember that if it were possible for me and you alone to suffer as much trouble as the whole world doth together, all that were not worthy of itself to bring us to the joy which we hope to have everlastingly. And therefore I pray you let the consideration of that joy put all worldly trouble out of your heart, and also pray that it may do the same in me.

(*Dialogue of Comfort Against Tribula-tion,* Everyman Edition.)

[4] Romans viii, 18.

Consider Well

Consider well that both by night and day
    While we most busily provide and care
For our disport, our revel, and our play,
    For pleasant melody and dainty fare,
    Death stealeth on full slily; unaware
He lieth at hand and shall us all surprise,
We wot not when nor where nor in what wise.

When fierce temptations threat thy soul with loss
    Think of His Passion and the bitter pain,
Think on the mortal anguish of the Cross,
    Think on Christ's blood let out at every vein,
    Think on His precious heart all rent in twain;
For thy redemption think all this was wrought,
Nor be that lost which He so dearly bought.

Saint Francis Xavier

Apostle of the Indies and Japan

1 5 5 2

(*December 3*)

In every age since Christ charged the Apostles to go and preach to all nations there have been saintly and heroic men who have journeyed to far lands in order to bring new peoples into the Christian fold. Among those who labored most zealously was the Jesuit, Francis Xavier, named by Pius X as official patron of foreign missions and of all work for spreading the faith. The first great missionary to the Orient in modern times, Xavier planted Christianity in western and southern India, in the then uncharted islands of the Indian Ocean, and in Japan. He died, four hundred years ago, while making a valiant effort to reach the people of China.

Xavier was born in 1506. It was fourteen years after Columbus' first voyage, and Spain was stirring with a ferment that was to result in ever greater achievements as the century advanced. His birthplace was the castle of Xavier, near Pampeluna, not far from the present French border. The family was highly placed, the mother being the heiress of the houses of Azpilqueta and Xavier, and the father, Don Juan de Jasso, councilor to the King of Navarre. Francis was the youngest of a large family, and special attention was given to his education. Since he had a taste for study, he was sent at seventeen to the University of Paris, to enter the College of St. Barbara. In 1530 he received the degree of Master of Arts, and afterwards taught Aristotelian philosophy in the university. Before receiving his degree he had come under the influ-

ence of a compatriot and fellow student, Ignatius Loyola, a former
soldier who was fifteen years his senior. Filled with a compelling
desire to save souls, Loyola had drawn around him a little band
of seven earnest men who, in 1534, formed themselves into the
Society of Jesus, dedicated to the service of God.[1] Francis was a
member of this group.

With his companions he was ordained to the priesthood three
years later in Venice, and shared in all the labors and vicissitudes
of the young organization. It was in 1540 that the King of Portugal,
John III, had his ambassador at the Vatican ask the Pope for
Jesuit missionaries to spread the faith in his new Indian possessions. Loyola promptly appointed Francis to join Simon Rodriguez,
another of the original seven, then in Portugal; together they
should undertake this work. On reaching Lisbon at the end of June,
Xavier went immediately to Rodriguez, and the two priests, while
waiting through the fall and winter for plans to mature, were
lodged in a hospital where they helped care for the sick; they also
catechized and taught in the hospital and in the city, and their
Sundays and holidays were often spent hearing confessions at
court. King John came to have so high a regard for them that he
decided to keep Rodriguez at Lisbon and was for a time uncertain
whether or not to let Xavier go. But at last he delivered to Xavier
four briefs from Pope Paul III, in which he was constituted papal
nuncio and recommended to the princes of the East.

In the spring Xavier, with two assistants, Brother Paul of
Camerino, an Italian, and Francis Mancias, a Portuguese layman,
joined an expedition bound for Goa, on the west coast of India.
They sailed on April 7, 1541, Xavier's thirty-fifth birthday. There
were five ships in the fleet, and the missionaries sailed on that of
the admiral, which also carried Don Martin de Sousa, newly appointed governor of India. Xavier had declined to take a servant,
saying that as long as he had the use of his hands and feet he could
wait on himself. When told it would be unbecoming for a papal

[1] The story of the founding of the Society of Jesus is told in more detail in
the life of *Ignatius Loyola,* which follows.

nuncio and scion of a noble Spanish house to cook his own food and wash his own linen on deck, he replied that he could cause no scandal so long as he did no evil. He took all on board under his spiritual care. He catechized the sailors, said Mass, and preached on deck every Sunday; he also had to settle quarrels and check disorders. When scurvy broke out on all the ships, he helped tend the sick. It took five months to round the Cape of Good Hope and reach Mozambique, where they wintered and rested for six months. Finally, on May 6, 1542, they landed at Goa, after a voyage of thirteen months, twice the usual period of time required.

Following quickly on the great voyages of discovery and exploration made by Magellan and Da Gama, the Portuguese had established themselves at Goa thirty years earlier. The Christian population had churches, clergy, and a bishop, but many of the Portuguese were ruled by ambition, avarice, and debauchery. They ignored the tenets and Sacraments of the Church and tended to shock and alienate the pagans by their behavior. There were a few preachers but no priests beyond the walls of Goa. Don Martin, the new governor, was a good man and tried to help Xavier in every way. To meet this challenging situation Xavier decided that he must begin by instructing the Portuguese themselves in the principles of faith, and give much of his time to the teaching of children. His mornings were usually spent in tending and comforting the distressed in hospital and prison; after that, he walked through the streets ringing a bell to summon the children and servants to Catechism. As they gathered about him, he led them into the church and taught them prayers, the Creed, and the rules of Christian conduct. On Sunday he said Mass for the lepers, preached to the Portuguese, then to the Indians, and finished the day by visiting in private homes.

By the gentleness of his words and behavior and his deep concern for souls, Francis won the people's respect. One of his most troublesome problems was the concubinage openly practiced by Europeans of all ranks with the native women. Xavier tried to meet the situation by methods that were not only moral, but sensible, humane, and tactful. To help simple people, he set Catholic doctrines to rhyme, to fit popular tunes, and these songs were sung everywhere, in fields and workshops, in streets and homes.

Xavier soon learned that along the Pearl Fishery Coast, which extends from Cape Comorin on the southern tip of India to the island of Manaar, off Ceylon, there was a low-caste people called Paravas, many of whom had been baptized ten years before, merely to please the Portuguese, who had helped them against their Mohammedan enemies, but who for lack of all teaching still kept their ancient superstitions. Accompanied by several native clerics from the seminary at Goa, he set sail for Cape Comorin in October, 1542. First he set himself to learn the language of the Paravas; he instructed those who had already been baptized, then preached to those still unsaved, and so great was the multitude he baptized that at times he was almost too weary to move his arms. With the high-caste Brahmins his efforts were unavailing, and at the end of a year he had made only one convert. But the common people accepted him and his message; he made himself one with them; his food was the same as that of the poorest, rice and water; he slept on the ground in a native hut. In his letters he reveals how intense was the joy that this labor gave him.

After fifteen months with the Paravas he returned to Goa to recruit help. The year following he was again working among them, with the help of Mancias, two native priests, and a lay catechist. In his letters from here we see how his work was made even more difficult by the unethical behavior of the Portuguese traders and settlers, who had not only been exploiting the poor people but also at times arousing the antagonism of the Indian rulers. He writes of one settler who stole a slave owned by the Rajah of nearby Travancore. "This act of injustice shuts me out from the Rajah, who is otherwise well disposed. . . . Would the Portuguese be pleased if, when one of the natives happened to quarrel with one of themselves, he were to take that Portuguese by force, put him in chains, and carry him off up country? Certainly not. The Indians must have the same feelings. . . ."

Xavier extended his activities up into Travancore, where he founded forty-five churches, and was hailed as the "Great Father." Village after village received him; he baptized the inhabitants and destroyed their temples and idols. As elsewhere, he enlisted the children and used them as helpers to the catechists, to teach others what they had just learned themselves. The Brahmin and Mohammedan authorities opposed Xavier with violence; time and again his hut was burned down over his head, and once he saved his life only by hiding among the branches of a large tree. His difficulties were increased too when the Christians of Comorin and Tuticorin were set upon by heathen tribes to the east, who robbed, massacred, and carried them into slavery. Xavier went to their relief and is said to have held off the raiders once by facing them alone, crucifix in hand. Again he was handicapped by the misdeeds of the Portuguese, whose local commandant was suspected of having secret dealings with the heathen.

Twice while in Travancore Xavier was credited with the miracle of bringing the dead to life. The miracles were probably one reason for his being invited to visit the island of Manaar, between Ceylon and the mainland. He could not himself leave Travancore at that time, but he sent a missionary to whom many came for instruction and baptism. The ruler of Jafanatapam in northern Ceylon, hearing of these successes, and fearing they might lead to a Portuguese conquest of Manaar, sent over an army that slew six hundred converts who, when questioned, bravely confessed Christ. Don Martin de Sousa gave orders for an expedition to avenge the massacre and depose its perpetrator in favor of a dethroned elder brother. Xavier went thither to join it, but the officers were diverted from their objective and Xavier made instead a journey of devotion to the shrine of St. Thomas at Mylapore,[2] near Madras.

Many incidents are told of Xavier's conversion of notorious

---

[2] According to tradition, St. Thomas, one of the Twelve Apostles, had journeyed east and established Christianity on the southeast coast of India, later suffering martyrdom there. In 1547, two years after St. Francis' visit, the Portuguese rebuilt his shrine at Mylapore.

European sinners during these travels. From Cochin in Travancore, early in 1545, he sent a long letter to King John with an account of his mission. He speaks boldly of the harm these adventurers were doing to the cause, and the danger that heathen who had been gathered into the Church might fall away,—"scandalized and terrified by the many grievous injuries and wrongs which they suffer, especially from your Highness' own servants. . . . For there is danger that when our Lord God calls your Highness to His judgment that your Highness may hear angry words from him: 'Why did you not punish those who were your subjects and owned your authority, and were enemies of Me in India?' " In another letter he is more explicit about the wickedness of the European colonists: "People scarcely hesitate to believe that it cannot be wrong to do what can be done so easily. . . . I never cease wondering at the number of novel inflexions which, in this new language of avarice, have been added to the usual forms in the conjugation of that ill-omened verb 'to rob.' " Plain speaking could not go much farther. Xavier's dedication to his task was complete; he ended one letter to the king with the words, "As I expect to die in these Indian regions and never to see your Highness again in this life, I beg you, my lord, to help me with your prayers, that we may meet again in the next world, where we shall certainly have more rest than here."

In the spring of 1545 Xavier moved on eastward to Malacca, on the Malay peninsula, and spent four months there. It was a large and prosperous city, which Albuquerque had captured for the Portuguese in 1511. Xavier was received with reverence and cordiality, and the people accepted in good part his efforts at correcting their licentiousness and greed. For the next eighteen months he was traveling into the almost unknown world of the Pacific, visiting islands which he speaks of as the Moluccas, probably those that are now known as the Spice Islands. On some of them he found Portuguese merchants and settlers. He suffered many physical hardships, but in spite of all he writes to Loyola: "The dangers to which I am exposed and the tasks I undertake for God are inexhaustible springs of spiritual joy, so much so that these islands are the places in all the world for a man to lose his sight by excess of weeping; but they are tears of joy. I do not remember ever to have tasted such inward delight; and these consolations take from me all sense of bodily hardships and of troubles from open enemies and not too trustworthy friends." On his return, Xavier sent three new Jesuit recruits from Europe to these islands.

Before leaving he heard for the first time of the existence of the Japanese archipelago. The news that there were still new worlds to conquer thrilled him. After visiting the Pearl Fishery Coast and Ceylon once more, he reached Goa in March. There, with a well-born Japanese convert whom he called Anger, he made plans for going to Japan. But first, five new Jesuits recently arrived from home must be stationed in various Portuguese settlements. A training house and a school were established at Goa. All the while preparations for Japan were going forward. At the end of a year Xavier set out with Father Torres, John Fernandez, Anger, henceforth known as Paul, and two native servants who had received baptism. After a short stay in Malacca they boarded a ship and sailed north, landing at Kagoshima, on the Japanese island of Kyushu, on the feast of the Assumption, 1549.

Kagoshima was Paul's native city, and he obtained from the prince of Satsuma province permission for Xavier to preach. While Paul translated and circulated the Creed, the Catechism, and some simple prayers, Xavier set himself to learn the Japanese language. As soon as he could use it fluently, he began to preach. But not long afterward the prince grew angry with the Portuguese merchants because they had abandoned his port of Kagoshima to carry on their trading at Hirado, a better harbor, a little to the north of modern Nagasaki. He withdrew the permission he had given Xavier and threatened to punish any Japanese who became a Christian. The few converts remained faithful and declared they were ready to suffer banishment or death rather than deny Christ. After a year at Kagoshima, Xavier decided to push on to Hirado, carrying on his back all the articles necessary for the celebration of Mass.

On the way he stopped to preach at the fortress of Ekandono, where the prince's steward and the prince's wife were secret believers in the new teaching. When he departed, Xavier left the converts in the steward's care, and twelve years later another missionary found this isolated little group still full of fervor and faithfully practicing their religion. At Hirado the missionaries baptized more converts in twenty days than they had done at Kagoshima in a whole year. Leaving these converts in charge of Father Torres, Xavier and his party set out for Kyoto, the imperial capital, on the main island of Hondo. They went by the beautiful Inland Sea to the port of Yamaguchi, and Xavier preached there, in public and before the local prince. The number of persons interested in his message was small.

After a month's stay at Yamaguchi, where he met with many affronts, Xavier resumed his journey with his companions. It was nearing the end of the year, and they suffered from inclement weather and bad roads. They reached Kyoto in February, and here Xavier found that he could not have an audience with the emperor without paying a large sum of money. Also, the city was in a state of civil disorder, and after a fortnight's stay he returned to Yamaguchi.

Having now learned that evangelical poverty had not the appeal in Japan that it had in Europe and in India, he decided to change his method of approach. Handsomely dressed, with his companions acting as attendants, he presented himself before Oshindono, the ruler of Nagate, and as a representative of the great kingdom of Portugal offered him the letters and presents, a musical instrument, a watch, and other attractive objects which had been given him by the authorities in India for the emperor. Oshindono, pleased with these attentions from an envoy of so great a power, gave Xavier leave to teach in his province, and provided an empty Buddhist temple for his residence. Under these auspices, Xavier preached to such effect that he baptized many.

Hearing after a time that a Portuguese ship had arrived at a port in the province of Bungo in Kyushu and that the prince there would like to see him, Xavier now set out southward again. Among the passengers on the ship was the traveler Fernao Mendez Pinto, who has left an entertaining account of how the seamen received the visits of the highly respected Xavier and of Civan, the young and friendly Japanese grandee who came with him. The Jesuit, in a fine cassock, surplice, and stole, was attended by thirty gentlemen and as many servants, all in their best clothes. Five of them bore on cushions valuable articles, including a portrait of Our Lady and a pair of velvet slippers, these not gifts for the prince, but solemn offerings to Xavier, to impress the onlookers with his eminence!

Thus he opened a way for preaching in Bungo. With the Buddhist priests he had long discussions and even made a few converts among them. One discussion, arranged by the prince, lasted for five days, according to Mendez Pinto. Some of the points argued were puerile, others so lofty that, "I avow," says Mendez, "that my wit is not capable of understanding them." Both he and Xavier mention the mental alertness of the Japanese and their openness to conviction by reasoning, agreeing that "their intellects are as sharp and sensible as any in the world." The threatened persecution of the Christians did not occur, and by the end of 1551 Xavier felt free to take passage on the Portuguese ship back to India, leaving the Japanese converts in charge of Father Torres and Brother Fernandez. He had been in Japan for about two years and had baptized, according to report, some seven hundred and sixty Japanese.

At Malacca he halted long enough to study the possibility of contriving an entry into China, where strangers were forbidden by law to set foot, on pain of death or imprisonment. The governor of Malacca was of the opinion that an informal embassy might be landed in a Chinese port in the name of the King of Portugal, professedly in the interests of mutual trade, and that a few missionaries might go with it. Meanwhile, early in February, 1552, Xavier was back in Goa receiving reports: Brother Gaspar Baertz had been making converts in the city and island of Ormuz, at the entrance to the Persian Gulf. On the Pearl Fishery Coast Christianity was flourishing, even though the native converts were still being terribly exploited by the Portuguese. There was also progress in Cochin, Mylapore, and the Moluccas. The Rajah of Tanore, whose dominions lay on the coast of Malabar, between Goa and Travancore, had been baptized, as had one of the rulers of Ceylon.

On the other hand, Father Antony Gomez, rector of the college at Goa, had been making such innovations in the internal discipline of the Society that Xavier felt obliged to dismiss him, and send him to a distant mission. He appointed Father Baertz rector and vice-provincial, distributed the newly-arrived recruits among all the missions, and obtained from the viceroy a commission for his friend, James Pereira, to go as Portuguese envoy to China. Having thus settled affairs at Goa, he wrote long, detailed letters to the King of Portugal, Loyola, and Simon Rodriguez. Then, after sending final instructions to his scattered missionaries, he bade farewell to his brethren, and with one priest and four lay helpers set sail once more for the east. This was on April 25, 1552.

At Malacca they found that a contagious fever was raging, and Xavier with his companions helped carry the sick people to hospitals. When the plague slackened, he took up the matter of the embassy to China with the new governor, Don Alvaro d'Ataide,[3] who had succeeded his brother, Don Pedro de Silva, Xavier's friend, and who had received instructions from the Viceroy in India to forward the project. But Don Alvaro had a personal grudge against Pereira, and refused to allow him to sail. After a month of fruitless persuasion, Xavier produced the briefs of Pope Paul, which contained his appointment as papal nuncio. He had kept these documents secret up to this time, except from the bishop of Goa. Don Alvaro ignored them; the most he would concede was that Xavier himself might go to China in Pereira's ship, but without its owner, a proposition to which Pereira agreed. As for missionary work in Malacca, it seems that Xavier labored

[3] Don Alvaro was a son of Vasco da Gama, discoverer of the sea-route to India.

harder for its regeneration than for any other place, with the poorest results. On leaving this time, he took off his shoes and beat out the dust of the place on a rock. "Are you leaving us forever?" the episcopal vicar asked him. "I hope that our Lord will soon send you back to us in peace." "That is as God wills," Xavier replied sadly, climbing into the boat.

Since the project for an embassy failed, Xavier sent three of the Jesuits he had with him on to Japan, and kept only one brother and a young Chinese. With these two he hoped to find a way to land secretly in China. Before leaving Malacca he wrote to thank Pereira, and suggested that he write the King of Portugal an account of the attempt and of the chances of future trade with China. He also wrote to Father Baertz, bidding him go to the bishop of Goa and arrange for the publication in Malacca of the excommunication which Don Alvaro and his abettors had incurred by impeding a papal envoy. Late in August, 1552, he reached the port of Shang-chuen, on an island near the mouth of the Su-kiang River, not far from Canton. From here he wrote more letters. He had found an interpreter, for the Chinese he had brought from Goa knew nothing of the language spoken at court. Then, with difficulty, he had hired a Chinese merchant to land him at night in some part of Canton, and had bound himself by oath never to reveal this man's name. There were some Portuguese traders on the island, and they were out to thwart him, fearing the Chinese would take vengeance on them for Xavier's daring. At this critical juncture Xavier fell ill of a fever. The Portuguese ships in harbor, all but one, departed, and he was reduced to extreme want. The Chinese merchant failed to come for him and the interpreter disappeared. On November 20 fever seized him a second time, and he felt a presentiment of death. He took refuge on the one remaining Portuguese ship, but the rocking of the ship made him feel worse; the next day he asked to be set on land again.

The sailors were afraid to show any kindness to Xavier for fear of offending Don Alvaro. They left him lying on the sands exposed to a piercing wind, until someone carried him into the shelter of a

SAINT LOUIS, KING OF FRANCE   El Greco

Domenikos Theotocopoulos (1541-1614) who painted in Spain, was known
as El Greco, "The Greek," because of his birth on the Isle of
Crete. Although he had studied in Italy, probably under
Titian, his style is completely individual. All of his work is
pervaded by a sense of mysticism, and the elongation of his
figures is most characteristic.

Saint Louis is shown with the crown of a king and his sceptre
tipped with a "Manus Dei," which are his most usual symbols.

SAINT THOMAS AQUINAS   M. Feuerstein

This modern painting of Saint Thomas Aquinas beholding the crucified Christ in a vision portrays the inspiration which led the Angelic Doctor to compose the office of the Blessed Sacrament which is still in use.

The open book and pen are characteristic of Saint Thomas Aquinas, as is a rayed chalice, emblematic of the Holy Eucharist.

native hut. For two weeks he lay there, lonely and deserted, praying ceaselessly between periods of delirium. His strength ebbed rapidly and on December 3, 1552, with eyes fixed on his crucifix, he murmured: *"In te, Domine, speravi. Non confundar in aeternam"* (In Thee, O Lord, have I put my hope. Let me never be confounded), and died. Although he was only forty-six years old, the severity of his exertions during the ten years of his mission had so aged him that his hair was almost white. The next evening his body was buried in a shallow grave. Only Antony, the Chinese youth, Francis d'Aghiar, the pilot, and two half-caste bearers were at the burial.

The following February the body was removed to Malacca, thence on to Goa, and there it still lies magnificently enshrined in the Church of the Good Jesus. Within a few weeks of Xavier's death Loyola wrote to recall him to Europe for the purpose of making him his successor, in recognition of his heroic work in the Orient. In 1622 Xavier was canonized, along with the founder of the Society of Jesus. Of the Apostle of the Indies Sir Walter Scott wrote: "One cannot deny him the courage and patience of a martyr, with the good sense, resolution, ready wit, and address of the best negotiator that ever went on a temporal embassy." This great mystic and ascetic, to whom the spiritual life was an ever-present reality, had those vital qualities of mind and personality which enabled him to speak to men's hearts and organize their efforts in the spreading of God's word.

Letter to the Society at Rome

(XLIV)

*M*ay the grace and love of Christ our Lord always help and favor us! Amen. . . . Now to speak of what I know you are most anxious to hear about—the state of religion in India. In this region of Travancore, where I now am, God has drawn very many to the faith of His Son Jesus Christ. In the space of one month I made Christians of more than ten thousand. This is the method I followed. As soon as I arrived in any heathen village where they had sent for me to give them baptism, I gave orders for all, men, women, and children, to be collected in one place. Then, beginning with the first elements of the Christian faith, I taught them there is one God, Father, Son, and Holy Ghost; and at the same time, calling on the three divine Persons and one God, I made them each make three times the sign of the Cross; then, putting on a surplice, I began to recite in a loud voice and in their own language the form of the general Confession, the Apostle's Creed, the Ten Commandments, the Lord's Prayer, the *Ave Maria*, and the *Salve Regina*. Two years ago I translated all these prayers into the language of the country, and learned them by heart. I recited them slowly so that all of every age and condition followed me in them.

Then I began to explain shortly the articles of the Creed and the Ten Commandments in the language of the country. Where the people appeared to me sufficiently instructed to receive baptism, I ordered them all to ask God's pardon publicly for the sins of their past life, and to do this with a loud voice and in the presence of their neighbors still hostile to the Christian religion, in order to touch the hearts of the heathen and confirm the faith of the good. All the heathen are filled with admiration at the holiness of the law of God, and express the greatest shame at having lived so long in ignorance of the true God. They willingly hear about the mysteries and rules of the Christian religion, and treat me, poor sinner as I am, with the greatest respect. Many, however, put away from them with hardness of heart the truth which they well know.

When I have done my instruction, I ask one by one all those who desire baptism if they believe without hesitation each of the articles of the faith. All immediately, holding their arms in the form of the Cross, declare with one voice that they believe all entirely. Then at last I baptize them in due form, and I give to each his name written on a ticket. After their baptism the new Christians go back to their houses and bring me their wives and families for baptism. When all are baptized I order all the temples of their false gods to be destroyed and all the idols to be broken in pieces. I can give you no idea of the joy I feel in seeing this done, witnessing the destruction of the idols by the very people who but lately adored them. In all the towns and villages I leave the Christian doctrine in writing in the language of the country, and I prescribe at the same time the manner in which it is to be taught in the morning and evening schools. When I have done all this in one place, I pass to another, and so on successively to the rest. In this way I go all round the country, bringing the natives into the fold of Jesus Christ, and the joy that I feel in this is far too great to be expressed in a letter, or even by word of mouth. . . .

You may judge from this alone, my very dear brothers, what great and fertile harvests this uncultivated field promises to produce. This part of the world is so ready, so teeming with shooting corn, as I may say, that I hope within this very year to make as many as a hundred thousand Christians. . . .

And now what ought you to do when you see the minds of these people so well prepared to receive the seed of the Gospel? May God make known to you His most holy will, and give you at the same time strength and courage to carry it out; and may He in His Providence send as many as possible of you into this country!

The least and most lonely of your brothers,

FRANCIS

From Cochin, January 27th, 1545.

To the Society at Rome

(LIV)

May the grace and love of Jesus Christ our Lord always help and favor us! Amen. . . .

. . . Nearly two hundred miles beyond Molucca there is a region which is called Maurica. Here, many years ago, a great number of the inhabitants became Christians, but having been totally neglected and left, as it were, orphans by the death of the priests who taught them, they have returned to their former barbarous and savage state. It is in every way a land full of perils, and especially to be dreaded by strangers on account of the great ferocity of the natives and the many kinds of poison which it is there common to give in what is eaten and drunk. The fear of this has deterred priests from abroad from going there to help the islanders.

I have considered in what great necessity they are, with no one to instruct them or give them the sacraments, and I have come to think that I ought to provide for their salvation even at the risk of my life. I have resolved to go thither as soon as possible, and to offer my life to the risk. Truly I have put all my trust in God, and I wish as much as is in me to obey the precept of our Lord Jesus Christ: "He that will save his life shall lose it; and he that shall lose his life for My sake shall find it." [4] Words easy in thought but not easy in practice. When the hour comes when life must be lost that you may find it in God, when danger of death is on you, and you see plainly that to obey God you must sacrifice life, then, I know not how, it comes to pass that what before seemed a very clear precept is involved in incredible darkness. . . . It is in such circumstances that we see clearly how great after all our weakness is, how frail and unstable is our human nature here.

Many friends of mine have prayed me earnestly not to go amongst so barbarous a people. Afterwards, when they saw they gained nothing by prayers or tears, they brought me each what he thought the best possible antidote against poison of all sorts; but I have unrelentingly sent them all back, lest after burdening myself with medicines, I should have another burden which before I was without, that of fear. I had put all my hope in the protection of Divine Providence, and I thought I ought to be on my guard, lest relying on human aid I should lose something of my trust in God. So I thanked them all and earnestly entreated them to pray God for me, for that no more certain remedy could possibly be found. . . .

From Amboyna [May, 1546]

(H. T. Coleridge, *Life and Letters of St. Francis Xavier*, 1872.)

[4] Matthew xvi, 25.

Saint Ignatius of Loyola
Founder of the Society of Jesus, Confessor
1 5 5 6
(*July 31*)

St. Ignatius of Loyola, with his new and dynamic conception of the religious life, has left an impress on the Church unparalleled in modern times. The founder of the Society of Jesus was a pragmatic idealist who devoted his mature years to revitalizing Catholicism and meeting the challenge of the Protestant Reformation. He was born on December 24, 1491, the year before Columbus discovered a New World and claimed it for Ferdinand and Isabella. His birthplace was the great castle of Loyola in Guipuzcoa, in the Basque country of northwest Spain. Both his father, Don Beltran, lord of Onaz and Loyola, and his mother were of ancient and illustrious lineage. There were three daughters and eight sons in the family, and Inigo, as Ignatius was christened, was the youngest. He was a slight, handsome, high-spirited boy, with the Spaniard's pride, physical courage, and ardent passion for glory. As a youth, Inigo was sent by his father to go and live in the household of Juan Velasquez de Cuellar, one of King Ferdinand's provincial governors, at Arevalo, a town of Castile. Here he remained for many years, but like most young men of his class, he was taught little more than how to be a good soldier, an accomplished horseman and courtier. This long period of training, inculcating the soldierly virtues of discipline, obedience, and prudence, probably exerted some influence on the form and general tone of the society he founded.

When he was twenty-five, he enlisted under a kinsman, the Duke

341

of Najera, saw service in border warfare against the French in northern Castile and Navarre, and won a captaincy. The event that utterly changed the course of his life was the defense of the fortress of Pampeluna, the capital of Navarre. During this hotly contested battle, which Inigo led, he showed great bravery against heavy odds, but when he was hit by a cannon ball that broke his right shin, the Spanish capitulated. The French looked after the young captain's wounds and then sent him in a litter to his father's castle, some fifty miles away. The shattered bone, badly set, was now rebroken and set again, a crude operation which left the end of a bone protruding. Anaesthesia was still in the distant future, and Inigo endured this, as well as having the bone sawed off, without being bound or held. Afterwards his right leg was always shorter than the left.

One day, while he was confined to his bed, he asked his sister-in-law for a popular romantic book, *Amadis of Gaul*, to while away the hours. This book about knights and their valorous deeds could not be found, and instead he was given *The Golden Legend*, a collection of stories of the saints, and a *Life of Christ*. He began to read with faint interest, but gradually became so immersed and so moved that he spent entire days reading and rereading these books. He had fallen in love with a certain lady of the court; he also at this time retained his strong feeling for knightly deeds. Now he gradually came to realize the vanity of these worldly passions and his dependence on things of the spirit. He observed that the thoughts which came from God filled him with peace and tranquillity, while the others, though they might delight him briefly, left his heart heavy. This cleavage, as he was to write in his book *Spiritual Exercises*, helps one to distinguish the spirit of God from that of the world.[1] Towards the end of his convalescence he reached the point of dedication; henceforth he would fight for victory on the battlefield of the spirit, and achieve glory as the saints had done.

[1] St. Antony of Egypt, twelve hundred years before, had told his disciples to use a similar test.

He began to discipline his body, rising at midnight to spend hours mourning for his sins. How grave these sins may have been we do not know, but as a young soldier he may well have shared in the loose and careless life around him. His eldest brother, Don Martin, who on the death of their father had become lord of Loyola, now returned from the wars. He tried his best to keep Inigo in the world, for he needed the strength and intelligence of this young brother in the management of their great estate. Inigo, however, was now set on his course. As soon as his condition permitted, he mounted a mule and went on pilgrimage, always the great resource of persons in trouble or in a state of indecision, to Our Lady of Montserrat,[2] a shrine in the mountains above Barcelona. One episode of this journey shows us that his understanding of Catholicism was still far from perfect. He fell in with a Moorish horseman, and as they jogged along they talked of their respective faiths. When the Moslem spoke slightingly of the Virgin Mary, Inigo was aroused to fury. After the two had angrily separated at a certain crossroad, Inigo let the mule follow its own bent: if it took the road towards Montserrat, he would forget the Moor; if it followed after him, he would fight and, if possible, kill the man. The mule, we are told, providentially took the road that led to the pilgrimage place. On arriving, Inigo took off his rich attire, left his sword at the altar, donned the pilgrim's sackcloth, provided himself with a staff and gourd. After full Confession, he took a vow to lead henceforth a life of penance and devotion to God. He soon met a holy man, Inez Pascual, who became his lifelong friend. A few miles away was the small town of Manresa, where Inigo retired to a cave for prayer and penance. He lived in the cave, on alms, through most of the year 1522.

As frequently happens, exaltation was followed by trials of doubt and fear. Depressed and sad, Inigo was at times tempted to

[2] Both Manresa and Montserrat, a Benedictine abbey, have locations of great natural beauty in the mountains of Catalonia and both have become pilgrim shrines of prime importance. A church dedicated to St. Ignatius was built above his cave at Manresa.

suicide. He began noting down his inner experiences and insights, and these notes slowly developed into his famous book, *Spiritual Exercises*. At length his peace of mind was fully restored and his soul again overflowed with joy. From this experience came the wisdom that helped him to understand and cure other men's troubled consciences. Years later he told his successor in the Society of Jesus, Father Laynez, that he learned more of divine mysteries in one hour of prayer at Manresa than all the doctors of the schools could ever have taught him. In February, 1523, Ignatius, as he was henceforth known, started on a long-anticipated journey to the Holy Land, where he proposed to labor and preach. He took ship from Barcelona and spent Easter at Rome, sailed from Venice to Cyprus and thence to Jaffa. His zeal was so conspicuous as he visited the scenes of Christ's life that the Franciscan Guardian of the Holy Places ordered him to depart, lest he antagonize the fanatical Turks and be kidnaped and held for ransom.

He returned to Barcelona by way of Venice. Feeling the need of more education, he entered a class in elementary Latin grammar, since all serious works were then written in Latin. A pious lady of the city, Isabel Roser, helped to support him. At thirty-three, he found the study of Latin difficult. His life as a soldier as well as his more recent period of retirement had prepared him poorly for such an undertaking. Only by viewing his concentration on religion as a temptation was he able to make progress. He bore with good humor the taunts of his school fellows.

After two years of study at Barcelona Ignatius went to the University of Alcalá, near Madrid, newly founded by the Grand Inquisitor, Ximenes de Cisneros. He attended lectures in logic, physics, and theology, and though he worked hard he learned little. Living at a hospice for poor students, he wore a coarse gray habit and begged his food. A part of his time was spent in holding services in the hospice and in teaching children the Catechism. Since he had no training or authority for this, the vicar-general accused him of presumption and had him imprisoned for six weeks. At the end of that time the vicar declared Ignatius innocent and released him, but still forbade him to give instruction in religion for three years or to wear any distinguishing dress.

On the advice of the archbishop of Toledo, Ignatius went to the ancient University of Salamanca. Here too, mainly because he could not temper his zeal for reform, he was suspected of harboring dangerous ideas. The vicar-general of Salamanca imprisoned him for a time, and afterward pronounced him innocent, orthodox, and a person of sincere goodness. Ignatius looked upon these sufferings as trials by which God was sanctifying his soul, and spoke no word against his persecutors. However, on recovering his liberty, he resolved to leave Spain, and in the middle of winter traveled on foot to Paris, where he arrived in February, 1528.

He studied at the College of Montaigu and later at the College of St. Barbara, where he perfected himself in Latin, and then took the undergraduate course in philosophy. In his vacations he went to Flanders, and once or twice over to England, to ask help of Spanish merchants who had settled there. For three and a half years he studied philosophy; but such was his desire to make the Catholic religion a vital force in men's lives that he was never content to be merely a student. He persuaded a few of his fellows, most of them much younger than himself, to spend their Sundays and holy days with him in prayer, and also to engage in good works on behalf of others. Several of these men were to form the inner core of the Society of Jesus. The highly conservative authorities were not slow in asserting themselves. Pegna, a master, thought these activities interfered with studying and complained of Ignatius to Govea, principal of the college. As a result, Ignatius was to be punished by a public flogging, that his disgrace might deter anyone from following his example. He was ready to suffer all things, but he feared that this scandal and his condemnation as a corrupter of youth would make the young souls he had reclaimed lose faith in him. He therefore went to the principal and modestly explained what he was trying to do. Govea listened intently, and, when Ignatius had finished, took him by the hand and led him into the hall where the whole college was assembled. There he turned and asked Ignatius' pardon, and said he now knew that Ignatius had no other aim than the salvation of souls. After this dramatic vindication, Pegna appointed another student, Peter Faber, to assist him in his studies, and with his help Ignatius finished the course in philosophy, took the degree of Master of Arts in 1535, and began work in theology. Ill health prevented him from going on to his doctorate.

By this time six other students of theology at Paris were associating themselves regularly with him in what he called his Spiritual Exercises. They were Peter Faber, Francis Xavier, a young Spaniard of noble family, Nicholas Bobadilla, Diego Laynez and Alfonso Salmeron, also Spaniards and fine scholars, and Simon Rodriguez, a Portuguese. They now agreed to take a vow of perpetual poverty and chastity and, as soon as their studies were completed, preach in Palestine, or, if that proved impossible, to offer themselves to the Pope to be used as he saw fit. This vow they solemnly took in a chapel on Montmartre on the feast of the Assumption in August, 1534, after having received Communion from Peter Faber, who had recently been ordained priest. Not long after, Ignatius went back to his native land for the sake of his health. He left Paris in the beginning of the year 1535, and was joyfully welcomed in Guipuzcoa. Instead of staying in his family's castle, however, he took up quarters in a hospital nearby, where he went on with his work of teaching Christian doctrine.

The seven men did not lose touch with one another and two years later they all met in Venice. Because of the war then raging between the Venetians and the Turks, they could find no ship sailing for Palestine. Ignatius' companions now went to Rome, where Pope Paul III received them graciously, and gave those who were not yet priests permission to receive Holy Orders from any bishop they pleased. All having been ordained, they retired together to a cottage near Vicenza to prepare themselves by fasting and prayer for taking up the ministry of the altar. Soon all had said Mass save Ignatius, who deferred the step until he had spent over a year in preparation. He said Mass for the first time in Rome, in the church of Santa Maria Maggiore, December, 1538, more than fifteen years after his "conversion." Still unable to go to the Holy Land, they resolved to place their services at the disposal of the Pope. If anyone asked what their association was, they would reply, "the Company of Jesus," [3] for their purpose was to fight against heresy and vice, apathy and decadence, under the standard of Christ. While praying in a little chapel at La Storta, on the road to Rome, Ignatius had a vision. God appeared, commending him to His Son, who shone radiantly beside Him, though burdened with a heavy cross, and a voice said, "I will be helpful to you at Rome." On this second visit, the Pope did in fact receive them cordially and accepted their services: Faber was appointed to teach the Scriptures and Laynez to expound theology in the Sapienza,[4] and Ignatius to continue to develop his Spiritual Exercises and to teach among the people. The four remaining members were assigned to other employment.

With a view to perpetuating and defining their ideas, it was now proposed that the seven form themselves into a religious order with a rule and organization of their own. After prayer and deliberation, they all agreed to this, and resolved to add to the vows of poverty and chastity a third vow, that of perpetual soldierly obedience. At their head should be a general who should hold office for life, with absolute authority over every member, himself subject only to the Pope. A fourth vow should require them to go wherever the Pope might send them for the salvation of souls. Professed Jesuits could own no real estate or revenues, either as individuals or in common; but their colleges might use incomes and rent for the maintenance of students. The teaching of the Catechism was to be one of their special duties. The cardinals appointed by the Pope

[3] This early military form of their title is still used in France, Spain, and Italy. "Company" was altered to "Society" in the bull of foundation. "Jesuit" was at first a rather hostile nickname, never used by Ignatius himself.

[4] The Sapienza (literally, the Wisdom) was the name given in the sixteenth century to the University of Rome, founded by Pope Boniface in 1303. It is now a secular institution.

to examine the new organization were at first inclined to disapprove it, on the ground that there were already too many orders in the Church. Eventually they changed their minds, and Pope Paul approved it by a bull, dated September 27, 1540. Ignatius, unanimously chosen general on April 7, 1541, reluctantly accepted the office in obedience to his confessor. A few days later his brothers all took the full vows, in the basilica of St. Paul-Outside-the-Walls.

Ignatius set himself to write out the constitutions of the Society. Its aims were to be, first, the sanctification of their own souls by a union of the active and the contemplative life; and, secondly, instructing youth in piety and learning, acting as confessors of uneasy consciences, undertaking missions abroad, and in general propagating the faith. They should wear the dress of the secular clergy. They should not be compelled to keep choir,[5] because their special business was evangelical work, not the services of the cloister. Before anyone could be admitted he must make a general Confession, spend a month going through the Spiritual Exercises, then serve a novitiate of two years, after which he might take the simple vows of poverty, chastity, and obedience. By these vows he consecrated himself irrevocably to God, but the general still had power to dismiss him. Dismissal, if it came, would free him from all obligation to the Society. The higher rank of Jesuits, called the "professed," after more years of study, took the same vows again, but this time publicly and with no reservations; they were forever binding on both sides. To them was added a vow to undertake any mission, whether to Christians or to infidels, at the Pope's command.

Ignatius was now fifty years old. The remainder of his life was passed in Rome, where he directed the activities of the Society of Jesus and interested himself in other foundations. He established a house for the reception of converted Jews during their period of instruction, and another for loose women who were anxious to reform but felt no call to the religious life. When told that the conversion of such women was seldom sincere or permanent, he

[5] That is, to say the Divine Office daily in choir.

answered, "To prevent only one sin would be a great happiness, though it cost ever so much pain." He set up two houses for poor orphans, and another as a home for young women whose poverty exposed them to danger.

Many princes and cities in Italy, Spain, Germany, and the Low Countries begged Ignatius for workers. He made it a rule that anyone sent abroad should be fluent in the language of the country, so that he could preach and serve effectively. As early as 1540, Fathers Rodriguez and Xavier had been sent to Portugal, and the latter had gone on to the Indies, where he won a new world for Christ. Father Gonzales went to Morocco to teach and help the enslaved Christians there. Four missionaries made their way into the Congo, and, in 1555, eleven reached Abyssinia; others embarked on the long voyage to the Spanish and Portuguese settlements of South America. Doctor Peter Canisius, famed for learning and piety, founded Jesuit schools in Germany, Austria, and Bohemia. Fathers Laynez and Salmeron assisted at the momentous Council of Trent.[6] Before their departure, Ignatius admonished them to be humble in all their disputations, to shun contentiousness and empty displays of learning. Jesuits landed in Ireland in 1542, while others bravely undertook the hazardous mission to England.

In Elizabethan England and Scotland Protestantism was now firmly established and adherents of the Roman Church suffered persecution. Ignatius prayed much for the conversion of England, and his sons still repeat in their prayers the phrase, "for all Northern nations." Many were the brothers who risked death to keep Mass said in places where it had been forbidden. Of the English and Welsh Catholic martyrs of the period, subsequently beatified, twenty-six were Jesuits. The activity of the Society in England was, however, but a small part of the work of Ignatius and his followers

---

[6] The Council of Trent, held in the Austrian Tyrol (1545-1563), was one of the longest and most important of all oecumenical councils. Summoned for the purpose of combatting Protestantism (Luther died the year before it was called), clarifying doctrine, and reforming the discipline of the Church, it adopted far-reaching decrees of reformation in discipline and morals.

in the movement which came to be known as the Counter-Reformation. The Jesuits carried encouragement to Catholics of other European countries where a militant Protestantism was in control. "It was," says Cardinal Manning, "exactly what was wanted at the time to counteract the revolt of the sixteenth century. The revolt was disobedience and disorder in the most aggressive form. The Society was obedience and order in its most solid compactness."

In 1551 Francis Borgia,[7] a minister of Emperor Charles V, joined the Society and donated a large sum to start the building of the Roman College of the Jesuits; later Pope Gregory XIII contributed to it lavishly. Ignatius planned to make it a model for all Jesuit institutions, taking great pains to secure able teachers and excellent equipment. The German College in Rome he designed for students from countries where Protestantism was making headway. Other colleges, seminaries, and universities were soon established. The type of academic, psychological, and spiritual education for which the Jesuits became so famous was well worked out before the founder's death. The tone remained religious; students must hear Mass every day, go to Confession every month, and begin their studies with prayer. Their master should take every fit occasion to inspire them with love of heavenly things, and encourage a fervent habit of prayer, which otherwise might easily be crowded out by the school routine.

Ignatius' chief work, *Spiritual Exercises,* begun at Manresa in 1522, was finally published in Rome in 1548, with papal approval. In essence, it is an application of Gospel precepts to the individual soul, written in such a way as to arouse conviction of sin, of justice, and judgment. The value of systematic retirement and religious meditation, which the book sets forth, had always been known, but the order and method of meditation prescribed by Ignatius were new, and, though many of the maxims he repeats had been laid

[7] St. Francis Borgia, a Spaniard of famous lineage, became in time the third general of the Jesuit Order; so effective was he in spreading its influence in Western Europe that he is sometimes called its "second founder."

down before by the Fathers, they were here singularly well arranged, explained, and applied. To perform the Exercises as directed requires a month. The first week is given to consideration
of sin and its consequences; the second, to our Lord's earthly life;
the third, to His Passion, and the fourth, to His Resurrection. The
object is to induce in the practitioner such a state of inner calm
that he can thereafter make a choice "either as to some particular
crisis or as to the general course of his life," unbiased "by any
excessive like or dislike; and guided solely by the consideration of
what will best forward the one end for which he was created—the
glory of God and the perfection of his own soul." A warning contained in the book runs as follows: "When God has appointed a
way, we must faithfully follow it and never think of another under
pretense that it is more easy and safe. It is one of the Devil's
artifices to set before a soul some state, holy indeed, but impossible
to her, or at least different from hers, so that by a love of novelty,
she may dislike, or be slack in her present state in which God has
placed her and which is best for her. In like manner, he represents
to her other acts as more holy and profitable to make her conceive
a disgust of her present employment."

Ignatius' tender regard for his brothers won the heart of each
one of them. He was fatherly and understanding, especially with
the sick. Obedience and self-denial were the two first lessons he
taught novices. In his famous letter to the Portuguese Jesuits on
the virtue of obedience, he says that it brings forth and nourishes
all the other virtues; he calls it the distinguishing virtue of the
Jesuits. True obedience reaches to the understanding as well as to
the will, and does not suffer a person even secretly to complain of
or to criticize any command of his superior, whom he must look
upon as vested with the authority of Jesus Christ. Even when
broken with age and infirmities, Ignatius said that, if the Pope
commanded it, he would with joy go on board the first ship he
could find, though it had neither sails nor rudder, and immediately
set out for any part of the globe. When someone asked what his
feelings would be if the Pope should decide to suppress the Com-

pany of Jesus, "A quarter of an hour of prayer," he answered, "and I should think no more about it." His perpetual lesson was: "Sacrifice your own will and judgment to obedience. Whatever you do without the consent of your spiritual guide will be imputed to willfulness, not to virtue, though you were to exhaust your bodies by labors and austerities."

Humility, the characteristic trait of all the saints, was to Ignatius the sister virtue of obedience. For a long time he had gone about in threadbare garments, and lived in hostels for the poor, despised and ignored, but finding joy in his humiliation. When he lived in a house with his brothers, he always shared in the humble daily tasks in an unobtrusive fashion. In matters where he did not feel competent, Ignatius always readily accepted the judgment of others. As he received rebuke with cheerfulness and thanks, he allowed no false delicacy to restrain him from rebuking those who stood in need of it. Although he encouraged learning, he was quick to reprimand anyone whose learning made him conceited, tedious, or lukewarm in religion. He would have each member of the Society take up whatever work, whether teaching, preaching, or missions abroad, that he could do best. Notwithstanding the fatigue which the government of the Society imposed on him, Ignatius was always on fire to help others. The motto, *"Ad majorem Dei gloriam"* (To the greater glory of God), was the end for which he and the Society existed. When asked the most certain way to perfection, he answered: "To endure many and grievous afflictions for the love of Christ. Ask this grace of our Lord; to whomever He grants it, He does many other signal favors that always attend this grace." The French historian Guizot, in his *History of Civilization,* wrote of the members of the order, "Greatness of thought as well as greatness of will has been theirs."

Ignatius directed the Society of Jesus for fifteen years. At the time of his death there were 13,000 members, dispersed in thirty-two provinces all over Europe, and soon they were to be established in the New World. The Society of Jesus served as the chief instrument of the Catholic Reformation. Its pursuits as a trading firm,

SAINT CATHERINE OF SIENA RECEIVING THE STIGMATA Sodoma
Giovanni Antonio de Bazzi, known as Il Sodoma (c. 1477-1549), was an
associate of Raphael in the decoration of the Vatican. However, most of his life was spent in Siena, where his most characteristic work is this painting of Siena's beloved Saint
Catherine.

Saint Catherine of Siena is represented by a lily and by the
stigmata. She is always shown in white Dominican robes.

JOAN OF ARC, HEROINE OF FRANCE   Ingres

Jean Auguste Dominique Ingres (1780-1867) was one of the first of the French Romantic painters of the nineteenth century. He won the Academy award in 1806 for study in Rome, where he was much influenced by the works of Raphael which he saw there. This painting hangs in the Louvre in Paris.

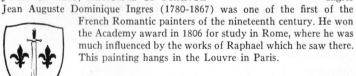

Saint Joan of Arc is symbolized by armor and the banner of the Annunciation. The fleur-de-lis, emblem of France as of the Holy Trinity is also one of her symbols.

followed for some years, reaped high returns but were disapproved by the papacy. Exclusive of the period of its suppression by papal brief, 1776–1814, and its suppression by various countries at different periods, largely by reason of these commercial activities, it has flourished in virtually all parts of the globe; its educational institutions are famous, and many individual Jesuits have achieved distinction as teachers and writers.

Towards the end of his life Ignatius became so worn and feeble that he was assisted by three fathers. He died, after a brief illness, on July 31, 1556. The brilliant Father Laynez succeeded him; he and Father Francis Borgia gave the Society its direction for years to come. In 1622 Ignatius was canonized by Pope Gregory XV, and in our own time Pope Pius XI declared him the patron of all spiritual exercises. His emblems are a chasuble, communion, a book, and the apparition of the Lord.

Excerpts from Spiritual Exercises

PRINCIPLE AND FOUNDATION

Man was created to praise, do reverence to and serve God our Lord, and thereby to save his soul; and the other things on the face of the earth were created for man's sake and to help him in the following out of the end for which he was created. Hence it follows that man should make use of creatures so far as they do help him towards his end, and should withdraw from them so far as they are a hindrance to him with respect to that end. Wherefore it is necessary to make ourselves indifferent toward all created things, in whatever is left to the liberty of our free choice and is not forbidden, so that we on our part should not wish for health rather than sickness, for riches rather than poverty, for honor rather than ignominy, for a long life rather than a short life, and in all other matters should desire and choose solely those things which may better lead us to the end for which we were created.

FIRST WEEK. SECOND EXERCISE

. . . The first point is the indictment of sins, that is to say, to bring to mind all the sins of my life, looking through it year by year or period by period. For this purpose three things are helpful; the first to look at the place and house where I have lived; the second at the dealings I have had with others; the third at the calling in which I have lived.

The second point is to weigh the sins, looking at the foulness and malice that any mortal sin committed has in itself, even though it was not forbidden.

The third, is to see who I am, belittling myself by examples; first, what am I in comparison with all mankind; secondly, what are all mankind in comparison with all the Angels and Saints in paradise; thirdly, to see what all creation is in comparison with God,—therefore in myself alone, what can I be? fourthly, to see all my corruption and foulness of body; fifthly, to look at myself as a sort of ulcer and abscess, from which have sprung so many sins and so many wickednesses and most hideous venom.

The fourth is to consider who God is against whom I have sinned, according to His attributes, comparing them with their contraries in me—His wisdom with my ignorance, His omnipotence with my weakness, His justice with my iniquity, His goodness with my malice.

The fifth, is a cry of wonder with a flood of emotion, ranging in thought through all creatures, how they have suffered me to live and have preserved me in life—how the Angels, being the sword of divine justice, have borne with me and guarded and prayed for me, how the Saints have interceded and prayed for me, and the heavens, sun, moon, stars and elements, fruits, birds, fishes and animals . . . and the earth, how it has not opened to swallow me up, creating new hells for my eternal torment therein.

To conclude with a colloquy on mercy, casting a reckoning and giving thanks to God that He has granted me life hitherto, proposing amendment for the time to come with His grace. Our Father.

SECOND WEEK. FIRST DAY. FIRST CONTEMPLATION

The usual preparatory prayer.

The first prelude is to recall the history of what I have to contemplate, which is here how the three Divine Persons were looking down upon the whole flat or round of the world full of men; and how, seeing that all were going down to hell, it was decreed in their eternity that the Second Person should become man to save the human race. And so it was done, when the fullness of time came, by sending the angel Saint Gabriel to our Lady.

The second, the composition [act of imagination], seeing the place. Here it will be to see the great room and round of the world, where dwell so many and such diverse nations. In like manner afterwards in particular, the house and apartments of our Lady, in the city of Nazareth, in the province of Galilee.

The third, to ask for what I want. It will be here to ask for an intimate knowledge of the Lord who was made man for me, that I may love Him more and follow Him. . . .

The first point is to see the persons, each and all of them; and, first, those on the face of the earth, in such variety both in dress and in mien, some white and others black, some in peace and others at war, some weeping and others laughing, some healthy, others sick, some just born and others dying, etc.

Secondly, to see and consider the three Divine Persons as on the royal seat or throne of the Divine Majesty, how they regard the whole face and circuit of the earth and all nations in such blindness, and how they are dying and going down to hell.

Thirdly, to see our Lady and the angel who salutes her, and to reflect how I may gather fruit from such a sight.

The second point, to hear what the persons on earth are saying, to wit, how they talk to one another, how they swear and blaspheme, etc. In like manner what the Divine Persons are saying, to wit: "Let us work the redemption of mankind"; and afterwards what our Lady and the angels are saying; and then to reflect so as to gather fruit from their words.

The third then, to study what the persons on the face of the earth are doing, to wit, smiting, slaying, going to hell, etc.; likewise what the Divine Persons are doing, namely, working the

most holy Incarnation, etc.; and in like manner what the angel
and our Lady are doing, to wit, the angel performing his office of
Ambassador, and our Lady humbling herself and returning thanks
to the Divine Majesty; and afterwards to reflect so as to gather
some fruit from each of these things.

At the end a colloquy is to be made, thinking what I ought to
say to the three Divine Persons, or to the Eternal Word Incarnate,
or to the Mother and our Lady, asking according as one feels in
oneself how better to follow and imitate our Lord, so newly Incarnate, saying Our Father.

SECOND WEEK. EXERCISE

Let the preparatory prayer be as usual.

The first prelude is the composition, seeing the place. It will be
here to see with the eye of the imagination the synagogues, towns,
and country places through which Christ our Lord preached.

The second, to ask the grace which I want. It will be here to ask
grace of our Lord that I be not deaf to His call, but prompt and
diligent to fulfill His most holy will.

The first point is to put before my eyes a human king, chosen
by God the Lord Himself, to whom all Christian princes and all
Christian men pay reverence and obedience.

The second, to mark how this king addressed all his people, saying: "My will is to conquer the whole land of the unbelievers;
therefore whoever shall wish to come with me must be content to
eat as I do, and to drink and dress, etc. as I do. In like manner he
must labor as I do by day, and watch at night, etc., so that in like
manner afterwards he may share with me in the victory as he shall
have shared in the labours."

The third, to consider what should be the answer of good subjects to a king so generous, such a man indeed; and how consequently, if anyone would not answer the request of such a king,
how worthy he would be of being despised by the whole world,
and reckoned a recreant knight, no gentleman, but a "skulker."

The second part of the Exercise consists of applying the aforesaid example of a temporal king to Christ our Lord according to the
said three points.

And touching the first point, if we pay regard to such a call of a temporal king on his subjects, how much more it is worth our consideration to see Christ our Lord, the eternal King, and before Him the whole world, to which and to every man in particular He cries and says: "My will is to overcome the whole world and all mine enemies and so to enter into the glory of my Father; therefore he who shall wish to come with me must labour with me, that following me in hardship he may likewise follow me in glory."

The second, to consider that all who have judgment and reason will offer their whole persons to labor. . . .

For the Second Week and thereafter it is very profitable to read at times from the books of the *Imitation of Christ,* and of the Gospels and the Lives of the Saints.

FOURTH WEEK. A CONTEMPLATION TO OBTAIN LOVE

. . . The usual prayer.

First prelude is a composition, which is here to see how I stand before God our Lord, the Angels, and the Saints interceding for me.

The second, to ask for what I want; it will be here to ask for an inward knowledge of the great good received, in order that I, being fully grateful for the same, may in all things love and serve His Divine Majesty.

The first point is to recall to memory the benefits received of creation, redemption, and particular gifts, pondering with deep affection how much God our Lord has done for me, and how much He has given me of what He has, and further, how the same Lord desires to give Himself to me so far as He can, according to His divine ordinance; and therewithal to reflect within myself, considering with much reason and justice what I on my part ought to offer for them, as one who offers with deep affection:—Take, O Lord, and receive all my liberty, my memory, my understanding, and all my will, all I have and possess; you have given it me; to you, Lord, I return it; all is yours, dispose of it entirely according to your will. Give me your love and grace, because that is enough for me. . . .

(*Spiritual Exercises,* translated by Father Rickaby, S. J.)

Saint Teresa of Avila

Virgin, Foundress

1 5 8 2

(October 15)

In the *Autobiography* which she completed towards the end of her life, Saint Teresa of Avila gives us a description of her parents, along with a disparaging estimate of her own character. "The possession of virtuous parents who lived in the fear of God, together with those favors which I received from his Divine Majesty, might have made me good, if I had not been so very wicked." A heavy consciousness of sin was prevalent in sixteenth-century Spain, and we can readily discount this avowal of guilt. What we are told of Teresa's early life does not sound in the least wicked, but it is plain that she was an unusually active, imaginative, and sensitive child. Her parents, Don Alfonso Sanchez de Capeda and Dona Beatriz Davila y Ahumada, his second wife, were people of position in Avila, a city of Old Castile, where Teresa was born on March 28, 1515. There were nine children of this marriage, of whom Teresa was the third, and three children of her father's first marriage.

Piously reared as she was, Teresa became completely fascinated by stories of the saints and martyrs, as was her brother Roderigo, who was near her own age and her partner in youthful adventures. Once, when Teresa was seven, they made a plan to run away to Africa, where they might be beheaded by the infidel Moors and so achieve martyrdom. They set out secretly, expecting to beg their way like the poor friars, but had gone only a short distance from home when they were met by an uncle and brought back to their anxious mother, who had sent servants into the streets to search for them. She and her brother now thought they would like to become hermits, and tried to build themselves little cells from stones they found in the garden. Thus we see that religious thoughts and influences dominated the mind of the future saint in childhood.

Teresa was only fourteen when her mother died, and she later wrote of her sorrow in these words: "As soon as I began to understand how great a loss I had sustained by losing her, I was very much afflicted; and so I went before an image of our Blessed Lady and besought her with many tears that she would vouchsafe to be my mother." Visits from a girl cousin were most welcome at this time, but they had the effect of stimulating her interest in superficial things. Reading tales of chivalry was one of their diversions, and Teresa even tried to write romantic stories. "These tales," she says in her Autobiography, "did not fail to cool my good desires, and were the cause of my falling insensibly into other defects. I was so enchanted that I could not be happy without some new tale in my hands. I began to imitate the fashions, to enjoy being well dressed, to take great care of my hands, to use perfumes, and wear all the vain ornaments which my position in the world allowed." Noting this sudden change in his daughter's personality, Teresa's father decided to place her in a convent of Augustinian nuns in Avila, where other young women of her class were being educated. This action made Teresa aware that her danger had been greater than she knew. After a year and a half in the convent she fell ill with what seems to have been a malignant type of malaria, and Don Alfonso brought her home. After recovering, she went to stay with her eldest sister, who had married and gone to live in the country. Then she visited an uncle, Peter Sanchez de Capeda, a very sober and pious man. At home once more, and fearing that an uncongenial marriage would be forced upon her, she began to deliberate whether or not she should undertake the religious life. Reading the *Letters of St. Jerome*,[1] helped her to reach a decision.

[1] For extracts from St. Jerome's letters, see above, p. 93.

St. Jerome's realism and ardor were akin to her own Castilian spirit, with its mixture of the practical and the idealistic. She now announced to her father her desire to become a nun, but he withheld consent, saying that after his death she might do as she pleased.

This reaction caused a new conflict, for Teresa loved her father devotedly. Feeling that delay might weaken her resolve, she went secretly to the Carmelite convent of the Incarnation [2] outside the town of Avila, where her dear friend Sister Jane Suarez was living, and applied for admission. Of this painful step, she wrote: "I remember . . . while I was going out of my father's house—the sharpness of sense will not be greater, I believe, in the very instant of agony of my death, than it was then. It seemed as if all the bones in my body were wrenched asunder. . . . There was no such love of God in me then as was able to quench the love I felt for my father and my friends." A year later Teresa made her profession, but when there was a recurrence of her illness, Don Alfonso had her removed from the convent, as the rule of enclosure was not then in effect. After a period of intense suffering, during which, on one occasion, at least, her life was despaired of, she gradually began to improve. She was helped by certain prayers she had begun to use. Her devout Uncle Peter had given her a little book called the *Third Spiritual Alphabet,* by Father Francis de Osuna, which dealt with "prayers of recollection and quiet." Taking this book as her guide, she began to concentrate on mental prayer, and progressed towards the "prayer of quiet," with the soul resting in divine contemplation, all earthly things forgotten. Occasionally, for brief moments, she attained the "prayer of union," in which all the powers of the soul are absorbed in God. She persuaded her father to apply himself to this form of prayer.

After three years Teresa went back to the convent. Her intel-

---

[2] The Carmelites were an order of mendicant friars claiming descent from hermits who lived on Mt. Carmel in Palestine in the sixth century. The order was founded in 1156, when a monastery was built on the mountain; the nuns of the order, which at this time were established in the Netherlands and Spain, were divided into three observances.

ligence, warmth, and charm made her a favorite, and she found
pleasure in being with people. It was the custom in Spain in those
days for the young nuns to receive their acquaintances in the
convent parlor, and Teresa spent much time there, chatting with
friends. She was attracted to one of the visitors whose company
was disturbing to her, although she told herself that there could
be no question of sin, since she was only doing what so many
others, better than she, were doing. During this relaxed period,
she gave up her habit of mental prayer, using as a pretext the
poor state of her health. "This excuse of bodily weakness," she
wrote afterwards, "was not a sufficient reason why I should
abandon so good a thing, which required no physical strength,
but only love and habit. In the midst of sickness the best prayer
may be offered, and it is a mistake to think it can only be offered
in solitude." She returned to the practice of mental prayer and
never again abandoned it, although she had not yet the courage to
follow God completely, or to stop wasting her time and talents. But
during these years of apparent wavering, her spirit was being
forged. When depressed by her own unworthiness, she turned to
those two great penitents, St. Mary Magdalen and St. Augustine,
and through them came experiences that helped to steady her will.
One was the reading of St. Augustine's *Confessions;* another was
an overpowering impulse to penitence before a picture of the suffering Lord, in which, she writes, "I felt Mary Magdalen come to
my assistance. . . . From that day I have gone on improving in
my spiritual life."

When finally Teresa withdrew from the pleasures of social inter-
course, she found herself able once more to pray the "prayer of
quiet," and also the "prayer of union." She began to have intellectual visions of divine things and to hear inner voices. Though
she was persuaded these manifestations came from God, she was at
times fearful and troubled. She consulted many persons, binding
all to secrecy, but her perplexities nevertheless were spread abroad,
to her great mortification. Among those she talked to was Father
Gaspar Daza, a learned priest, who, after listening, reported that

she was deluded, for such divine favors were not consistent with a life as full of imperfections as hers was, as she herself admitted. A friend, Don Francis de Salsedo, suggested that she talk to a priest of the newly formed Society of Jesus. To one of them, accordingly, she made a general Confession, recounting her manner of prayer and extraordinary visions. He assured her that she experienced divine graces, but warned her that she had failed to lay the foundations of a true spiritual life by practices of mortification. He advised her to try to resist the visions and voices for two months; resistance proved useless. Francis Borgia, commissary-general of the Society in Spain, then advised her not to resist further, but also not to seek such experiences.

Another Jesuit, Father Balthasar Alvarez, who now became her director, pointed out certain traits that were incompatible with perfect grace. He told her that she would do well to beg God to direct her to what was most pleasing to Him, and to recite daily the hymn of St. Gregory the Great, *"Veni Creator Spiritus!"* One day, as she repeated the stanzas, she was seized with a rapture in which she heard the words, "I will not have you hold conversation with men, but with angels." For three years, while Father Balthasar was her director, she suffered from the disapproval of those around her; and for two years, from extreme desolation of soul. She was censured for her austerities and ridiculed as a victim of delusion or a hypocrite. A confessor to whom she went during Father Balthasar's absence said that her very prayer was an illusion, and commanded her, when she saw any vision, to make the sign of the cross and repel it as if it were an evil spirit. But Teresa tells us that the visions now brought with them their own evidence of authenticity, so that it was impossible to doubt they were from God. Nevertheless, she obeyed this order of her confessor. Pope Gregory XV, in his bull of canonization, commends her obedience in these words: "She was wont to say that she might be deceived in discerning visions and revelations, but could not be in obeying superiors."

In 1557 Peter of Alcantara, a Franciscan of the Observance,

came to Avila. Few saints have been more experienced in the inner life, and he found in Teresa unmistakable evidence of the Holy Spirit. He openly expressed compassion for what she endured from slander and predicted that she was not at the end of her tribulations. However, as her mystical experiences continued, the greatness and goodness of God, the sweetness of His service, became more and more manifest to her. She was sometimes lifted from the ground, an experience other saints have known. "God," she says, "seems not content with drawing the soul to Himself, but he must needs draw up the very body too, even while it is mortal and compounded of so unclean a clay as we have made it by our sins."

It was at this time, she tells us, that her most singular experience took place, her mystical marriage to Christ, and the piercing of her heart. Of the latter she writes: "I saw an angel very near me, towards my left side, in bodily form, which is not usual with me; for though angels are often represented to me, it is only in my mental vision. This angel appeared rather small than large, and very beautiful. His face was so shining that he seemed to be one of those highest angels called seraphs, who look as if all on fire with divine love. He had in his hands a long golden dart; at the end of the point methought there was a little fire. And I felt him thrust it several times through my heart in such a way that it passed through my very bowels. And when he drew it out, methought it pulled them out with it and left me wholly on fire with a great love of God." The pain in her soul spread to her body, but it was accompanied by great delight too; she was like one transported, caring neither to see nor to speak but only to be consumed with the mingled pain and happiness.[3]

Teresa's longing to die that she might be united with God was tempered by her desire to suffer for Him on earth. The account which the *Autobiography* gives of her revelations is marked by sincerity, genuine simplicity of style, and scrupulous precision. An unlettered woman, she wrote in the Castilian vernacular, setting

[3] This event is commemorated by the Carmelites on August 27.

down her experiences reluctantly, out of obedience to her confessor, and submitting everything to his judgment and that of the Church, merely complaining that the task kept her from spinning. Teresa wrote of herself without self-love or pride. Towards her persecutors she was respectful, representing them as honest servants of God.

Teresa's other literary works came later, during the fifteen years when she was actively engaged in founding new convents of reformed Carmelite nuns. They are proof of her industry and her power of memory, as well as of a real talent for expression. *The Way of Perfection* she composed for the special guidance of her nuns, and the *Foundations* for their further edification. *The Interior Castle* was perhaps meant for all Catholics; in it she writes with authority on the spiritual life. One admiring critic says: "She lays bare in her writings the most impenetrable secrets of true wisdom in what we call mystical theology, of which God has given the key to a small number of his favored servants. This thought may somewhat lessen our surprise that an unlearned woman should have expounded what the greatest doctors never attained, for God employs in His works what instruments He wills."

We have seen how undisciplined the Carmelite nuns had become, how the convent parlor at Avila was a social gathering place, and how easily nuns might leave their enclosure. Any woman, in fact, who wanted a sheltered life without much responsibility could find it in a convent in sixteenth-century Spain. The religious themselves, for the most part, were not even aware of how far they fell short of what their profession demanded. So when one of the nuns at the House of the Incarnation began talking of the possibility of founding a new and stricter community, the idea struck Teresa as an inspiration from Heaven. She determined to undertake its establishment herself and received a promise of help from a wealthy widow, Doña Guiomar de Ulloa. The project was approved by Peter of Alcantara and Father Angelo de Salazar, provincial of the Carmelite Order. The latter was soon compelled to withdraw his permission, for Teresa's fellow nuns, the local nobility, the magistrates, and others united to thwart the project. Father Ibanez, a

Dominican, secretly encouraged Teresa and urged Doña Guiomar to continue to lend her support. One of Teresa's married sisters began with her husband to erect a small convent at Avila in 1561 to shelter the new establishment; outsiders took it for a house intended for the use of her family.

An episode famous in Teresa's life occurred at this time. Her little nephew was crushed by a wall of the new structure which fell on him as he was playing, and he was carried, apparently lifeless, to Teresa. She held the child in her arms and prayed. After some minutes she restored him alive and sound to his mother. The miracle was presented at the process for Teresa's canonization. Another seemingly solid wall of the convent collapsed during the night. Teresa's brother-in-law was going to refuse to pay the masons, but Teresa assured him that it was all the work of evil spirits and insisted that the men be paid.

A wealthy woman of Toledo, Countess Louise de la Cerda, happened at the time to be mourning the recent death of her husband, and asked the Carmelite provincial to order Teresa, whose goodness she had heard praised, to come to her. Teresa was accordingly sent to the woman, and stayed with her for six months, using a part of the time, at the request of Father Ibanez, to write, and to develop further her ideas for the convent. While at Toledo she met Maria of Jesus, of the Carmelite convent at Granada, who had had revelations concerning a reform of the order, and this meeting strengthened Teresa's own desires. Back in Avila, on the very evening of her arrival, the Pope's letter authorizing the new reformed convent was brought to her. Teresa's adherents now persuaded the bishop of Avila to concur, and the convent, dedicated to St. Joseph, was quietly opened. On St. Bartholomew's day, 1562, the Blessed Sacrament was placed in the little chapel, and four novices took the habit.

The news soon spread in the town and opposition flared into the open. The prioress of the Incarnation convent sent for Teresa, who was required to explain her conduct. Detained almost as a prisoner, Teresa did not lose her poise. The prioress was joined in her disapproval by the mayor and magistrates, always fearful that an unendowed convent would be a burden on the townspeople. Some were for demolishing the building forthwith. Meanwhile Don Francis sent a priest to Madrid, to plead for the new establishment before the King's Council. Teresa was allowed to go back to her convent and shortly afterward the bishop officially appointed her prioress. The hubbub now quickly subsided. Teresa was henceforth known simply as Teresa of Jesus, mother of the reform of Carmel. The nuns were strictly cloistered, under a rule of poverty and almost complete silence; the constant chatter of women's voices was one of the things that Teresa had most deplored at the Incarnation. They were poor, without regular revenues; they wore habits of coarse serge and sandals instead of shoes, and for this reason were called the "discalced" or shoeless Carmelites. Although the prioress was now in her late forties, and frail, her great achievement still lay in the future.

Convinced that too many women under one roof made for relaxation of discipline, Teresa limited the number of nuns to thirteen; later, when houses were being founded with endowments and hence were not wholly dependent on alms, the number was increased to twenty-one. The prior general of the Carmelites, John Baptist Rubeo of Ravenna, visiting Avila in 1567, carried away a fine impression of Teresa's sincerity and prudent rule. He gave her full authority to found other convents on the same plan, in spite of the fact that St. Joseph's had been established without his knowledge.

Five peaceful years were spent with the thirteen nuns in the little convent of St. Joseph. Teresa trained the sisters in every kind of useful work and in all religious observances; but whether at spinning or at prayer, she herself was always first and most diligent. In August, 1567, she founded a second convent at Medina del Campo. The Countess de la Cerda was anxious to found a similar house in her native town of Malagon, and Teresa went to advise her about it. When this third community had been launched, the intrepid nun moved on to Valladolid, and there founded a fourth; then a fifth at Toledo. On beginning this work, she had no more than four or five ducats (approximately ten dollars), but she said, "Teresa and this money are nothing; but God, Teresa, and these ducats suffice." At Medina del Campo she encountered two friars who had heard of her reform and wished to adopt it: Antony de Heredia, prior of the Carmelite monastery there, and John of the Cross. With their aid, in 1568, and the authority given her by the prior general, she established a reformed house for men at Durelo, and in 1569 a second one at Pastrana, both on a pattern of extreme poverty and austerity. She left to John of the Cross, who at this time was in his late twenties, the direction of these and other reformed communities that might be started for men. Refusing to obey the order of his provincial to return to Medina, he was imprisoned at Toledo for nine months. After his escape he became vicar-general of Andalusia, and strove for papal recognition of the order. John, later to attain fame as a poet, mystic confessor, and finally saint, became Teresa's friend; a close spiritual bond developed between the young friar and the aging prioress, and he was made director and confessor in the mother house at Avila.

The hardships and dangers involved in Teresa's labors are indicated by a little episode of the founding of a new convent at Salamanca. She and another nun took over a house which had been occupied by students. It was a large, dirty, desolate place, without furnishings, and when night came the two nuns lay down on their piles of straw, for, Teresa tells us, "the first furniture I provided wherever I founded convents was straw, for, having that, I reckoned I had beds." On this occasion, the other nun seemed very nervous, and Teresa asked her the reason. "I was wondering," was the reply, "what you would do alone with a corpse if I were to die here now." Teresa was startled, but only said, "I shall think of that when it happens, Sister. For the present, let us go to sleep."

At about this time Pope Pius V appointed a number of apostolic visitors to inquire into the relaxations of discipline in religious orders everywhere. The visitor to the Carmelites of Castile found great fault with the Incarnation convent and sent for Teresa, bidding her to assume its direction and remedy the abuses there. It was hard to be separated from her own daughters, and even more distasteful to be brought in as head of the old house which had long opposed her with bitterness and jealousy. The nuns at first refused to obey her; some of them fell into hysterics at the very idea. She told them that she came not to coerce or instruct but to serve and to learn from the least among them. By gentleness and tact she won the affection of the community, and was able to reestablish discipline. Frequent callers were forbidden, the finances of the house were set in order, and a more truly religious spirit reigned. At the end of three years, although the nuns wished to keep her longer, she was directed to return to her own convent.

Teresa organized a nunnery at Veas and while there met Father Jerome Gratian, a reformed Carmelite, and was persuaded by him to extend her work to Seville. With the exception of her first convent, none proved so hard to establish as this. Among her problems there was a disgruntled novice, who reported the nuns to the Inquisition,[4] charging them with being Illuminati.[5]

The Italian Carmelite friars had meanwhile been growing alarmed at the progress of the reform in Spain, lest, as one of their number said, they might one day be compelled to set about reforming themselves, a fear shared by their still unreformed Spanish brothers. At a general chapter at Piacenza several decrees were passed restricting the reform. The new apostolic nuncio dismissed Father Gratian from his office as visitor to the reformed Carmelites. Teresa was told to choose one of her convents and retire to it, and abstain from founding others. At this point she turned to her friends in the world, who were able to interest King Philip II [6] in her behalf, and he personally espoused her cause. He

[4] The Spanish Inquisition had been set up a century before by Ferdinand and Isabella. It was less severe in Teresa's day than it had been earlier.

[5] The Illuminati was a heretical secret society that denied dependence on the Church and claimed that salvation came through the enlightenment of each individual by his own vision of God.

[6] Philip II, son of the Emperor Charles V and husband of the English Catholic Queen, Mary, was a devout champion of the faith against Protestantism.

SAINT RITA   Zandrino

This modern Italian painting is an example of devotional art which successfully avoids the sentimental and banal. Such a painting may
well become an art treasure of the future.

Saint Rita, shown in the habit of her order, is symbolized by
the roses. Often she is shown with a wound on her forehead,
mark of her devotion to the crown of thorns.

SIR THOMAS MORE   Holbein

Hans Holbein (1497-1543) was born in Bavaria, but became the court painter
to Henry VIII of England. During his first visit to England in 1526, he came
under the patronage of Sir Thomas More, who was later to be martyred, and
painted this portrait, which is now owned by the Frick Collection. It
is reproduced by permission of the Frick Collection.

At the time this portrait was painted, Thomas More was a member of the
King's Council and confidant and assistant to Cardinal Wolsey. He succeeded
Wolsey as Chancellor of England, the first layman to achieve the office. No
symbolism is attached to his portrait.

summoned the nuncio to rebuke him for his severity towards the
discalced friars and nuns. In 1580 came an order from Rome
exempting the reformed from the jurisdiction of the unreformed
Carmelites, and giving each party its own provincial. Father Gratian was elected provincial of the reformed branch. The separation,
although painful to many, brought an end to dissension.

Teresa was a person of great natural gifts. Her ardor and lively
wit was balanced by her sound judgment and psychological insight.
It was no mere flight of fancy when the English Catholic poet,
Richard Crashaw,[7] called her "the eagle" and "the dove." She
could stand up boldly and bravely for what she thought was right;
she could also be severe with a prioress who by excessive austerity
had made herself unfit for her duties. Yet she could be gentle as
a dove, as when she writes to an erring, irresponsible nephew,
"God's mercy is great in that you have been enabled to make so
good a choice and marry so soon, for you began to be dissipated
when you were so young that we might have had much sorrow on
your account." Love, with Teresa, meant constructive action, and
she had the young man's daughter, born out of wedlock, brought
to the convent, and took charge of her upbringing and that of his
young sister.

One of Teresa's charms was a sense of humor. In the early years,
when an indiscreet male visitor to the convent once praised the
beauty of her bare feet, she laughed and told him to take a good
look at them for he would never see them again—implying that in
the future he would not be admitted. Her method of selecting
novices was characteristic. The first requirement, even before piety,
was intelligence. A woman could attain to piety, but scarcely to
intelligence, by which she meant common sense as well as brains.
"An intelligent mind," she wrote, "is simple and teachable; it sees
its faults and allows itself to be guided. A mind that is dull and
narrow never sees its faults even when shown them. It is always

[7] Crashaw left England when Charles I was beheaded, became a Catholic
priest, and spent his later years in Italy. One of his most eloquent poems is
the "Hymn to the Adorable St. Teresa."

pleased with itself and never learns to do right." Pretentiousness and pride annoyed her. Once a young woman of high reputation for virtue asked to be admitted to a convent in Teresa's charge, and added, as if to emphasize her intellect, "I shall bring my Bible with me." "What," exclaimed Teresa, "your Bible? Do not come to us. We are only poor women who know nothing but how to spin and do as we are told."

In spite of a naturally sturdy constitution, Teresa continued throughout her life to suffer from ailments which physicians found baffling. It would seem that sheer will power kept her alive. At the time of the definitive division of the Carmelite Order she had reached the age of sixty-five and was broken in health. Yet during the last two years of her life she somehow found strength to establish three more convents. They were at Granada, in the far south, at Burgos, in the north, and at Soria, in Portugal. The total was now sixteen. What an astounding achievement this was for one small, enfeebled woman may be better appreciated if we recall the hardships of travel. Most of this extensive journeying was done in a curtained carriage or cart drawn by mules over the extremely poor roads; her trips took her from the northern provinces down to the Mediterranean, and west into Portugal, across mountains, rivers, and arid plateaus. She and the nun who accompanied her endured all the rigors of a harsh climate as well as the steady discomfort of rude lodgings and scanty food.

In the autumn of 1582, Teresa, although ill, set out for Alva de Tormez, where an old friend was expecting a visit from her. Her companion of later years, Anne-of-St. Bartholomew, describes the journey. Teresa grew worse on the road, along which there were few habitations. They could get no food save figs, and when they arrived at the convent, Teresa went to bed in a state of exhaustion. She never recovered, and three days later, she remarked to Anne, "At last, my daughter, I have reached the house of death," a reference to her book, *The Seven Mansions*. Extreme Unction was administered by Father Antony de Heredia, a friar of the Reform, and when he asked her where she wished to be buried, she plaintively

replied, "Will they deny me a little ground for my body here?"
She sat up as she received the Sacrament, exclaiming, "O my Lord,
now is the time that we shall see each other!" and died in Anne's
arms. It was the evening of October 4. The next day, as it happened, the Gregorian calendar came into use. The readjustment
made it necessary to drop ten days, so that October 5 was counted
as October 15, and this latter date became Teresa's feast day. She
was buried at Alva; three years later, following the decree of a
provincial chapter of Reformed Carmelites, the body was secretly
removed to Avila. The next year the Duke of Alva procured an
order from Rome to return it to Alva de Tormez, and there it has
remained.

Teresa was canonized in 1662. Shortly after her death, Philip II,
keenly aware of the Carmelite nun's contribution to Catholicism,
had her manuscripts collected and brought to his great palace of
the Escorial, and there placed in a rich case, the key of which he
carried on his person. These writings were edited for publication
by two Dominican scholars and brought out in 1587. Subsequently
her works have appeared in uncounted Spanish editions, and have
been translated into many languages. An ever-spreading circle of
readers through the centuries have found understanding and courage in the life and works of this nun of Castile, who is one of the
glories of Spain and of the Church. Teresa's emblems are a heart,
an arrow, and a book.

Excerpts from Interior Castle

*T*his body has one fault, that the more people pamper it, the
more its wants are made known. It is strange how much it
likes to be indulged. How well it finds some good pretext to deceive
the poor soul! . . . Oh, you who are free from the great troubles
of the world, learn to suffer a little for the love of God without
everyone's knowing it! . . .

And remember our holy fathers of past times and holy hermits
whose life we try to imitate; what pains they endured, what loneli-

ness, what cold, what hunger, what burning suns, without having anyone to complain to except God. Do you think that they were of iron? No, they were as much flesh as we are; and as soon as we begin, daughters, to conquer this little carcass, it will not bother us so much. . . . If you don't make up your mind to swallow, once and for all, death and loss of health, you will never do anything. . . .

God deliver us from anybody who wishes to serve Him and thinks about her own dignity and fears to be disgraced. . . . No poison in the world so slays perfection as these things do. . . .

There are persons, it seems, who are ready to ask God for favors as a matter of justice. A fine sort of humility! Hence He who knows all does well in giving it to them hardly ever; He sees plainly they are not fit to drink the chalice. . . .

Sometimes the Devil proposes to us great desires, so that we shall not put our hand to what we have to do, and serve our Lord in possible things, but stay content with having desired impossible ones. Granting that you can help much by prayer, don't try to benefit all the world, but those who are in your company, and so the work will be better for you are much bounden to them. . . . In short, what I would conclude with is that we must not build towers without foundations; the Lord does not look so much to the grandeur of our works as to the love with which they are done; and if we do all we can, His Majesty will see to it that we are able to do more and more every day, if we do not then grow weary, and during the little that this life lasts—and perhaps it will be shorter than each one thinks—we offer to Christ, inwardly and outwardly, what sacrifice we can, for His Majesty will join it with the one He made to the Father for us on the Cross, that it may have the value which our will would have merited, even though our works may be small.

Epilogue

Although, as I told you, I felt reluctant to begin this work, yet now it is finished I am very glad to have written it, and I think my trouble is well spent, though I confess it has cost me but little.

Considering your strict enclosure, the little recreation you have, my sisters, and how many conveniences are wanting in some of your convents, I think it may console you to enjoy yourselves in this Interior Castle, where you can enter, and walk about at will, at any hour you please, without asking leave of your superiors.

It is true you cannot enter all the mansions by your own power, however great it may appear to you, unless the Lord of the Castle Himself admits you. Therefore I advise you to use no violence if you meet with any obstacle, for that would displease Him so much that He would never give you admission to them. He dearly loves humility: if you think yourselves unworthy to enter the third mansion, He will grant you all the sooner the favor of entering the fifth. Then if you serve Him well there, and often repair to it, He will draw you into the mansion where He dwells Himself, where you need never depart, unless called away by the Prioress, whose commands the sovereign Master wishes you to obey as if they were His own. If, by her orders, you are often absent from His presence chamber, whenever you return He will hold the door open for you. When once you have learned how to enjoy this Castle, you will always find rest, however painful your trials may be, in the hope of returning to your Lord, which no one can prevent.

Although I have only mentioned seven mansions, yet each one contains many more rooms, above, below, and around it, with fair gardens, fountains, and labyrinths, besides other things so delightful that you will wish to consume yourself in praising the great God for them, Who has created the soul in His own image and likeness. If you find anything in the plan of this treatise which helps you to know Him better, be certain that it is sent by His Majesty to encourage you, and whatever you find amiss in it is my own.

In return for my strong desire to aid you in serving Him, my God and my Lord, I implore you, whenever you read this, to praise His Majesty fervently in my name, and to beg Him to prosper His Church, to give light to the Lutherans, to pardon my sins, and to free me from purgatory, where perhaps I shall be, by the mercy of God, when you see this book, provided it is given to you after having been examined by the theologians. If these writings contain any error, it is through my ignorance; I submit in all things to the teachings of the Holy Catholic Roman Church, of which I am now a member, as I protest and promise both to live and die. May our Lord God be forever praised and blessed. Amen. Amen.

The writing of this was finished in the convent of Saint Joseph of Avila, in the year 1577, on the vigil of Saint Andrew, to the glory of God, Who liveth and reigneth for ever and ever. Amen.

(*Interior Castle and Mansions*. London, 1912.)

Saint Charles Borromeo

Archbishop, Cardinal

1 5 8 4

(*November 4*)

Among the great reformers of the troubled sixteenth century was Charles Borromeo, who, with St. Francis of Loyola, St. Philip Neri, and others, led the movement to combat the inroads of the Protestant Reformation. His father, Count Gilbert Borromeo, was a man of piety and ability, and his mother was a member of the famous Medici family of Milan, sister of Angelo de Medici, later to become Pope Pius IV. The second of two sons in a family of six children, Charles was born in the castle of Arona on Lake Maggiore, on October 2, 1538. He was so devout that at the age of twelve he received the tonsure. At this time his paternal uncle, Julius Caesar Borromeo, turned over to him the income from a rich Benedictine abbey, one of the ancient perquisites of this noble family. In spite of his youth, Charles had a sense of responsibility, and he made plain to his father that all revenues from the abbey beyond what was required to prepare him for a career in the Church belonged to the poor and could not be applied to secular use. To take such a scrupulous stand in a period of corruption and decadence was unusual, and most significant as an indication of Charles' integrity of character.

The young man attended the University of Pavia, where he applied himself to the study of civil and canon law. Due to a slight impediment of speech, he was regarded as slow; yet his thoroughness and industry more than compensated for the handicap, and his strict behavior made him a model for his fellow students, who, in this era of the Renaissance, were for the most part pleasure-loving and dissipated. Charles now accepted a sufficient income from the abbey to meet the expenses of the kind of household a young nobleman was expected to maintain. By the time he took his doctor's degree at twenty-two his parents were dead and his elder brother, Frederick, was head of the family. Charles had no sooner returned home than the news came that his uncle, Cardinal Angelo de Medici, had been elected Pope Pius IV. A few months later the new Pope sent for his nephew to come to Rome, and within a very short time Charles was the recipient of such a wealth of honors, offices, and powers that he became a leading figure at the papal court. He was appointed cardinal-deacon and administrator of the see of Milan, although he was not to take up his work there for many years; he was named legate of Bologna, Romagna, and the March of Ancona; protector of Portugal, the Low Countries, and the Catholic cantons of Switzerland; supervisor of the Franciscan and Carmelite Orders, and of the Knights of Malta, and administrator of the papal states. The Pope's confidence in him was not misplaced, for Charles displayed great energy, ability, and diplomacy in fulfilling these various duties. Methodical and diligent, he learned how to despatch business affairs with speed and efficiency.

Yet in spite of his heavy tasks, Charles found time for recreation in music and physical exercise. He had the many-sidedness which we associate with men of the Renaissance, and was deeply interested in the advancement of learning. He set up at the Vatican a literary academy of clergy and laymen, and some of the studies and talks growing out of it were published as *Noctes Vaticanae*, to which Charles himself was a contributor. It was the custom for one in his position to live in magnificent state, but splendid trappings meant nothing to him. He remained modest and humble in spirit, and wholly aloof from the worldly temptations of Rome.

When the Venerable Bartholomew de Martyribus, archbishop of Braga, came to Rome, Charles consulted him as to his future. "You know what it is," he is recorded as saying, "to be the nephew of a pope, and a beloved nephew; nor are you ignorant of what it is to live at the court of Rome. The dangers are infinite. What ought I to do, young as I am, and without experience? God has given me ardor for penance, and an earnest desire to prefer Him to all things; and I have some thought of going into a monastery, to live as if there were only God and myself in the world." The prelate advised Charles to stay on at Rome, where he was so greatly needed. This proved to be excellent counsel, for an even greater opportunity for service to the Church was to come to the young man.

The Pope, soon after his election, announced the reassembling of the Council of Trent, which had been suspended ten years earlier, in 1552. Charles now devoted himself to plans for the resumption of deliberations, and was in attendance during the two years that the Council continued in session at Trent (Italian, Trento), a city of northern Italy. Its purpose was to conclude the work of formulating and codifying Church doctrine and to bring about a genuine reform of abuses. It defined original sin, decreed the perpetuity of the marital tie, pronounced anathema against those who rejected the invocation of saints or the veneration of relics, or who denied the existence of Purgatory or the validity of indulgences. It also dealt with episcopal jurisdiction, the education of seminarists, and discipline for the clergy. Some of the points proved so controversial that several times the Council almost broke up with its labors unfinished. Charles is credited with helping to heal the rifts and spurring the prelates and theologians on to the conclusion of their historic task. He is also conceded to have had a large share in drawing up the Tridentine Catechism. His training in diplomacy at the papal court had served him well.

In this flowering time of all the arts, Church music showed remarkable development. Among Charles' duties was the commissioning of composers to write liturgical music. The renowned Palestrina, later to become Vatican choir master, composed at this time the glorious Mass called "Papae Marcelli," and other choral works that set a new standard for polyphonic music.

While the Council of Trent was in session, Charles' elder brother died, and as head of the family Charles became proprietor of extensive land holdings. Since he was only in minor orders, people thought that he would now marry, but Charles remained true to the course he had marked out for himself. Yielding his family position to his Uncle Julius, he entered the priesthood in September, 1563. Three months later he became bishop of Milan, as well as cardinal-priest, with the title of St. Prassede. For a long time Charles had been concerned over the see of Milan, to which, years before, he had been appointed administrator. Catholics were falling away from the Church, chiefly because there had been no resident bishop at Milan for eighty years. The new bishop was welcomed with joy and he set to work vigorously to reform this important diocese. Soon he was called back to Rome to assist the Pope on his deathbed, at which Philip Neri, another future saint, was also present. The new Pope, Pius V, who was to follow in the noble tradition of his predecessor, urged Charles to remain with him for a time. Soon, however, with the Pope's blessing, he returned to Milan.

Charles now concentrated his great abilities on the establishment of schools, seminaries, and convents. But more important than the improvement of the physical structures through which the Church must carry on its work was the need for reform of the priestly function itself. Throughout the region religious practices were profaned by grave abuses; the Sacrament was neglected, for many priests were both lazy and ignorant; the monasteries were relaxed in discipline and full of disorders. These widespread faults had been engendered in part by the decay of medieval society and in part by the revival of the ideas of pagan antiquity. By remonstrance and exhortation Charles worked to raise the level of spiritual life, and to put into effect the ecclesiastical changes indicated by the Council of Trent. He founded the Confraternity of Christian Doctrine, with its Sunday Schools for the teaching of the Catechism to children. Historically these were the first Sunday Schools, and are said to have numbered 740. He instituted a secular fraternity whose members, called the Oblates of St. Ambrose, pledged obedience to their bishop and were used by him in religious work in any manner he thought wise. The bishop's income from his family estates was considerable, and nearly all of it was turned over to an almoner for the relief of the poor; plate and other valuables were sold for the same purpose. In conformity with the decrees of the Council of Trent, the cathedral of Milan was cleared of its gorgeous tombs, banners, and arms. In his zeal for reform Charles came into conflict with the governor of the province and the senate, who feared the Church was encroaching upon the civil jurisdiction. The opposition to Charles and the complaints against him were carried to King Philip II of Spain, who had sovereignty over this part of Italy, and to the Pope; in the end Charles was completely exonerated. His days were filled with duties and cares; at night he would take off his bishop's robes, don a tattered old cassock, and pass the evening in study and prayer. He lived as simply as it was possible to do. One cold night when someone wanted to have his bed warmed, he said, "The best way not to find a bed cold is to go to bed colder than the bed is." However, he did not allow his rigorous self-discipline to weaken him for the work he had to do.

The almost inaccessible Alpine valleys lying in the northern part of his diocese had been virtually abandoned by the clergy. The bishop did not hesitate to undertake journeys to these remote valleys and mountain tops. He discussed theology with peasants and taught the Catechism to herdboys. Everywhere he preached and effected reforms, replacing unworthy priests by those who were zealous to restore the faith. In 1576 he successfully met another challenge. There was famine at Milan due to crop failures, and later came an outbreak of the plague. The city's trade fell off, and along with it the people's source of income. The governor and many members of the nobility fled the city, but the bishop remained, to organize the care of those who were stricken and to minister to the dying. He called together the superiors of all the religious communities in the diocese, and won their cooperation. He used up his own funds and went into debt to provide food for the hungry. Finally he wrote to the governor, and shamed him into coming back to his post.

The bishop's reforms were opposed by the Humiliati (Brothers of Humility), a decayed penitential order which, although reduced to about 170 members, owned some ninety monasteries. Three of its priors hatched a plot to assassinate Charles, and he was actually fired upon while at evening prayers with his household. Charles refused to have the would-be assassin sought out and punished. The Humiliati at length submitted to the reform of their order.

Many English Catholics had fled to Italy at this time because of the persecutions under Queen Elizabeth. The bishop had a Welshman, Dr. Griffith Roberts, as canon theologian, and an Englishman, Thomas Goldwell, as vicar-general. He carried about on his person a little picture of St. John Fisher, who, with St. Thomas More, had been martyred for the faith during the reign of Henry VIII.

Travels in his diocese, especially in the difficult Alpine country, had weakened the bishop's constitution. In 1584, during his annual retreat at Monte Varallo, he was stricken with ague, and on returning to Milan grew rapidly worse. After receiving the Last Sacraments, the beloved bishop died quietly on November 4, at the age of forty-six. Canonization followed in 1610. St. Charles Borromeo's sermons were published at Milan in the eighteenth century and have been widely translated. Two years after his death the Borromean League was formed in the Catholic cantons of Switzerland, for the expulsion of heretics. Contrary to his wishes, a memorial was erected in the Milan cathedral, where his body now rests, and at Arona, his birthplace, stands an impressive statue in his honor. For his piety, energy, and effectiveness this eminent churchman soon became known as a "second Ambrose." He is the patron of Lombardy; his emblems are the Holy Communion and a coat of arms bearing the word *Humilitas*.

Saint Philip Neri

Confessor

1 5 9 5

(*May 26*)

Philip Neri was born in Florence in the year 1515, one of four children of the notary Francesco Neri. The mother died while the children were very young, her place being filled by a capable stepmother. From infancy Philip had a docile, merry disposition. They called him "Pippo buono," "good little Phil," for he was a dutiful, attractive, cheerful lad, popular with all who knew him.

At eighteen Philip was sent to the town of San Germano, to live with a childless kinsman who had a business there and would be likely to make Philip his apprentice and heir. It is hard to imagine anyone with less aptitude for business than Philip. Soon after his arrival he had a mystical experience which in after years he spoke of as his "conversion," and which radically changed his life. He left his kinsman's house, to set out for Rome without money or plan, trusting entirely to God's providence. In Rome he found shelter under the roof of a former Florentine, one Galeotto Caccia, a customs official, who offered him an attic and the bare necessaries of life, in return for which Philip was to give lessons to Caccia's two small sons. Under his tutoring the little boys improved rapidly in all respects, according to their grateful mother. This promised well for Philip's future human relationships. Indeed, as we shall see, he had a natural talent for bringing out the best in people of all ages and conditions.

Except for the hours he devoted to his pupils, Philip seems to have passed his first two years at Rome as a recluse, spending much time in prayer in his bare, uncomfortable attic. He ate frugal meals of bread, water, and a few olives or vegetables. It was a period of intense preparation, and at its close he emerged from obscurity with his spirit strengthened, his resolve to live for God confirmed. He now took courses in philosophy and theology at the Sapienza and at St. Augustine's monastery. For three years he worked so hard that he was considered an unusually promising scholar. Then, quite suddenly, moved by some inner prompting, he put an end to classes and studying, sold most of his books, and launched on a mission to the people of Rome.

Religion was at a low ebb in the papal city, which had not yet recovered from the atrocious depredations of the German and Spanish armies of 1527, a decade earlier. There were also grave abuses within the Church, and although they had long been recognized, too little was being done to cure them. Elections to the Sacred College were controlled by the Medici family,[1] with the result that the cardinals, with a few notable exceptions, were princes of the state, worldlings who thought in terms of power and politics, rather than men dedicated to God and the Church. The enthusiasm for classical writers and the tendency towards scepticism, fostered by the humanists of the Renaissance, had gradually substituted pagan for Christian ideals in Italian intellectual circles. Indifference and luxury, if not corruption, were rife among the clergy, many of whom allowed their churches to fall into disrepair, seldom said Mass, and completely neglected their flocks. Little wonder that the laity were lapsing into cynicism and disbelief! To fill the people of Rome with new ardor, to re-evangelize the city, became Philip Neri's life work.

He began in the most direct way possible, making acquaintances on street corners and in the public squares, where people were inclined to loiter. At first he interested himself especially in the young Florentines who were employed in the banks and shops of the busy Sant'Angelo quarter near the Vatican. He has been com-

[1] The Medici family, the ruling dynasty of Florence since the fourteenth century, had during the past fifty years extended its power to include the papacy.

pared to Socrates for the way he could seize on opportunities for engaging in conversation and then lead his hearers on by questions and suggestions to consider a better way of life. His warm friendliness and lively sense of humor would quickly catch the attention of passersby, and once caught, they found it difficult to break away. By this warm, personal approach he gradually prevailed on many to give up their careless way of life. His customary question, "Well, brothers, when shall we begin to do good?" soon brought a response, provided he led the way. Losing no time in converting good intentions into action, he would take them to wait on the sick in the hospitals or to pray in the Seven Churches, one of Philip's own favorite devotions. His days were wholly given up to others, but towards evening it was his habit to retire into solitude, to spend the night in a church porch or in the catacombs beside the Appian Way, gathering strength for another day's work.

In one of the grottoes along the Appian Way he had an experience which affected him profoundly. He was praying on the eve of Pentecost, 1544, when there appeared to him what seemed to be a globe of fire; it entered his mouth and afterwards he felt a dilation of the heart. Immediately he was filled with such paroxysms of divine love that he fell to the ground exclaiming, "Enough, enough, Lord, I can bear no more!" When he had come to himself and risen up, he discovered a swelling over his heart, though neither then nor later did it give him pain. From that day on, under stress of spiritual emotion, he was apt to be seized with palpitations; at such times he would ask God to mitigate His visitations lest he should die of love.

In the year 1548, when Philip had been carrying out his informal mission for some ten years, he founded, with the help of his confessor, Father Persiano Rossa, a confraternity of poor laymen who met for spiritual exercises in the church of San Salvatore in Campo. He popularized the devotion of the Forty Hours,[2] and undertook

[2] This consists of a solemn exposition of the Blessed Sacrament for forty hours, usually on three successive days, in honor of the forty hours Christ is considered to have spent in the tomb.

to provide for needy pilgrims, a work which led to the building of
the famous hospital Santa Trinita. During the Year of Jubilee of
1575 it cared for no less than a hundred and forty-five thousand
pilgrims. Later it received convalescents also.

Thus by the time he was thirty-four, Philip had accomplished a
great deal. His confessor, however, was convinced that as a priest
his work would be even more effective. Philip's humility made him
shrink from taking Holy Orders, but at last, on May 23, 1551, he
was ordained. He went to live with Father Rossa and other priests
at San Girolamo and thereafter carried on his mission mainly
through the confessional. Starting before daybreak and continuing
hour after hour, he sat in the tribunal of penance, while men and
women of all ages and ranks flocked to him. Sometimes he conducted informal discussions with those who desired to lead a better
life, or he would read aloud to them, choosing the lives of the saints,
martyrs, and missionaries. The story of the heroic life and death
of St. Francis Xavier so inspired Philip that he himself considered
service in the foreign mission field: a Cistercian whom he consulted
persuaded him that Rome was to be his Indies.

To accommodate the increasing number of those who attended
Philip's discussions, a large room was built over the nave of
San Girolamo. Several other priests were appointed to assist him.
The people called them "Oratorians" because they rang a little
bell to summon the faithful to prayers in their "oratory." The
actual foundation of the Congregation of the Priests of the Oratory
was laid a few years later, when Philip presented five of his young
followers for ordination and sent them to serve the church of San
Giovanni, which had been put in his charge by fellow Florentines
living in Rome. The future cardinal and Church historian, Caesar
Baronius, was among them. Philip drew up for them some simple
rules: they were to share a common table and perform spiritual
exercises under his direction, but they were not to bind themselves
to the life by vow or to renounce their property. The organization
grew rapidly, although it met with opposition in certain quarters.
In 1575, the Congregation received the formal approbation of Pope

Gregory XIII, who later bestowed on it the ancient church of Santa Maria in Vellicella. The building was in a ruinous condition and far too small. Philip was not long in deciding to demolish it and rebuild on a large scale.

He had no money, but contributions poured in from his friends, rich and poor. Pope Gregory and Charles Borromeo gave generously, as did other prominent men. Cardinals and princes were now among Philip's disciples, though he sometimes shocked them by his impulsiveness. His desire was always to establish a close, human bond with others, even though it meant indulging in a wine-drinking contest, practical joking, or other undignified behavior. He acted in a jocular manner to conceal his deep emotion, or to put himself on a level with those around him. Humility was the virtue he strove most of all to practice, but of course he could not conceal his extraordinary gifts or sanctity. More than once he foretold events which later came to pass. He lived in such a state of spiritual exaltation that at times it was with difficulty that he carried on his daily labors. Men declared that his face often glowed with a celestial radiance.

By April, 1577, work on the Nuova Chiesa, or New Church, had advanced sufficiently for the Congregation of the Oratory to be transferred there. Philip stayed at San Girolamo for another seven years before he moved to quarters in the New Church. Although he ate his meals apart from the group, he was far from leading the life of a solitary. Not only did his spiritual sons have free access to him, but his room was constantly crowded by others. Rich and poor mounted the steps that led to his refuge at the top of the house, with its balcony looking over the roofs of Rome. The Italian people loved and venerated him, and visitors came from other countries to speak with him. Thus he continued his apostolate when the infirmities of age prevented him from leading an active life. The College of Cardinals frequently sought his advice, and although he refrained from becoming involved in political matters, he broke this rule when he persuaded Pope Clement VII to withdraw the excommunication and anathema laid on Henry IV of France.

In the words of one of his biographers, "He was all things to all men. . . . When he was called upon to be merry, he was so; if there was a demand upon his sympathy, he was equally ready. . . . In consequence of his being so accessible and willing to receive all comers, many went to him every day, and some continued for the space of thirty, nay, forty years, to visit him very often both morning and evening, so that his room went by the agreeable nickname of the "Home of Christian mirth." The tradition of this genial saint was very much alive two hundred years later, when the German poet Goethe was living in Rome. He heard so much of Neri that he studied the sources and wrote a highly appreciative essay about him, entitled, "The Humorous Saint."

Two years before his death Neri retired from his office of Superior in favor of his disciple, Caesar Baronius. He obtained permission from the Pope to celebrate Mass daily in a little Oratory adjoining his room. So enraptured did he become at such times that it was the practice of those who attended to retire respectfully at the *Agnus Dei*. On the Feast of Corpus Christi, May 25, 1595, Philip was in a radiantly happy mood, and his physician told him that he had not looked so well for ten years. He alone realized that his hour had come. All day he heard confessions and saw visitors as usual, but before retiring he said: "Last of all, we must die." About midnight, he had a severe haemorrhage and the fathers in the house were called to his bedside. He was dying, and Baronius read the commendatory prayers, and then besought him to say a parting word or at least to bless his sons once more. Unable to speak, Philip raised his hand, and in the act of benediction passed to his reward. He had reached the ripe age of eighty and his work was done. His body rests in the New Church, which the Oratorians still serve.[3] Six years later he was beatified; Pope Gregory XV canonized him in 1622. Even during his lifetime he had received the title of "Apostle of Rome."

One of the most famous members of the Oratorian order, Car-

[3] The Oratorians continue to live in communities, each congregation being independent.

dinal Newman, wrote [4] of Neri nearly three hundred years after his death, "he contemplated as the idea of his mission, not the propagation of the faith, nor the exposition of doctrine, nor the catechetical schools; whatever was exact and systematic pleased him not; he put from him monastic rule and authoritative speech, as David refused the armor of his king. . . . He came to the Eternal City and he sat himself down there, and his home and his family gradually grew up around him, by the spontaneous accession of materials from without. He did not so much seek his own as draw them to him. He sat in his small room, and they in their gay, worldly dresses, the rich and the wellborn, as well as the simple and the illiterate, crowded into it. In the mid-heats of summer, in the frosts of winter, still was he in that low and narrow cell at San Girolamo, reading the hearts of those who came to him, and curing their souls' maladies by the very touch of his hand. . . . And they who came remained gazing and listening till, at length, first one and then another threw off their bravery, and took his poor cassock and girdle instead; or, if they kept it, it was to put haircloth under it, or to take on them a rule of life, while to the world they looked as before."

[4] *The Idea of a University,* Discourse IX, 9.

Saint Rose of Lima
Virgin
1 6 1 7
(August 30)

Rose of Lima has a special claim on our interest for she has the honor of being the first person born in the Western Hemisphere to be canonized by the Church. Only a little more than half a century before her birth, the fabulous land of Peru had been discovered and seized for Spain by the explorer Francisco Pizarro. In 1533 this enterprising conquistador subdued the native population and took over as his capital the inland city of Cuzco, with its strange Inca temples, palaces, and great fortress. Two years later the seat of government was transferred to Lima, a city on the coast, which came to be called the "royal city of kings," because of its architectural splendors. Dominican friars and the representatives of other religious orders were in the vanguard of a great migration from Spain and Portugal that meant a long, dangerous journey across the Atlantic, across the Isthmus of Panama, and down the western coast of South America. To implant Christianity in the new empire was a major aim; while the civilian population, European and native, were working the mines and raising products for export, the friars and priests were intensely active. They taught, preached, learned the native languages, tried to win the love and confidence of the Indians, and soon were engaged in building churches, hospitals, and schools.

The child who became St. Rose of Lima was born on April 20, 1586, of a Spaniard, Gaspar de Flores, and Maria d'Olivia, a woman who had Inca blood in her veins. The infant, one of ten children born to the couple, was baptized Isabel, after an aunt, Isabel de Herrara, who acted as godmother. This ceremony took place at home, for the baby was extremely weak. Several weeks later the tiny infant was carried to the nearby church of San Sebastian for baptism by the priest, Don Antonio Polanco. By the time she was confirmed by Archbishop Toribio of Lima, the name Isabel had been replaced by Rose, and this was the name now bestowed on her. Rose had a fresh, lovely complexion, and she was worried by the thought that this name had been given as a tribute to her beauty. So sensitive was her conscience that she had genuine scruples over bearing the name, and on one occasion, after hearing someone praise her comeliness, she rubbed pepper into her face to mar it; another time, she put lime on her hands, inducing acute suffering. This was her way—a way conditioned by the time and place—of fighting a temptation to vanity. Such self-imposed cruelties, as we have seen in the lives of some of the other saints, have not been uncommon, particularly among those of a mystical bent.

Rose seems to have taken for her model St. Catherine of Siena, and, like the earlier saint, she experienced so ardent a love of God whenever she was in the presence of the Blessed Sacrament that exaltation completely filled her soul. Yet Rose was not without a practical side. Her father had been well-to-do, but when he lost money in mining ventures, the family's fortunes reached a very low ebb. Rose helped out by selling her fine needlework; she also raised beautiful flowers and these too were taken to market. One of her brothers, Ferdinand, was sympathetic and understanding toward this sister who was so markedly "different." As she grew to maturity, her parents were anxious to have Rose marry, and indeed there were several worthy aspirants for her hand. Rose did not wish marriage, and, to end the arguments and offers, she joined the Third Order of St. Dominic, donned the habit, and took a vow of perpetual virginity.

For many years Rose lived virtually as a recluse. There was a little hut in the family garden, and this she used as an oratory. She often wore on her head a circlet of silver studded on the inside with sharp points, in memory of the Lord's crown of thorns. Other forms of penitence which she inflicted on her body were floggings, administered three times daily, the wearing of a hair shirt, and the dragging of a heavy, wooden cross about the garden. She rubbed her lips with gall and often chewed bitter herbs to deaden the sense of taste. Both eating and sleeping were reduced to a minimum. Naturally her health was affected, but the physical disorders which resulted from this regime—stomach ailments, asthma, rheumatism, and fevers—were suffered uncomplainingly. This manner of life offended her family, who preferred their daughter to follow the more conventional and accepted ways of holiness. Finally, when Rose began to tell of visions, revelations, visitations, and voices they deplored her penitential practices more than ever. She endured their disapproval and grew in spiritual fortitude.

In spite of the rigors of her ascetic life, Rose was not wholly detached from happenings around her, and her awareness of the suffering of others often led her to protest against some of the practices of the Spanish overlords. In the new world, the discovery of unbelievable mineral resources was doing little to enrich or ennoble the lives of the Peruvian natives. The gold and silver from this land of El Dorado was being shipped back to strengthen the empire and embellish the palaces and cathedrals of Old Spain, but at its source there was vice, exploitation, and corruption. The natives were oppressed and impoverished, in spite of the missionaries' efforts to alleviate their miseries and to exercise a restraining hand on the governing class. Rose was cognizant of the evils, and spoke out against them fearlessly. Sometimes she brought sick and hungry persons into her own home that she might better care for them.

For fifteen years Rose bore the disapproval and persecution of those close to her, as well as the more severe trial of desolation of soul. At length an examination by priests and physicians was indicated, and this resulted in the judgment that her experiences were indeed supernatural. Rose's last years were passed in the home of a government official, Don Gonzalo de Massa. During an illness towards the end of her life, she was able to pray, "Lord, increase my sufferings, and with them increase Thy love in my heart." This remarkable woman died on August 25, 1617, at the age of thirty-one.

Not until after her death was it known how widely her beneficent influence had extended, and how deeply venerated she was by the common people of Lima. When her body was borne down the street to the cathedral, a great cry of mourning arose from the crowd. For several days it was impossible to perform the ritual of burial on account of the great press of sorrowing citizens around her bier. She was finally laid to rest in the Dominican convent at Lima. Later, when miracles and cures were being attributed to her intervention, the body was transferred to the church of San Domingo. There it reposes today in a special chapel. Rose of Lima was declared patroness of South America and the Philippines; she was canonized by Pope Clement in 1671, August 30 being appointed her feast-day. This holy woman is highly honored in all Spanish-American countries. The emblems associated with her are an anchor, a crown of roses, and a city.

Saint Francis de Sales

Bishop, Doctor of the Church

1 6 2 2

(*January 29*)

Francis de Sales was born at the Château de Sales in Swiss Savoy on August 21, 1567, and at his baptism in the parish church of Thorens was named Francis Bonaventura, for two greatly loved Franciscan saints. The room in which he was born was known as the "St. Francis room," from an old painting on the wall showing the friar of Assisi preaching to the birds; and it was this lover of all living creatures whom Francis de Sales was to choose as his patron in later years. His father, the Seigneur de Nouvelles, was an aristocrat who had served his country well in war and peace. On his marriage to the only child of Melchior de Sionnaz, who brought as her dowry the Signory of Boisy, he took the name of Boisy. When Francis was born, the eldest of thirteen children, his mother was only fifteen. The boy was frail at birth, but with devoted care he grew to vigorous maturity.

Young as she was, Francis' mother kept his early education largely in her own hands; after a few years she was aided by the excellent Abbé Deage, who acted as the boy's tutor and companion. Francis was obedient, truthful, and habitually generous to those less fortunate than himself. He was responsive in matters of religion, and seems to have loved books and knowledge. At the age of eight he was sent to the nearby college of Annecy, and there, in the church of St. Dominic (now called St. Maurice), he made his First Communion and received Confirmation. A year later he was permitted to take the tonsure, for he was set even then on consecrating himself to the Church, and this was regarded as the first step. His father, a worldly man, who planned a brilliant career for his son in public life, attached little importance to the ceremony. In his fourteenth year Francis went to the University of Paris, accompanied by the Abbé Deage. The University, with its fifty-four colleges, was still the most famous center of learning in Europe. Monsieur de Boisy had selected for his son the College of Navarre, for it was frequented by the sons of the noble families of Savoy, but Francis resolved to go to the College of Clermont, which was under Jesuit direction, and renowned for both piety and scholarship.

At the College of Clermont Francis soon excelled in rhetoric and philosophy, and other subjects arousing his most fervent enthusiasm were theology and the Scriptures. To please his father, he took lessons in riding, dancing, and fencing, but cared for none of these gentlemanly accomplishments. During this time his heart became more and more fixed on giving himself to God, and he took a vow of perpetual chastity, placing himself under the special protection of the Blessed Virgin. He was, nevertheless, not free from trials. The love of God had always meant more to him than anything else, and now he became prey to the fear that he had lost God's favor. This obsession haunted him day and night. It was a heroic act of pure love that finally brought him deliverance. "O Lord," he cried, "if I am never to see Thee in Heaven, this at least grant me, that I may never curse or blaspheme Thy holy name. If I may not love Thee in the other world—for in Hell none praise Thee—let me at least every instant of my brief existence here love Thee as much as I can." Directly afterwards, as he knelt in the church, all fear and despair suddenly left him and he was filled with peace. This experience of his youth taught him to deal understandingly with the spiritual crises of those who, at a later period, looked to him for guidance.

After six years in Paris he was called home by his father, who sent him to the University of Padua to study jurisprudence. He was at Padua for four years, and there, as at Paris, he won a name for scholarship and virtuous conduct. At twenty-four he was given the degree of Doctor of Law. A pilgrimage to Loreto and a short stay at Rome followed, then he returned to his father's château. For some eighteen months, he led, at least outwardly, the life of a conventional young nobleman. That his son and heir should now settle down and marry was Boisy's desire, and this autocratic father had already chosen for him a charming bride. Francis, by his distant though courteous manner to the young lady, soon made it plain that in this matter, as in many others, he could not carry out his father's wishes. Not long afterwards he again annoyed his father by declining the honor offered him by the prince of Savoy of a seat in the senate, an unusual compliment to one so young.

The Catholic bishop of Geneva, Claude de Granier, was living at Annecy, his own diocese now being in Calvinist hands. The bishop, impressed by Francis' character, is reported to have made this prophetic utterance to those about him: "This young man will be a great personage some day! He will become a pillar of the Church and my successor in this see." So far Francis had confided only to his mother and a few friends his desire for a life in the Church; an explanation to his father now became inevitable. Monsieur de Boisy had been much chagrined by his son's refusal to marry and also by his rejection of the senatorship, but he was not prepared for this new disappointment. He withheld his consent. The unexpected death just then of the provost of the chapter of cathedral canons made Francis' cousin, Canon Louis de Sales, hope that Francis might be appointed to this honorable post, in which case his father might yield. The post was offered, Francis accepted it, and thus he finally obtained his father's permission to enter the priesthood. The young man was already so well prepared by his purity of life and by his theological studies that there was no need for the usual delay. On the very day his father gave his consent, Francis put on ecclesiastical dress and three weeks later took minor orders. Six months afterwards, on December 18, 1593, at the age of twenty-six, he was ordained priest by the bishop of Geneva in the parish church of Thorens.

Before offering the Holy Sacrifice, Francis went into a short retreat, during which he made several important resolutions. One of these was to use every moment of the day as a preparation for the morrow's Mass, so that if he were asked, "What are you doing at this moment?" he could always truly answer, "Preparing to celebrate Mass." On the feast of St. Thomas, December 21, in the cathedral of Annecy, he consecrated the Host for the first time, his parents being among those who received Communion at his hands. A few days later he was installed provost of the chapter of Geneva. He took up his duties with an ardor that never abated. He ministered lovingly to the poor and in the confessional devoted himself to the needs of the humblest with special care. His style of preaching was so simple that it charmed his hearers; scholar though he was, he refrained from filling his sermons with Greek and Latin quotations and theological subtleties, in the prevailing fashion.

Before long he was called on to undertake a far more difficult task. The Chablais, a section of Savoy on the south shore of Lake Geneva, had been invaded about sixty years earlier by militant Protestants from Berne, who took over the western part of it as well as the Pays de Vaud and the Pays de Gex, on the north shore of the lake. Catholic worship was outlawed, and churches were burned or razed when not appropriated for Protestant use. Religious orders were suppressed and priests expelled. Thirty years later the duke of Savoy, by giving up his claim to Vaud, had got back the Chablais and Gex, but on condition that the Catholic religion remain forbidden. In 1589 the Protestants of Berne again invaded the Chablais only to be repulsed, and by the Treaty of Nyon had agreed to allow the reestablishment of Catholic worship in the province and to restrict Protestant teaching to three towns, of which Thonon, the capital, was not to be one. But they soon broke their agreement and made a fresh attempt to conquer both the Chablais and Gex.

As soon as hostilities ceased, the duke appealed to the bishop of Geneva to send Catholic missionaries into the district. The pious ecclesiastic who undertook this mission was a timid soul who eventually withdrew in fear of personal violence and in despair of ever achieving success. The bishop now summoned his canons and put the situation before them, disguising none of the difficulties. When the bishop had concluded, Francis stood up to offer himself, saying simply, "Monseigneur, if you think I am capable, tell me to go. I am ready, and should rejoice to be chosen." To his delight, the bishop accepted Francis at once. Monsieur de Boisy tried to stop his son, but nothing could shake Francis' resolution. He departed without his father's blessing.

Traveling on foot with little money, Francis, accompanied by his cousin, Canon Louis de Sales, set out in September of 1594 to win the Chablais back to its ancient faith. The Château des Allinges, six or seven miles from Thonon, was a Catholic stronghold where the governor of the province was stationed with a garrison of soldiers, and to this fortress the two cousins were to return each night for the sake of safety. At Thonon, the Catholic population of the city had been reduced to about twenty persons, who were too intimidated to declare themselves openly. Francis sought them out one by one for private interviews and inspired them with renewed courage. He and his cousin gradually extended their efforts to the villages of the surrounding countryside.

The long walk night and morning to and from Allinges was a heavy tax on their strength and during the winter it exposed them to real dangers. Once Francis was set upon by wolves and only escaped by spending the night in a tree. When daylight came he was discovered by some peasants in such an exhausted condition that had they not helped him to reach their hut and revived him with food and warmth, he would have died. These good people were Calvinists. With his thanks Francis spoke words of enlightenment and charity and his rescuers were later restored to the faith. Twice in January, 1595, he was waylaid by Protestant fanatics who had sworn to take his life. On both occasions he was saved, seemingly, by a miracle.

Although at first the missionaries had little reward for their labors, they did not lose heart. Francis continually sought new ways to reach the minds of the people. He began to write brief leaflets, setting forth the leading dogmas of the Church as opposed to the tenets of Calvinism. These little papers, on which he worked in spare moments, were copied and recopied by hand and widely distributed. Later they were collected and printed in a volume called *Controversies*. Copies of these leaflets in the original written form are still preserved in the convent at Annecy.

To this work Francis added the spiritual direction of the soldiers quartered in the Château des Allinges, who, though nominally Catholic, were ignorant and dissolute. He instructed them and persuaded many to reform their lives. In the summer of 1595 he climbed the mountain of Voiron to restore an oratory to the Blessed Virgin which had been destroyed by the Bernese. On the way he was attacked by a hostile crowd, who beat him and drove him back. Soon after this his sermons at Thonon were drawing larger congregations. The little tracts or leaflets, scattered abroad, proved quietly effective, and in time there was a stream of lapsed Catholics asking for reconciliation with their Church.

Francis now went to live openly at Thonon. Oblivious of calumny and danger, he preached in the market place and held public disputations with leading Calvinist ministers of the district. Later on he was commissioned by Pope Clement VIII to debate with Theodore Beza, a distinguished Calvinist scholar. Francis was not able to bring Beza back into the Church, but many Protestants were convinced that Francis had the truth on his side. When, after three or four years, Bishop de Granier came to visit the mission, the results of Francis' untiring zeal were plain to see. Catholic faith and worship had been reestablished in the province, and by 1598 the whole district was once more predominantly Catholic.

Francis was very tender in his reception of sinners and apostates who had returned to the faith. He would greet them with the warmth of a father, saying, "Come, my dear children, come, let me put my arms around you. Ah, let me hide you in the bottom of my heart! God and I will help you, all I ask of you is not to despair; I will take on myself the rest of the burden." His affectionate care of them extended even to their bodily wants, and his purse was open to them as well as his heart. When told that his generosity would only encourage sinners, he replied: "Has not our Blessed Lord shed His blood for them, and shall I refuse them my tears? These wolves will be changed into lambs; a day will come when, cleansed of their sins, they will be more precious in the sight of God than we are. If Saul had been cast off, we should never have had St. Paul."

The bishop had long been considering Francis as a coadjutor and successor, but Francis declined the honor, thinking himself unworthy. In the end he yielded. No sooner was his decision made than he fell dangerously ill with a fever. When he had regained his strength, he started for Rome, accompanied by the Abbé de Chisse, who was to handle diocesan matters and arrange for the coadjutorship. At Rome Cardinal de Medici presented Francis to Pope Clement VIII. Having heard much praise of the young provost, the Pope suggested that he be examined in his presence. On the appointed day there was an assemblage of learned theologians, including the Church historian Baronius, Cardinal Robert Bellarmine, and Cardinal Federigo Borromeo. They put to Francis thirty-five questions on points of theology. He answered all of them simply and modestly, yet in a way that demonstrated his profound understanding. The Pope declared himself completely satisfied, and embraced and congratulated the candidate. Francis' appointment as coadjutor for the diocese of Geneva was confirmed, and he returned to take up his local work with fresh energy. The following year, his father, aged seventy-nine, died at the Château de Sales, comforted during his last hours by his eldest son.

Early in 1602 Bishop de Granier sent Francis to Paris to negotiate with King Henry IV [1] on behalf of the French section of

1 Henry IV, King of Navarre, after ten years of struggle and conflict, had asserted his sovereignty over all France. He had been educated as a Protestant, but later, as he faced the problem of re-uniting his war-torn country and establishing himself firmly on the throne, he professed conversion to Catholicism.

the diocese of Geneva. During his stay he was invited to preach a course of sermons in the Chapel Royal, which soon proved too small to hold the crowds that came to listen to his uncompromising words of truth. He was in high favor with King Henry, who said of him, "Monseigneur de Genève has every virtue and not a fault." The King offered many inducements to Francis to remain in France, and renewed his persuasions when Francis was again in Paris some years later. But the young bishop would not forsake "my poor bride," as he called his mountain diocese.

On the death of Bishop de Granier in the autumn of 1602, he succeeded to the see of Geneva and took up residence at Annecy, living in a style appropriate to the office but with a household conducted on lines of strict economy. His personal life was one of evangelical poverty. He fulfilled his episcopal duties with devotion and along with the administrative work continued to preach and serve in the confessional. He instituted the teaching of the Catechism throughout his diocese, and at Annecy gave the instruction himself with such fervor that years after his death the "Bishop's Catechisms" were still remembered. Children loved him and followed him about, eager for his blessing.

Through an immense correspondence he brought encouragement and guidance to innumerable persons. For sixteen years a sharer in his work was Jeanne Françoise Fremyot (St. Jane Frances de Chantal), with whom he became acquainted in 1604, while he was preaching at Dijon. The baroness of Chantal was only twenty-four when, after the death of her husband, she decided to enter the religious life. One result of her meeting with Francis was the foundation, in 1610, of the Order of the Visitation, to meet the needs of widows and lonely women in poor health, "strong souls with weak bodies," who were deterred from joining other orders because of their physical condition. Some of St. Francis' best thought is to be found in the letters he wrote to this great woman, who was herself canonized in 1767. What is perhaps his most famous book, the *Introduction to the Devout Life*, grew out of a series of casual letters written to another woman, a cousin by marriage, Madame de Chamoisy, who had placed herself under his guidance. This little collection of short practical lessons on true piety and everyday living was published in 1608. It was soon translated into many languages, and has continued to find readers.

In 1610 came the heavy sorrow of Madame de Boisy's death. Francis was to survive his mother by twelve years—probably the most laborious of his life. His young brother, Jean-François de Sales, was consecrated bishop in 1621 and appointed coadjutor in the diocese of Geneva. His help was welcome to Francis, whose health was failing under the ever-increasing duties. The following year the duke of Savoy, traveling in state to meet King Louis XIII in Languedoc, invited the good bishop of Geneva to join him. Anxious to obtain from Louis certain religious privileges for the French part of his diocese, Francis accepted, although the journey promised to be chilly and uncomfortable. Before leaving Annecy he set his affairs in order, as if he had no expectation of returning. On his arrival at Avignon, he avoided the pomp and entertainments of the brilliant court gathered there, and tried to lead his customary austere life. But the famous bishop was much sought after; people wanted to see him and to hear him preach.

He was worn out, therefore, when he stopped at Lyons on his return. The convent of the Visitation provided him with a cottage on their grounds, where he stayed for a month. He spared himself no labor, giving the nuns instruction and advice, and continuing his preaching and ministrations through Christmas. On December 27 he had a paralytic seizure. He recovered speech and consciousness, and after receiving the Last Sacraments, he murmured words of Scripture, expressing all confidence in God's mercy. On December 28, while those kneeling about his bed recited the litany for the dying, he breathed his last. He was fifty-six, and in the twentieth year of his episcopacy. In his *Treatise on the Love of God,* Francis had written, "The measure of love is to love without measure," a precept which he had consistently taught and lived.

His body was embalmed and brought, all save the heart, to Annecy. It remained in a tomb near the high altar in the church

DEATH OF SAINT FRANCIS XAVIER   Henniger

One of a series of paintings of the life of Saint Francis by a modern painter,
this shows his death off the coast of China in 1552. Others
show his conversion, his commission by Saint Ignatius, his
work in India and in Japan.

Saint Francis Xavier is recognized by the crucifix in his hand,
and by the ship standing off shore. Often he carries a pilgrim's staff.

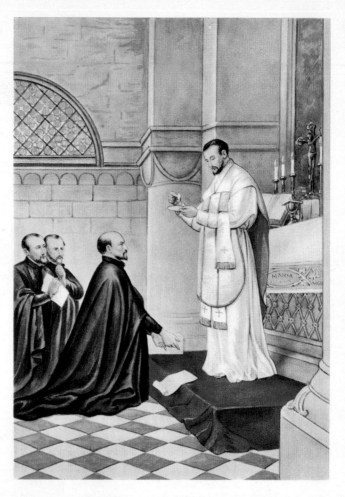

FIRST VOWS OF IGNATIUS AND HIS COMPANIONS   Henniger

The same painter whose "Death of Saint Francis Xavier" is shown facing

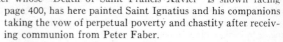

page 400, has here painted Saint Ignatius and his companions taking the vow of perpetual poverty and chastity after receiving communion from Peter Faber.

None of the usual symbols of Saint Ignatius are used in this painting. Generally he is symbolized with a rayed IHC, or with a sword and lance upon an altar.

of the first convent of the Visitation until the French Revolution, when it was removed for fear of desecration. Since then it has been restored to the church of the reconstructed convent at Annecy. Francis was beatified by Alexander VII in 1661,[2] canonized by him in 1665, and proclaimed a Doctor of the Church during the pontificate of Pope Pius IX, in 1877. His heart was preserved in the church of the Visitation at Lyons, in a golden shrine given by Louis XIII.

Introduction to a Devout Life

AUTHOR'S PREFACE

. . . *Almost all who have hitherto treated of devotion have had* in view the instruction of persons wholly retired from the world, or have taught a kind of devotion leading to this absolute retirement; whereas my intention is to instruct such as live in towns, in families, or at court, and who by their condition are obliged to lead, as to the exterior, a life in society; who frequently, under imaginary pretense of impossibility, will not so much as think of undertaking a devout life, believing that as no beast dares taste the seed of the herb *Palma Christi,* so no man ought to aspire to the palm of Christian piety as long as he lives in the bustle of temporal affairs. Now to such I shall prove that as the mother pearl lives in the sea without receiving a drop of salt water, and as towards the Chelidonian islands springs of fresh water may be found in the midst of the sea, and as the firefly passes through flames without burning its wings, so a vigorous and resolute soul may live in the world without being infected by any of its humors, may discover sweet springs of piety amidst its salt waters, and fly amongst the flames of earthly concupiscences without burning the wings of the holy desires of a devout life. . . .

2 For a letter from St. Vincent de Paul to Pope Alexander recommending the canonization of Francis de Sales, see below, p. 425.

CHAPTER I

. . . There are some virtues of such general utility as not only to require an exercise of themselves apart but also to communicate their qualities to the practice of other virtues. Occasions are seldom presented for the exercise of fortitude, magnanimity, and magnificence, but meekness, temperance, modesty, and humility are virtues wherewith all the actions of our life should be tempered. It is true there are other virtues more agreeable, but the use of these is more necessary. Sugar is more agreeable than salt but the use of salt is more necessary and general. Therefore we must constantly have a good store of these general virtues in readiness, since we stand in need of them almost continually. . . .

Among the virtues unconnected with our particular duty we must prefer the excellent to the glittering and showy. Comets appear greater than stars and apparently occupy a greater space, whereas in reality they can neither in magnitude nor quality be compared to the stars; for as they only seem great because they are nearer and appear in a grosser manner than the stars, so there are certain virtues, which, on account of their proximity become more noticeable, or, to use the expression, more material, that are highly exteemed and always preferred by the vulgar. Hence it is that so many prefer corporal alms before spiritual, the hair-shirt, fasting, going barefoot, using the discipline, and other such corporal mortifications before meekness, mildness, modesty, and other mortifications of the heart. Choose then, Philothea,[3] the best virtues, not the most esteemed; the most noble, not the most apparent; those that are actually the best, not those that are the most ostensible or shining. . . .

CHAPTER II

. . . There are certain things which many esteem as virtues which in reality are not; I mean ecstasies or raptures, insensibili-

---

[3] In preparing for publication this series of letters, originally written for the instruction of Madame de Chamoisy, Francis substituted for her name the Greek Philothea, "lover of God."

ties,[4] impassibilities, deific unions, elevations, transformations, and similar perfections, treated of in certain books, which promise to elevate the soul to a contemplation purely intellectual, to an essential application of the spirit, and a supernatural life. But observe well, Philothea, these perfections are not virtues but rather the recompense of virtues, or small specimens of the happiness of the life to come, which God sometimes presents to men to make them enraptured with the whole piece which is only to be found in heaven.

But we must not aspire to these favors, since they are by no means necessary to the serving and loving of God which should be our only pretension, neither are they such as can be obtained by labor and industry, since they are rather experiences than actions, which we may indeed receive, but cannot produce in ourselves. . . . Let us leave these super-eminent favors to elevated souls; we merit not so high a rank in the service of God; we shall be too happy to serve Him in his kitchen or to be his domestics in much lower station. If he should hereafter think proper to admit us into his cabinet or privy council, it will be through the excess of his bountiful goodness. Yea, Philothea, the King of Glory does not recompense his servants according to the dignity of the offices they hold, but according to the measure of the love and humility with which they exercise them. Saul, seeking the asses of his father, found the kingdom of Israel.[5]

CHAPTER IX

One of the best exercises of meekness we can perform is that the object of which is within ourselves, in never fretting at our own imperfections; for though reason requires that we should be sorry when we commit any fault, yet we must refrain from that bitter, gloomy, spiteful, and passionate displeasure for which many are greatly to blame who, being overcome by anger, are angry for having been angry and vexed to see themselves vexed; for by this means they keep their heart perpetually steeped in passion, and

[4] St. Francis lists here certain mystic states to which previous saints had attained.

[5] I Kings ix, 3-20.

though it seems as if the second anger destroyed the first, it serves nevertheless to open a passage for fresh anger on the first occasion that shall present itself. Besides, this anger and vexation against ourselves tend to pride and flow from no other source than self-love, which is troubled and disquieted to see itself imperfect. We must be displeased at our faults but in a peaceable, settled, and firm manner; for as a judge punishes malefactors much more justly when he is guided in his decisions by reason and proceeds with the spirit of tranquillity than when he acts with violence and passion . . . so we correct ourselves much better by a calm and steady repentance than by one that is harsh, turbulent, and passionate; for repentance exercised with violence proceeds not according to the quality of our faults but according to our inclinations. . . .

If, for example, I had formed a strong resolution not to yield to the sin of vanity, and yet had fallen into it, I would not reprove my heart after this manner: 'Art thou not wretched and abominable that after so many resolutions hast suffered thyself to be thus carried away by vanity? Die with shame; lift up no more thine eyes to heaven, blind, impudent traitor as thou art, a rebel to thy God!' but I would correct it thus, rationally saying, by way of compassion: 'Alas, my poor heart, behold we are fallen into the pit we had so firmly resolved to avoid. Well, let us rise again and quit it forever; let us call on the mercy of God and hope that it will assist us to be more constant for the time to come; and let us enter again the path of humility. Let us be encouraged, let us from this day be more on our guard. God will help us; we shall do better.' . . .

However, if anyone should find his heart not sufficiently moved with this mild manner of reprehension, he may use one more sharp and severe to excite it to deeper confusion provided that he afterward closes up all grief and anger with a sweet and consoling confidence in God. . . .

Raise up your heart then again whenever it falls, but fairly and softly, humbling yourself before God through the knowledge of your own misery but without being surprised at your fall, for it is no wonder that weakness should be weak or misery wretched; detest, nevertheless, with all your power the offense God has received through you and return to the way of virtue, which you had forsaken, with great courage and confidence in his mercy.

CHAPTER X

. . . Undertake then all your affairs with a calm and peaceable mind, and endeavor to despatch them in order, one after another; for if you make an effort to do them all at once or in disorder, your spirit will be so overcharged and depressed that it will probably sink under the burden without effecting anything.

In all your affairs rely wholly on divine Providence, through which alone you must look for success; labor, nevertheless, quietly on your part to cooperate with its designs, and then you may be assured, if you trust as you ought in God; the success which shall come to you shall be always that which is the most profitable for you, whether it appear good or bad according to your private judgment. Imitate little children who, as they with one hand hold fast by their father, and with the other gather strawberries or blackberries along the hedges; so you, gathering and handling the goods of this world with one hand, must with the other always hold fast the hand of your heavenly Father, turning yourself towards him from time to time to see if your actions or occupations be pleasing to him; but above all things take heed that you never leave his protecting hand nor think to gather more, for should he forsake you, you will not be able to go a step further without falling to the ground.

My meaning is, Philothea, that amidst those ordinary affairs and occupations that require not so earnest an attention, you should look more on God than on them; and when they are of such importance as to require your whole attention, that then also you should look from time to time towards God, like mariners, who, to arrive at the port to which they are bound, look more up towards heaven than down on the sea on which they sail. Thus will God work with you, in you, and for you, and your labor will be followed by consolation.

(Introduction to the Devout Life, New York, n.d.)

Saint Isaac Jogues

Martyr

1 6 4 6

(September 26)

The labors of the Jesuit and Franciscan missionaries in the New World form an important chapter in the history of the Church and of the Western Hemisphere. These missionaries were for the most part men of culture and learning, carefully chosen and rigorously trained. Many of them gave up important careers in the Church to endure the dangers and privations of the wilderness. In New France, as Canada was then called, where Isaac Jogues spent his missionary years, their lot was hardship, disease, solitude, and, not infrequently, torture or violent death. The perils of forest and trail, the intense cold, the wretched food and verminous huts of the Indians, changed them, after a few years, into haggard old men; yet their spirits remained undaunted, strengthened as they were by an indomitable faith. What the American historian, Francis Parkman, in *The Jesuits of North America*, wrote of Father Brébeuf, Jesuit leader in Canada, applies almost equally to the other members of this noble band: "His was the ancient faith uncurtailed, redeemed from the decay of centuries, kindled with new life, and stimulated to a preternatural growth and fruitfulness."

The pioneer French explorers, Cartier and Champlain, were men of piety, eager to have the aid of the religious orders in opening up the new continent, and both Jesuits and Franciscans were encouraged to establish Catholicism in Canada. Jesuits led the way here, while Franciscans and Dominicans became active in the southwest of the United States and in South America. Early in the seventeenth century the Jesuits began to arrive in Quebec; they would quickly push on into the interior, to be engulfed by the forest or to be taken prisoner by the Indians and treated as slaves or objects of barter; yet at times they met with a heartening response. Among the more notable of these men were Brébeuf, Daniel, Massé, Lalemant, Chabanel, Ragueneau, Garnier, Jogues, and Le Jeune. It was Le Jeune, a Huguenot in early life, who conceived the plan for keeping his superiors of the Society of Jesus, as well as the European laity, informed of the great undertaking, by the careful compilation of missionaries' letters, which described in detail their experiences and impressions. Every summer, for a period of forty years, these reports were despatched back to Paris, where they were published serially under the title of *Jesuit Relations*. They form an historical chronicle of the highest value, and it is to them that we are mainly indebted for our knowledge of Father Jogues.

Called the "Apostle of the Mohawks," and known to the Mohawks themselves as Ondessonk, "the indomitable one," Isaac Jogues has been selected to represent this group of North American saints. He was born on January 10, 1607, at Orleans, France, into a good bourgeois family; at the age of seventeen he entered the Jesuit novitiate school at Rouen. Later he studied at the royal college of La Fleche, which Henry IV had founded a short time before. From one of the teachers there, Louis Lalemant, who had two brothers and a nephew serving as missionaries in Canada, the young man heard stories that may well have turned his thoughts towards the New World. He also had meetings with the pioneers, Brébeuf and Massé, on their return from Canada in 1629, when Quebec was captured by the English. Three years later the province was again in French hands, and Richelieu had formed the Company of One Hundred Associates, which was to control New France for the next thirty odd years. Isaac Jogues continued his education at the College of Clermont, University of Paris, and in due time was ordained and accepted for missionary service. He was already recognized as an able scholar, with talents for writing and teaching. In the summer of 1636, at the age of twenty-nine, he embarked for Canada with several of his fellows, among them Charles Garnier. Drawings of Jogues made at about this time reveal features of unusual refinement; this air of delicacy was, however, deceptive, for beneath it lay heroic powers of physical endurance.

Sailing on the same ship with the young missionaries was Sieur Huault de Montmagny, the new French governor sent out to replace Champlain, who had died a few months before. After a stormy voyage, they sailed up the St. Lawrence to the lofty citadel of Quebec. On arrival Jogues wrote as follows to his mother: "I do not know what it is to enter Heaven, but this I know—that it would be difficult to experience in this world a joy more excessive and more overflowing than I felt in setting foot in the New World, and celebrating my first Mass on the day of the Visitation." His later letters show the same exaltation of spirit.

Father Jogues' companions were at once sent on westward to join Father Brébeuf, who in 1626 had established an outpost on the peninsula of Lake Huron, to minister to the Huron Indians, one of the less warlike tribes. Jogues went with them as far as the settlement of Trois Rivières, and there, some weeks later, he saw a flotilla of canoes descending the St. Lawrence. In the first, wielding a paddle, was Father Anthony Daniel, one of Brébeuf's co-workers, exhausted and emaciated, his cassock in tatters. He was bound for Quebec for a period of recuperation, and Jogues was to replace him. The young missionary lost no time in organizing the expedition. The post was nine hundred miles away, up the river, through forests, across portages. On long trips such as these the missionaries and their guides had to carry provisions, and sometimes stored corn in *caches* by the way.

Arriving at last at the Lake Huron post, Father Jogues collapsed in Brébeuf's arms. Almost at once he fell ill of a fever, which in turn struck down others. At this time the fathers were living in crude huts, and their food was poor and scanty. When the missionaries had recovered, a similar epidemic broke out among the Indians, who, blaming it on the Black Coats, as they called the Jesuits, threatened to kill them all. Brébeuf conciliated them and by the following year relations had so improved that he was able to write in one of his reports: "We are gladly heard, and there is scarcely a village that has not invited us to go to it. . . . And at last it is understood from our whole conduct that we have not come to buy skins or to carry on any traffic, but solely to teach them, and to procure for them their souls' health." Indian good will, however, was fickle, and before long the medicine men had fomented so much hostility that in a tribal council the Indians decided that the Jesuit priests must die. Once more the Indians were pacified.

For six years Father Jogues labored here. He learned the language and ways of the Hurons, developed into a skilled woodsman with great stamina, and often went on missions. He and Garnier were chosen to go south to the Petun Indians, called the Tobacco Nation, with the Gospel, and he and Raymbault were sent to make the acquaintance of the Indians further north. On this latter trip, traversing uncharted lands and waterways, they may have been the first white men to stand on the shore of Lake Superior, at the site of the present city of Sault Ste. Marie. About 2,000 Ojibways were gathered there to celebrate their Feast of the Dead, and Jogues addressed them. He erected a cross facing west towards the country of the Sioux, who were settled around the headwaters of the Mississippi. This was thirty years before Père Marquette set out to explore the great river. With the good will of the Indians in these parts gained, the way was prepared for Marquette and others, who were able to carry on their work without suffering martyrdom.

Back on the Huron peninsula, near the mouth of the Wye River, the Jesuits established their main settlement, calling it Ste. Marie. A church, living quarters, a cemetery, a hospital, and a fort were eventually built, and a way of life that was half monastic, half patriarchal grew up in this remote spot. The surrounding lands were cleared and cultivated, food was stored against famine, and here the Indians came in times of sickness and trouble, as well as on Sundays and feast days. Although no tangible evidence of the Jesuits' enterprise survives today save a part of the foundation of the fort, archeologists are of the opinion that the buildings were well-designed and impressive; the achievement is noteworthy in view of the scarcity of materials and the primitive nature of the available tools. Here in the lonely north woods the missionaries tried to create order and organization and to demonstrate in their manner of life the teachings of their religion.

The year 1642 brought a very poor harvest and much sickness among the Indians. Also Father Raymbault was ill and needed medical treatment. Father Jogues was appointed to lead an expedition to Quebec for supplies and reinforcements. The journey was safely made, but unfortunately they had been sighted on the way down by a Mohawk scouting party. The Mohawks were members of the confederation of Five Nations into which the great Iroquois people had banded themselves, and were the sworn enemies of the Hurons. More Mohawk warriors were recruited by the scouting party and they lay in wait for the Black Robes and their detested Huron converts as the flotilla traveled back upstream.

Father Jogues was in command of the twelve canoes, carrying in all some forty persons; there were but three white men—William Couture, René Goupil, and himself. Goupil was a young Frenchman who had failed of admission to the Society of Jesus because of poor health, but he had nevertheless taken up the study of medicine and had come to Canada to offer his services to the missionaries. Couture was another layman of great courage and integrity. Among the company was a noted Huron chief, a Huron medicine man and his young niece Thérèse, who had been trained by the Ursulines in Quebec and was returning to teach her people. The canoes were loaded with vestments, altar vessels, bread and wine for the Eucharist, writing materials, tools, and food. About a day's journey beyond Trois Rivières, the main body of warriors fell upon them, killing or maiming some and taking many prisoners, including the girl Thérèse. The more agile of the Hurons escaped to the woods. Father Jogues could also have escaped, but gave himself up when he saw that Goupil had been taken. Couture was singled out for severe torture later because in the fray he had slain a Mohawk leader.

The white men and the Huron prisoners were led south to the home ground of the Mohawks in east central New York. At the southern end of Lake Champlain is a small island, now called Jogues Island, which is believed to have been the scene of barbarous cruelties inflicted on the prisoners. Jogues wrote: "We were made to go up from the shore between two lines of Indians who were armed with clubs, sticks, and knives. I was the last and blows were showered on me. I fell on the ground and thought my end had come, but they lifted me up all streaming with blood and carried me more dead than alive to the platform." Worse tortures followed. The Iroquois were especially cruel to the Huron converts. At this time and during subsequent torturings Father Jogues suffered the loss of two fingers.

The horrible journey south continued. Their destination was Ossernenon, a village on the banks of the Mohawk River, a little above where the Schoharie flows into the larger stream. Known as the Lower Castle, it was in fact a very strong fortress which served to protect the Mohawks against their enemies as well as from the rigors of winter. It consisted of a double palisade, with a trench between, and, inside the enclosure, a number of communal dwellings called Long Houses, each of which was large enough to accommodate several families or clans. The captives were exposed to mistreatment there and in the other Mohawk villages of Teonontogen and Andaragon. Couture was left in one of them, while Jogues and Goupil were brought back to Ossernenon, where the Indians apparently intended to burn them alive. The news of their capture soon reached the Protestant Dutch settlement of New Amsterdam at the mouth of the Hudson, and Commandant Van Corlear came up in person to ransom them. His overtures were rejected, but the Indians decided not to kill such valuable captives

—perhaps in the hope of getting an even higher ransom from the French.

Before long, however, Goupil was tomahawked from behind by an Indian who had observed him making the sign of the cross on the head of an Indian girl, a gesture which, according to the Indian medicine men, brought bad luck. Jogues, who happened to be nearby, took the dying man in his arms, and gave him the last absolution before he died. The Indians snatched the body away from the grieving priest and concealed it in a stream. Guided by a friendly Indian, Jogues went in search of the corpse, and on finding it, hid it deeper in the stream, hoping to return and give it proper burial before he too was killed. The Indians thwarted him by destroying the body. Father Jogues wrote of the young doctor's death: "Thus on the 28th of September this angel of innocence and martyr of Jesus Christ was immolated in his thirty-fifth year, for Him who had given His life for his ransom. He had consecrated his heart and soul to God and his life and labor to the welfare of the poor Indians."

Jogues' slavery lasted for more than a year. His record of it, written for his Superior, has been studied by scholars who are amazed at his endurance. "He would sometimes escape," Parkman wrote, ". . . and wander in the forest, telling his beads and repeating passages of Scripture. In a remote and lonely spot he cut the bark in the form of a cross from the trunk of a great tree; and here he made his prayers. This living martyr, half clad in shaggy furs, kneeling in the snow among the icicled rocks and beneath the gloomy pines, bowing in adoration before the emblem of his faith in which was his only consolation and his only hope, is alike a theme for the pen and a subject for the pencil." Later Jogues was to report to his spiritual guide, "The only sin I can remember during my captivity is that I sometimes looked on the approach of death with complacency." The Indians were not without respect for their strange captive, naming him "the indomitable one." He had at least one good friend among the Mohawks, an old woman whom he called "aunt." She tried to heal his wounds and to warn and protect him when danger threatened. His days were passed in menial work, learning the language, and comforting Huron prisoners who were sometimes brought in. He was taken on fishing and hunting expeditions, when he suffered much from hunger and exposure. As opportunity offered, he baptized children he found dying. During the year he baptized some seventy persons, New York State's first Catholic baptismal record.

The Dutch hoped to rescue him, though they did not wish to jeopardize their own fairly peaceful relations with the Mohawks. Their efforts finally freed Jogues. His captors were lured into bringing him to Fort Orange, at Rensselaerwyck, now Albany. The Dutch told him on arrival that it would be possible to escape that night to a boat lying offshore in the Hudson which was ready to sail for Bordeaux. He and his Indian guards were to sleep in a Dutch farmer's big barn. Before dawn, guided by a farm hand, he picked his way over the sleeping Indians around him, and got to the river. Rowing out to the anchored vessel, he was taken on board and concealed. The enraged Mohawks were soon on his trail, threatening reprisals against the Dutch for their part in the affair. Learning of this, Jogues insisted on going back on shore. "If this trouble has been caused by me," he said, "I am ready to appease it at the loss of my life. I have never wished to escape if it meant injury to the least man in the colony." But the Indians were now persuaded to relinquish all claim to his person for the sum of 300 livres, which the Dutch paid. Yet Jogues' life continued in jeopardy, and for the next six weeks, while awaiting another boat, he was kept in close, uncomfortable confinement, befriended by the Dutch pastor, Dominie Megalolensis.

At last, Jogues got passage down the river to New Amsterdam, on the island of "Manhatte." His descriptions of the fort and the town, now New York City, have been incorporated in the official records of the state. He was the first Catholic priest to visit the settlement, and to the two Catholics living there at the time he offered the comforts and rites of the Church. "No religion is publicly exercised here but the Calvinist," he noted, "and orders are to admit none but Calvinists; but this is not observed. There are in the colony Catholics, Puritans, Lutherans, Anabaptists, etc."

On November 5, 1643, Jogues sailed, and towards the end of December reached the coast of Cornwall. He was able to get aboard a collier bound for France and on Christmas Day was put ashore in Brittany. Kindly people helped him reach the town of Rennes. At the rector's house, he sent word by a servant that he was the bearer of news from New France. Unknown to Jogues, his own fate was a matter of widespread concern in France, for the latest volume of *Jesuit Relations* had contained the details of his capture. When the rector came to the door, after an exchange of courtesies, he asked the shabbily-dressed man if he had known Father Jogues. "Very well indeed," was the answer. "Have they murdered him?" "No, Father, he is alive and free—and I am he!"

The astonishing news spread quickly. Jogues reported to his superiors, and such was his fame that ladies, courtiers, and even the Queen Regent desired to meet him and do him honor. Jogues was received by Anne of Austria, and told his story. At its conclusion, the Queen arose and stooped to kiss the mutilated hands, which the priest habitually kept covered by the folds of his cassock. But public acclaim was the last thing the modest priest desired; he even refrained from going to see his mother, wishing to spare her the pain of another parting and the sight of his maimed hands. He feared that their condition would debar him from saying Mass, but Pope Urban VIII abrogated in his case the canonical ruling.

Father Jogues' only desire was to get back to Canada, and in June, 1644, he was again in Quebec. From there he was sent to Montreal, to spend his time helping to build up that new outpost, until the cessation of warfare would permit him to return to the Hurons. Two years later an embassy of Iroquois came to Trois Rivières to discuss terms of truce and the ransom of prisoners. Many fine speeches were made and gifts were exchanged. The Jesuit priest participated in these conclaves. After the deliberations were concluded, the French thought it prudent to send a conciliatory deputation to meet with other Iroquois chieftains at

Ossernenon. This embassy was led by Father Jogues and Sieur Jean Bourdon, an engineer, who represented the government of New France. "Oh, how I should regret to lose so glorious an occasion," wrote the priest to his superior before starting, "when it may depend only on me that some souls be saved! I hope that His goodness, which has not abandoned me in the hour of trial, will aid me still."

The party traveled south, stopping first at Fort Orange, where the priest saw again his Dutch friends and reimbursed them for his ransom of the year before. The Dutch were astonished to learn that he was going back to the scene of his painful captivity. Ondessonk indeed deserved his name! The Mohawks, too, when he appeared among them, were impressed by his courage and disarmed by his gentleness, for he showed no trace of ill-will. The old "aunt" greeted with friendly words the man who had been the tribe's despised captive and who now returned as an envoy of peace. "With us you will always have a mat to lie on and a fire to warm yourself," she told him. Gifts were exchanged between Frenchmen and Indians, and belts of wampum offered for the release of the Hurons held captive. Thus the purpose of the visit was achieved, the pact confirmed, and Jogues went back to Quebec. He was to return to spend the winter among the Mohawks, now that friendly relations were established.

In the meanwhile, after Jogues and Bourdon had left Ossernenon, an epidemic broke out, caterpillars ate the crops, and famine threatened. As usual, the Mohawks blamed all their troubles on Black Coat, even though, on his latest trip, he had not worn priestly garb. But had he not left with them a mysterious box? True, he had showed them its contents, which consisted of personal necessaries, but he had locked it up and asked them to keep it. No doubt a devil was concealed in the box, to bring upon them all manner of evils. They threw the box into the river. Totally unaware of the mounting tension and antagonism, Jogues, with John Lalande, a lay missionary, once more started south for Ossernenon. On the trail they were met by a party of Mohawks on the warpath. The three or four Hurons serving Jogues as guides turned back to escape capture, while the two Frenchmen were led on as prisoners. At Ossernenon Jogues' arguments seemed to affect his hearers. "I am a man like yourselves," he replied to their charges. "I do not fear death or torture. I do not know why you wish to kill me. I come here to confirm the peace and show you the way to Heaven, and you treat me like a dog." In the councils the majority were ready to give the brave Ondessonk his freedom, but the minority faction, members of the Bear clan, took matters into their own hands. They invited Jogues to pay them a visit, and as he unsuspectingly entered the cabin of the Bear chief, he was brutally tomahawked. The next day Lalande met the same fate, and both bodies were thrown into a nearby ravine. Their heads were cut off and placed on poles facing the trail by which they had come, as if in warning to other Black Robes. When the news of the martyrdom was carried to Fort Orange, the Dutch pastor hastened to Ossernenon to denounce the Mohawks for their crime. Later on some of the Indians went to the fort with Father Jogues' breviary, missal, and cassock, hoping to make a profitable trade, and the pastor again censured them.

The Iroquois now once more began to attack and plunder the Huron villages, sparing neither Christians nor non-Christians. Garnier, Daniel, Gabriel, Lalemant, and Brébeuf were killed. But in the Mohawk Valley the example of Jogues' heroism was not forgotten, for the gentle priest had possessed in high degree the virtue the Indians most admired, bravery. And when, some years later, there was peace, the three Jesuit priests sent from Canada to establish the Mission of the Martyrs were well received. Before long Mohawk converts were traveling to the seminary in Quebec to be trained as Christian leaders. Today, near the town of Auriesville, New York, which on the best archeological authority is accepted as the site of Ossernenon, there is a famous Catholic shrine and pilgrimage place. It was dedicated in 1885 to the Martyrs of North America and to their Indian converts. Here pilgrims come to honor the memory of the Jesuits of the seventeenth century who

SAINT TERESA OF AVILA   Suter

A modern painting of Saint Teresa receiving inspiration from the Holy Spirit
as she writes "either to suffer or to die," a reflection of her
desire to suffer for God on earth and to be united with Him
in death.

Saint Teresa is symbolized by the dove, and by a book and
pen.

SANTA ROSA LIMENSIS   H. L. Camusat de Riancey
An example of the particularly ornate work which was lavished on holy pictures in earlier days, this picture of Saint Rose in the habit of
a Dominican nun copies the style of Italian painters of the
Renaissance.

Saint Rose of Lima is shown with a crown of thorns and with
a spray of lilies, the emblem of purity.

faced death in the wilderness. The eight martyrs—Jogues, Lalande, Brébeuf, Lalemant, Garnier, Daniel, Goupil, and Chabanel—were solemnly beatified in 1925 and canonized in 1930.

Letter to a Friend [1]

. . . *The Iroquois have come to make some presents to our* governor, ransom some prisoners he held, and treat of peace with him in the name of the whole country. It has been concluded, to the great joy of France. It will last as long as pleases the Almighty.

To maintain, and see what can be done for the instruction of these tribes, it is here deemed expedient to send them some father. I have reason to think I shall be sent, since I have some knowledge of the language and country. You see what need I have of the powerful aid of prayers while amidst these savages. I will have to remain among them, almost without liberty to pray, without Mass, without Sacraments, and be responsible for every accident among the Iroquois, French, Algonquins, and others. But what shall I say? My hope is in God, who needs not us to accomplish his designs. We must endeavor to be faithful to Him and not spoil His work by our shortcomings. . . .

My heart tells me that if I have the happiness of being employed in this mission, *Ibo et non redibo* (I shall go and shall not return); but I shall be happy if our Lord will complete the sacrifice where He has begun it, and make the little blood I have shed in that land the earnest of what I would give from every vein of my body and my heart.

In a word, this people is "a bloody spouse" to me (Exodus iv,25). May our good Master, who has purchased them in His blood, open to them the door of His Gospel, as well as to the four allied nations near them.

Adieu, dear Father. Pray Him to unite me inseparably to Him.

ISAAC JOGUES, S.J.

[1] This letter was written to one of the Canadian fathers, just before Jogues started south on his last journey.

Saint Vincent de Paul

Founder of the Vincentians

1 6 6 0

(July 19)

Like his fellow saint, Francis de Sales, who was his friend and
contemporary, Vincent de Paul performed an invaluable service to the Catholic Church in a period of confusion and laxness.
But unlike the aristocratic bishop of Geneva, Vincent was born
in poverty, of peasant stock. His birthplace was Pouy, near Dax
in Gascony, in southwest France; the year was 1576. Jean de Paul
and Bertrande de Moras, his parents, were sturdy farming people
who reared a family of four sons and two daughters. Observing
young Vincent's quick intelligence, his father sent him to be educated by the Cordelier Brothers [1] at Dax. When the boy had been
at school for four years, a lawyer of the town engaged him as
tutor to his children, thus enabling Vincent to go on with his
studies without further expense to his parents. Vincent continued
his education at the Spanish University of Saragossa, and then
returned to France to attend the University of Toulouse. At the
age of twenty-four he was ordained priest by the bishop of
Perigueux, but remained at Toulouse for another four years to
take the degree of Doctor of Theology.

Beyond an aptitude for study and a certain persistence in
achieving his ends, there is nothing in Vincent's life up to this time
to suggest his future fame and sanctity. He now went on a short
journey which was to change his whole life. The scholarly young
priest was to be captured at sea by pirates and sold as a slave in

[1] Cordeliers was a name popularly given to the stricter branch of the Franciscan Order.

Africa! This extraordinary happening came about in the following way. Vincent, having returned home after receiving his degree, went back to Toulouse to recover by process of law a small legacy which had been left him by an old woman of that city. Homeward bound, he made the trip from Marseilles to Narbonne by water, on board a small coastwise vessel. The ship was set upon by three brigantines manned by Barbary pirates, who were at this time a menace to all Mediterranean shipping. When the Christians refused to strike their flag, the infidels attacked them with arrows. Three were killed and several, including Vincent, were wounded. Those who remained alive were put in chains, and the pirates straightway sailed to Africa with their human cargo. Landing at Tunis, the pirates led their prisoners through the streets of the city, after which they were brought back to the vessel and sold to the highest bidder, like cattle. Vincent, bought by a fisherman, was sold again to an aged Moslem, a humane man, who had spent fifty years in search of the "philosopher's stone." He grew fond of his slave, to whom he gave long lectures on alchemy and Mohammedanism; he even promised to make Vincent his heir and also to communicate to him all the secrets of his science if he adopted the religion of Islam. The young priest, terrified that his faith would be corrupted in this alien environment, prayed for divine protection, particularly for the intercession of the Blessed Virgin.

Vincent continued firm in his faith and lived on with the old man until his death, when he became the property of his master's nephew, who soon sold him to a renegade Christian, a native of Nice. This man, a convert to Mohammedanism, had three wives, one of whom was a Turkish woman. She often wandered into the field where the new Christian slave was at work, and out of idle curiosity would ask him to sing songs in praise of his God. With tears running down his cheeks Vincent would obediently sing certain Psalms, among which was Psalm cxxxvii, "By the waters of Babylon," in which the Jews bewailed their captivity. The Turkish woman now began to reproach her husband for abandoning his religion, and kept on until, without herself accepting the faith, she made him return to it. He repented of his apostasy, and he and Vincent made their escape from Africa together. They crossed the Mediterranean safely in a small boat, landed near Marseilles, in June, 1607, then traveled up to Avignon. There the apostate confessed, and abjured Mohammedanism before the papal vice-legate. The following year, accompanied by Vincent, he went to Rome, where he entered the order of the Brothers of St. John of God,[2] who serve in hospitals.

Vincent now returned to France and chanced to be brought to the attention of Queen Marguerite of Valois, who appointed him her almoner. This office gave him the income from a small abbey. For a time he lodged in the same house as a lawyer, who was one day robbed of a considerable sum. He openly charged Vincent with the theft and spoke against him to all his friends. Vincent did nothing save quietly deny the charge, adding, "God knows the truth." For six years he bore the slander, making no further denial, and at last the real thief confessed. Speaking as though the victim had been someone else, Vincent once told this story at a conference with his priests, in order to show that patience, silence, and resignation are generally the best defense of innocence.

Vincent soon came to know a famous priest of Paris, Monsieur de Bérulle, afterwards a cardinal. Father Bérulle, who at that time was founding a branch of the Congregation of the Oratory in France, recognized Vincent's worth. He found for him a curacy at Clichy, in the outskirts of Paris, and later through his influence Vincent became tutor to the children of Philip de Gondi, Count of Joigny and general of the galleys of France. The countess, a serious-minded woman, was so impressed by Vincent that she eventually chose him as her spiritual director.

In 1617, while the family was at its country seat at Folleville, in the diocese of Amiens, Vincent was sent for to hear the confession of a peasant who lay dangerously ill. In the course of his

---

[2] John of God was a Portuguese shepherd who turned soldier, and later devoted his life to the care of the sick. He became head of the Brothers of Charity, a lay society which was later raised to an order under Augustinian Rule.

questioning, Vincent learned that every one of the peasant's previous confessions had been sacrilegious. On his recovery the man declared, in the presence of the countess, that he would have been eternally lost if he had not spoken with Vincent. Unlike the majority of noble women of this period, who felt no responsibility for their dependents, this good lady was concerned about the spiritual welfare of her tenantry. She persuaded Vincent to preach in the parish church of Folleville and instruct the people. Such crowds came to confess that he called the Jesuits of Amiens to his aid. The Congregation of the Mission had its inception at this time.

Vincent left the household of the count that same year to become pastor of the parish of Chatillon-les-Dombes, which had long been neglected, its church virtually abandoned to the elements. By restoring the church, by instituting the habit of regular worship, he created a new spirit which helped to regenerate the whole district. He converted the notorious count of Rougemont and many other aristocrats from their dissolute lives. Seeing how effective Vincent's labors were, the countess now offered him a large sum of money to found a perpetual mission in whatever place and manner he thought fit. Nothing at first came of the idea, for Vincent seemed reluctant to undertake so important an enterprise. Meanwhile the countess secured her husband's help in organizing a company of zealous missionaries to work among their own vassals and the peasants of the countryside. They also discussed the plan for a perpetual mission with the count's brother, Jean François de Gondi, archbishop of Paris, who gave them the College des Bons Enfants as a reception house for the proposed new community.

The countess had obtained from Vincent a promise to continue as her spiritual director while she lived and to assist her at the end. She was in failing health and died in the summer of 1625, whereupon Vincent went to Paris to establish himself at the College des Bons Enfants. Now, at the age of forty-nine, he was free to assume the position of director. He drew up rules and constitutions for the house, and these were approved by Pope Urban VIII in 1632. In that year they were given the priory of St. Lazare, henceforth the chief house of the congregation. The Fathers of the Mission thus came to be called Lazarists, although they are more generally known as Vincentians. The Congregation consisted then, as it still does, of priests and laymen who, after a period of probation, take four simple vows, poverty, chastity, obedience, and stability. They live from a common fund and devote themselves to sanctifying their own spirits and to converting sinners. They are employed in missions, especially to country people, teaching the Catechism, preaching, reconciling differences, and performing charitable deeds. Some of them conduct seminaries. Their institutions now flourish in all parts of the world. Vincent lived to see twenty-five more communities founded in France, northern Italy, Poland, and elsewhere.

Extensive and rewarding as this work was, it did not satisfy Vincent's passion for helping suffering people. He started confraternities to seek out and care for the sick in every parish. From these groups, under the leadership of Louise de Marillac, sprang the Sisters of Charity,[3] "whose chapel is the parish church, whose cloister the streets of the city and wards of the hospitals." Vincent persuaded a number of noble and wealthy Parisian women, who had hitherto never given a thought to the misery of others, to band together as Ladies of Charity, to collect funds and assist in many practical ways. He made plans for the founding of several hospitals to serve the needy sick, foundlings, and the aged. At Marseilles a home was opened for exhausted galley-slaves. It was the custom at this time in France to punish criminals by condemning them to service in the war galleys of the state. Under the lash and chained to their benches, they performed the cruelly hard labor of rowing these cumbersome vessels with their many-tiered banks of oars. After a few years the prisoners were broken and

---

[3] Blessed Louise de Marillac was one of the first women to be drawn into the movement. The Congregation of Sisters of Charity was founded in 1634. They are active, unenclosed nuns who devote their lives to serving the needy and the ill. The habit resembles a French peasant dress—blue-gray gown with wide sleeves and apron, white linen cap and "wings." The order is worldwide and now numbers some thirty-seven thousand members.

useless; now for the first time they had a hospital and various other forms of aid.

For men about to take Holy Orders, Vincent devised a set of spiritual exercises, and special exercises also for those desiring to make general Confession, or to settle on a vocation. He conferred frequently with the clergy on the correction of the shocking slackness, ignorance, and abuses that were all around them. To the Biblical injunction, "Thou art thy brother's keeper," he gave new practical meaning, by laying down patterns of philanthropy that have been followed ever since. To the worldly society of seventeenth-century Paris he presented a much-needed example of selfless charity.

The great political and religious conflict known as the Thirty Years War was now raging. Vincent, on hearing of the wretchedness of the people of Lorraine, collected alms for them in Paris. He sent missionaries to other countries affected by the war. Recalling his own sorrows as a slave in Tunisia, he raised enough money to ransom some twelve hundred Christian slaves in Africa. He had influence with the powerful Cardinals Richelieu and De Retz, directors of French foreign policy; and was sent for by King Louis XIII, to minister to him as he lay dying. The king's widow, Anne of Austria, now Queen Regent, had him made a member of the Council of Conscience of the five-year-old prince, the future Louis XIV. Vincent continued to be in favor at court, and during the civil war of the Fronde, tried to persuade the Queen Regent to give up her unpopular minister, Cardinal Mazarin, to help pacify and unify the people.

Thus, although he had no advantages of birth, fortune, or handsome appearance, or any showy gifts at all, Vincent de Paul's later years became one long record of accomplishment. In the midst of great affairs, his soul never strayed from God; always when he heard the clock strike, he made the sign of the cross as an act of divine love. Under setbacks, calumnies, and frustrations, and there were many, he preserved his serenity of mind. He looked on all events as manifestations of the Divine will, to which he was perfectly resigned. Yet by nature, he once wrote of himself, he was "of a bilious temperament and very subject to anger." Without divine grace, he declared, he would have been "in temper hard and repellent, rough and crabbed." With grace, he became tender-hearted to the point of looking on the troubles of all mankind as his own. His tranquillity seemed to lift him above petty disturbances. Self-denial, humility, and an earnest spirit of prayer were the means by which he attained to this degree of perfection. Once when two men of exceptional learning and ability asked to be admitted to his congregation, Vincent courteously refused them, saying: "Your abilities raise you above our low state. Your talents may be of good service in some other place. As for us, our highest ambition is to instruct the ignorant, to bring sinners to a spirit of penitence, and to plant the Gospel spirit of charity, humility, and simplicity in the hearts of all Christians." One of his rules was that, so far as possible, a man ought not to speak of himself or his own concerns, since such discourse usually proceeds from and strengthens pride and self-love.

Vincent was deeply concerned at the rise and spread of the Jansenist heresy.[4] He protested hotly against a view of God that seemed to limit His mercy, and no priest teaching that error could remain in his congregation. "I have made the doctrine of grace the subject of my prayer for three months," he said, "and every day God has confirmed my faith that our Lord died for us all and that He desires to save the whole world."

As the end of his long life drew near, Vincent endured much suffering. On September 27, 1660, he received the Last Sacraments, and died calmly in his chair, being then eighty-five years old. He was buried in the church of St. Lazare, Paris. In 1729 he was beatified by Benedict XIII, and canonized by Clement XII in 1737. Pope Leo XIII proclaimed him patron of all charitable societies. His emblem is, most appropriately, children.

---

[4] Jansenism was a heresy propounded by Cornelius Jansen, bishop of Ypres. It denied the freedom of the will and the ability of man to contribute to his own salvation. God, it held, had predestined some to eternal life and others to be forever lost. Jansenism had won many believers in France at this time.

Letter of St. Vincent de Paul to Pope Alexander VII

Most Holy Father: *June 6, 1659*

I know that the whole of France and many other nations are urgently beseeching Your Holiness to deign to inscribe on the calendar of Saints the name of the Most Illustrious and Most Reverend Francis de Sales, Bishop of Geneva. I am also aware that Your Holiness, filled with admiration for the rare virtues that shone in him, and the books of lofty devotion which he composed, holds his memory in profound veneration, and, consequently, that Your Holiness seems inclined to carry out this design, without there being any need of petitions from others and, especially, from such a wretched and unknown individual as myself. Nevertheless, Most Holy Father, as I was on rather familiar terms with this servant of God, who often deigned to hold converse with me, either about the Institute of the Religious of the Visitation of Holy Mary, which he established and founded, or on other pious matters, I have admired so many, and so great, virtues in him, that it is hard for me now to keep silence; I cannot be the only person who says nothing.

Faith, Hope, Charity, and the other cardinal and moral Christian virtues seemed almost innate in him and, taken together, formed in him, at least to my way of thinking, such a fund of goodness that, during an illness which occurred to me shortly after a conversation with him, I turned over in my mind his sweetness and exquisite meekness, and often repeated to myself: 'Oh! how good must God be, since the Bishop of Geneva is so kind.'

If I were alone, Most Holy Father, in thus thinking about him, I might believe I was deceiving myself but, as the whole world shares these sentiments, what else is needed, Most Holy Father, but a word from Your Holiness to consummate such a holy enterprise, by resolving to inscribe his name in the catalogue of the saints, and setting him up for the veneration of the whole world! All the priests of our Congregation and myself prostrate at the feet of Your Holiness, now most humbly beg you to do so. May God Almighty deign to grant you many long years for the welfare of His Church!

Most Holy Father, etc., etc.

> (*Letters of St. Vincent de Paul.* Burns, Oates, 1937.)

Saint Margaret Mary Alacoque

Virgin

1 6 9 0

(*October 17*)

In seventeenth-century France the faith of the people had been badly shaken; there was rebellion against the Church and neglect of its teachings; the rise of Protestantism and the spread of the heresy of Jansenism [1] both had a part in the weakening of the structure built up through the ages. But as every threat brings its response, so now there rose up fresh, strong forces to counter these trends. Three famous religious, who are today venerated as saints, were particularly effective: John Eudes and Claude de la Columbière were French Jesuit priests and writers; Margaret Mary Alacoque was a simple nun of the order of the Visitation. Their special work was to popularize the devotion to the Sacred Heart of Jesus. To represent this trio and this movement, we have chosen Margaret Mary Alacoque.

She was born in 1647 at Janots, a small town of Burgundy, the fifth of seven children, of Claude and Philiberte Alacoque. Her father was a prosperous notary; the family owned a country house and farmland, and had some aristocratic connections. Margaret's godmother was a neighbor, the Countess of Corcheval. As a small child Margaret spent a great deal of time with her, but these visits were brought to a sudden end by the death of the countess. The father died of pneumonia when Margaret was about eight, and this was another severe shock to the little girl. Claude had loved his family dearly but had been short-sighted and extravagant. His

[1] For Jansenism, see *St. Vincent de Paul*, n. 5.

death put them in hard straits. However, Margaret was sent to school with the Urbanist Sisters at Charolles. She loved the peace and order of the convent life, and the nuns were so impressed by her devotion that she was allowed to make her First Communion at the age of nine. A rheumatic affliction kept her bedridden for four years. During this time she was brought home, where some of her father's relatives had moved in and taken over the direction of the farm and household. She and her mother were disregarded, and treated almost as servants. This painful situation grew more acute after Margaret's recovery, for the relatives tried to regulate all her comings and goings. Not allowed to attend church as often as she pleased, the young girl was sometimes seen weeping and praying in a corner of the garden. It grieved her deeply that she could not ease things for her mother. Her eldest brother's coming of age saved the day, for the property now reverted to him, and the family again had undisputed possession of their home.

Philiberte expressed a hope that Margaret would marry; the girl considered the step, inflicting severe austerities upon herself during a period of indecision. At the age of twenty, inspired by a vision, she put aside all such thoughts and resolved to enter a convent. While awaiting admission, she tried to help and teach certain neglected children of the village. At twenty-two she made her profession at the convent of the Visitation at Paray-le-Monial. The nuns of the Order of the Visitation, founded in the early years of the seventeenth century by St. Francis de Sales, were famed for their humility and selflessness. As a novice Margaret excelled in these virtues. When she made her profession, the name of Mary was added and she was called Margaret Mary. She began a course of mortifications and penances which were to continue, with more or less intensity, as long as she lived. We are told that she was assigned to the infirmary and was not very skillful at her tasks.

Some years passed quietly in the convent, and then Margaret Mary began to have experiences which seemed to be of supernatural origin. The first of these occurred on December 27, 1673, when she was kneeling at the grille in the chapel. She felt suffused

by the Divine Presence, and heard the Lord inviting her to take
the place which St. John had occupied at the Last Supper. The
Lord told her that the love of His heart must spread and manifest
itself to men, and He would reveal its graces through her. This
was the beginning of a series of revelations covering a period of
eighteen months. When Margaret Mary went to the Superior,
Mother de Saumaise, with an account of these mystical experiences, claiming that she, an humble nun, had been chosen as the
transmitter of a new devotion to the Sacred Heart, she was reprimanded for her presumption. Seriously overwrought, Margaret
Mary suffered a collapse, and became so ill that her life was
despaired of. Now the Mother Superior reflected that she might
have erred in scorning the nun's story and vowed that if her life
were spared, she would take it as a sign that the visions and messages were truly from God. When Margaret Mary recovered, the
Superior invited some theologians who happened to be in the town
—they included a Jesuit and a Benedictine—to hear the story.
These priests listened and judged the young nun to be a victim
of delusions. Their examination had been a sheer torture to
Margaret Mary. Later a Jesuit, Father Claude de la Columbière,
talked to her and was completely convinced of the genuineness of
the revelations. He was to write of the nun and to inaugurate this
devotion in England.

For many years the nun suffered from despair, from self-in-
flicted punishments, and also from the slights and contempt of
those around her. In 1681 Father Claude returned to the convent
and died there the following year. Margaret Mary was appointed
assistant and novice-mistress by a new Mother Superior who was
more sympathetic towards her. Opposition ceased—or at least was
restrained—after an account of Margaret Mary's visions was read
aloud in the refectory from the writings left by Father Claude,
who had taken it upon himself to make known to the world the
nun's remarkable experiences. That she was finally vindicated was
to her a matter of indifference. When she was forty-three, while
serving a second term as assistant superior, Margaret Mary fell ill.

Sinking rapidly, she received the Last Sacraments, saying, "I need nothing but God, and to lose myself in the heart of Jesus."

Although the devotion to the Sacred Heart of Jesus was practiced before this time, it now gained a strong new impetus through the work of Father John Eudes and the writings of Father Claude. The Sacred Heart is regarded as "the symbol of that boundless love which moved the Word to take flesh, to institute the Holy Eucharist, to take our sins upon Himself, and, dying on the Cross, to offer Himself as a victim and sacrifice to the eternal Father." The cult first became popular in France, then spread to Poland and other countries, including, at a later period, the United States. The first petition to the Holy See for the institution of the feast was from Queen Mary, consort of James II of England. The month of June is appointed for this devotion, and since 1929 the feast has been one of the highest rank.

Saint John Baptist de la Salle

Founder, Confessor

1 7 1 9

(*May 15*)

John Baptist de la Salle, educational pioneer, founder of the world-wide Institute of the Brothers of the Christian Schools, commonly called the Christian Brothers, was born in the cathedral town of Rheims, France, on April 30, 1651. His parents were people of standing, his father holding a judicial post. From childhood he gave evidence of such unusual piety that he was designated for the priesthood. At eleven he received the tonsure and at sixteen became a canon of the cathedral chapter at Rheims. Later he was sent to the seminary of St. Sulpice to complete his studies. The young canon, handsome in appearance and scholarly in his tastes, seemed destined for high ecclesiastical preferment. Soon after his return to Rheims he was to discover his true life work—the education of the poor. It was to be a long, hard struggle, with few tangible rewards, but he unquestionably started a movement which was to result in furthering free elementary instruction.

The social orders of seventeenth-century France were still cast in a rigid mold. Education, with rare exceptions, was for the rich and noble, and quite beyond the dreams of the great mass of the people. Their pitiful ignorance became the lifelong concern of John Baptist de la Salle. From the outset of his career he was thrown into contact with poor children. His first post was spiritual director of the Sisters of the Holy Infant and the orphanage they conducted. Through this work he came into contact with a wealthy woman, one of his own relations, who urged him to found a similar

430

refuge for orphaned boys. A lay teacher, Arien Nigel, joined him, and such a home and school opened its doors. It was so successful that soon another institution of the same type was set up in the diocese. Father John now saw the way clear before him—he must devote his whole energy to the cause of education. But to educate you must have teachers, and the preparation of young school-masters to teach in these schools was his initial task. He invited a number of them to come and live in his own home that he might have more time to train and counsel them. His brothers objected to having their house taken over in this manner, so Father John moved with his group to more suitable quarters.

Since only a religious community could furnish a permanent and continuing supply of teachers serving without pay, an Institute, a sort of teaching brotherhood of young men who were attracted to a life of service, was formed. The novice teachers took the three usual vows, but not Holy Orders. Another vow, that they would dedicate their lives to teaching the poor, specializing as catechists, was added. A rule was drawn up; it provided that the Brothers should be laymen and that no priests could ever become members.

Father John Baptist soon decided to resign his canonry to devote his full attention to the establishment of schools and the training of teachers. He had inherited a considerable fortune, and this might have been used to further his aims, but on the advice of a saintly priest, Father Barre, of Paris, and after much prayer for God's guidance, he decided against this course. He sold what he had and sent the money to the poor of the province of Champagne, where a famine was causing great suffering. His enterprises must henceforth depend on the charity of others, and from this time on his own life was lived in the true ascetic pattern.

The Institute grew rapidly, and soon there were so many applications from young men of fifteen to twenty years of age that a junior novitiate was formed. Also, from many parts of France, parish priests were sending their promising young men to be trained so they might return to serve as schoolmasters in their own villages. What may be considered the first Normal School was now functioning, and this became the first novice house of the order. Here Father John Baptist wrote his *Manual for Christian Schools*, setting forth his original and practical ideas of education. To him we owe the separation of pupils into classes according to their stage of mental maturity. He also introduced teaching in the vernacular, that is, the use of French instead of Latin. He knew the importance of the eye in learning, and made great use of the blackboard. Included in the curriculum were courses in ethics, literature, physics, philosophy, and mathematics.

Such a movement was sure to arouse opposition, and many obstacles and protests had to be overcome. The schools for poor boys in Paris were attacked by Jansenists, by lay teachers and tutors, who perhaps felt their own position and livelihood jeopardized; and by others who on principle did not approve of education for the "lower orders," save training in the manual crafts and trades. After a time it became evident that the schools had come to stay, and the persecutions gradually ceased.

Although the schools had originally been founded for orphans and the children of the poor, a new departure was made at the request of King James II of England, who was then living in exile. He urged the founding of a college for the sons of his adherents, mainly Irish, who were living in France, and Father John opened such a school for fifty young men of gentle birth. At about the same time he started a school for boys of the artisan class. Here technical instruction was combined with religious exercises, and this type of school became very popular. There were also schools started for "troublesome boys," now usually called "juvenile delinquents." Efforts were thus being made to meet the needs of all types and classes of boys and young men. This constantly expanding work required insight and adaptability in an unusual degree.

Father John Baptist's later years were spent at the College of St. Yon, in Rouen, where the novitiate had been transferred in 1705, after it had functioned for some years in Paris. In 1716 he resigned from the active direction and government of the Institute, and from then on would give no orders, and lived like the humblest of the brothers, teaching the novices and young boarders. He wrote for them several treatises, including *A Method of Mental Prayer*. Worn out by illness and austerities, he passed away on Good Friday, April 7, 1719, at the age of sixty-seven. Six years after his death, the Christian Brothers' institute was recognized by Pope Benedict XIII, and its rule approved. Father John was canonized in 1900. To his valiant efforts we owe in large part the acceptance of the idea of universal education.

In spite of internal difficulties, chiefly concerning the degree of austerity to be observed by the Brothers, the schools spread and flourished up to the French Revolution. During that period of persecution, the Christian Brothers were at one point reduced to twenty active members. However, when the ban was lifted by Napoleon I in 1799, the community sprang back to life with remarkable resilience. During the nineteenth century the schools expanded steadily; then, from 1904 to 1908, there was another setback: 1285 establishments were closed by legislative decree in France. Meanwhile the Brothers had established themselves in other countries of Europe, in England, Ireland, the Levant, North and South America, the West Indies, and Australia. Their first school in the United States was founded in 1846; today many of them are on the college level.

Saint Bernadette Soubirous
Virgin, Patroness of Lourdes

1 8 7 9

(*February 11*)

Bernadette's canonization in 1933 was the culmination of a process which had been started nearly three-quarters of a century earlier: she is, therefore, a saint of modern times, and the remarkable facts of her life are readily accessible to all. Her story even challenges the interest of those who do not share the Catholic faith. Christianity had its beginnings among humble people without influence or riches, such as Bernadette. Perhaps it is a natural human instinct to rejoice when the lowly are lifted up to the heights, and especially when a child, neglected and untaught, is chosen for special grace and favor, thus becoming an instrument for good.

Born in Lourdes, France, on January 7, 1844, Bernadette was the first child of François and Louise Soubirous. At the time of her birth, François was a miller, operating a mill which had belonged to his wife's people. He was a good-natured, easy-going man, with little ability for carrying on a business, and before many years the mill had been forfeited for debt. During most of Bernadette's childhood he was an odd-job man, picking up a day's work as opportunity offered, and, from time to time, escaping from his problems and responsibilities by turning to the delusive comfort of alcohol. His wife and children, naturally, were the chief sufferers from his ineffectualness. Louise, whose family was of somewhat better economic status than her husband's, was a hard worker, a warm-hearted neighbor, and exemplary in her

434

observance of Catholic rites. Within a short space of years many children were born to her, only five of whom survived infancy. After Bernadette, there was another girl, Toinette Marie, and three boys. To help feed and clothe them it was often necessary for their harassed mother to go out to work by the day, doing laundry and other rough tasks for the more prosperous citizens, and, on one occasion, at least, helping to harvest a crop of grain. A peasant woman of the region has told of seeing little Bernadette, then about twelve, carrying the youngest baby to Louise in the field, to be nursed during the noon-day rest period. As a child, Bernadette not only did more than might be expected in caring for the smaller children, but helped in their moral and religious training as well.

Bernadette was never strong, and from the age of six she showed symptoms of the respiratory ailment that later became a chronic affliction. It is not clear at this early stage whether she suffered from asthma or tuberculosis, but we know that her mother was anxious about her health and made an effort to provide special food for her. When Bernadette was thirteen she was sent to the neighboring mountain hamlet of Bartrès, to the home of one Marie Arevant, her foster mother. It was here that Bernadette had been taken for a few months when she was still an infant, to be nursed by Madame Arevant, who had just lost a baby. The woman now had a large family and little Bernadette made herself useful in the house and in the fields. One of her duties was to tend a small flock of sheep that grazed on a hillside nearby; it is this brief phase of her girlhood that has inspired artists to picture her as a shepherdess. Her life was a lonely one, and we get the impression that she was overworked and homesick while she remained in this peasant home. At all events she sent word to her parents that she wished to leave Bartrès. One thing seemed especially to disturb her at this time; although she was now fourteen, she had not made her First Communion. Her foster mother had tried half-heartedly to prepare her, but after one or two sessions had impatiently given it up, saying that Bernadette was too dull to learn.

When Bernadette went back to Lourdes, it made her very happy to be admitted to the day school conducted by the Sisters of Charity and Christian Instruction. This was a teaching and nursing order whose mother-house is at Nevers, in central France. A hospice, a day school, and a boarding school were maintained at Lourdes by these devout nuns, who were, as a group, unusually well trained. Thus Bernadette at last began her secular education, and, under Abbé Pomian, continued to prepare for First Communion. She was also learning a little French, for up to this time she spoke only the local dialect. The nuns discovered that beneath a quiet, modest exterior, Bernadette had a winning personality and a lively sense of humor. This might have been a happy and constructive time for the little girl had it not been for the ever-increasing shadows of poverty at home.

After moving from one poor location to another, the Soubirous family was now living in a single room of a dilapidated structure in the rue des Pétits Fosses; this damp, unwholesome place had once served as a jail and was known as Le Cachot, the Dungeon. Above loomed an ancient fortress, and the narrow cobbled street had once been a part of the moat. The town of Lourdes, itself very old, is situated in one of the most picturesque parts of France, lying in the extreme southwest, near the Spanish frontier, where the Pyrenees mountains rise sharply above the plains. From the craggy, wooded heights, several valleys descend to converge at this site, and the little river Gave rushes through the town, its turbulent current turning the wheels of many mills. There are escarpments of rock in and around Lourdes, the most famous being the Massabeille, a great mound jutting out from the base of a plateau. On the side facing the river it had an arch-shaped opening which led into a sizeable grotto—a grotto that was soon destined to become famous in every part of the world. At this time the Massabeille had, if not exactly an aura of evil, a touch of the sinister. According to legend, it had been sacred to the pagans of prehistoric times; now it served as a shelter for fishermen or herdsmen caught by sudden storms.

It was very cold on February 11, 1858, the day that was to mark the beginning of such an extraordinary series of events at the rock of Massabeille. When Bernadette returned from school her mother gave her permission to go down by the river to pick up driftwood and fallen branches. Toinette Marie, aged nine, and Marie Abadie, aged twelve, a neighbor's child, went with her. When the three girls reached the Massabeille, the two younger ones took off their wooden shoes to wade across an icy mill-stream which here joined the river. Bernadette, more sensitive, hung behind. Standing alone beside the river, she had started to remove her stockings when she heard a noise like a sudden rush of wind. Looking up towards the grotto she saw some movement among the branches, then there floated out of the opening a golden cloud, and in the midst of it was the figure of a beautiful young girl who placed herself in a small niche in the rock, at one side of the opening and slightly above it. In the crannies around this niche grew stunted vines and shrubs, and in particular a white eglantine. Bernadette, staring in fascination, saw that the luminous apparition was dressed in a soft white robe, with a broad girdle of blue, and a long white veil that partially covered her hair. Her eyes were blue and gentle. Golden roses gleamed on her bare feet. When the vision smiled and beckoned to Bernadette, the girl's fear vanished and she came a few steps nearer, then sank reverently to her knees. She drew her rosary from her pocket, for, in moments of stress, she habitually said her beads. The mysterious being also had a rosary, of large white beads, and to quote Bernadette's own account: "The Lady let me pray alone; she passed the beads of the rosary between her fingers, but said nothing; only at the end of each decade did she say the Gloria with me." When the recitation was finished, the Lady vanished into the cave and the golden mist disappeared with her. This experience affected Bernadette so powerfully that, when the other girls turned back to look for her, she was still kneeling, a rapt, faraway look on her face. They chided her, thinking she had passed the time praying to escape the task of gathering fuel. Tying up their twigs and branches into faggots, they started for home. Too full of her vision to keep quiet about it, before they had gone far Bernadette burst out with the whole wondrous story; she asked the girls to say nothing at home. But Toinette told Madame Soubirous that same evening, and soon the news spread further. Bernadette wished to go back to the Massabeille the next day, but her mother, after talking the matter over with a sister, refused her permission.

Bernadette now showed the independence of spirit—some were to characterize it as obstinacy—that became one of her outstanding traits. When she told her confessor of the apparition, Abbé Pomian made light of it, thinking the girl suffered from hallucinations. Nevertheless, on the following Sunday Bernadette asked if she might go to the grotto and her father told her she might go if she took a flask of holy water with her, to exorcise the apparition should it prove to be a demon. Bernadette, advancing ahead of several little friends who accompanied her, knelt before the grotto and soon the vision appeared as before. On their return the excited girls, although they had seen nothing, naturally began to tell their versions of the affair, and soon the town buzzed with varying reports and rumors. On the next market day the peasants heard of these strange happenings. The story reached the Mother Superior of the convent, who took a firm stand: she announced to the class preparing for Communion, comprising Bernadette's friends and companions for the most part, that they must stop talking and thinking of this matter. Bernadette's teacher, Sister Marie Thérèse Vauzous, was even hostile.

The apparition was manifest to Bernadette for the third time on Thursday, February 18, when she went to the grotto accompanied by two women of Lourdes who thought the "damiezelo," as Bernadette called her, was the returning spirit of a young woman, one of their dear friends, who had died a few months before. On this occasion the same little figure appeared to Bernadette, smiled warmly, and spoke, asking Bernadette to come every day for fifteen days. Bernadette promised to come, provided she was given permission to do so. Since neither her god-mother, who was her mother's sister, nor the priest actually forbade it, Bernadette's parents offered no objection. On the following day her mother and aunt went with her, and on subsequent visits great crowds of people gathered on the Massabeille, or down by the river, hoping to see or hear something miraculous. During these two weeks the excitement increased to such a pitch that the civil authorities felt obliged to take action. The police were not content to threaten the Soubirous family; they must take Bernadette to the local police office for questioning and try to make her admit that it was all an elaborate hoax. Bernadette emerged from this and many another ordeal somewhat shaken but obdurate. The authorities continued to try to discredit her. They even gave currency to the report that the whole thing had been thought up by Bernadette's poverty-stricken parents, so that they might derive some profit from it. François and Louise Soubirous, from being puzzled, worried, and uncertain at the outset, had now come to believe in the supernatural character of their daughter's experiences, and stood loyally by her. They did not dream of exploiting the affair in their own interest. As a matter of fact, pious, well-meaning people were bringing them gifts of money and food, sometimes asking for a token from Bernadette. These offerings were declined; even Bernadette's small brothers were cautioned to accept nothing. The girl herself was adamant in her determination to have no part in any kind of trafficking; the record of her complete honesty and disinterestedness is clear and unquestioned. However, she found the sudden notoriety unpleasant, and this sensitivity to being stared at and talked about and pointed out was to last throughout her life. People began to gather at the grotto in the middle of the night, awaiting her appearance. It was rumored that she had a miraculous, healing touch. Several cures were attributed to her.

On Sunday, February 21, a number of persons went with her to the grotto, including citizens who had been highly skeptical. On this occasion, Bernadette reported later, the apparition said to her: "You will pray to God for sinners." On February 26, while she was in the trance-like state which lasted as long as she saw the vision, Bernadette crawled inside the grotto, and, at the Lady's bidding, uncovered with her bare hands a little trickle of water from which she drank and with which she bathed her face, still at the Lady's direction. This tiny spring continued to well up and by the next day was flowing steadily down into the river: to this day it has never ceased to gush forth from the grotto. The people regarded its discovery by Bernadette as a miracle.

On March 2 Bernadette saw the apparition for the thirteenth time. It was on this day that the Lady bade Bernadette to tell the priests that "a chapel should be built and a procession formed." Bernadette had no thought but to obey, in spite of the open hostility of the curé of Lourdes. Dean Peyramale, an imposing man of excellent family and background, received Bernadette and reprimanded her harshly, asking her to inquire the name of her visitant, and to tell her she must perform a real miracle, such as making the eglantine bloom out of season, to prove herself. During the preceding weeks he had ordered the priests to have nothing to do with the grotto, for it was the general practice of the clergy to discourage or ignore religious visionaries. Very often such persons were ill-balanced or suffering from delusions. As a matter of fact, Bernadette's experiences were proving contagious, and before long many others, young and old, were claiming to have had supernatural visions at the grotto and elsewhere. Dean Peyramale's stand of determined opposition was based on the necessity of restoring order in the parish.

On March 25, Lady Day, Bernadette started for the grotto at dawn. When the vision appeared to her, Bernadette said: "Would you kindly tell me who you are?" When the girl had repeated the question twice more, the Lady replied: "I am the Immaculate Conception. I want a chapel here." This answer, when reported by Bernadette, caused the local excitement to rise to a still higher pitch and the feeling grew that Bernadette's visitor was the Blessed Virgin. Only four years before the dogma of the Immaculate Conception had been promulgated. The seventeenth apparition took place on April 7, and the final one, more than three months later, on July 16. By that time, the grotto, which the people were trying to make into a sanctuary and place of worship, had been barricaded by the town authorities to discourage worshipers and curiosity-seekers from congregating there. During the twenty-one years that she was to remain on earth, Bernadette never again saw the vision. The accounts of what she had seen and heard, which she was obliged to repeat so often, never varied in any significant detail.

Meanwhile the news of the phenomenal happenings at Lourdes had reached the very highest ecclesiastical and government circles: the bishop, the prefect, even Emperor Napoleon III and his pious wife Eugènie, became actors in the drama. On October 5, the mayor of Lourdes, on orders from above, had the grotto reopened. It was thought that the empress herself had had a voice in this decision. At all events, it seemed to be the only appropriate response to the overwhelming demand of the people for a shrine. Bernadette's visions, the new spring, and the cures that were being reported, all had taken a profound hold on the popular imagination.

Due to a lucky turn, Bernadette's family was now more comfortably situated, and, to escape visitors, Bernadette went to live at the convent. Even there, intrusions upon her privacy were allowed; these she bore as patiently as she could. While her fame not only continued but steadily grew, Bernadette herself withdrew more and more. At the age of twenty she decided to take the veil. Since the state of her health precluded the more ascetic orders, it was considered best for her to join the Sisters who had taught and sheltered her. At twenty-two, therefore, she traveled to the motherhouse of the convent. Her novitiate was full of trials and sorrows. Acting under the quite unfounded notion that Bernadette's visions and all the attendant publicity might have made the young woman vain or self-important, Sister Marie Thérèse Vauzous, now novicemistress at Nevers, was very severe with her former pupil. Although she made life difficult for Bernadette, the little novice met all tests with perfect humility. She cheerfully performed the menial

tasks assigned to her, at first in the convent kitchen, although this
work must have taxed her strength. Later, when it was noted that
her sympathetic manner made her a favorite with sick people, she
was appointed assistant infirmarian. Her step and touch were light,
and her very presence brought comfort. But during these years,
Bernadette was suffering from the chronic disease which was
slowly draining her life away. She was finally given work in the
sacristy, where cleverness with the needle made her work admired
and cherished. She displayed a real gift for design and color in
embroidering the sacred vestments. To all tasks she brought a pure
grace of spirit and an utter willingness to serve.

In September, 1878, Bernadette made her perpetual and final
vows. Her strength was ebbing away, but even when she was confined to wheel chair or bed, she went on with the fine needlework.
And now she had more time for prayer and meditation. There is
little outward drama in the life of a nun, but in Bernadette's case
there was steady activity, steady growth, in things of the spirit.
She had been told by her vision that she would not attain happiness in this world. Her childhood had been sad, and maturity had
brought no easing of the burden she must carry. During the last
two years of life a tumor developed on one knee, which was followed by caries of the bone. She suffered excruciating pain. One
day, when a Superior came to visit her and said, "What are you
doing in bed, you lazy little thing?" Bernadette simply replied, "I
am doing my stint. I must be a victim." She felt that such was the
Divine plan for her.

The nuns, the novice mistress, and the Superior had all long
since come to regard her as the vessel of Divine grace and to believe in the reality of those visitations of her youth. She still suffered from the curiosity of visiting strangers. Not only did nuns
and priests come to Nevers but celebrities from Paris and other
parts of France came to see for themselves the now famous Bernadette. Disliking publicity as she did, yet not wishing to remain
isolated and aloof if a glimpse of her could help or inspire any
other human soul, she met this test too—and sometimes with a

native cleverness. Once a visitor stopped her as she was passing down a corridor and asked where she could get a glimpse of Sister Bernadette. The little nun said, "Just watch that doorway and presently you will see her go through." And she slipped away through the door. Such was the prestige her presence gave to the order that many young women now joined it.

On her death-bed, in a spasm of pain, Bernadette pressed the crucifix closer to her, and cried, "All this is good for Heaven!" That afternoon, as the nuns of the convent knelt round her bed to repeat the prayers for the dying, they heard her say in a low voice, "Blessed Mary, Mother of God, pray for me! A poor sinner, a poor sinner—" She could not finish. The date was April 16, 1879. As soon as the news spread, people came streaming towards the convent, chanting, "The saint is dead! The saint is dead!" Bernadette's body was placed in a casket which was sealed, then buried near the chapel of St. Joseph in the convent grounds. When it was exhumed in 1908 by the commission formed to forward the examination of Bernadette's life and character, it was found to be intact and uncorrupted. In August, 1913, Pope Pius X conferred the title of Venerable upon her, and in June, 1925, the ceremony of beatification took place. Since then, her body, reposing in a handsome glass reliquary, lies in the convent chapel, guarded above by a statue of the Blessed Virgin, and by the nuns who keep vigil. In Rome, on December 8, 1933, the Feast of the Immaculate Conception, amidst a brilliant setting and the fanfare of silver trumpets, Bernadette Soubirous was admitted to the company of saints. This little nun, humble, unlettered, honest, and obedient, is venerated by the great host of Catholic worshipers throughout the world. Tens of thousands of them journey annually to the glorious shrine at Lourdes.

The story of Lourdes as a pilgrimage place forms a strange contrast to Bernadette's retired life of prayer and service. Its growth from a sleepy country town to its present status as the most popular pilgrimage place in Christendom has been phenomenal. A railroad line from Pau was built, facilitating the influx of visitors who, from the very first year, were drawn to Lourdes. Dean Peyramale and his superior, the bishop of Pau, who at first had scoffed, came to believe most ardently; it was the aged dean who found the money for raising the great basilica to Our Lady, which was completed in 1876. Participating in the ceremony were thirty-five prelates, a cardinal, and three thousand priests. Sister Bernadette had no share in these rites. Another church at the base of the basilica was erected and consecrated in 1901. The entire district has been enhanced by architecture and landscaping to make it an impressive sanctuary, with a background of great natural beauty.

Of the cures at Lourdes it can be said that even non-believers have observed something here that medical science cannot explain. The commission of physicians, known as the Bureau of Constatations, who examine evidence and report on their findings, operate with great caution and circumspection. The alleged cure must be immediate and permanent to be regarded as a miracle. Medical records prior to the trip are studied, as well as the patient's subsequent medical history. The patient may himself be a witness, and it is most moving to hear the words, "I was sick and now I am well," which give such comfort and hope to others who are ailing. Only a few cures each year stand up against these rigid tests, but those few are enough. The thousands—the lame, the halt, the blind —continue to come, to be washed in the waters of the spring, to share in the processions, the singing, the prayers, the impressive rites, and breathe the pure air of faith. The Canticle of Bernadette hovers in that air, and even those well persons who go to Lourdes simply searching for a renewal of faith find themselves amply rewarded, for the spirit of the child Bernadette is still a potent inspiration.

Saint John Bosco

Founder of the Salesian Society

1 8 8 8

(August 13)

I n his life the supernatural became the natural and the extraordinary the ordinary." So spoke Pope Pius XI of the beloved Don
Bosco, renowned for his educational pioneering and his affectionate care for the fatherless. Born Giovanni Melchior Bosco in 1815,
the future saint was the youngest son of a peasant farmer in the
hamlet of Becchi, in the Piedmont district of north Italy. He lost
his father at the age of two and was brought up by a devoted and
industrious mother, Margaret Bosco, who had a hard struggle
maintaining the home and the three children, all of them boys. A
dream that little Giovanni had at the age of nine revealed to him
his vocation. He seemed to be surrounded by a mob of fighting and
swearing children whom he tried in vain to pacify, at first by arguments and then by hitting them. Suddenly there appeared a mysterious woman who said: "Softly, softly . . . if you wish to win
them! Take your shepherd's staff and lead them to pasture." Even
as she spoke, the children were transformed first into wild beasts
and then into gentle lambs. From that time on, the boy thought,
it was his clear duty to lead and help other boys.

He began with those of his own village, teaching them the
Catechism and bringing them to church. As an inducement, he
would amuse them first with acrobatic and conjuring tricks, at
which he became very clever. One Sunday morning when an
itinerant juggler and gymnast was holding the children spellbound
by his performance, young John challenged him to a competition

445

and beat him at his own tricks. Then he marched off to church, followed by his admiring audience. It was more or less by chance that this talented boy learned to read. He was staying with an aunt who was servant to the priest, and when the priest was told of John's ambition, he taught him gladly. But John didn't want to stop with reading and writing; he wished to study for the priesthood. Many difficulties had to be overcome before he could even begin his preliminary studies. When, at sixteen, he entered the seminary at Chieri, he was so poor that money for his maintenance and his clothes had to be supplied by charity. The village mayor contributed a hat, one friendly person gave him a cloak, and another a pair of shoes. People were eager to help a boy who was himself so eager and ambitious. After his ordination as deacon, he attended the theological school at nearby Turin, finding time to continue his volunteer work with homeless or neglected boys. Having won the approbation of his superiors for what he was doing, he began to gather around him regularly on Sunday afternoons a band of these waifs and young apprentices.

After taking Holy Orders, his first appointment was assistant chaplain of a home for girls, founded by the Marchesa Barolo, a wealthy and philanthropic woman. This post left Don Bosco free on Sundays to devote himself to his group of boys. He set up for them a sort of combined Sunday School and recreation center on grounds belonging to the Marchesa, which he called "the festive Oratory." But the Marchesa quickly withdrew her permission, because the boys were, naturally, noisy and unruly, and sometimes even made so bold as to pick the flowers in the garden. For more than a year the group was regarded as a nuisance and sent from pillar to post. No property owner was able to put up with them for long. When at last Don Bosco was able to hire an old shed as a meeting place, and the future seemed promising, the Marchesa delivered herself of an ultimatum. He must choose between giving up the boys—who now numbered several hundred—or resigning his post at the girl's orphanage. Don Bosco promptly resigned, to devote himself wholly to the boys.

In the midst of these anxieties, he was prostrated by a severe attack of pneumonia that came near ending his life. As soon as he had recovered, he went to live in some poor rooms adjoining a new Oratory, or gathering place, with his mother as housekeeper. For ten years this good woman served as his adjutant and loyal helper, extending her motherly care over all the waifs and strays her son brought to her. Don Bosco now applied himself to consolidating his work and planning for the years to come. A night school which had been opened the previous year took shape, and as the Oratory was soon overcrowded, he opened two more youth centers in other parts of Turin. About the same time he began housing a few destitute boys. His next step was to build for his flock a small church which he placed under the patronage of his favorite saint, Francis de Sales. With that completed, he started to build a home for his steadily growing family. No one knew just how he managed to raise the money for these various projects, but his natural persuasiveness had much to do with it.

Those enrolled as boarders in the school were of two sorts: young apprentices and craftsmen, and other youths of more than average intelligence in whom Don Bosco discerned future helpers, with, possibly, vocations to the priesthood. At first they attended classes outside, but, as more teachers were enlisted, academic and technical courses were given at the house. By 1856 a hundred and fifty boys were in residence; there were four workshops, including a printing shop, and four Latin classes, with ten young priests as instructors; all this in addition to the oratories with their five hundred children. He cultivated in all of them a taste for music, and he was a believer in the therapeutic value of play. Don Bosco's understanding of young people, their needs, and their dreams, gave him great influence. He could manage them without punishment. "I do not remember to have used formal punishment," he wrote, "and with God's grace I have always obtained—and from apparently hopeless children—not alone what duty exacted but what my wish simply expressed." With an approach that seems quite modern, he planned programs that combined play, song, study, prayer, and manual work. He knew that straight academic learning was not enough. "Knowledge gives more power in the exercise of good or evil," he said, "but alone it is an indifferent weapon, lacking guidance."

Don Bosco's outgoing personality made him popular as a preacher, and there were many demands on his time to speak to various congregations. As a third form of activity, in the few hours that remained to him, he wrote useful and popular books for boys. In that day there was almost no attractive reading matter written especially for young people, and Don Bosco set himself to fill this need. He wrote stories based on history, and sometimes popular treatises on the faith. Often he toiled far into the night, until, in later life, his failing eyesight compelled him to give up writing.

A plan for some sort of religious order, to carry on the work when he had passed away, had long been in Don Bosco's mind, and at last he felt he had the strong nucleus of helpers that was required. "On the night of January 26, 1854, we were assembled in Don Bosco's room," writes one of the men present. "Besides Don Bosco, there were Cagliero, Rocchetti, Artiglia, and Rua. It was suggested that with God's help we should enter upon a period of practical works of charity to help our neighbors. At the close of the period, we might bind ourselves by a promise which could subsequently be transformed into a vow. From that evening, the name of Salesian was given to all who embarked on that form of apostolate." The name of course honored the great bishop of Geneva, St. Francis de Sales. It was not a propitious time for launching a new order, for in all its history Piedmont had never been so anti-clerical. The Jesuits and the Sisters of the Sacred Heart had been expelled, many convents suppressed, and laws were being passed curtailing the rights of religious orders. The statesman Urbano Rattazzi, one of those most responsible for the anti-clerical legislation, was deeply interested in popular education. As a resident of Turin, Rattazzi was familiar with Father John's activities, and, on meeting him by chance one day, urged

SAINT FRANCIS DE SALES   Unknown

The painting by an unknown seventeenth century painter hangs in Turin, Italy. It bears the date 1618 and thus was painted four years before the death of the Bishop in 1622. Accordingly, it may be a painting from life, although this is not known.

Saint Francis de Sales is shown here as a Bishop. His usual symbols are a heart and crown of thorns rayed, or a flaming heart.

SAINT ISAAC JOGUES AND COMPANIONS   Lloyd Ostendorf
A modern painting, this shows the saint and his two companions, William
Couture and Rene Goupil, who shared his captivity by the Mohawk Indians.

No symbols are peculiar to this modern saint, but the frontiersman's dress
and the crucifix are emblematic of his mission to the American Indians.

him to found a society to further his valuable work, promising the support of the government.

The project grew, and in 1858 John went to Rome, taking with him the rules of the institution. From Pope Pius IX he received preliminary approbation. Sixteen years later he obtained full sanction, together with permission to present candidates for Holy Orders. The new society grew rapidly. Within five years there were thirty-nine Salesians; at the time of the founder's death there were eight hundred, and by 1929 the number had increased to about eight thousand. One of Father John's dreams was realized when he sent his first missionaries to the bleak and faraway land of Patagonia; other areas of South America were soon the scene of missionary endeavor. He lived to see twenty-six houses started in the New World and thirty-eight in the Old.

His next great work was the foundation in 1862 of an order of women to do for poor girls what the Salesians were doing for boys. The original group consisted of twenty-seven young women to whom he gave the name of Daughters of St. Mary Auxiliatrix, the Helper. The organization now numbers many thousands, with elementary schools in Italy, Brazil, and Argentina. To supplement the work of these two congregations, Father John organized his outside lay helpers into a new kind of Third Order, which he called Salesian Cooperators. They were men and women of all classes who pledged themselves to assist in practical ways the educational labors of the Salesians.

Any account of the life of this saint would be incomplete without some mention of his achievements as a builder of churches. His first little church of St. Francis de Sales soon proved inadequate, and he undertook the construction of a much larger building. This he finished in 1868, dedicating it to St. Mary the Helper. Later he found means to put up another spacious and much-needed church in a poor quarter of Turin, and this he placed under the patronage of St. John the Evangelist. But the immense effort of money-raising had left Don Bosco weary and depleted. He was not allowed time to recover his strength before another task was put before him. During the last years of Pope Pius IX, a project had been formed of building at Rome a church in honor of the Sacred Heart of Jesus, and Pius himself had donated money to buy the site. His successor, Leo XIII, was eager for the work to be carried forward, but there was difficulty in raising funds. It was suggested to the Pope that this was something that Don Bosco did better than anyone else, and when he was asked to undertake it, he accepted the challenge.

After obtaining a considerable sum in Italy, Don Bosco went to France, where devotion to the cult of the Sacred Heart was particularly intense at this time. He was successful in his appeals, money came flowing in, and the early completion of the church was assured. As the day appointed for its consecration drew near, he was sometimes heard to murmur that if there were any delay, he would not live to witness it. Two years before the doctors had said that this generous-hearted man had worn himself out and that complete retirement offered the only chance of prolonging his life. Don Bosco had the joy of living a few months beyond the consecration of the church, which took place on May 14, 1887. He said one Mass before the new high altar.

Later in the year it became plain that his days were numbered; he gradually weakened, and on the morning of January 31, 1888, he died in his home city of Turin. Forty thousand persons came to the church to do honor to Don Bosco, and the entire city turned out as his remains were borne to their resting place. His memory was cherished and his work carried on by his followers. Not many years had elapsed before a movement was begun for his beatification. He was declared Venerable by Pope Pius X in 1907, beatified by Pius XI in 1929, and canonized by him in 1934. Don Bosco exemplified a new trend in the treatment of children, anticipating in some respects the practices of modern psychologists. Intuitively he knew that the loving care and attention of a wise, interested adult was essential to the healthy growth of every child, and he gave his very best to those children who had the least.

Saint Thérèse of Lisieux
Virgin
1 8 9 7
(*October 3*)

The spread of the cult of St. Thérèse of Lisieux is one of the impressive religious manifestations of our time. During her few years on earth this young French Carmelite was scarcely to be distinguished from many another devoted nun, but her death brought an almost immediate awareness of her unique gifts. Through her letters, the word-of-mouth tradition originating with her fellow-nuns, and especially through the publication of *Histoire d'un âme,* Thérèse of the Child Jesus or "The Little Flower" soon came to mean a great deal to numberless people; she had shown them the way of perfection in the small things of every day. Miracles and graces were being attributed to her intercession, and within twenty-eight years after death, this simple young nun had been canonized. In 1936 a basilica in her honor at Lisieux was opened and blessed by Cardinal Pacelli; and it was he who, in 1944, as Pope, declared her the secondary patroness of France. "The Little Flower" was an admirer of St. Teresa of Avila, and a comparison at once suggests itself. Both were christened Teresa, both were Carmelites, and both left interesting autobiographies. Many temperamental and intellectual differences separate them, in addition to the differences of period and of race; but there are striking similarities. They both patiently endured severe physical sufferings; both had a capacity for intense religious experience; both led lives made radiant by the love of Christ.

The parents of the later saint were Louis Martin, a watchmaker of Alençon, France, son of an army officer, and Azélie-Marie Guérin, a lacemaker of the same town. Only five of their nine children lived to maturity; all five were daughters and all were to become nuns. Françoise-Marie Thérèse, the youngest, was born on January 2, 1873. Her childhood must have been normally happy, for her first memories, she writes, are of smiles and tender caresses. Although she was affectionate and had much natural charm, Thérèse gave no sign of precocity. When she was only four, the family was stricken by the sad blow of the mother's death. Monsieur Martin gave up his business and established himself at Lisieux, Normandy, where Madame Martin's brother lived with his wife and family. The Guérins, generous and loyal people, were able to ease the father's responsibilities through the years by giving to their five nieces practical counsel and deep affection.

The Martins were now and always united in the closest bonds. The eldest daughter, Marie, although only thirteen, took over the management of the household, and the second, Pauline, gave the girls religious instruction. When the group gathered around the fire on winter evenings, Pauline would read aloud works of piety, such as the *Liturgical Year* of Dom Gueranger. Their lives moved along quietly for some years, then came the first break in the little circle. Pauline entered the Carmelite convent of Lisieux. She was to advance steadily in her religious vocation, later becoming prioress. It is not astonishing that the youngest sister, then only nine, had a great desire to follow the one who had been her loving guide. Four years later, when Marie joined her sister at the Carmel, Thérèse's desire for a life in religion was intensified. Her education during these years was in the hands of the Benedictine nuns of the convent of Notre-Dame-du-Prè. She was confirmed there at the age of eleven.

In her autobiography Thérèse writes that her personality changed after her mother's death, and from being childishly merry she became withdrawn and shy. While Thérèse was indeed developing into a serious-minded girl, it does not appear that she became markedly sad. We have many evidences of liveliness and fun, and the oral tradition, as well as the many letters, reveal an outgoing nature, able to articulate the warmest expressions of love for her family, teachers, and friends.

On Christmas Eve, just a few days before Thérèse's fourteenth birthday, she underwent an experience which she ever after referred to as "my conversion." It was to exert a profound influence on her life. Let her tell of it—and its moral effect—in her own words: "On that blessed night the sweet infant Jesus, scarcely an hour old, filled the darkness of my soul with floods of light. By becoming weak and little, for love of me, He made me strong and brave: He put His own weapons into my hands so that I went on from strength to strength, beginning, if I may say so, 'to run as a giant.' " An indelible impression had been made on this attuned soul; she claimed that the Holy Child had healed her of undue sensitiveness and "girded her with His weapons." It was by reason of this vision that the saint was to become known as "Thérèse of the Child Jesus."

The next year she told her father of her wish to become a Carmelite. He readily consented, but both the Carmelite authorities and Bishop Hugonin of Bayeux refused to consider it while she was still so young. A few months later, in November, to her unbounded delight, her father took her and another daughter, Céline, to visit Notre-Dame des Victoires in Paris, then on pilgrimage to Rome for the Jubilee of Pope Leo XIII. The party was accompanied by the Abbé Reverony of Bayeux. In a letter from Rome to her sister Pauline, who was now Sister Agnes of Jesus, Thérèse described the audience: "The Pope was sitting on a great chair; M. Reverony was near him; he watched the pilgrims kiss the Pope's foot and pass before him and spoke a word about some of them. Imagine how my heart beat as I saw my turn come: I didn't want to return without speaking to the Pope. I spoke, but I did not get it all said because M. Reverony did not give me time. He said immediately: 'Most Holy Father, she is a child who wants to enter Carmel at fifteen, but its superiors are considering the matter at the moment.' I would have liked to be able to explain my case, but there was no way. The Holy Father said to me simply: 'If the good God wills, you will enter.' Then I was made to pass on to another room. Pauline, I cannot tell you what I felt. It was like annihilation, I felt deserted. . . . Still God cannot be giving me trials beyond my strength. He gave me the courage to sustain this one."

Thérèse did not have to wait long in suspense. The Pope's blessing and the earnest prayers she offered at many shrines during the pilgrimage had the desired effect. At the end of the year Bishop Hugonin gave his permission, and on April 9, 1888, Thérèse joined her sisters in the Carmel at Lisieux. "From her entrance she astonished the community by her bearing, which was marked by a certain majesty that one would not expect in a child of fifteen." So testified her novice mistress at the time of Thérèse's beatification. During her novitiate Father Pichon, a Jesuit, gave a retreat, and he also testified to Thérèse's piety. "It was easy to direct that child. The Holy Spirit was leading her and I do not think that I ever had, either then or later, to warn her against illusions. . . . What struck me during the retreat were the spiritual trials through which God wished her to pass." Thérèse's presence among them filled the nuns with happiness. She was slight in build, and had fair hair, gray-blue eyes, and delicate features. With all the intensity of her ardent nature she loved the daily round of religious practices, the liturgical prayers, the reading of Scripture. After entering the Carmel she began to sign letters to her father and others, "Thérèse of the Child Jesus."

In 1889 the Martin sisters suffered a great shock. Their father, after two paralytic strokes, had a mental breakdown and had to be removed to a private sanatarium, where he remained for three years. Thérèse bore this grievous sorrow heroically.

On September 8, 1890, at the age of seventeen, Thérèse took final vows. In spite of poor health, she carried out from the first all the austerities of the stern Carmelite rule, except that she was not permitted to fast. "A soul of such mettle," said the prioress, "must not be treated like a child. Dispensations are not meant for her." The physical ordeal which she felt more than any other was the cold of the convent buildings in winter, but no one even suspected this until she confessed it on her death-bed. And by that time she was able to say, "I have reached the point of not being able to suffer any more, because all suffering is sweet to me."

In 1893, when she was twenty, she was appointed to assist the novice mistress, and was in fact mistress in all but name. She comments, "From afar it seems easy to do good to souls, to make them love God more, to mold them according to our own ideas and views. But coming closer we find, on the contrary, that to do good without God's help is as impossible as to make the sun shine at night."

In her twenty-third year, on order of the prioress, Thérèse began to write the memories of her childhood and of life at the convent; this material forms the first chapters of *Histoire d'un âme*, the *History of a Soul*. It is a unique and engaging document, written with a charming spontaneity, full of fresh turns of phrase, unconscious self-revelation, and, above all, giving evidence of deep spirituality. She describes her own prayers and thereby tells us much about herself. "With me prayer is a lifting up of the heart, a look towards Heaven, a cry of gratitude and love uttered equally in sorrow and in joy; in a word, something noble, supernatural, which enlarges my soul and unites it to God. . . . Except for the Divine Office, which in spite of my unworthiness is a daily joy, I have not the courage to look through books for beautiful prayers. . . . I do as a child who has not learned to read, I just tell our Lord all that I want and he understands." She has natural psychological insight: "Each time that my enemy would provoke me to fight I behave like a brave soldier. I know that a duel is an act of cowardice, and so, without once looking him in the face, I turn my back on the foe, hasten to my Saviour, and vow that I am ready to shed my blood in witness of my belief in Heaven." She mentions her own patience humorously. During meditation in the choir, one of the sisters continually fidgeted with her rosary, until Thérèse was perspiring with irritation. At last, "instead of trying not to hear it, which was impossible, I set myself to listen as though it had been some delightful music, and my meditation, which was *not* the 'prayer of quiet,' passed in offering this music to our Lord." Her last chapter is a paean to divine love, and concludes, "I entreat Thee to let Thy divine eyes rest upon a vast number of little souls; I entreat Thee to choose in this world a legion of little victims of Thy love." She counted herself among these. "I am a very little soul, who can offer only very little things to the Lord."

In 1894 Louis Martin died, and soon Céline, who had of late been taking care of him, made the fourth sister from this family in the Carmel at Lisieux. Some years later, the fifth, Léonie, entered the convent of the Visitation at Caen.

Thérèse occupied herself with reading and writing almost up to the end of her life. That event loomed ever nearer as tuberculosis made a steady advance. During the night between Holy Thursday and Good Friday, 1896, she suffered a pulmonary haemorrhage. Although her bodily and spiritual sufferings were extreme, she wrote many letters, to members of her family and to distant friends, as well as continuing *Histoire d'un âme*. She carried on a correspondance with Carmelite sisters at Hanoi, China; they wished her to come out and join them, not realizing the seriousness of her ailment. She had a great yearning to respond to their appeal. At intervals moments of revelation came to her, and it was then that she penned those succinct reflections that are now repeated so widely. Here are three of them that give the flavor of her mind: "I will spend my Heaven doing good on earth." "I have never given the good God aught but love, and it is with love that He will repay." "My 'little way' is the way of spiritual childhood, the way of trust and absolute self-surrender."

A further insight is given us in a letter Thérèse wrote, shortly before she died, to Père Roulland, a missionary in China. "Sometimes, when I read spiritual treatises, in which perfection is shown with a thousand obstacles in the way and a host of illusions round about it, my poor little mind soon grows weary, I close the learned book, which leaves my head splitting and my heart parched, and

I take the Holy Scriptures. Then all seems luminous, a single word opens up infinite horizons to my soul, perfection seems easy; I see that it is enough to realize one's nothingness, and give oneself wholly, like a child, into the arms of the good God. Leaving to great souls, great minds, the fine books I cannot understand, I rejoice to be little because 'only children, and those who are like them, will be admitted to the heavenly banquet.' "

In June, 1897, Thérèse was removed to the infirmary of the convent. On September 30, with the words, "My God . . . I love Thee!" on her lips she died. The day before, her sister Céline, knowing the end was at hand, had asked for some word of farewell, and Thérèse, serene in spite of pain, murmured, "I have said all . . . all is consummated . . . only love counts."

The prioress, Mother Marie de Gonzague, wrote in the convent register, alongside the saint's act of Profession: ". . . The nine and a half years she spent among us leave our souls fragrant with the most beautiful virtues with which the life of a Carmelite can be filled. A perfect model of humility, obedience, charity, prudence, detachment, and regularity, she fulfilled the difficult discipline of mistress of novices with a sagacity and affection which nothing could equal save her love for God. . . ."

The Church was to recognize a profound and valuable teaching in 'the little way'—connoting a realistic awareness of one's limitations, and the wholehearted giving of what one has, however small the gift. Beginning in 1898, with the publication of a small edition of *Histoire d'un âme,* the cult of this saint of 'the little way' grew so swiftly that the Pope dispensed with the rule that a process for canonization must not be started until fifty years after death. Almost from childhood, it seems, Thérèse had consciously aspired to the heights, often saying to herself that God would not fill her with a desire that was unattainable. Only twenty-six years after her death she was beatified by Pope Pius XI, and in the year of Jubilee, 1925, he pronounced her a saint. Two years later she was named heavenly patroness of foreign missions along with St. Francis Xavier.

Saint Frances Xavier Cabrini

Virgin, Foundress

1 9 1 7

(December 22)

As a saint of our own time and as the first United States citizen to be elevated to sainthood, Mother Cabrini has a double claim on our interest. Foundress of the Missionary Sisters of the Sacred Heart and pioneer worker for the welfare of dispersed Italian nationals, this diminutive nun was responsible for the establishment of nearly seventy orphanages, schools, and hospitals, scattered over eight countries in Europe, North, South, and Central America. Still living are pupils, colleagues, and friends who remember Mother Cabrini vividly; her spirit continues to inspire the nuns who received their training at her hands. Since the record remains fresh in memory, and since the saint's letters and diaries have been carefully preserved, we have more authentic information about her, especially of the formative years, than we have concerning any other saint.

Francesca Cabrini was born on July 15, 1850, in the village of Sant' Angelo, on the outskirts of Lodi, about twenty miles from Milan, in the pleasant, fertile Lombardy plain. She was the thirteenth child of a farmer's family, her father Agostino being the proprietor of a modest estate. The home into which she was born was a comfortable, attractive place for children, with its flowering vines, its gardens, and animals; but its serenity and security was in strong contrast with the confusion of the times. Italy had succeeded in throwing off the Austrian yoke and was moving towards unity. Agostino and his wife Stella were conservative people who took no part in the political upheavals around them, although some of their relatives were deeply concerned in the struggle, and one, Agostino Depretis, later became prime minister. Sturdy and pious, the Cabrinis were devoted to their home, their children, and their Church. Signora Cabrini was fifty-two when Francesca was born, and the tiny baby seemed so fragile at birth that she was carried to the church for baptism at once. No one would have ventured to predict then that she would not only survive but live out sixty-seven extraordinarily active and productive years. Villagers and members of the family recalled later that just before her birth a flock of white doves circled around high above the house, and one of them dropped down to nestle in the vines that covered the walls. The father took the bird, showed it to his children, then released it to fly away.

Since the mother had so many cares, the oldest daughter, Rosa, assumed charge of the newest arrival. She made the little Cecchina, for so the family called the baby, her companion, carried her on errands around the village, later taught her to knit and sew, and gave her religious instruction. In preparation for her future career as a teacher, Rosa was inclined to be severe. Her small sister's nature was quite the reverse; Cecchina was gay and smiling and teachable. Agostino was in the habit of reading aloud to his children, all gathered together in the big kitchen. He often read from a book of missionary stories, which fired little Cecchina's imagination. In her play, her dolls became holy nuns. When she went on a visit to her uncle, a priest who lived beside a swift canal, she made little boats of paper, dropped violets in them, called the flowers missionaries, and launched them to sail off to India and China. Once, playing thus, she tumbled into the water, but was quickly rescued and suffered only shock from the accident.

At thirteen Francesca was sent to a private school kept by the Daughters of the Sacred Heart. Here she remained for five years, taking the course that led to a teacher's certificate. Rosa had by this time been teaching for some years. At eighteen Francesca passed her examinations, *cum laude,* and then applied for admission into the convent, in the hope that she might some day be sent as a teacher to the Orient. When, on account of her health, her application was turned down, she resolved to devote herself to a life of lay service. At home she shared wholeheartedly in the domestic tasks. Within the next few years she had the sorrow of losing both her parents. An epidemic of smallpox later ran through the village, and she threw herself into nursing the stricken. Eventually she caught the disease herself, but Rosa, now grown much gentler, nursed her so skillfully that she recovered promptly, with no disfigurement. Her oval face, with its large expressive blue eyes, was beginning to show the beauty that in time became so striking.

Francesca was offered a temporary position as substitute teacher in a village school, a mile or so away. Thankful for this chance to practice her profession, she accepted, learning much from her brief experience. She then again applied for admission to the convent of the Daughters of the Sacred Heart, and might have been accepted, for her health was now much improved. However, the rector of the parish, Father Antonio Serrati, had been observing her ardent spirit of service and was making other plans for her future. He therefore advised the Mother Superior to turn her down once more.

Father Serrati, soon to be Monsignor Serrati, was to remain Francesca's lifelong friend and adviser. From the start he had great confidence in her abilities, and now he gave her a most difficult task. She was to go to a disorganized and badly run orphanage in the nearby town of Cadogno, called the House of Providence. It had been started by two wholly incompetent laywomen, one of whom had given the money for its endowment. Now Francesca was charged "to put things right," a large order in view of her youth—she was but twenty-four—and the complicated human factors in the situation. The next six years were a period of training in tact and diplomacy, as well as in the everyday, practical problems of running such an institution. She worked quietly and effectively, in the face of jealous opposition, devoting herself to the young girls under her supervision and winning their affection and cooperation. Francesca assumed the nun's habit, and in three years took her vows. By this time her ecclesiastical superiors were impressed by her performance and made her Mother Superior of the institution. For three years more she carried on, and then, as the foundress had grown more and more erratic, the House of Providence was dissolved. Francesca had under her at the time seven young nuns whom she had trained. Now they were all homeless.

At this juncture the bishop of Lodi sent for her and offered a suggestion that was to determine the nun's life work. He wished her to found a missionary order of women to serve in his diocese. She accepted the opportunity gratefully and soon discovered a house which she thought suitable, an abandoned Franciscan friary in Cadogno. The building was purchased, the sisters moved in and began to make the place habitable. Almost immediately it became a busy hive of activity. They received orphans and foundlings, opened a day school to help pay expenses, started classes in needlework and sold their fine embroidery to earn a little more money. Meanwhile, in the midst of superintending all these activities, Francesca, now Mother Cabrini, was drawing up a simple rule for the institute. As one patron, she chose St. Francis de Sales, and as another, her own name saint, St. Francis Xavier. The rule was simple, and the habit she devised for the hard-working nuns was correspondingly simple, without the luxury of elaborate linen or starched headdress. They even carried their rosaries in their pockets, to be less encumbered while going about their tasks. The name chosen for the order was the Missionary Sisters of the Sacred Heart.

With the success of the institute and the growing reputation of its young founder, many postulants came asking for admission, more than the limited quarters could accommodate. The nuns' resources were now, as always, at a low level; nevertheless, expansion seemed necessary. Unable to hire labor, they undertook to be their own builders. One nun was the daughter of a bricklayer, and she showed the others how to lay bricks. The new walls were actually going up under her direction, when the local authorities stepped in and insisted that the walls must be buttressed for safety. The nuns obeyed, and with some outside help went on with the job, knowing they were working to meet a real need. The townspeople could not, of course, remain indifferent in the face of such determination. After two years another mission was started by Mother Cabrini, at Cremona, and then a boarding school for girls at the provincial capital of Milan. The latter was the first of many such schools, which in time were to become a source of income and also of novices to carry on the ever-expanding work. Within seven years seven institutions of various kinds, each founded to meet some critical need, were in operation, all staffed by nuns trained under Mother Cabrini.

In September, 1887, came the nun's first trip to Rome, always a momentous event in the life of any religious. In her case it was to mark the opening of a much broader field of activity. Now, in her late thirties, Mother Cabrini was a woman of note in her own locality, and some rumors of her work had undoubtedly been carried to Rome. Accompanied by a sister, Serafina, she left Cadogno with the dual purpose of seeking papal approval for the order, which so far had functioned merely on the diocesan level, and of opening a house in Rome which might serve as headquarters for future enterprises. While she did not go as an absolute stranger, many another has arrived there with more backing and stayed longer with far less to show.

Within two weeks Mother Cabrini had made contacts in high places, and had several interviews with Cardinal Parocchi, who became her loyal supporter, with full confidence in her sincerity and ability. She was encouraged to continue her foundations elsewhere and charged to establish a free school and kindergarten in the environs of Rome. Pope Leo XIII received her and blessed the work. He was then an old man of seventy-eight, who had occupied the papal throne for ten years and done much to enhance the prestige of the office. Known as the "workingman's Pope" because of his sympathy for the poor and his series of famous encyclicals on social justice, he was also a man of scholarly attainments and cultural interests. He saw Mother Cabrini on many future occasions, always spoke of her with admiration and affection, and sent contributions from his own funds to aid her work.

A new and greater challenge awaited the intrepid nun, a chance to fulfill the old dream of being a missionary to a distant land. A burning question of the day in Italy was the plight of Italians in foreign countries. As a result of hard times at home, millions of them had emigrated to the United States and to South America in the hope of bettering themselves. In the New World they were faced with many cruel situations which they were often helpless to meet. Bishop Scalabrini had written a pamphlet describing their misery, and had been instrumental in establishing St. Raphael's Society for their material assistance, and also a mission of the Congregation of St. Charles Borromeo in New York. Talks with Bishop Scalabrini persuaded Mother Cabrini that this cause was henceforth to be hers.

In America the great tide of immigration had not yet reached its peak, but a steady stream of hopeful humanity from southern Europe, lured by promises and pictures, was flowing into our ports, with little or no provision made for the reception or assimilation of the individual components. Instead, the newcomers fell victim at once to the prejudices of both native-born Americans and the earlier immigrants, who had chiefly been of Irish and German stock. They were also exploited unmercifully by their own *padroni*, or bosses, after being drawn into the roughest and most dangerous jobs, digging and draining, and the almost equally hazardous indoor work in mills and sweatshops. They tended to cluster in the overcrowded, disease-breeding slums of our cities, areas which were becoming known as "Little Italies." They were in America, but not of it. Both church and family life were sacrificed to mere survival and the struggle to save enough money to return to their native land. Cut off from their accustomed ties, some drifted into the criminal underworld. For the most part, however, they lived forgotten, lonely and homesick, trying to cope with new ways of living without proper direction. "Here we live like animals," wrote one immigrant; "one lives and dies without a priest, without teachers, and without doctors." All in all, the problem was so vast and difficult that no one with a soul less dauntless than Mother Cabrini's would have dreamed of tackling it.

After seeing that the new establishments at Rome were running smoothly and visiting the old centers in Lombardy, Mother Cabrini wrote to Archbishop Corrigan in New York that she was coming to aid him. She was given to understand that a convent or hostel would be prepared, to accommodate the few nuns she would bring. Unfortunately there was a misunderstanding as to the time of her arrival, and when she and the seven nuns landed in New York on March 31, 1889, they learned that there was no convent ready. They felt they could not afford a hotel, and asked to be taken to an inexpensive lodging house. This turned out to be so dismal and dirty that they avoided the beds and spent the night in prayer and quiet thought. But the nuns were young and full of courage; from this bleak beginning they emerged the next morning to attend Mass. Then they called on the apologetic archbishop and outlined a plan of action. They wished to begin work without delay. A wealthy Italian woman contributed money for the purchase of their first house, and before long an orphanage had opened its doors there. So quickly did they gather a houseful of orphans that their funds ran low; to feed the ever-growing brood they must go out to beg. The nuns became familiar figures down on Mulberry Street, in the heart of the city's Little Italy. They trudged from door to door, from shop to shop, asking for anything that could be spared—food, clothing, or money.

With the scene surveyed and the work well begun, Mother Cabrini returned to Italy in July of the same year. She again visited the foundations, stirred up the ardor of the nuns, and had another audience with the Pope, to whom she gave a report of the situation in New York with respect to the Italian colony. Also, while in Rome, she made plans for opening a dormitory for normal-school students, securing the aid of several rich women for this enterprise. The following spring she sailed again for New

SAINT VINCENT DE PAUL   Unknown

A nineteenth-century Swiss picture, this painting reflects the humility and
benevolence of Saint Vincent de Paul although it is not very great art. The
costumes of the children represent the era in which the picture was painted.

Saint Vincent is symbolized, very simply, by the baby in his arms and the
children surrounding him.

OUR LADY OF LOURDES   R. M. Dougherty
This painting represents the vision of Saint Bernadette at the grotto of
Lourdes. Our Lady appears with golden roses on her feet, with a rosary of
large white beads. On her nimbus is written "I am the Immaculate Conception."

Another saint too modern to have accepted symbols in art, Saint Bernadette
is identified by the grotto and the details of her vision.

York, with a fresh group of nuns chosen from the order. Soon after her arrival she concluded arrangements for the purchase from the Jesuits of a house and land, now known as West Park, on the west bank of the Hudson. This rural retreat was to become a veritable paradise for children from the city's slums. Then, with several nuns who had been trained as teachers, she embarked for Nicaragua, where she had been asked to open a school for girls of well-to-do families in the city of Granada. This was accomplished with the approbation of the Nicaraguan government, and Mother Cabrini, accompanied by one nun, started back north overland, curious to see more of the people of Central America. They traveled by rough and primitive means, but the journey was safely achieved. They stopped off for a time in New Orleans and did preparatory work looking to the establishment of a mission. The plight of Italian immigrants in Louisiana was almost as serious as in New York. On reaching New York she chose a little band of courageous nuns to begin work in the southern city. They literally begged their way to New Orleans, for there was no money for train fare. As soon as they had made a very small beginning, Mother Cabrini joined them. With the aid of contributions, they bought a tenement which became known as a place where any Italian in trouble or need could go for help and counsel. A school was established which rapidly became a center for the city's Italian population. The nuns made a practice too of visiting the outlying rural sections where Italians were employed on the great plantations.

The year that celebrated the four hundredth anniversary of Columbus' voyage of discovery, 1892, marked also the founding of Mother Cabrini's first hospital. At this time Italians were enjoying more esteem than usual and it was natural that this first hospital should be named for Columbus. Earlier Mother Cabrini had had some experience of hospital management in connection with the institution conducted by the Congregation of St. Charles Borromeo, but the new one was to be quite independent. With an initial capital of two hundred and fifty dollars, representing five contributions of fifty dollars each, Columbus Hospital began its existence on Twelfth Street in New York. Doctors offered it their services without charge, and the nuns tried to make up in zeal what they lacked in equipment. Gradually the place came to have a reputation that won for it adequate financial support. It moved to larger quarters on Twentieth Street, and continues to function to this day.

Mother Cabrini returned to Italy frequently to oversee the training of novices and to select the nuns best qualified for foreign service. She was in Rome to share in the Pope's Jubilee, celebrating his fifty years as a churchman. Back in New York in 1895, she accepted the invitation of the Archbishop of Buenos Aires to come down to Argentina and establish a school. The Nicaraguan school had been forced to close its doors as a result of a revolutionary overthrow of the government, and the nuns had moved to Panama and opened a school there. Mother Cabrini and her companion stopped to visit this new institution before proceeding by water down the Pacific Coast towards their destination. To avoid the stormy Straits of Magellan they had been advised to make the later stages of the journey by land, which meant a train trip from the coast to the mountains, across the Andes by mule-back, then another train trip to the capital. The nuns looked like Capuchin friars, for they wore brown fur-lined capes. On their unaccustomed mounts, guided by muleteers whose language they hardly understood, they followed the narrow trail over the backbone of the Andes, with frightening chasms below and icy winds whistling about their heads. The perilous crossing was made without serious mishap. On their arrival in Buenos Aires they learned that the archbishop who had invited them to come had died, and they were not sure of a welcome. It was not long, however, before Mother Cabrini's charm and sincerity had worked their usual spell, and she was entreated to open a school. She inspected dozens of sites before making a choice. When it came to the purchase of land she seemed to have excellent judgment as to what location would turn out to be good from all points of view. The school was for girls of wealthy families, for the Italians in Argentina were, on the average, more prosperous than those of North America. Another group of nuns came down from New York to serve as teachers. Here and in similar schools elsewhere, today's pupils became tomorrow's supporters of the foundations.

Not long afterward schools were opened in Paris, in England, and in Spain, where Mother Cabrini's work had the sponsorship of the queen. From the Latin countries in course of time came novice teachers for the South American schools. Another southern country, Brazil, was soon added to the lengthening roster, with establishments at Rio de Janeiro and Sao Paulo. Back in the United States Mother Cabrini started parochial schools in and around New York and an orphanage at Dobbs Ferry. In 1899 she founded the Sacred Heart Villa on Fort Washington Avenue, New York, as a school and training center for novices. In later years this place was her nearest approach to an American home. It is this section of their city that New Yorkers now associate with her, and here a handsome avenue bears her name.

Launching across the country, Mother Cabrini now extended her activities to the Pacific Coast. Newark, Scranton, Chicago, Denver, Seattle, Los Angeles, all became familiar territory. In Colorado she visited the mining camps, where the high rate of fatal accidents left an unusually large number of fatherless children to be cared for. Wherever she went men and women began to take constructive steps for the remedying of suffering and wrong, so powerful was the stimulus of her personality. Her warm desire to serve God by helping people, especially children, was a steady inspiration to others. Yet the founding of each little school or orphanage seemed touched by the miraculous, for the necessary funds generally materialized in some last-minute, unexpected fashion.

In Seattle, in 1909, Mother Cabrini took the oath of allegiance to the United States and became a citizen of the country. She was then fifty-nine years old, and was looking forward to a future of lessened activity, possibly even to semi-retirement in the mother house at Cadogno. But for some years the journeys to and fro across the Atlantic went on; like a bird, she never settled long in one place. When she was far away, her nuns felt her presence, felt she understood their cares and pains. Her modest nature had always kept her from assuming an attitude of authority; indeed she even deplored being referred to as "head" of her Order. During the last years Mother Cabrini undoubtedly pushed her flagging energies to the limit of endurance. Coming back from a trip to the Pacific Coast in the late fall of 1917, she stopped in Chicago. Much troubled now over the war and all the new problems it brought, she suffered a recurrence of the malaria contracted many years before. Then, while she and other nuns were making preparations for a children's Christmas party in the hospital, a sudden heart attack ended her life on earth in a few minutes. The date was December 22, and she was sixty-seven. The little nun had been the friend of three popes, a foster-mother to thousands of children, for whom she had found means to provide shelter and food; she had created a flourishing order, and established many institutions to serve human needs.

It was not surprising that almost at once Catholics in widely separated places began saying to each other, "Surely she was a saint." This ground swell of popular feeling culminated in 1929 in the first official steps towards beatification. Ten years later she became Blessed Mother Cabrini, and Cardinal Mundelein, who had officiated at her funeral in Chicago, now presided at the beatification. Heralded by a great pealing of the bells of St. Peter's and the four hundred other churches of Rome, the canonization ceremony took place on July 7, 1946. Hundreds of devout Catholics from the United States were in attendance, as well as the highest dignitaries of the Church and lay noblemen. Saint Frances Xavier Cabrini, the first American to be canonized, lies buried under the altar of the chapel of Mother Cabrini High School in New York City.

Scriptural Saints

Saint Michael
Archangel

(September 29)

St. Michael, who ranks among the seven archangels, is also one of the three angels mentioned by name in the Scriptures, the others being St. Raphael and St. Gabriel. St. Michael is spoken of twice in the Old Testament, and twice in the New. The first reference occurs in the Book of Daniel (chapter x), where Michael comes to comfort Daniel after he has had a vision, and promises to be his helper in all things. In Daniel xii, Michael is called "the great prince who standeth for the children of Thy people." In these references Michael is represented as Israel's great support during the seventy years of the Babylonian captivity. Daniel, wise and holy leader that he was, wanted his people to understand that God had not forgotten them, and that, even though enslaved, they had a royal champion. In the New Testament (Jude ix), we are told that Michael disputed with the devil over the body of Moses; this episode is not mentioned elsewhere in the Bible.

In the Apocalypse (chapter xii) we find the most dramatic reference to St. Michael. Here John recounts the great battle in Heaven, when the wicked angels under Lucifer revolt against God, and how Michael, leading the faithful angels, defeats the hosts of evil and drives them out. In this role he has been painted by many artists, and the poet Milton, in book vi of *Paradise Lost*, recounts the famous struggle. Because of this victory, St. Michael is revered in Catholic tradition and liturgy as the protector of the Church, as once he was regarded as the protector of the Israelites. In the Eastern Church, as well as among many theologians in the West, St. Michael is placed over all the angels, as prince of the Seraphim. He is the special patron of sick people, mariners, and grocers; in Asia Minor many curative springs were dedicated to him. His cult has also been popular in Egypt, Rome, France, and Germany. His emblems are a banner, a sword, a dragon, and scales. The name Michael is a variation of Micah, meaning in Hebrew, "Who is like God?"

Saint Gabriel
Archangel

(*March 24*)

The Jews venerated Gabriel as the angel of judgment, and in both Jewish and Christian tradition he is one of the seven archangels. Gabriel is also known to the Mohammedans, who believe him to be the angel who served as the mouthpiece of God in dictating the Koran to their prophet. Mention of St. Gabriel occurs four times in the Scriptures. He first appears to Daniel in the guise of a man and proceeds to interpret a vision Daniel has had of a ram with two horns, which is overcome by a he-goat. Gabriel explains that the ram is the empire of the Medes and the Persians which will be destroyed by the he-goat, the king of the Greeks (Alexander the Great). This vision came to Daniel in the year 554 B.C., while the Israelites were in captivity in Babylonia. The prophecy was to be fulfilled nearly two hundred years later. The angel Gabriel again appears to Daniel (Daniel ix, 21-27) to foretell the coming of the Messiah and the destruction of Jerusalem

and its sanctuary. The next appearance of Gabriel is recorded in
Luke i, 11-20, where he predicts to the priest Zachary as he is burning incense at the altar in the temple that his wife is to bear a son
whose name shall be John. The final mention of Gabriel is found
a little later in the same chapter of Luke, where he goes to the
Blessed Virgin Mary with the tidings that she is to be the Mother
of the Messiah. Thus we see that Gabriel comes as the bearer of
good tidings and as the comforter and helper of men. In Milton's
Paradise Lost, book iv, Gabriel is placed at the eastern gate of
Paradise as chief of the angelic guards. Christian tradition holds
that Gabriel was the unnamed angel who appeared to Jesus in the
Garden of Gethsemane. A fresco of this angel figures prominently
in a chapel on the Appian Way, indicating that he was honored
very early in the history of the Church. The Hebrew word from
which Gabriel is derived means "hero of God."

Saint Anne

Mother of the Blessed Virgin

(*July 26*)

Of St. Anne we have no certain knowledge. She is not mentioned
in the New Testament, and we must depend on apocryphal
literature, chiefly the Protoevangelium of James, which dates back
only to the second century. In this document we are told that
Anne, wife of Joachim, was advanced in years and that her prayers
for a child had not been answered. Once as she prayed beneath a
laurel tree near her home in Galilee, an angel appeared and said
to her, "Anne, the Lord hath heard thy prayer and thou shalt con-

ceive and bring forth, and thy seed shall be spoken of in all the world." Anne replied, "As the Lord my God liveth, if I beget either male or female, I will bring it as a gift to the Lord my God; and it shall minister to Him in holy things all the days of its life." And thus Anne became the mother of the Blessed Virgin Mary. The cult of St. Anne was known in the East in the fifth century, but it was not diffused in the West until the thirteenth. A shrine at Douai, in northern France, was one of the early centers of the cult. In 1382 her feast was extended to the whole Western Church, and she became very popular, especially in France. Her two most famous shrines are at St. Anne d'Auray in Brittany and at St. Anne-de-Beaupré in the province of Quebec. She is patroness of housewives, women in labor, cabinet-makers, and miners. Her emblem is a door. St. Anne has been frequently represented in art, and the lovely face depicted by Leonardo da Vinci comes first to mind in this connection. The name Anne derives from the Hebrew Hannah, meaning "grace."

Saint Joachim
Father of the Blessed Virgin

(August 6)

Nothing is known of St. Joachim save what is told in apocryphal literature. He was a man of Galilee, husband of Anne, and both he and Anne were in the decline of life when Mary was born. Tradition relates that while Joachim was away from home he had a vision that Anne was to be blessed with a child, and that on his return home, his wife ran forth to tell of the visitation of an angel who had revealed to her the same good tidings. There was an ancient belief that a child born of an elderly mother who had given up hope of having offspring was destined for some high purpose and would be blessed by all the world. Parallels occur in the Old Testament in the cases of Rachel, mother of Joseph, and that of Hannah, mother of Samuel. The traditional tomb of St. Anne and St. Joachim was rediscovered in Jerusalem in 1889.

Saint Joseph
Foster Father of the Lord
c. 2 0
(*March 19*)

St. Joseph, in all likelihood, was born in Bethlehem, and it is generally assumed that he died at Nazareth before Jesus began his ministry. The Bible tells us very little of Joseph, but from the early chapters of Matthew and Luke we glean that he was a carpenter by trade, a just and pious man, and a most excellent husband and father. The geneology given in Matthew i, 1-17, traces his line from Abraham and King David. In accordance with the Jewish ritual, he was betrothed to the Virgin Mary, who was also of the race of David. Later, having learned that she was with child, though he had not been near her, he was privately considering putting her away. Yet he hesitated, for he was a kindly man, and he did not wish to expose the young woman to the reproach which such an action would bring. It was at this time of uncertainty that the angel of the Lord appeared to Joseph in a dream and revealed to him the Mystery of the Incarnation. "Do not be afraid, Joseph, son of David," said the angel, "to take to thee Mary thy wife, for that which is begotten of her is of the Holy Spirit. And she shall bring forth a son, and thou shall call his name Jesus; for he shall save the people from their sins" (Luke i, 20-21).

Joseph now accepted without question the two-fold office with which he was charged, protector of Mary's honor and foster father of the child that was to be born. He took Mary with him from Nazareth to Bethlehem, when, in compliance with the Roman edict, it was necessary to return there for the census-taking. Then came the birth of the Lord. We know that Joseph was at the stable of the inn beside his wife when the three wise men, following a star, came there out of the East to honor the newborn child with precious gifts. The infant was duly circumcized, and when the forty days prescribed by Mosaic law were passed, Joseph and Mary took him to the temple in Jerusalem. A certain holy man named Simeon, to whom it had been revealed that he would not die until he had seen the Christ, was in the temple on that day, and when he saw Jesus, he knew that this was the promised Messiah. The priest blessed Joseph and Mary and spoke of the glory that had come to them.

The angel of the Lord again appeared to Joseph to tell him to flee with his family into Egypt to escape the wrath of the jealous King Herod. Obediently Joseph hastened to comply, and the family stayed in Egypt until word came of Herod's death, when it was safe for them to return to their homeland. Back in the pleasant hill-town of Nazareth, Joseph carried on his trade, teaching it to Jesus as the boy grew older. The important event of every year was the Passover, when the pious traveled to Jerusalem to share in the ceremonies. Joseph and Mary were in the habit of going on this journey, and we are told that Joseph shared his wife's anxiety when, on one such occasion, the twelve-year-old Jesus became separated from them, and was later found debating with the learned men in the temple. Thus all we know of Joseph adds to the picture of the gentle, protective father and husband.

Veneration of this saint played no part in primitive Christianity. Recognition seems to have developed first among the Copts, a branch of Eastern Christendom. Devotion to St. Joseph was practiced from very early times in Ireland, and in the Middle Ages in

Europe many fanciful stories were woven about his name. In spite of this popularity, it was not until 1870, under Pope Pius IX, that he was proclaimed patron of the Universal Church, and Wednesdays in March were set for special devotion to him. The great number of churches dedicated to St. Joseph is an indication of the breadth and depth of this veneration. St. Joseph is patron of carpenters and of a happy death; his symbols are the rod and the plane.

Saint Elizabeth
Mother of John the Baptist

(*November 5*)

The name Elizabeth, which has been borne by several saints, means in Hebrew "worshiper of God." All that we know of Elizabeth, wife of Zachary and mother of John the Baptist, is to be found in the book of Luke. A descendant of the priestly line of Aaron, she was a kinswoman—how close we are not told—of the Virgin Mary. According to the Gospel, Elizabeth had lived a blameless life with her husband in one of the hill-towns of Judaea. Having reached an advanced age with her prayers for a son unanswered, she thought that her barrenness was a reproach. One day, while Zachary was serving in the temple, the Angel Gabriel appeared at the right of the altar, and announced that a son would be born to Elizabeth. It was in the sixth month of her pregnancy that the Virgin Mary came to visit her—a touching and beautiful scene pictured by many great artists. The Angel Gabriel, having lately announced to Mary the destiny that awaited her, also told her that her kinswoman Elizabeth was with child. The Virgin Mary, eager to share in Elizabeth's happiness and to confide that she too would bear a child, traveled down the dusty road from Nazareth. On Mary's arrival, she was amazed when Elizabeth, having foreknowledge, greeted her as "mother of my Lord." Elizabeth's salutation was in these words: "Blessed art thou among women and blessed is the fruit of thy womb. And how have I deserved that the mother of my Lord should come to me? For behold, the moment that the sound of thy greeting came to my ears, the babe in my womb leapt for joy. And blessed is she who has believed, because the things promised her by the Lord shall be accomplished." The Gospel story tells us further that at Elizabeth's delivery her friends and neighbors rejoiced with her, and when the child was brought to be circumcized, they were going to call him after his father Zachary, but his mother said, "His name shall be John."

Saint Zachary
Father of John the Baptist

(*November 5*)

S t. Zachary, whose feast is celebrated on the same day as that of St. Elizabeth, his wife, was of the tribe of Abia, and a member of the priestly class. It was customary for the priests whose week it was to serve in the temple to cast lots each day for the performance of the various rituals. One day, during Zachary's period of service, the privilege of offering incense on the altar in the holy place fell to him, and while he was alone before the altar performing this rite, the Angel Gabriel appeared to him, standing at the right of the altar. Zachary was troubled and afraid. Then

Gabriel spoke, saying that the prayers of the priest and his wife would be answered; a son was to be born to them, and his name was to be John. Zachary found this hard to believe, for both he and Elizabeth were advanced in years. Overcoming his fear, he asked the angel for some sign. Because he doubted, the angel announced that Zachary would be stricken dumb and would regain the power of speech only when the prophecy was fulfilled. Then the angel disappeared and Zachary came forth from the temple. The people saw that he was unable to speak and they knew then that he had received a vision from the Lord.

Elizabeth conceived and gave birth to the one who was to be the Precursor of the Lord. After eight days, when the child was about to be circumcized, Elizabeth told the people that he was to be named John; and Zachary, still unable to speak, asked for a tablet, and on it he wrote the words, "John is his name." At this moment Zachary's tongue was loosed, and he began to praise the Lord. The New Testament tells us nothing further concerning St. Zachary. In Hebrew his name means "Jehovah hath remembered."

Saint John the Baptist
The Precursor
3 2
(*June 24*)

We are given the story of the ministry of John the Baptist, called the Precursor or Forerunner of the Lord, with some variation of detail, in the three synoptic Gospels of Matthew, Mark, and Luke, as well as in the Book of John. Luke tells us of the birth of John the Baptist in a town of Judaea, about six months before the birth of the Saviour. The attendant circumstances, which we have already recounted under the headings of *St. Elizabeth* and *St. Zachary*, his parents, suggest the miraculous and wonderful. The New Testament tells us nothing of John's early years, but we know that his pious, virtuous parents must have reared the boy with care, conscious always of the important work to which he was appointed, and imbuing him with a sense of his destiny.

When John began final preparations for his mission, he was probably in his thirty-second year. He withdrew into the harsh, rocky desert beyond the Jordan to fast and pray, as was the ancient custom of holy men. We are told that he kept himself alive by eating locusts and wild honey and wore a rough garment of camel's hair, tied with a leathern girdle. When he came back to start preaching in the villages of Judaea, he was haggard and uncouth, but his eyes burned with zeal and his voice carried deep conviction. The Jews were accustomed to preachers and prophets who gave no thought to outward appearances, and they accepted John at once; the times were troubled, and the people yearned for reassurance and comfort. So transcendant was the power emanating from the holy man that after hearing him many believed he was indeed the long-awaited Messiah. John quickly put them right, saying he had come only to prepare the way, and that he was not worthy to unloose the Master's sandals. Although his preaching and baptizing continued for some months during the Saviour's own ministry, John always made plain that he was merely the Forerunner. His humility remained incorruptible even when his fame spread to Jerusalem and members of the higher priesthood came to make inquiries and to hear him. "Repent, for the Kingdom of Heaven is at hand,"—this was John's oft-repeated theme. For the evils of the times his remedy was individual purification. "Every tree," he said, "that is not bringing forth good fruit is to be cut down and thrown into the fire." The reformation of each person's life must be complete— the wheat must be separated from the chaff and the chaff burned "with unquenchable fire."

SAINT JOHN BOSCO   Crida
This painting of the Apostle of Youth is a modern painting after a drawing
of the saint, probably made from life. He is shown in the habit of his order,
and the artist has very simply done nothing to detract from the kindly
ruggedness of his face.

No symbolism is attached to this saint who was canonized in 1934.

SAINT THERESE OF LISEUX   Unknown
This painting by an unknown artist portrays extremely well the youthful-
ness and serenity of Saint Therese who described herself as a "little soul."

Although no symbols are attributed to this modern saint, Saint Therese can
be recognized by her Carmelite habit and the armful of roses.

The rite of baptism, a symbolic act signifying sincere repentance as well as a desire to be spiritually cleansed in order to receive the Christ, was so strongly emphasized by John that people began to call him "the baptizer." The Scriptures tell us of the day when Jesus joined the group of those who wished to receive baptism at John's hands. John knew Jesus for the Messiah they had so long expected, and at first excused himself as unworthy. Then, in obedience to Jesus, he acquiesced and baptized Him. Although sinless, Jesus chose to be baptized in order to identify Himself with the human lot. And when He arose from the waters of the Jordan, where the rite was performed, "the heavens opened and the Spirit as a dove descended. And there came a voice from the heavens, Thou art my beloved Son, in Thee I am well pleased" (Mark i, 11).

John's life now rushes on towards its tragic end. In the fifteenth year of the reign of the Roman emperor, Tiberias Caesar, Herod Antipas was the provincial governor or tetrarch of a subdivision of Palestine which included Galilee and Peraea, a district lying east of the Jordan. In the course of John's preaching, he had denounced in unmeasured terms the immorality of Herod's petty court, and had even boldly upbraided Herod to his face for his defiance of old Jewish law, especially in having taken to himself the wife of his half-brother, Philip. This woman, the dissolute Herodias, was also Herod's niece. Herod feared and reverenced John, knowing him to be a holy man, and he followed his advice in many matters; but he could not endure having his private life castigated. Herodias stimulated his anger by lies and artifices. His resentment at length got the better of his judgment and he had John cast into the fortress of Machaerus, near the Dead Sea. When Jesus heard of this, and knew that some of His disciples had gone to see John, He spoke thus of him: "What went you to see? A prophet? Yea, I say to you, and more than a prophet. This is he of whom it is written: Behold I send my angel before thy face, who shall prepare thy way before thee. For I say to you, amongst those that are born of women there is not a greater prophet than John the Baptist" (Matthew xi, 10-12).

Herodias never ceased plotting against the life of John, who was not silenced even by prison walls. His followers now became even more turbulent. To Herodias soon came the opportunity she had long sought to put an end to the trouble-maker. On Herod's birthday he gave a feast for the chief men of that region. In Matthew xiv, Mark vi, and Luke ix, we are given parallel accounts of this infamous occasion which was to culminate in John's death. At the feast, Salome, fourteen-year-old daughter of Herodias by her lawful husband, pleased Herod and his guests so much by her dancing that Herod promised on oath to give her anything that it was in his power to give, even though it should amount to half his kingdom. Salome, acting under the direction and influence of her wicked mother, answered that she wished to have the head of John the Baptist, presented to her on a platter. Such a horrible request shocked and unnerved Herod. Still, he had given his word and was afraid to break it. So, with no legal formalities whatever, he despatched a soldier to the prison with orders to behead the prisoner and return with it immediately. This was quickly done, and the cruel girl did not hesitate to accept the dish with its dreadful offering and give it to her mother. John's brief ministry was thus terminated by a monstrous crime. There was great sadness among the people who had hearkened to him, and when the disciples of Jesus heard the news of John's death, they came and took the body and laid it reverently in a tomb. Jesus, with some of his disciples, retired "to a desert place apart," to mourn.

The Jewish historian Josephus, giving further testimony of John's holiness, writes: "He was indeed a man endued with all virtue, who exhorted the Jews to the practice of justice towards men and piety towards God; and also to baptism, preaching that they would become acceptable to God if they renounced their sins, and to the cleanness of their bodies added purity of soul." Thus Jews and Christians unite in reverence and love for this prophet-saint whose life is an incomparable example of both humility and courage.

Saint Stephen
The First Martyr
c. 3 5
(*December 26*)

All that we know of the life, trial, and death of St. Stephen, the first martyr, is found in the Book of Acts, chapters vi and vii. In the long chronicle of Christian martyrs, the story of Stephen stands out as one of the most moving and memorable. Although his name is Greek (from Stephanos, meaning crown), Stephen was a Jew, probably among those who had been born or who had lived beyond the borders of Palestine, and therefore had come under the influence of the prevailing Hellenistic culture. The New Testament does not give us the circumstances of his conversion. It would seem, however, that soon after the death of the Messiah he rose to a position of prominence among the Christians of Jerusalem and used his talents especially to win over the Greek-speaking residents of the city.

The earliest mention of Stephen is when he is listed among the seven men chosen to supervise the public tables. We recall that these first Christians held their property in common, the well-to-do sharing what they possessed with the poor; and at this time, as always in the wake of war, there were many "displaced persons" in need of charity. We read in Acts that the Hellenists, as the Greek-speaking Christians were called, thought that they, particularly the widows among them, were being discriminated against at the public tables. The Apostles were informed of these complaints, but they were too busy to deal with the problem. Therefore seven good and prudent men were selected to administer and supervise the tables. The seven, on being presented to the Apostles, were prayed over and ordained by the imposition of hands. Associated in these charitable tasks with Stephen, whose name heads the list as "a man full of faith and the Holy Spirit," were Philip, known as "the Evangelist," Prochorus, Nicanor, Timon, Parmenas, and Nicholas—all Greek names. The title of deacon, which came to be linked with their function, derives from the Greek verb meaning "to minister." These men served the Christian community in temporal and charitable affairs; later on they were to assume minor religious offices.

Stephen, already a leader, now began to speak in public with more vigor and, "full of grace and power, was working great wonders and signs among the people." By this time a number of Jewish priests had been converted to the new faith, but they still held to the old traditions and rules as laid down in Mosaic law. Stephen was prepared to engage in controversy with them, eager to point out that, according to the Master, the old law had been superseded. He was continually quoting Jesus and the prophets to the effect that external usages and all the ancient holy rites were of less importance than the spirit; that even the Temple might be destroyed, as it had been in the past, without damage to the true and eternal religion. It was talk of this sort, carried by hearsay and rumor about the city, and often misquoted, intentionally or not, that was to draw down upon Stephen the wrath of the Jewish priestly class.

It was in a certain synagogue of Jews "called that of the Freedmen, and of the Cyrenians and of the Alexandrians and of those from Cilicia and the province of Asia" that Stephen chiefly disputed. Perhaps they did not understand him; at all events, they could not make effective answer, and so fell to abusing him. They bribed men to say that Stephen was speaking blasphemous words against Moses and against God. The elders and the scribes were stirred up and brought him before the Sanhedrin, the supreme Jewish tribunal, which had authority in both civil and religious matters. False witnesses made their accusations; Stephen defended himself ably, reviewing the long spiritual history of his people;

finally his defense turned into a bitter accusation. He concluded thus:

"Yet not in houses made by hands does the Most High dwell, even as the prophet says. . . . Stiff-necked and uncircumcized in heart and ear, you always oppose the Holy Spirit; as your father did, so do you also. Which of the prophets have not your fathers persecuted? And they killed those who foretold the coming of the Just One, of whom you have now been the betrayers and murderers, you who received the Law as an ordinance of angels and did not keep it."

Thus castigated, the Jews could contain their anger no longer. They rushed upon Stephen, drove him outside the city to the place appointed, and stoned him. At this time Jewish law permitted the death penalty by stoning for blasphemy. Stephen, full of "grace and fortitude" to the very end, met the great test without flinching, praying the Lord to receive his spirit and not to lay this sin against the people. So perished the first martyr, his dying breath spent in prayer for those who killed him. Among those present at the scene and approving of the penalty meted out to Stephen was a young Jew named Saul, the future Paul, Apostle to the Gentiles: his own conversion to Christianity was to take place within a few short months.

In the fifth century the priest Lucian writes of the discovery of the relics of Stephen, which now, it is believed, repose in the church of St. Lawrence in Rome.

Saint Jude

Apostle

FIRST CENTURY

(*October 28*)

We have little knowledge of the life of this Apostle, who is known mainly as the author of the Epistle of St. Jude, the book immediately preceding the Apocalypse of St. John in the New Testament. At the outset of this Epistle Jude identifies himself as "the brother of James." This is taken to mean St. James the Less, bishop of Jerusalem, who is known for his authorship of the Epistle bearing his name. Jude, also known by the name of Thaddeus, and James the Less were sons of Cleophas and Mary, the latter, possibly, a cousin of the Blessed Virgin. We find a reference (Matthew xiii, 55) to Judge as one of the brethren of the Lord, but we are mindful of the fact that near relatives were often called brothers in ancient times.

The history of St. Jude after the Ascension continues to be obscure, and indeed is as uncertain as that of St. Simon, whom the Church calendar honors on the same day. There are traditions that Jude preached in Judaea, Samaria, and Mesopotamia; St. Paulinus, writing hundreds of years later, declared that Jude planted the faith in faraway Libya. According to one tradition, he died at Beirut; another tells us that he and St. Simon suffered martyrdom at Suanis, a city of Persia, where they had gone as missionaries. But if concrete facts as to the life and death of St. Jude are wanting, we may at least glean something from his Epistle as to the kind of man he was. This letter was probably written before the fall of Jerusalem, between the years 62 and 65. In it there is evidence that heresies had already arisen, for Jude denounces the evil life of heretics and warns of the judgment to come. He condemns the impious, the lustful, and those "who cultivate people for the sake of gain." He charges Christians to "build up yourself upon your most holy faith, praying in the Holy Spirit; keep yourselves in the law of God, looking for the mercy of our Lord Jesus Christ unto life everlasting." The letter bears a close resemblance in tone and expression to the Second Epistle of St. Peter, and it seems likely that St. Peter was familiar with it.

Saint Paul
Apostle to the Gentiles
6 7 (?)
(*June 30*)

The historic records bearing on St. Paul are fuller than those for any Scriptural saint. We have Paul's own wonderful writings, the fourteen letters included in the New Testament, which outline his missionary journeys, exhort and admonish the various Christian congregations, discuss ethics and doctrinal matters; and in the midst of all this we get a revelation of the man himself, his inner character, his problems and fears. St. Luke's Acts of the Apostles and certain apocryphal books are other sources of our knowledge of St. Paul. Of all the founders of the Church, Paul was perhaps the most brilliant and many-sided, the broadest in outlook, and therefore the best endowed to carry Christianity to alien lands and peoples.

Born into a well-to-do Jewish family of Tarsus, the son of a Roman citizen, Saul (as we shall call him until after his conversion) was sent to Jerusalem to be trained in the famous rabbinical school headed by Gamaliel. Here, in addition to studying the Law and the Prophets, he learned a trade, as was the custom. Young Saul chose the trade of tent-making. Although his upbringing was orthodox, while still at home in Tarsus he had come under the liberalizing Hellenic influences which at this time had permeated all levels of urban society in Asia Minor. Thus the Judaic, Roman, and Greek traditions and cultures all had a part in shaping this great Apostle, who was so different in status and temperament from the humble fishermen of Jesus' initial band of disciples. His missionary journeys were to give him the flexibility and the deep sympathy that made him the ideal human instrument for preaching Christ's Gospel of world brotherhood.

In the year 35 Saul appears as a self-righteous young Pharisee, almost fanatically anti-Christian. He believed that the trouble-making new sect should be stamped out, its adherents punished. We are told in Acts vii that he was present, although not a participator in the stoning, when Stephen, the first martyr, met his death. It was very soon afterwards that Paul experienced the revelation which was to transform his life. On the road to the Syrian city of Damascus, where he was going to continue his persecutions against the Christians, he was struck blind. On arriving in Damascus, there followed in dramatic sequence his sudden conversion, the cure of his blindness by the disciple Ananias, and his baptism. Paul accepted eagerly the commission to preach the Gospel of Christ, but like many another called to a great task he felt his unworthiness and withdrew from the world to spend three years in "Arabia" in meditation and prayer before beginning his apostolate. From the moment of his return, Paul—for he had now assumed this Roman name—never paused in his labors. It proved to be the most extraordinary career of preaching, writing, and church-founding of which we have record. The extensive travels by land and sea, so replete with adventure, are to be traced by anyone who reads carefully the New Testament letters. We cannot be sure, however, that the letters and records now extant reveal the full and complete chronicle of Paul's activities. He himself tells us he was stoned, thrice scourged, thrice shipwrecked, endured hunger and thirst, sleepless nights, perils and hardships; besides these physical trials, he suffered many disappointments and almost constant anxieties over the weak and widely-scattered communities of Christians.

Paul began his preaching in Damascus. Here the anger of the orthodox Jews against this renegade was so great that he had to make his escape by having himself let down from the city wall in a basket. Going down to Jerusalem, he was there looked on with suspicion by the Jewish Christians, for they could not at first believe that he who had so lately been their persecutor had turned advocate. Back in his native city of Tarsus once more, he was joined by Barnabas, and together they journeyed to Syrian Antioch,[1] where they were so successful in finding followers that a church, later to become famous in the annals of early Christianity, was founded. It was here that the disciples of Jesus were first given the name of Christians (from the Greek *christos,* anointed). After again returning to Jerusalem to bring aid to members of the sect who were suffering from famine, these two missionaries went back to Antioch, then sailed to the island of Cyprus; while there they converted the Roman proconsul, Sergius Paulus. Once more on the mainland of Asia Minor, they crossed the Taurus Mountains and visited many towns of the interior, particularly those having Jewish settlements. It was Paul's general practice in such places first to visit the synagogues and preach to the Jews; if rejected by them, he would then preach to the Gentiles. At Antioch in Pisidia Paul delivered a memorable discourse to the Jews, concluding with these words (Acts xiii, 46-47): "It was necessary that the word of God should be spoken to you first, but since you reject it and judge yourselves unworthy of eternal life, behold, we now turn to the Gentiles. For so the Lord commanded us, I have set thee for a light to the Gentiles, to be a means of salvation

---

[1] Antioch, in northwestern Syria, founded by one of the generals of Alexander the Great in about 300 B.C., had become a rich and beautiful city, ranking close to Alexandria under the Roman Empire.

to the very ends of the earth." After this, the Jews drove Paul and Barnabas out from their midst, and a little later the missionaries were back in Jerusalem, where the elders were debating the attitude of the Christian Church, still predominantly Jewish in membership, towards Gentile converts. The question of circumcision proved troublesome, for most Jews thought it important that Gentiles should submit to this requirement of Jewish law; Paul's side, the more liberal, standing against circumcision, won out eventually.

The second missionary journey, which lasted from 49 to 52, took Paul and Silas, his new assistant, to Phrygia and Galatia, to Troas, and across to the mainland of Europe, to Philippi in Macedonia. The physician Luke was now a member of the party, and in the book of Acts he gives us the record. They made their way to Thessalonica, then down to Athens and Corinth. At Athens Paul preached in the Areopagus, and we know that some of the Stoics and Epicureans heard him and debated with him informally, attracted by his vigorous intellect, his magnetic personality, and the ethical teachings which, in many respects, were not unlike their own. Passing over to Corinth, he found himself in the very heart of the Graeco-Roman world, and his letters of this period show that he is aware of the great odds against him, of the ceaseless struggle to be waged in overcoming pagan skepticism and indifference. He nevertheless stayed at Corinth for eighteen months, and met with considerable success. Two valuable workers there, Aquila and Priscilla, husband and wife, returned with him to Asia. It was during his first winter at Corinth that Paul wrote the earliest extant missionary letters. They show his supreme concern for conduct and his belief in the indwelling of the Holy Spirit which gives men power for good.

The third missionary journey covered the period of 52 to 56. At Ephesus, an important city of Lydia, where the cult of the Greek-Ionic goddess Diana was very popular, Paul raised a disturbance against the cult and the trade in silver images of the goddess which flourished there. Later, in Jerusalem, he caused a commotion by visiting the temple; he was arrested, roughly handled, and bound with chains; but when he was brought before the tribune, he defended himself in a way that impressed his captors. He was taken to Caesarea, for it was rumored that some Jews at Jerusalem, who falsely accused him of having admitted Gentiles to the temple, were plotting to kill him. He was kept in prison at Caesarea awaiting trial for about two years, under the proconsuls Felix and Festus. The Roman governors apparently wished to avoid trouble with both Jews and Christians and so postponed judgment from month to month. Paul at last appealed to the Emperor, demanding the legal right of a Roman citizen to have his case heard by Nero himself. He was placed in the custody of a centurion, who took him to Rome. The Acts of the Apostles leave him in the imperial city, awaiting his hearing.

It would appear that Paul's appeal was successful, for there is some evidence of another missionary journey, probably to Macedonia. On this last visit to the various Christian communities, it is believed that he appointed Titus bishop in Crete and Timothy at Ephesus. Returning to Rome, he was once more arrested, and after two years in chains suffered martyrdom, presumably at about the same time as the Apostle Peter, bishop of the Roman Church. Inscriptions of the second and third century in the catacombs give evidence of a cult of SS. Peter and Paul. This devotion has never diminished in popularity. In Christian art St. Paul is usually depicted as a bald man with a black beard, rather stocky, but vigorous and intense. His relics are venerated in the basilica of St. Paul and in the Lateran Church at Rome.

Because of the pressure of his work, Paul usually dictated his letters, writing the salutation in his own hand. The most quoted of New Testament writers, Paul has given us a wealth of counsel, aphorisms, and ethical teachings; he had the power of expressing spiritual truths in the simplest of words, and this, rather than the building up of a systematic theology, was his contribution to the early Church. A man of action, Paul reveals the dynamic of his whole career when he writes, "I press on towards the goal, to the

prize of God's heavenly calling in Christ Jesus." Although he himself was forever pressing onwards, his letters often invoked a
spirit of quiet meditation, as when he ends his epistle to the
Philippians with the beautiful lines: "Whatever things are true,
whatever honorable, whatever just, whatever holy, whatever lovable, whatever of good repute, if there be any virtue, if anything
worthy of praise, think upon these things."

Saint Peter

Prince of the Apostles

6 7 (?)

(*June 29*)

S t. Peter is mentioned so often in the New Testament—in the
Gospels, in the Acts of the Apostles, and in the Epistles of
St. Paul—that we feel we know him better than any other person
who figured prominently in the life of the Saviour. In all, his name
appears 182 times. We have no knowledge of him prior to his conversion, save that he was a Galilean fisherman, from the village of
Bethsaida or Capernaum. There is some evidence for supposing
that Peter's brother Andrew and possibly Peter himself were followers of John the Baptist, and were therefore prepared for the
appearance of the Messiah in their midst. We picture Peter as a
shrewd and simple man, of great power for good, but now and
again afflicted by sudden weakness and doubt, at least at the outset
of his discipleship. After the death of the Saviour he manifested
his primacy among the Apostles by his courage and strength. He
was "the Rock" on which the Church was founded. It is perhaps
Peter's capacity for growth that makes his story so inspiring to other

erring humans. He reached the lowest depths on the night when he denied the Lord, then began the climb upward, to become bishop of Rome, martyr, and, finally, "keeper of the keys of Heaven."

Our first glimpse of Peter comes at the very beginning of Jesus' ministry. While He was walking along the shore of the Sea of Galilee, He saw two brothers, Simon Peter and Andrew, casting a net into the water. When He called to them, "Come, and I will make you fishers of men," they at once dropped their net to follow Him. A little later we learn that they visited the house where Peter's mother-in-law was suffering from a fever, and Jesus cured her. This was the first cure witnessed by Peter, but he was to see many miracles, for he stayed close to Jesus during the two years of His ministry. All the while he was listening, watching, questioning, learning, sometimes failing in perfect faith, but in the end full of strength and thoroughly prepared for his own years of missionary preaching.

Let us recall a few of the Biblical episodes in which Peter appears. We are told that after the miracle of the loaves and fishes, Jesus withdrew to the mountain to pray, and his disciples started to sail home across the Lake of Galilee. Suddenly they saw Him walking on the water, and, according to the account in Matthew, Jesus told them not to be afraid. It was Peter who said, "Lord, if it is Thou, bid me come to Thee over the water." Peter set out confidently, but suddenly grew afraid and began to sink, and Jesus stretched forth His hand to save him, saying, "O thou of little faith, why didst thou doubt?"

Then we have Peter's dramatic confession of faith, which occurred when Jesus and his followers had reached the villages of Caesarea Philippi. Jesus having asked the question, "Who do men say that I am?" there were various responses. Then Jesus turned to Peter and said, "But who do you say that I am?" and Peter answered firmly, "Thou art the Christ, son of the living God." (Matthew xvi, 13-18; Mark viii, 27-29; Luke ix, 18-20.) Then Jesus told him that his name would henceforth be Peter. In the Aramaic tongue which Jesus and his disciples spoke, the word was *kepha,* meaning rock. Jesus concluded with the prophetic words, "Thou art Peter, and upon this rock shall be built My church, and the gates of hell shall not prevail against it."

There seems to be no doubt that Peter was favored among the disciples. He was selected, with James and John, to accompany Jesus to the mountain, the scene of the Transfiguration, to be given a glimpse of His glory, and there heard God pronounce the words, "This is my beloved Son in whom I am well pleased."

After this, the group had gone down to Jerusalem, where Jesus began to prepare his disciples for the approaching end of his ministry on earth. Peter chided Him and could not bring himself to believe that the end was near. When all were gathered for the Last Supper, Peter declared his loyalty and devotion in these words, "Lord, with Thee I am ready to go both to prison and to death." It must have been in deep sorrow that Jesus answered that before cockcrow Peter would deny Him thrice. And as the tragic night unrolled, this prophecy came true. When Jesus was betrayed by Judas as he prayed in the Garden of Gethsemane, and was taken by soldiers to the Jewish high priest, Peter followed far behind, and sat half hidden in the courtyard of the temple during the proceedings. Pointed out as one of the disciples, Peter three times denied the accusation. But we know that he was forgiven, and when, after the Ascension, Jesus manifested himself to his disciples, He signaled Peter out, and made him declare three times that he loved Him, paralleling the three times that Peter had denied Him. Finally, Jesus charged Peter, with dramatic brevity, "Feed my sheep." From that time on Peter became the acknowledged and responsible leader of the sect.

It was Peter who took the initiative in selecting a new Apostle in place of Judas, and he who performed the first miracle of healing. A lame beggar asked for money; Peter told him he had none, but in the name of Jesus the Nazarene bade him arise and walk. The beggar did as he was bidden, cured of his lameness. When, about two years after the Ascension, the spread of the new religion brought on the persecutions that culminated in the martyrdom of

St. Stephen, many of the converts scattered or went into hiding. The Apostles stood their ground firmly in Jerusalem, where the Jewish temple had become the spearhead of opposition to them. Peter chose to preach in the outlying villages, farther and farther afield. In Samaria, where he preached and performed miracles, he was offered money by Simon Magus, a magician, if he would teach the secret of his occult powers. Peter rebuked the magician sternly, saying, "Keep thy money to thyself, to perish with thee, because thou hast thought that the gift of God may be purchased by money."

With his vigorous outspokenness, Peter inevitably came into conflict with the Jewish authorities, and twice the high priests had him arrested. We are told that he was miraculously freed of his prison chains, and astonished the other Apostles by suddenly appearing back among them. Peter now preached in the seaports of Joppa and Lydda, where he met men of many races, and in Caesarea, where he converted the first Gentile, a man named Cornelius. Realizing that the sect must win its greatest support from Gentiles, Peter helped to shape the early policy towards them. Its growing eminence led to his election as bishop of the see of Antioch. How long he remained there, or how or when he came to Rome, we do not know. The evidence seems to establish the fact that his last years were spent in Rome as bishop. The belief that he suffered martyrdom there during the reign of Nero in the same year as St. Paul is soundly based on the writings of three early Fathers, St. Irenaeus, Clement of Alexandria, and Tertullian.[1]

The only writings by St. Peter which have come down to us are his New Testament Epistles I and II, both of which are thought to have been written from Rome to the Christian converts of Asia Minor. The First Epistle is filled with admonitions to mutual helpfulness, charity, and humility, and in general outlines the duties

[1] For *St. Irenaeus,* see below; Clement of Alexandria was a Christian writer who died about the year 215; Tertullian was a Roman convert who lived and wrote in Carthage, dying about 230.

of Christians in all aspects of life. At its conclusion (I Peter v, 13) Peter sends greetings from "the church which is at Babylon." This is accepted as further evidence that the letter was written from Rome, which in the Jewish usage of the time was called "Babylon." The second Epistle warns against false teachings, speaks of the Second Coming of the Lord, and ends with the beautiful doxology, "But grow in grace and knowledge of our Lord and Saviour, Jesus Christ. To him be the glory, both now and the day of eternity."

The latest archeological findings indicate that St. Peter's Church in Rome rises over the site of his tomb, as Pius XII announced at the close of the Holy Year of 1950. In the catacombs many wall writings have been found which link the names of St. Peter and St. Paul, showing that popular devotion to the two great Apostles began in very early times. Paintings of later date commonly depict Peter as a short, energetic man with curly hair and beard; in art his traditional emblems are a boat, keys, and a cock.

SAINT FRANCES XAVIER CABRINI   Gonippo Raggi

This lovely painting of Mother Cabrini as the Patron Saint of Immigrants is a mural in the chapel of an orphanage run by the Missionary Sisters of the Sacred Heart, and is used with their permission.

Saint Frances Cabrini is too modern a saint to have acquired traditional symbolism. However, she is most often shown against a background of New York harbor with the Statue of Liberty.

SOROR BENEDICTA DE MARIA · ORDINIS
FRANCISCALIVM S. CLARAE · BEATI PII X
INTERVENTV · STATIM PERFECTEQVE
LIBERATA EST a TVMORE MALIGNO ABDOMINALI

SAINT PIUS X HEALS SISTER BENEDICT MARIA   Unknown
This picture of one of the miracles of Saint Pius X was especially commissioned for the canonization of the saint in 1954 and was hung in Saint Peter's
for the ceremonies. It shows Sister Benedict Maria being instantaneously
healed of a malignant tumor through the intercession of Blessed Pius X. The
reproduction is copyright by Time, Incorporated, and is used by courtesy
of *Life* Magazine.

Again, no symbols are attributed to this most recent saint. He is portrayed
as a Pope.

Saint Pius X

Pope

1 9 1 4

(*August 20*)

Perhaps nowhere in the history of the Church is there a better example of a man possessed of so many of the saintly virtues —piety, charity, deep humility, pastoral zeal, and simplicity— than in one of the newest of God's elect, St. Pius X. Yet the parish priest of Tombolo, who remained a country priest at heart throughout his life, faced the problems and evils of a strife-torn world with the spiritual fervor of a crusader. The inscription on his tomb in the crypt of the basilica of St. Peter's gives the most eloquent testimony to a life spent in the service of God:

> "Born poor and humble of heart,
> Undaunted champion of the Catholic faith,
> Zealous to restore all things in Christ,
> Crowned a holy life with a holy death."

St. Pius X was born Giuseppe Melchiorre Sarto on June 2, 1835 in the little Italian town of Riese, in the province of Treviso near Venice. His father was Giovanni Sarto, a cobbler by trade, who was also caretaker of the city hall and the town's postmaster; his mother was Margherita Sanson, a seamstress. The family had few worldly goods and the early life of young Giuseppe, eldest of eight surviving children, was a difficult one. He attended the parish school and while there, his intelligence and high moral character attracted the notice of the pastor, who arranged a scholarship for the lad at the high school in Castelfranco, a larger town two miles

497

from Riese. After completing the course of instruction at Castel-franco, he made known that he had felt the call to the priesthood for some time, but had considered the means of attaining this end beyond his grasp. However, his parents saw that the will of God was in their son's calling, and they did all in their power to encourage him, while the pastor again came to the rescue by arranging another scholarship to the seminary at Padua. In November of 1850, young Sarto arrived at Padua and was immediately taken up with the life and studies of the seminary. The same high qualifications of intellect and spirit, later to blossom forth in his work as bishop and Pope, were much in evidence as a seminarian. Giuseppe worked hard and finally on September 18, 1858, Father Sarto was ordained at the cathedral in Castelfranco.

The young priest's first assignment was as curate at Tombolo, a parish of 1500 souls in the Trentino district of Italy. Here, for eight years, Father Sarto labored among his favorite parishioners, the poor. He also organized a night school for the general education of adults, and trained the parish choir to a high degree of skill in Gregorian Chant. His pastor at Tombolo, Father Constantini, recognizing the worth of the young priest, wrote a prophetic summary of his assistant. "They have sent me as curate a young priest, with orders to mould him to the duties of pastor; in fact, however, the contrary is true. He is so zealous, so full of good sense, and other precious gifts that it is I who can learn much from him. Some day or other he will wear the mitre, of that I am sure. After that—who knows?"

In July of 1867, Father Sarto, then 32 years of age, was appointed pastor of Salzano, one of the most favored parishes in the diocese of Treviso. Soon his concern and help toward the poor became well known throughout the parish, and his two sisters, who acted as his housekeepers, were often at wit's end as their brother gave away much of his own clothing and food to the needy. The new pastor arranged for the instruction of young and old in the fundamentals of Christian Doctrine. The firm conviction that devotion meant little if its meaning was not understood was later to be embodied in the encyclical *Acerbo nimis,* "On the Teaching of Christian Doctrine." After nine years at Salzano, Father Sarto was rewarded for his labors by the appointment as Canon of the Cathedral at Treviso and as Chancellor of that diocese. In addition, he became Spiritual Director of the seminary. Canon Sarto took a deep interest in this work of forming Christ in the hearts of young priests. However, in spite of these many duties, he remained ever the teacher; he often journeyed from the seminary into the city to teach catechism to the children, and he organized Sunday classes for those children who attended public schools, where religion was banned. When the diocese of Mantua fell vacant in 1884, Pope Leo XIII named Canon Sarto as bishop of that diocese.

Bishop Sarto found a troubled diocese in which to begin his labors. There was a general opposition of the government to religion manifested in many ways—monasteries had been suppressed, many religious institutions were government-managed, and Church property was heavily taxed. All these political disturbances had a far-reaching effect on both the clergy and the laiety. The seminaries of Mantua were depleted and a general laxity among the younger priests was evident; dangerous errors of thought had crept into the clergy, and the faults of the shepherds had spread to the flock. In general, a pall of religious indifference and secularism had spread over the diocese. With characteristic energy and spiritual strength, Bishop Sarto set to work to put his see in order. He gave first attention to the seminary, where by his own example of zeal and teaching, he won back the clergy to full and faithful service. The laxity of the people was attributed to neglect of parish priests in the instruction of the catechism; Bishop Sarto often taught such classes himself, and in his pastoral visits and letters, he urged the establishment of the Confraternity of Christian Doctrine in all parishes. God blessed this work on behalf of all classes of His flock, and in 1893, His Holiness, Leo XIII, elevated Bishop Sarto to Cardinal and appointed him Patriarch of Venice.

As Patriarch of Venice, it was Tombolo, Salzano, and Mantua all over again, but on a widening scale—the same care for his clergy and for the seminaries, the ever-willing hand and heart given to the poor, the long hours spent in teaching young and old—only the red of his new office had replaced the purple and black of former days. Social and economic problems were of prime concern to the new cardinal, and any worthy social action organization was assured of his help. When the Workingmen's Society was founded in Venice, the name of Cardinal Sarto was at the top of the list and he paid regular dues as a member! Once it seemed that an important diocesan newspaper would go into bankruptcy, and the cardinal declared, "I would rather sell my crozier and my robes of office than let that paper go under."

On July 20, 1903, the reign of Leo XIII came to a close, and the world mourned the death of a great Pontiff. Cardinals from all over the world came to Rome for the conclave which would elect the new Pope, and it is again typical of Cardinal Sarto that, due to his many charities, he was short of funds necessary to make the trip; so sure was he that he would never be elected that the problem was solved by the purchase of a return ticket to Venice! With the conclave in solemn session, the voting began, and with each successive ballot, Cardinal Sarto gained more votes. As his cause continued to gain strength, he all the more strongly pleaded that he was neither worthy nor capable enough for the office. When it was finally announced that he had gained sufficient votes to be elected, he bent his head, broke into tears, and whispered, "Fiat voluntas tua" (Thy will be done). He accepted, took the name of Pius X, and on August 9, 1903, was crowned as Vicar of Christ on earth.

The world was now the parish of the new Pontiff, and in his first encyclical he announced the aim of his reign. It was his desire, in the words of St. Paul, "to restore all things in Christ." (Eph 1:10). The prime means of accomplishing this restoration was clearly seen by Pius to be through the clergy, and throughout his reign, the Pope exhorted bishops to reorganize the seminaries and to obtain the best possible training for these men who would instill in others the knowledge of God. The Pontiff published an encyclical, "Exhortation to the Catholic Clergy," in which he pointed out that only through a trained and disciplined clergy could a program of return to Christ be realized.

The religious instruction of young and old became the second most important means toward the Christian restoration, and in his encyclical *Acerbo nimis,* "On the Teaching of Christian Doctrine," Pius X firmly stated his position. The evils of the world were traceable to an ignorance of God, he said, and it was necessary for priests to make the eternal truths available to all and in a language that all could understand. Ever an example, he himself gave Sunday instruction to the people in one of the Vatican courtyards. However, no reform of Pius' was more widely acclaimed than the Decrees on Holy Communion, and Pius X is often called "the Pope of the Eucharist." These decrees, issued from 1905 through 1910, allowed the reception of first Holy Communion at an earlier age than had formerly been required, encouraged the frequent reception of the Holy Eucharist by all Catholics, and relaxed the fast for the sick.

In the field of Christian social action the Pope had always been an ardent champion, and in 1905, he published *Il fermo proposito,* "On Catholic Social Action." In this work, the Pontiff listed practical recommendations for the solution of the social problem; he reaffirmed the need and power of prayer, but said that society would not be Christianized by prayer alone. Action is needed, he pointed out, as had been shown in the lives of the Apostles and of saints like Francis Xavier. The Pope likewise vigorously promoted reforms within the liturgy of the Church, since he felt that these were long overdue. In his *Motu proprio on the Restoration of Church Music,* he listed the aims of such music to be sanctity, beauty of form, and universality. Gregorian Chant, the Pope felt, was the music best suited to attain those aims. However, he felt that an attempt to make all Church music Gregorian was an exaggerated fad, and modern compositions were always welcomed by the Pontiff as long as they fulfilled the prescribed norms. Pius also reformed the Breviary, and was founder of the Biblical Institute for the advancement of scholarship in the study of the Scriptures. Even more important for the internal structure of the Church, he initiated and closely supervised the construction of the Code of Canon Law.

The familiar notion of Pius X as the Teacher of Christian Truth and the firm guide and staunch foe of error was forceably illustrated in 1907 when he issued more than fourteen pronouncements against the growth of Modernism. This subtle philosophy, in which Pius saw the poison of all heresies, pretended to "modernize" the Church and to make it keep pace with the changing times. In reality, its end would have been the destructions of the foundation of faith. The crowning achievement of the Pontiff's writings and pronouncements against this philosophy came in the encyclical, *Pascendi dominici gregis*, "On the Doctrines of the Modernists." In this work, which was a death blow to Modernism, he gave a systematic exposition of the errors involved, their causes, and provisions for combatting the errors by definite preventive measures.

Pius X labored for the Master until the very last days of his life. His 79 years had not set too heavily upon him, but overwork and anxiety over the impending doom of a World War began to take their toll. Pius saw clearly the horrors of the coming conflict and felt helpless that he could not prevent it. A little more than a month after the outbreak of the war, the Pope was seized with an attack of influenza, and his weakened constitution could not combat the illness. The end for the Christ-like Pius came peacefully on August 20, 1914, and the world, though in the throes of a death struggle, paused to mourn the gentle and humble man whose last will and testament gave such an insight into his character. It read, in part, "I was born poor, I lived poor, I die poor." Shortly after his death, the faithful began to make pilgrimages to his tomb, bringing flowers, prayers, and petitions for favors. Accounts of miraculous favors and cures, some even accomplished during his lifetime and granted through his intercession, were announced and given widespread acclaim. In 1923, the Church, always cautious in such matters, began inquiry into the life and

virtues of Pius X, and in February of 1943, the first official step
in his Cause was taken when the necessary decree was signed by
the present Pontiff, Pius XII. In honor of the work which Pius X
had accomplished in its behalf, the Confraternity of Christian Doctrine actively contributed in promoting the Cause for his beatification and canonization. On June 3, 1951, Pius X was declared
Blessed, and finally on May 29, 1954, amid the traditional pealing
of the bells in the great churches of Rome, Giuseppe Sarto, the
humble parish priest of the world, was canonized a saint of God.

Excerpts from the Encyclical *Il fermo proposito*, On Catholic Action

. . . *Immense is the field of Catholic action;* it excludes absolutely
nothing which in any way, directly or indirectly, belongs to the
divine mission of the Church.

It is plainly necessary to take part individually in a work so
important, not only for the sanctification of our own souls, but also
in order to spread and more fully open out the Kingdom of God in
individuals, families, and society, each one working according to his
strength for his neighbor's good, by the diffusion of revealed truth,
the exercise of Christian virtue, and the spiritual and corporal
works of charity and mercy. Such is the conduct worthy of God
to which St. Paul exhorts us, so as to please Him in all things,
bringing forth fruits of all good works, and increasing in the
knowledge of God: "That you may walk worthy of God in all
things pleasing; being fruitful in every good work, and increasing
in the knowledge of God."

Besides these benefits, there are many in the natural order,
which, without being directly the object of the Church's mission,
nevertheless flow from it as one of its natural consequences. Such
is the light of Catholic revelation that it vividly illuminates all
knowledge; so great is the strength of the Gospel maxims that the
precepts of the natural law find in them a surer basis and a more

energetic vigor; such, in fine, is the power of the truth and morality taught by Jesus Christ that even the material well-being of individuals, of the family, and of human society, receive from them support and protection.

The Church, while preaching Jesus crucified, who was a stumbling-block and folly to the world, has been the first inspirer and promoter of civilization. She had spread it whenever her apostles have preached, preserving and perfecting what was good in ancient pagan civilization, rescuing from barbarism and raising to a form of civilized society the new peoples who took refuge in her maternal bosom, and giving to the whole of human society, little by little, no doubt, but with a sure and ever onward march, that characteristic stamp which it still everywhere preserves. The civilization of the world is Christian civilization; the more frankly Christian it is, so much is it more true, more lasting, and more productve of precious fruit; the more it withdraws from the Christian ideal, so much the feebler is it, to the great detriment of society. . . .

. . . *To restore all things in Christ* has ever been the Church's motto, and it is specially Ours, in the perilous times in which we live. To restore all things, not in any fashion, but in Christ; "that are in heaven, and on earth, in Him," adds the Apostle; to restore in Christ not only what depends on the divine mission of the Church to conduct souls to God, but also, as We have explained, that which flows spontaneously from this divine mission, namely, Christian civilization in each and every one of the elements which compose it.

To dwell only on this last part of the restoration, you see well what support is given to the Church by those chosen bands of Catholics whose aim is to unite all their forces in order to combat anti-Christian civilization by every just and lawful means, and to repair in every way the grievous disorders which flow from it; to reinstate Jesus Christ in the family, the school, and society; to re-establish the principle that human authority represents that of God; to take intimately to heart the interests of the people, especially those of the working and agricultural classes, not only by the inculcation of religion, the only true source of comfort in the sorrows of life, but also by striving to dry their tears, to soothe their sufferings, and by wise measures to improve their economic condition; to endeavor, consequently, to make public laws conformable to justice, to amend or suppress those which are not so; finally, with a true Catholic spirit, to defend and support the rights of God in everything, and the no less sacred laws of the Church.

All these works, of which Catholic laymen are the principal supporters and promoters, and whose form varies according to the special needs of each nation, and the particular circumstances of each country, constitute what is generally known by a distinctive, and surely a very noble name: *Catholic Action* or *Action of Catholics*. . . .

(trans. in *Publications of the Catholic Truth Society,* vol. 83, London, 1910.)

Excerpts from the Encyclical Letter *Acerbo nimis,* On the teaching of Christian Doctrine

. . . *How many and how grave are the consequences of ignorance in matters of religion!* And on the other hand, how necessary and how beneficial is religious instruction! It is indeed vain to expect the fulfillment of the duties of a Christian by one who does not even know them.

We must now consider upon whom rests the obligation to dissipate this most pernicious ignorance and to impart in its stead the knowledge that is wholly indispensable. There can be no doubt, Venerable Brothers, that this most important duty rests upon all those who are pastors of souls. On them, by command of Christ, rest the obligations of knowing and of feeling the flocks committed to their care; and to feed implies, first of all, to teach. "I will give you pastors after my own heart," God promised through Jeremias, "and they shall feed you with knowledge and doctrine." Hence the Apostle Paul said: "Christ did not send me to baptize, but to preach the Gospel," thereby indicating that the first duty of all those who are entrusted in any way with the government of the Church is to instruct the faithful in the things of God. . . .

. . . Here then it is well to emphasize and insist that for a priest there is no duty more grave or obligation more binding than this. Who, indeed, will deny that knowledge should be joined to holiness of life in the priest? "For the lips of the priest shall keep knowledge." The Church demands this knowledge of those who are to be ordained to the priesthood. Why? Because the Christian people expect from them knowledge of the divine law, and it was for that end that they were sent by God. "And they shall seek the law at his mouth; because He is the messenger of the Lord of Hosts." Thus the bishop speaking to the candidates for the priesthood in the ordination ceremony says: "Let your teaching be a spiritual remedy for God's people; may they be worthy fellow-workers of our order; and thus meditating day and night on His law, they may believe what they read, and teach what they shall believe.". . .

. . . In order to enkindle the zeal of the ministers of God, We again insist on the need to reach the ever-increasing number of those who know nothing at all of religion, or who possess at most such knowledge of God and Christian truths as befits idolaters. How many there are, alas, not only among the young, but among adults and those advanced in years, who know nothing of the chief mysteries of faith; who on hearing the name of Christ can only ask: "Who is He . . . that I may believe in Him?" In consequence of this ignorance, they do not consider it a crime to excite and nourish hatred against their neighbor, to enter into most unjust contracts, to do business in dishonest fashion, to hold the funds of others at an exhorbitant interest rate, and to commit other iniquities not less reprehensible. They are, moreover, ignorant of the law of Christ which not only condemns immoral actions, but also forbids deliberate immoral thoughts and desires. Even when for some reason or other they avoid sensual pleasures, they nevertheless entertain evil thoughts without the least scruple, thereby multiplying their sins above the number of hairs of the head. These persons are found, we deem it necessary to repeat, not merely among the poorer classes of the people or in sparsely settled districts, but also among those in the higher walks of life, even, indeed, among those puffed up with learning, who, relying upon a vain erudition, feel free to ridicule religion . . .

. . . What We have said so far demonstrates the supreme importance of religious instruction. We ought, therefore, to do all that lies in our power to maintain the teaching of Christian doctrine with full vigor, and where such is neglected, to restore it; for in the words of Our predecessor, Benedict XIV, "There is nothing more effective than catechetical instruction to spread the glory of God and to secure the salvation of souls."

(trans. by J. B. Collins in *Catechetical Documents of Pope Pius X*, Paterson, N. J., 1946.)

Calendar of Saints

. Apostle; **Ab.** Abbot; **Abs.** Abbess; **An.** Anchoret; **Ar.** Archbishop; **Ard.** Archdeacon; **B.** Bishop;
. Confessor; **Car.** Cardinal; **D.** Doctor; **Dc.** Deacon; **Emp.** Emperor; **Eps.** Empress; **Ev.** Evangelist;
. Hermit; **K.** King; **Lec.** Lector; **M.** Martyr; **MM.** Martyrs; **Ma.** Matron; **Mg.** Magus; **Mo.** Monk;
. Pope; **PP.** Popes; **Pat.** Patriarch; **Pc.** Prince; **Pen.** Penitent; **PM.** Protomartyr; **Pn.** Patron;
Pr. Priest; **Q.** Queen; **V.** Virgin; **VV.** Virgins; **W.** Widow.
Note: Figures indicate life span, or date of death.

January 1
ulgentius, B.C., 468-533
lmachius or Telemachus, 400
larus, Ab.
oncordius, M., 178
ugendus, Ab.
anchea, V., 585
elix of Bourges, B., 580
dilo or Olon, Ab., 1049
Villiam, Ab., 1031

January 2
lacarius of Alexandria, An., 394
delhard or Adelard, Ab., 827
spasius, B., 560
lunchin, 640
incencianus, H., 672

January 3
enevieve or Genovefa, V., 422-512
ntherus, P.
ertilia, V., 705
lorentius, B.M., 275
ordius, M.
eter Balsam, M., 311
heopemptus, B.M., end of 3rd Cent.

January 4
itus, B.
erriolus, B.
regory, B.
haraildis, V.
igobert, or Robert, Ar., 745

January 5
imeon Stylites, C., 459
emiliana, V.
erlac, H.
yncletica, V., 400
elesphorus, P.

January 6
lelanius, B.C., 490 or 530
rminold, A.M.
uarinus
eter Thomas, B.Ar.Pat., 1366
Viltrudis, W., 986

January 7
edd, B., 664
ldric, B., 800-856
ntony of Egypt, Ab.Pat., 356
anute, K.M.
entigerna, W.
ucian, Pr.M., 312
einold, M.
illo, C., 8th Cent.
alentinus, B.

January 8
pollinaris, The Apologist, B., 175
lbert, Ar.
tticus, B.
aldwin, M., 670
rhard, B., late in 7th Cent.
rodobertus or Frobert, Ab.
aribaldus, B., 762
udule, V.
ucian, M.
atiens, B.

January 8 (Cont'd)
Pega, V., early in 8th Cent.
Severnus, Ab.A., 5th Cent.
Severnus, B., 6th Cent.
Wulsin or Vulsin, B., 1005

January 9
Peter of Sebaste, B.C., 387
Adrian, Ab.C., 710
Brihtwald, Ar., 8th Cent.
Felan, Ab.
Julian and Basilissa, VV.
Marciana, V.M., 2nd Cent.
Paschasia, V.M., 178
Waningus or Vaneng, 683

January 10
William, C.Ar., 1209
Agatho, P., 681
John Camillus Bonus, C.B.
Marcian, Pr.C., 5th Cent.
Peter Urseolus or Orseolo, C., 987
Sethrida or Saethryth, V., 660

January 11
Theodosius, The Cenobiarch, 423-529
Egwin, B.C., 717
Hyginus, P., 142
Leucius, B.C.
Palaemon, H.
Salvius or Sauve, B., 625
Vitalis, Mo.

January 12
Benedict Biscop, commonly called Bennet, 690
Aelred, Ab., 1167
Arcadius, M.
Caesaria, V.
Tatiana, V.M.
Tigrius and Eutropius, MM.
Victorianus, Ab.

January 13
Kentigern or Mungho, B.C., 516-601
Agrecius, B.
Potitus, M.
Veronica of Milan, 1497

January 14
Hilary, B.C.D., 368
Barbasymas or Barbashemin, M.
Datius, B.
Felix of Nola
Macrina the Elder, W.
Sabas, Ar.

January 15
Paul, The First Hermit, 342
Alexander Akimetes, C, 430
Bonitus, B.
Ceolwulf, K.C.
Emebert, B.C.
Ephysius
Isadore, Pr.H.
Ita or Ida or Mida, Abs., 570
John Calybites, 450
Malard, B.C.
Maurus
Tarsitia, V.

January 16
Macarius, The Elder, 300-390
Ferriolus, B.
Fursey, 648
Honoratus, Ar.
James, B.
Marcellus, P.M.
Priscilla, Ma.
Tarantaise
Triverius, H.Mo.

January 17
Antony, Ab.Pat., 251-356
Genulfus or Genou, B., 250
Julian Sabas, H., 377
Mildgytha, V.
Richimirus, Ab.
Sabinas, B.C.
Speusippus, Eleusippus, and Meleusippus, MM.
Sulpicius or Sulpice, B.C.

January 18
Deicolus, Ab.
Prisca, V., 1st or 3rd Cent.
Ulfrid, 1028
Volusianus, 496

January 19
Wulstan, B.C., 1095
Canutus or Knut, M.
Germanicus, M., 156
Lomer or Launomar, Ab., 590
Marius, Martha, Audifax, and Abachum, MM.
Nathalan, B.
Regimus, B.

January 20
Fabian, P.M., 250
Sebastian, M., 283
Euthymius, Ab., 473
Fechin or Vigeanus, Ab., 665

January 21
Agnes, V.M., 303 or 304
Epiphanius, B.
Fructuosis, B.M.
Meinrad, H.M.
Patroclus, M.
Vinim or Wynnin, or Gwynnin, B.C.M.

January 22
Anastasius, M., 628
Blaesilla, W.
Brihtwold, B.C.
Dominic of Sora, Ab.
Vincent, M.

January 23
John the Almoner, C.Pat., 619
Asclas
Barnard, Ar.C.
Clement of Ancyra and Agathangelus, MM.
Erementiana, V.M.
Eusebius, Ab.
Ildephonsus, Ar.
Lufthild
Maimbod, M.
Raymund of Pennafort

January 24
Timothy, B.M., 97
Arthemius, B.C.
Babylas, B.M., 250
Cadocus or Cadoc, Ab.
Felician, B.M.
Macedonius, An.
January 25
Juventinus and Maximinus, MM., 363
Apollo, H.
Artemas, M.
Poppo, Ab., 987
Praejectus, B.M., 676
Publius, Ab., 380
January 26
Polycarp, B.M., 166
Conan, B.
Paula, W., 347
January 27
John Chrysostom, Ar.D., 344-407
Julian, B.C.
Marius, Ab.
Vitalian, P., 657
January 28
Cyril, Pat., 444
John, Ab.
Paulinus, Pat.
January 29
Francis De Sales, B.C.D., 1566-1622
Gildas
Sabinianus, M.
Sulpicius Severus, Ar., 425
Valerius, B., 100
January 30
Bathildes or Baldechilde, Q., 680
Adelemus, Ab.
Aldegund, V. Abs.
Barsimaeus (Barsamja), B.M., 250
Hyacintha Mariscotti, V., 1585-1640
Martina, V.M.
January 31
Peter Nolasco, C., 1189-1258
Aidanus, B.
Cyrus and John, MM.
Eusebius, H.M.
Germinianus, B., 348
Marcella, W.
Ulphia, V.
February 1
Ignatius, B.M., 107
Bridget, V.Abs.
Kinnea
Pionius, M.Pr.
Sigebert, K.
February 2
Laurence, Ar., 619
February 3
Blaise, B.M., 316
Anscharius, Ar., 865
Margaret, 1192
Wereburghe, Abs.Pn., 7th Cent.
February 4
Andrew Corsini, B.C., 1302-1373
Gilbert, Ab.
Isadore of Pelusium, Pr.Mo.
Joan or Jane, of Valois, Q.
Joseph of Leonissa
Modan, Ab.
Phileas and Philoromus, MM.
Rembert, Ar.
February 5
Agatha, V.M., 251
Abraamius, B.
Alice or Adelaide, Abs., 1015
Avitis, Ar.
Philip of Jesus, O.S.F., M.Pn.
February 6
Dorothy, V.M.
Amandus, B.C.
Barsanuphius, An.

February 6 (Cont'd)
Vedast, B.
February 7
Romuald, Ab.C., 956-1027
Richard, K.C., 722
Augulus, B.M.
Theodorus of Heraclea, 319
Tresain, Pr.
February 8
John of Matha, 1169-1218
Cuthman, 8th Cent.
Paul, B., 631
Stephen of Grandmont, 1124
February 9
Nicephorus, M., 260
Ansbert, Ar.
Apollonia, V.M., 249
Attracta or Tarahata
Erhard
Theliau, B., 580
February 10
Scholastica, V., 543
Erlulph, M., 830
Soteris, V.M.
William of Maleval, H., 1157
February 11
Saturninus, Dativus, MM., 304
Bernadette Soubirous, V.Pn., 1844-1879
Severinus, Ab.
Theodora, Eps.
February 12
Benedict of Anian, Ab., 821
Anthony Cauleas, Pat., 896
Eulalia, V.M.
Meletius, Pat.M.
February 13
Catharine De Ricci, V., 1522-1589
Gregory II, P.
Kentigern
Licinius, B.
Martinianus, H., 400
Modomnoc, or Dominick of Ossory
Polyeuctus, M., 250
Stephen, Ab.
February 14
Valentine, P.M., 270
Abraames, B., 422
Auxentius, H.
Conran, B.
Gilbert
Maro, Ab.
February 15
Faustinus and Jovita, MM., 121
Sigefride or Sigfrid, B.A.
February 16
Onesimus, 95
Elias, Jeremy, Isaias, Samuel, Daniel, Pamphilus and Porpherius, MM., 1309
Gregory X, P.C.
Juliana, M.
Tanco or Tatta, B.M.
February 17
Flavian, M.Ar., 449
Finnan, Mo.B., 661
Fintan, Ab.
Loman or Luman, B.
Silvin of Auchy, B.C.
Theodulas and Julian, MM.
February 18
Simeon, B.M., 116
Colman, B.C.
Leo and Paregorius, MM.
February 19
Barbatus or Barbas, C.B., beginning of 7th Cent.-682
Gabinus, Pr.M.
Georges, B.
Mansuetus, B.
February 20
Tyrannio, B.M. and Zenobius, M., 304

February 20 (Cont'd)
Eleutherius, B.
Eucherius, B.
Mildred, Abs.
Sadoth, B.M.
Ulrick, 1154
February 21
Severianus, M.B., 452 or 453
Daniel, Pr.M., Verda, V.M., 344
German, Ab.M. and Randaut, M 666
February 22
Margaret of Cortona, Pen., 1297
Baradat
Thelassius and Limneus
February 23
Milburge, V., 7th Cent.
Serenus, M., 327
February 24
Matthias, A.
Ethelbert, K.C., 616
Lethard, B.
Montanus, Lucius, Flavian, Julian, Victoricus, Primolus, Rhenus, and Donatian, MM. 259
Pretextatus or Prix, Ar.M.
February 25
Tarasius, C.Pat., middle of 8th Cent.-806
Caesarius of Nazianius
Victorinus, M.
Walberge, Abs.
February 26
Alexander, C.Pat., 326
Ethelbert, K.C.
Porphyrius, B.
Victor or Vittre of Arcis, An.
February 27
Leander, C.B., 596
Alnoth, An.
Galmier
Julian, Chronion, and Besas, MM.
Nestor, B.M., 250
Thalilaeus
February 28
Romanus, Ab., 460
Proterius, Pat.M.
February 29
Oswald, B.Ar., 992
March 1
David, Ar.Pn., 544
Albinus, B.
Monan, M., 874
Swidbert or Swibert, B.
March 2
Ceada or Chad, B.C., 673
Charles, M.
Joavin or Joevin, B.
Marman, B.
Simplicius, P.
March 3
Cunegundes, Eps., 1040
Aelred, Ab.
Emeterius and Chelidonius, MM.
Lamalisse
Marinus and Asterius, MM., 272
Winwaloe or Winwaloc, Mo.
March 4
Casimir, Pc., 1458-1484
Adrian, B.
Lucius, P.M., 253
March 5
Adrian and Eubulus, MM., 309
John Joseph of the Cross, 1654-1739
Kiaran or Kenerin
Philip of Jesus, O.S.F., Pn.
Roger
March 6
Chrodegang, B.C., 766
Baldrede

March 6 (Cont'd)

adroe
olette, Abs.
ridolin, Ab.
ineburge, Kineswide, and Tibba

March 7

homas Aquinas, C.D., 1225-1274
aul, An.
erpetua, Felicitas, and their Companions, MM., 203

March 8

ohn of God, C., 1495-1550
pollonius, Philemon, MM.
uthak, 1253
elix, B.M., 642
ohn of Avila
ilian, Ab., 690
salmod, An.
ose of Viterbo
nan, Ab.B.

March 9

rances of Rome, W., 1384-1440
atherine of Bologna, Abs., 1413
ominic Savio, 1842-1857
regory of Nyssa
acian, B.

March 10

roctovaeus, Ab., 590
ackessoge or Kessoge, B.

March 11

ulogius of Cordova, Pr.M., 859
engus, B.
onstantine, M., 576
ophronius, Pat.

March 12

regory the Great, P.C., 540-604
aximilian
aul, B.

March 13

uphrasia, V., 410
erald, B.
ennocha, V., 1007
ochemomoc, in Latin, Pulcherius, Ab.
icephorus, Pat.
heophanes, Ab.

March 14

aud, or Mathildis, Q., 968
cepsimas, B., Joseph, Pr., and Aithilahas, Dc.,MM.
oniface, B.

March 15

braham, H. and his niece, Mary, Pen., 360
ement Hofbauer, C., 1751-1820
achary, P.

March 16

lian of Cilicia, M.
nian

March 17

atrick, B.C.Ap., 464
oseph of Arimathea
ertrude, Abs., 626

March 18

dward, K.M., 979
lexander
nselm, B., 1086
yril, Ar., 386
ridian, B.

March 19

oseph, Foster Father of the Lord
dmund, M.

March 20

uthbert, C.B., 687
ulfran, Ar.

March 21

enedict, Ab. Pat., 480-543
nna or Endeus, Ab.
erapion, Ab. of Arsinoe
erapion, B. of Thmuis
erapion, "The Sindonite"

March 22

atharine of Sweden, V., 1373

March 22 (Cont'd)

Basil of Ancyra
Deogratias, B.
Lea, W.
Paul, B.

March 23

Alphonsus Turibius, C.Ar., 1538-1606
Edelward, Pr.
Joseph Oriol, 1650-1702
Victorian, M.

March 24

Irenaeus, M.B., 304
Gabriel the Archangel
Simon and William, MM.

March 25

Cammin, Ab.

March 26

Ludger, B.A., 743-809
Bernadine of Fossa, 1420-1503
Braulio, B.
Dismas, The Good Thief

March 27

John of Egypt, H., 305-394
John Damascene, D.
Rupert or Robert, B.

March 28

Priscus, Malchus, and Alexander, MM., 260
Gontran, K.
John Capistran
Sixtus III, P., 440

March 29

Jonas and Barachisius, MM., 327
Armogastes, Archinimus, and Saturas, MM.
Eustasius, Ab.
Gundleus
Mark, B.

March 30

John Climacus, Ab., 525-605
Regulus or Rieul, B.
Zosimus, B., 660

March 31

Benjamin, M.Dc., 424
Acasius or Achates, B.
Guy, Ab.

April 1

Hugh, C.B., 1053-1132
Gilbert, B., 1240
Melito, B.C.

April 2

Francis of Paula, C., 1416-1508
Apian, M., 306
Bronacha
Ebba
Nicetius, Ar.
Theodosia, V.M.

April 3

Agape, Chionia, and Irene, MM., 304
Nicetas, Ab.
Richard, B.C., 1253
Ulpian, M.

April 4

Isidore, B., 636
Plato, Ab.

April 5

Vincent Ferrer, C., 1357-1419
Becan, Ab.A.
Gerald, Ab.
Tigernach, B.C.

April 6

Sixtus, or Xistus I, P.M., Second Age
Celestine, P.
Celsus, B.
Prudentius, B.
William, Ab.

April 7

Aibert
Aphraates, An.
Finian
Hegesippas

April 8

Dionysius of Corinth, B.C.
Aedecius, M.
Walter, Ab.

April 9

Mary of Egypt, Fifth Age
Dotto, Ab., 6th Cent.
Eupsychius, M.
Gaucher, Ab.
Waltrude, W.
Zosimus

April 10

Bademus, Ab.M., 376

April 11

Leo the Great, P.D., 461
Aid, Ab.
Antipas, M.
Guthlake, H.Pn.
Maccai, Ab.

April 12

Sabas the Goth, M., 372
Julius, P.
Victor of Braga
Zeno, B.M.C.

April 13

Hermenegild, M., 586
Caradoc, Pr.H., 1124
Guinoch

April 14

Tiburtius, Valerian, and Maximus, MM., 229
Anthony, John, and Euatachius, MM.
Benezet, Pn.
Carpus, B.
Justin, M.

April 15

Peter Gonzales, commonly called Telm or Elm, C.Pn., 1190-1246
Basilissa and Anastasia, MM.
Munde, Ab.
Paternus, B.
Ruadhan, Ab. A., 584

April 16

Encratis or Engratia, V. M., 304
Benedict Joseph Labre, C., 1748-1783
Druon, or Drugo, Pn.
Encratis or Engratia, V.M., 304
Fructuosis, Ar.
Joachim of Sienna
Mans or Magnus
Optatus, M.
Turibius, B.

April 17

Stephen, C. Ab., 1134
Anicetus, P.M.
Simeon, B.M.
Stephen (Harding), Ab.

April 18

Apollonius the Apologist, M., 186
Galdin, Ar.
Laserian, B.

April 19

Leo IX, P.C., 1002-1054
Elphege, Ar.M., 1012
Ursmar, B.

April 20

Agnes of Monte Pulciano, V. Abs., 1317
James of Scavonia or Illyricum, 1485
Serf, B.A.

April 21

Anselm, C.Ar.D., 1033-1109
Anastasius, Pat.
Anastasius the Sinaite, An.
Anastasius, The Younger, Pat.
Beuno, B.
Eingan, K.
Malrubius, M.

April 22

Soter and Caius, PP. and MM.
Caius, P., 296

April 22 (Cont'd)
Azades and Tharba, MM., 341
Epipodius and Alexander, MM.
Leonides, M.
Opportuna, V.Abs.
Rufus, An.
Theodorus of Siceon, B.

April 23
George, M., 303
Adalbert, B.
Gerard, B.
Ibar or Ivor, B., 500

April 24
Mellitus, Ar.C., 624
Bona and Doda, both Abs.
Fidelis of Sigmarengen

April 25
Mark, Ev.Pn.
Anianus, B.
Ivea, B.
Kebius, B.
Macull
Phaebadius, B.

April 26
Cletus, P.M.
Marcellinus, P.M., 304
Pascharius Radbert, Ab.
Peter Canisius, S.J., D., 1521-1596
Richarius, Ab.An.

April 27
Zita, V., 1272
Anastasius, P.
Anthimus, B.M.
Egbert, 729

April 28
Vitalis, M., 62
Pollio, Lec.M., 304
Cronan, Ab.
Didymus and Theodora, MM.
Louis Marie Grignion, 1673-1716
Patricius, B.M.
Paul of the Cross, 1694-1775
Peter Chanel, M., 1803-1841

April 29
Peter, M., 1205-1252
Fiachna, Mo.
Hugh, Ab.
Robert, Ab., 1109

April 30
Catharine of Sienna, V., 1347-1380
Ajutre or Adjuntr
Erconwald, B.
James and Marian, MM., 259
Maximus, M.
Sophia, V.M., Third Age

May 1
Philip, A.
Acius and Acheolus, MM.
Andeolus, M.
Asaph, B.
Brieuc, B.
James the Less, A.
Marcou or Marculfus, Ab. 1558
Sigismund, K. M.

May 2
Athanasius, Pat.D.B., 296-373

May 3
Alexander, P.M., 119

May 4
Monica, W., 332-387
Godard, B.

May 5
Pius V, P.C., 1504-1572
Angelus, An.M.
Avertin, Dc.
Hilary, Ar.
Honoratus
Mauront, Ab., 634

May 6
John Before the Latin Gate, 95
Eadbert, B.
John Damascen

May 7
Stanislas, M.B., 1030-1079
Benedict II, P.
John of Beverley, B.M.

May 8
Peter, Ar., 1174
Gybrian or Gobrian, Pr., 8th Cent.
Joan of Arc, V., 1412-1431
Odrian, B.
Victor, M., 303
Wiro, B.

May 9
Gregory Nazianzen, B.C.D., 389
Brynoth, B.
Hermas
Nicholas, B.

May 10
Isidore of Madrid, Pn., 1170
Antoninus ("Little Anthony"), Ar.
Catuldus, Mo.B.
Comgall, Ab.
Gordian

May 11
Mammertus, C.Ar., 477
Maieul, in Latin Majolus, Ab.

May 12
Nereus, Achilleus, and Flavia Domitilla, MM.
Epiphanius, Ar.
Germanus, Pat.
Pancras
Rictrudes, Abs.

May 13
John The Silent, B.C., 454-559
Peter Regalati, 1456
Robert Bellarmine, C.B.D., 1542-1622
Servatius
Walburga

May 14
Boniface, M., 307
Garthagh or Carthage the Younger, B.
Michael, 1797-1863
Pachomius
Pontius, M., 258

May 15
Peter and Andrew, MM., 250
Dympna, V.M.
Genebrard or Genebern, M.
John Baptist De La Salle, C., 1651-1719

May 16
John Nepomucen, M., 1330-1383
Abdas, M.B.
Abdjesus or Habedjesus, M.B.
Brendan the Elder, Ab.
Honoratus, B., 660
Simon Stock
Ubaldus, B.

May 17
Paschal Baylon, C., 1540-1592
Cathan, B.
Maden or Madern
Maw
Possidius, B.
Silvae or Silan, B.

May 18
Eric, M.K., 1151
Potamon, B.M.
Theodotus, M.
Venantius, M.

May 19
Dunstan, B.C., 988
Peter Celestine
Pudentiana

May 20
Bernardin of Sienna, C., 1444
Ethelbert, K.

May 21
Godrick, H., 1170
Felix of Cantalicio

May 21 (Cont'd)
Hospitius

May 22
Yvo, C., 1253-1303
Basiliscus, M., 312
Bobo, 985
Castus and Aemilius, MM.
Conall, Ab.
Rita, W., 1386-1457

May 23
Julia, V.M., Fifth Age
Desiderius, B.M.
Desiderius, B.M., 612
John Baptist De Rossi, 16
1764

May 24
Vincent of Lerins, C., 450
Donatian and Rogatian, MM.
John De Prado, M.
Mary Magdalen Postel, V., 17
1846

May 25
Gregory VII, P.C., 1085
Aldhelm, B.
Dumhade of Ireland, Ab.
Madeleine Sophie Barat, 1779-1865
Mary Magdalen of Pazzi
Maximus and Venerand, MM.
Urban, P.M.

May 26
Elutharius, P.M., late half 2 Cent.
Francis Geronimo, C., 1642-17
Oduvald, Ab.
Philip Neri, C., 1595
Quadratus, B.

May 27
Bede, C.D., 673-735
John, P.
Julius M., 302

May 28
Augustine, B.C.A., 604
Germanus, C.B., 469-576
Caraunus or Caro, Fifth Age

May 29
Cyril, M.
Conon, M., 275
Maximinus
Sisinnius, Martyrius, and Ale ander, MM.

May 30
Ferdinand III, C.K., 1198-124
Felix I, P.M.
John Neopmucen, M.
Maguil or Madelgisilus
Walstan

May 31
Petronilla, V.
Angela Merici, V., 1474-1540
Cantius, Cantianus, and Canti nilla, MM., 304
Gabriel Possenti, C.P., 1838-18

June 1
Pamphilus, P.M., 309
Caprais, Ab., 430
Justin
Peter of Pisa
Wistan, M.Pc.

June 2
Pothinus, B., Sanctus, Dc., A talus, and Blandina, MM., 1
Erasmus, B.M., 303
Marcellinus and Peter

June 3
Clotildis or Clotilda, Q., 545
Cecilius
Coeingen or Keivin, B., 618
Genesius B., 656
Lifard, Ab.

June 4
Quirinus, B.M., 304
Breaca, V.
Burian

July 18 (Cont'd)
Bruno, B.
Frederick, B.M.
Odulph
Philastrius, B.

July 19
Vincent of Paul, C., 1660
Arsenius, An.
Machrina
Symmachus, P., 498

July 20
Joseph Barsabas, C.
Aurelius, Ard.Ar.
Ceslas
Jerome Aemiliani
Justa and Rufina, MM.
Margaret, M.
Ulmar or Wulmar, Ab.

July 21
Praxedes, V.
Arbogastus, B.
Barhadbesciabus, M.
Victor of Marseilles, M.
Zoticus, B.M., 204

July 22
Mary Magdalen
Dabius or Davius
Joseph of Palestine (Count Joseph)
Mineve, Ab.
Vandrille or Wandre Gisilus, Ab.

July 23
Apollinaris, M.B.
Liborius, B., 348

July 24
Lupus, C.B., 478
Christina, M.
Francis Solano
Kinga or Cunegundes
Lewine, V.M.
Romanus and David, MM.
Wulfhad and Ruffin, MM.

July 25
James the Great, A.
Christopher, M., 3rd Cent.
Cucufas or Cougat, M.
Nissen, Dc.Ab.
Thea, V.M.
Valentine, V.M.
Paul, M.

July 26
Anne, Mother of the Blessed Virgin
Germanus, B., 380

July 27
Pantaleon, M., 303
Congall, Ab.
Luican
Maximian, Malchus, Martinian, Dionysius, John, Serapion, and Constantin, MM.—"The Seven Sleepers," 479

July 28
Nazarius and Celsus, MM., 68
Innocent I, P., 402
Sampson, B., 496
Victor, P.

July 29
Martha, V.
Felix, P.M.
Olaus, K. (Norway)
Olaus, K. (Sweden), M.
Simplicius and Faustinus (brothers) and Beatrice (their sister), MM.
William Pinchon, B.

July 30
Abdon and Sennen, MM., 250
Julitta, M.

July 31
Ignatius of Loyola, C., 1556
Helen of Skofde
John Columbini, 1367

August 1
Ethelwolf, B.
Faith, Hope, and Charity (sisters), VV., MM.
Pellegrini or Peregrinus, H.

August 2
Stephen, P.M., 257
Alphonsus Mary de Ligouri, D., 1696-1787
Etheldritha or Alfrida

August 3
Gamaliel, D.
Nicodemus
Walthen, Ab.

August 4
Dominic, C., 1170-1221
Luanus or Lugid, Ab., 622

August 5
Oswald, K.M.
Afra and her Companions, MM.
Memmius, B.A.

August 6
Joachim, Father of the Blessed Virgin
Juatus and Pastor, MM.Pns.
Xystus or Sixtus II, Dc.P.M.

August 7
Cajetan of Thienna, C., 1547
Donatus, B.M.
Hilarinus, Mo.M.

August 8
Cyriacus, Largus, Smaragdus, and their Companions, MM., 303
Hormisdas, M.

August 9
Romanus, M., 258
Fedlimid or Felimy, B., 6th Cent.
John Baptist Vianney (The Cure D'Ars), 1786-1859
Nathy or David, Pr.Pn.

August 10
Laurence, M., 258
Blaan, B., 446
Deusdedit

August 11
Tiburtius, M., and Chromatius, C., 286
Equitius, Ab.
Gery or Gaugericus, B.
Susanna, M.

August 12
Clare, V.Abs., 1253
Euplius, M., 304
Muredach, B., 440

August 13
Hippolytus, M., 252
Cassian, M.
John Berchmans, C., 1599-1621
John Bosco, 1815-1888
Radegundes, Q.
Wigbert, Ab.

August 14
Eusebius, Pr.M., 3rd Cent.
Eusebius, Pr.C. (Rome) M.

August 15
Alipius, B.
Arnoul or Arnulphus, B.
Mac-cartin (called Ard or Aed), B.

August 16
Hyacinth, C., 1257
Roch, 1327

August 17
Mamas, M., 275
Liberatus, Ab. (and Six Monks) MM.

August 18
Helen or Helena, W.Eps., 328
Agapetus, M., 275
Clare of Montefalco, V., 1268-1308

August 19
Timothy, Agapius, and Thecla, MM., 304

August 19 (Cont'd)
Cumin, B.
John Eudes, C., 1601-1680
Lewis, B.
Mochteus, B.

August 20
Bernard, Ab.D., 1153
Oswin, K.M.
Pius X, P., 1835-1914

August 21
Jane Frances de Chantal, W.Abs, 1641
Bernard Ptolemy, 1272
Bonosus and Maximilian, MM 363
Richard, B.

August 22
Hippolytus, B.M., 3rd Cent.
Andrew, Dc.
Phillibert, Ab.
Symphorian
Timothy, M., 311

August 23
Philip Beniti, C., 1285
Apollinaris Sidonius, B., 431
Claudius, Asterius, Neon, Domnina, and Theonilla, MM.
Eugenius, B.
Justinian, H.M.
Theonas, Ar.

August 24
Bartholomew, A.
Irchard or Erthad, B.
Ouen or Audoen, B.

August 25
Louis, K.C., 1270
Ebba or Tabbs
Gregory, Ab.

August 26
Zephyrinus, P., 219
Gelasinus
Genisius, M.
Genisius of Arles, M.

August 27
Caesarius, Ar.C., 542
Hugh of Lincoln, 1255
Joseph Calasanctius
Malrubius, H.M.
Poemen or Pastor, Ab.
Syagrius, B.

August 28
Augustine, B.C.D., 430
Hermes, M., 132
Julian, M.

August 29
Merri or Medericus, 7th Cent.
Sabina, M.
Sebbi or Sebba

August 30
Rose of Lima, V., 1617
Agilus or Aile, Ab.
Felix and Adauctus, MM.
Fiaker, An.
Pammarchus

August 31
Aidan or Aedan, C.B.
Cuthburge, Q.V.Abs.
Isabel
Raymond Nonnatus, Car.

September 1
Giles, Ab., 7th Cent.
Felix, Sabrinianus, Arontius, Honoratus, Fortunatus, Sabinianus, Septimeus, Januarius, another Felix, Vitalis, Satyrus and Repositus (The Twelve Brothers), MM., 258
Fiacre
Firminus II, B.
Lupus of Leu, Ar.

September 2
Stephen, K.C., 1038
Justus, Ar.
William, B.

September 3
Simeon Stylites, The Younger, 512-592
Macnisius, B.
Mansuet, B.A.
Remaclus, Ab.B.
September 4
Marcellus and Valerian, MM., 179
Ida, W.
Rosa of Viterbo
Rosalia
Ultan, B., 656
September 5
Laurence Justinian, C.Pat., 1380-1455
Alto of Ireland, Mo.
Bertin
September 6
Pambo of Nitria, Ab., 385
Bega or Bees, V., 7th Cent.
Eleutherius, Ab.
Macculindus, B., 497
September 7
Cloud, C., 522-560
Alchmund and Tilberht, BB.
Eunan, B.
Evurtius, B.
Grimonia or Germana, V.M.
Madelberte, Abs.
Regina or Reine, M.
September 8
Adrian, M., 306
Corbinian, H.B.
Disen or Disibode, Mo.
Eusebius, Nestorius, Zeno, and Nestor, MM.
Sidronius, M.
September 9
Gorgonius, Dorotheus, and Companions, MM., 304
Bettelin or Beccelin, H.
Kiarin or Kierin, Ab.
Omer, B.
Osmanna, V.
Peter Claver, S.J., A., 1581-1654
September 10
Nicholas of Tolentino, C., 1245-1306
Finian or Winin, 6th Cent.
Macanisius
Nemecianus, Felix, Lucius, Jader, Davitus, another Felix, and their Companions, part MM., part CC.
Pulcheria, Emp.
Salvius, B.
September 11
Protus and Hyacinthus (brothers), MM., 3rd Cent.
Paphnutius, B.
Patiens, Ar.
September 12
Eanswide, V.Abs., Seventh Age
Albeus, B.Pn.
Guy or Guido
September 13
Eulogius, C.Pat., 608
Amatus or Ame
Amatus or Ame, Ab. (Lorraine)
Maurilius, B.
September 14
Catherine of Genoa, W., 1447
Cormac, K.B.
September 15
John (the Dwarf), An.
Aicard or Achard, B., 486
Aper or Evre
Nicetas, M., Fourth Age
Nicomedes, Pr.M.
September 16
Cornelius, P.M., 252
Cyprian, Ar.
Editha or Eadgith (daughter of

September 16 (Cont'd)
King Edgar), 961
Editha (daughter of King Frewald)
Euphemia, V.M., 307
Germianus, M.
Lucia, W.M.
Ninian or Nynias, B.A.
September 17
Lambert, B.Pn., 709
Columba, M., 853
Hildegardis, Abs., 1098
Peter Arbues, M., 1441-1485
Rouen, Ab.
Socrates and Stephen, MM.
September 18
Thomas of Villanova, C.Ar.A., 1488-1555
Ferreol, M.
Joseph of Cupertino
Methodius, B.
September 19
Januarius, B., and his Companions, MM., 305
Eustochius, B.
Lucy, V.
Peleus, Pa-termuthes, and their Companions, MM.
Sequanus or Seine, Ab.
Theodore, Ar.
September 20
Eustachus and his Companions, MM.
Agapetus, P.
September 21
Matthew, A.Ev.
Lo or Laudus, B.
Maura, V.
September 22
Maurice and his Companions, MM., 286
Emmeran, Pn.B., 653
September 23
Linus, P.M.
Adamnan of Ireland, Ab.
Thecla, V.P.M.
September 24
Gerard, B.M., 1046
Chuniald or Conald of Ireland
Germer or Geremar, Ab
Rusticus or Rotiri, An.B.
September 25
Ceolfrid, Ab., 716
Aunaire, B., 570
Barr or Finbarr, B.
Firman, B.
September 26
Cyprian and Justina, MM., 304
Colman Elo, Ab.
Eusebius, P.
Isaac Jogues, M., 1646
Nilus the Younger, Ab., 1005
September 27
Cosmas and Damian, MM., 303
Elzear (1295-1323), and Delphina (1293-1369)
September 28
Wenceslas, M., 938
Eustochium, V.
Euxuperius, B.
Lioba
September 29
Michael the Archangel
Theodata, M.
September 30
Jerom or Jerome, C.D., 420
Gregory, B.
Honorius, Ar., 653
October 1
Remigius, Ar.C., 439-533
Bavo, An.
Fidharleus of Ireland, Ab., 762
Piat, M.
Wasnulf or Wasnon, Mo.

October 2
Thomas, B.C.
Leodegarius or Leger, M.
Thomas Cantelupe, B.
October 3
Dionysius the Areopagite, B.M.
Ewalds (Two) (brothers), Prs.
Gerard, Ab.
Therese of Lisieux, V., 1873-1897
October 4
Francis of Assisi, C., 1182-1226
Ammon, H.
Aurea, Abs.
Edwin, 633
Marcus and Marcian (brothers), and their Companions, MM., 304 or 305
October 5
Placidus, Ab., Eutychius, and 30 others, their Companions, MM., 546
Galla, W.
October 6
Bruno, C.Ab., 1030-1101
Bruno, B. (Segni)
Bruno, B. (Wurzburg)
Faith or Fides, V.M.
October 7
Osith, V.M., 870
Justina of Padua, V.M., 304
Marcellus and Apeleius, MM.
Mark, P., 336
Sergius and Bacchus, MM.
October 8
Bridget, W., 1304-1373
Keyna, V.H.
Pelagia, H., Fifth Age
Thais
October 9
Dionysius or Denis, B., and his Companions, MM.
Domninus, 304
Guislain, Ab.
Lewis Bertrand
October 10
Paulinus, Ar.C.
Francis Borgia, 1572
John of Bridlington, 1397
October 11
Tarachus, Probus, and Andronicus, MM., 304
Ethelburge or Edelbirge, Abs.
Canice, Canicus, or Kenny, Ab., 599
Gummar or Gomer
John Leonardi, 1541-1609
October 12
Wilfrid, B.C., 634-709
Salvinus, B.
October 13
Edward, K.C., 1066
Colman, M., 1012
Comgan, Ab.
Faustus, Januaris, and Martialis, MM., 304
Gerald, Pn., 855
October 14
Calixtus or Callistus, P.M.
Burckard, B.
Dominic Loricatus, Pr., 1060
Donatian, B.Pn.
October 15
Teresa, V.Abs., 1515-1582
Tecla, Abs.
Hospicius, An.
October 16
Gall, Ab., 646
Gerard Majela, 1726-1755
Lullus or Lullon, Ar.
Mummolin or Mommolin, B.
October 17
Hedwiges or Avoice, W., 1243
Andrew of Crete, M., 761
Anstrudis or Anstru, Abs.

October 17 (Cont'd)
Margaret Mary Alacoque, V., 1647-1690

October 18
Luke the Evangelist
Julian, H.
Justin or Justus, M.
Monon, M., 7th Cent.

October 19
Peter of Alcantara, C., 1499-1562
Ethbin or Egbin, Ab.
Frideswide, V.Pns.
Ptolomy, Lucius, and their Companion, MM., 166

October 20
Artemius, M., 362
Aidan B., 768
Barsabias, Ab., and his Companions, MM.
John Cantius, Pn., 1473
Sindulphus of Sendou, Pr.
Zenobius, B., Pn.
Hilarion, Ab., 371

October 21
Fintan Munno, Ab.
Ursula and Companions, VV., MM., 451

October 22
Philip, B., and Companions, MM., 304
Donatus, B.
Mark, B.
Mello, B.
Nunilo and Alosia, VV.MM.

October 23
Theodoret, Pr.M., 362
Ignatius, Pat.
John Capistran, Mo.
Romanus, Ar.
Severin, Ar.

October 24
Proclus, C.Ar., 447
Felix, B.M., 247-303
Magliore, B.H.Ab.

October 25
Chrysanthus and Darias, MM., 3rd Cent.
Crispin and Crispinian, MM., 287
Boniface, P.C.
Gaudentius of Brescia, B.
John of Beverley, Mo.Ar.
Thaddeus Machar, B.

October 26
Evaristus, P.M., 112
Bean, B.
Lucian and Marcian, MM.

October 27
Frumentius, B.C.A., Fourth Age
Abban, Ab.
Elesbaan, K.
Otteran, B., 6th Cent.

October 28
Simon the Zealot, A.
Jude, A., 1st Cent.
Faro, B.
Neot, An.

October 29
Narcissus, B., 2nd Cent.
Bede, D.
Chef or Theuderius, Ab., 573
Colman, Pn.

October 30
Marcellus the Centurion, M., 298
Alphonsus Rodriguez, S.J., 1531-1617
Asterius, B.
Germanus, B.

October 31
Quintin, M., 287
Foillan
Wolfgang, B.

November 1
All Saints
Austremonius, 3rd Cent.

November 1 (Cont'd)
Benignus, Pr.M.A.
Caesarius, M., 300
Fortunatus, B.
Harold VI, K.M.
Marcellus, B., Fourth Age
Mary, M.

November 2
Marcian, An.
Victorinus, B.M., 304
Vulgan

November 3
Malachy, C.Ar., 1148
Wenefride or Winefride, V.M.Pn.
Flour, A.B.
Hubert, B.C., 727
Papoul or Papulus, Pr.M.
Rumwald, Pn.

November 4
Charles Borromeo, Ar.Car.C., 1538-1584
Brinstan, B., 941
Clarus, M.
Joannicius, Ab.
Vitalis and Agricola, MM., 300

November 5
Bertille, Abs., 692
Elizabeth, Mother of John the Baptist
Zachary, Father of John the Baptist

November 6
Leonard, H.C., Sixth Age
Iltutus or Iltyd, Ab.
Winoc, Ab.

November 7
Willibrord, C.B., 658-738
Jean Gabriel Perboyre, M., 1802-1840
Prosdecimus, B.
Werenfrid, Pr.Mo.

November 8
Godfrey, B.
Willehad, B.A.

November 9
Benignus or Benen, B.
Mathurin, Pr.
Theodorus Tyro, M.
Vanne or Vitonius, B.Mo.

November 10
Andrew Avellino, C., 1520-1608
Justus, B.Ar.
Milles, B., Ambrosimus, Pr., and Sina, Dc.,MM.
Nympha, V.M.
Trypho and Respicius, MM.

November 11
Martin, C.B., 316-397
Mennas, M. (an Egyptian)
Mennas, M. (of Lybia)

November 12
Martin, P.M., 655
Lebwin or Liafwin, Ar.Pn.
Livin, B.M.
Nilus, An.

November 13
Stanislas Kostka, C.Pn.
Brice, B.
Chillen or Killian, Pr.
Constant, Pr.An.
Didacus or Diego, H.Mo.
Homobonus
Mitrius, M.

November 14
Laurence, C.Ar., 1180
Dubricius, B.
Erconwald, Pc., 7th Cent.
Josaphat, B.M., 1580-1623

November 15
Gertrude, V.Abs., 1221-1292
Eugenius, M.
Jose Mania Pignatelli, 1737-1811
Leopold
Malo or Maclou, B.

November 16
Edmund, C.Mo.Ar., 1242
Eucherius, B.

November 17
Hugh, C.B., 1140-1200
Anian or Agnan, B.
Dionysius the Great, D.
Gregory of Tours, B.
Gregory Thaumaturgus, B.

November 18
Alphaeus, Zacaeus, Romanus, an Barulus, MM.
Hilda or Hild, Abs.
Odo, Ab.

November 19
Elizabeth of Hungary, W., 1207 1231
Balaam, M.
Pontian, P.M.

November 20
Edmund, K.M., 870
Bernward, B.
Humbert, B.M.
Maxentia of Ireland, V.M.

November 21
Columban of Ireland, Ab., 6t Cent.
Gelasius, P.

November 22
Cecily or Cecilia, V.M.Pn., 230
Philemon and Appia
Theodorus the Studite, Ab.

November 23
Clement, P.M., 100
Amphilochius, B.
Daniel, B.
Tron, Pr.

November 24
John of the Cross, C., 1542-159
Ceanan or Kenan, B.
Chrysogonus
Flora and Mary, VV.MM.

November 25
Catherine, V.M.Pn., 310
Erasmus of Elme, H.M.

November 26
Peter, B.M., 311
Conrad, B.
Leonard of Port Maurice, O.S.F., 1676-1751
Nicon Metanoite
Sylvester Gozzolini, Ab.

November 27
James Intercisus, M.
Cungar or Docunus, Ab., 711
Maharsapor, Pc.M.
Maximus, B.
Secundin or Seachnal, B.
Virgil, B.

November 28
Stephen the Younger, M., 714-764
James of La Marca of Ancona

November 29
Saturninus, B.M., 257
Radbod, B.
Saturninus, M., 304

November 30
Andrew, A.
Narses, B., and his Companions, MM.
Sapor and Isaac, BB., and Mahanes, Abraham, and Simeon, MM.

December 1
Eligius or Eloy, C.B., 588-659
Didacus
Nessan, Pn.

December 2
Bibiana, V.M., 363
Finian, B., 6th Cent.

December 3
Francis Xavier, C.A., 1506-1552
Birinus, B., 7th Cent.
Lucius, K., Second Age

Index

521

onstant, Pr.An., 516
onstantin, M., 514
onstantine, M., 511
onran, B., 510
orbinian, H.B., 515
orentin, B., 517
ormac, K.B., 515
ormac, Ab., 517
ornelius, P.M., 515
osmas, M., 515
ougat or Cucufas, M., 514
arus, Ab., 509
rescentia, M., 513
rispin, M., 516
rispinian, M., 516
ronan, Ab., 512
ucufas or Cougat, M. 514
umin, B., 514
unegundes, Eps., 510
unegundes or Kinga, 514
ungar or Docunus, Ab., 516
ure D'Ars (John Baptist Vianney), 514
uthbert, C.B., 511
uthburge, Q.V.Abs., 514
uthman, 510
ybar, 513
yprian, Ar., 515
yprian, M., 515
yriacus, M., 514
yril, Pat., 510
yril, Ar., 511
yril, M., 512
yril, B.A., 513
yril, B.Pn., 517
yrus, M., 510

D

abius or Davius, 514
airchilla (alias for Molingus), 513
amasus, P.C., 517
amhnade, V., 513
amian, M., 515
aniel, B., 516
aniel the Stylite, 517
aniel, M., 510
aniel, Pr.M., 510
arias, M., 516
atius, B., 509
ativa, M., 517
ativus, M., 510
avid, Ar.Pn., 510
avid, M., 514
avid or Nathy, Pr.Pn., 514
avitus(one of six; part CC.-part MM.), 515
avius or Dabius, 514
eicolus, Ab., 509
elphina, 515
enis or Dionysius, B., and his Companions, MM., 515
eodatus or Die, B., 513
eogratias, B., 511
esiderius, B.M., 512
esiderius, B.M., 512
eusdedit, 514
idacus, 516
idacus or Diego, H.Mo., 516
idymus, M., 512
ie or Deodatus, B., 513
iego or Didacus, H.Mo., 516
ionysia, M., 517
ionysius of Corinth, B.C., 511
ionysius The Areopagite, B.M., 515
ionysius The Great, D., 512
ionysius, M., 514
ionysius or Denis, B., and his Companions, MM., 515
isen or Disibode, Mo., 515
ismas, The Good Thief, 511
ocmael, 513

Docunus or Cungar, Ab., 516
Doda, Abs., 512
Dominic of Sora, Ab., 509
Dominic Savio, 511
Dominic C., 223;514
Illustration faces Pg 289
Dominic Loricatus, Pr., 515
Dominick of Ossory, or Modomnoc, 510
Domnina, M., 514
Domninus, 515
Donatian, B.Pn., 515
Donatian, M., 510;512
Donatus, B.M., 514
Donatus, B., 516
Dorotheus, M., 515
Dorotheus of Tyre, M., 513
Dorotheus, The Theban, 513
Dorothy, V.M., 510
Dotto, Ab., 511
Droatan, Ab., 513
Droctovaeus, Ab., 511
Drugo or Druon, Pn., 511
Dubricius, B., 516
Dumhade of Ireland, Ab., 512
Dunstan, B.C., 512
Duthak, 511
Dympna, V.M., 512

E

Eadbert, B., 512
Eadburghe, Abs., 517
Eadgith or Editha (daughter of King Edgar), 515
Eanswide, V.Abs., 515
Ebba, 511
Ebba or Tabbs, 514
Edaena or Edana, V., 513
Edberge or Idaberga, 513
Edburge, V., 517
Edelbirge or Ethelburge, Abs., 515
Edelburga, 513
Edelward, Pr., 511
Editha or Eadgith (daughter of King Edgar), 515
Editha (daughter of King Frewald), 515
Edmund, C.Mo.Ar., 516
Edmund, K.M., 516
Edward, K.M., 511
Edward, K.C., 515
Edwin, 515
Egbert, B., 512
Egbin or Ethbin, Ab., 516
Egwin, B.C., 509
Eingan, B., 511
Elesbaan, K., 516
Eleusippus, M., 509
Eleutherius, B., 510
Eleutherius, Ab., 515
Elias, M., 510
Elier, H.M., 513
Eligius or Eloy, C.B., 516
Elizabeth, Abs., 513
Elizabeth, Mother of John the Baptist, 477;516
Illustration faces Pg 49
Elizabeth, Q., 513
Elizabeth of Hungary, W., 516
Elm or Telm, or Peter Gonzales, C.Pn., 511
Eloy or Eligius, C.B., 516
Elphege, Ar.M., 511
Elutharius, P.M., 512
Elzear, 515
Emebert, B.C., 509
Emeterius, M., 510
Emiliana, V., 517
Emma, W., 513
Emmeran, Pn.B., 515
Encratis or Engratia, V.M., 511
Endeus or Enna, Ab., 511

Engratia or Encratis, V.M., 511
Enna or Endeus, Ab., 511
Ennodus, B., 513
Ephraim the Syrian, D., 513
Ephrem of Edessa, C.D., 513
Ephysius, 509
Epimachus, M., 517
Epiphanius, B., 509
Epiphanius, Ar., 512
Epipodius, M., 512
Erasmus, B.M., 512
Erasmus of Elme, H.M., 516
Equitius, Ab., 514
Erconwald, Pc., 516
Erconwald, 517
Erconwald, B., 512
Erementiana, V.M., 509
Erhard, B., 509
Erhard, 510
Eric, M.K., 512
Erlulph, M., 510
Erminold, A.M., 509
Erthad or Irchard, B., 514
Eskill, B.M., 513
Ethbin or Egbin, Ab., 516
Ethelbert, K.C., 510
Ethelbert, K.C., 510
Ethelbert, K., 512
Ethelburge or Edelbirge, Abs., 515
Etheldreda or Audry, V.Abs., 513
Etheldritha or Alfrida, 514
Ethelwolf, B., 514
Euatachius, M., 511
Eubulus, M., 510
Eucherius, B., 510
Eucherius, B., 516
Eugendus, Ab., 509
Eugenia, V.M., 517
Eugenius, B., 513
Eugenius, B., 514
Eugenius, M., 516
Eulalia, V.M., 510
Eulogius of Cordova, Pr.M., 511
Eulogius, C.Pat., 515
Eunan, B., 515
Euphemia, V.M., 515
Euphrasia, V., 511
Euplius, M., 514
Eupsychius, M., 511
Eusebius, Ab., 509
Eusebius, H.M., 510
Eusebius, B.M., 513
Eusebius, Pr.C.(Rome) M., 514
Eusebius, Pr.M., 514
Eusebius, M., 515
Eusebius, P., 516
Eusebius, B., 517
Eustachus and Companions, MM., 515
Eustasius, Ab., 511
Eustathius, C.Pat., 513
Eustochium, V., 515
Eustochius, B., 515
Euthymius, Ab., 509
Eutropius, M., 509
Eutychius, M., 515
Evaristus, P.M., 516
Everilidis, V., 513
Evre or Aper, 515
Evroul, Ab., 517
Evurtius, B., 515
Ewalds (Two) (brothers), Prs., 515
Exuperius, B., 515

F

Fabian, P.M., 509
Faith or Fides, V.M., 515
Faith, V.M., 514
Fanchea, V., 509
Fara, Abs., 517
Faro, B., 516
Faustinus, M., 510;514